The May 1970 Rebellion, Volume 2

Frank Gormlie

Published by Frank Gormlie, 2024.

While every precaution has been taken in the preparation of this book, the publisher assumes no responsibility for errors or omissions, or for damages resulting from the use of the information contained herein.

THE MAY 1970 REBELLION, VOLUME 2

First edition. October 13, 2024.

Copyright © 2024 Frank Gormlie.

ISBN: 979-8990401723

Written by Frank Gormlie.

Table of Contents

FRANK'S INTRODUCTION 1
ACKNOWLEDGEMENTS 3
INTRODUCTION TO THE MAY 1970 REBELLION 4
Chapter 5 SATURDAY MAY 9 – SUNDAY MAY 10 13
Chapter 6 MONDAY, MAY 11 – SUNDAY, MAY 17 66
Chapter 7 MONDAY MAY 18 – SUNDAY MAY 24 249
Chapter 8 MONDAY MAY 25 – SUNDAY MAY 31 305
EPILOGUE 329
AFTERWORD for VOLUME 2 343
CHAPTER END NOTES, Volume 2 355

DEDICATION

To Alan Canfora for inspiring me – he was wounded at Kent State in May 1970 and kept the story of the massacre alive for the university and the nation for fifty years, and to Patty Jones for supporting me and enabling me to research and write the book.

THE MAY 1970 REBELLION, Vol. 2

Day to Day Narrative of the National Student Strike

by
Frank Gormlie

Published by
Ocean Beach Rag Press, 2024

Published by
Ocean Beach Rag Press
c/o OB Rag
8161 Lincoln Street
Lemon Grove, CA 91945
or
PO Box 7012
San Diego, CA 92167
U.S.A.
obragblog@gmail.com
(619) 962-4804
The May 1970 Rebellion, Vol. 2
Copyright August 23, 2024 by Frank Gormlie
ISBN 979-8-9904017-0-9 (pbk Vol.1)
ISBN 979-8-9904017-2-3 (pbk Vol.2)
ISBN 979-8-9904017-1-6 (ebook)
Cover art by Forrest Seguin

All rights reserved. Without limiting the rights under copyright reserved above, no part of this publication may be reproduced, stored in or introduced into a retrieval system, or transmitted, in any form, or by any means (electronic, mechanical, photocopying, recording, or otherwise) without the prior written permission of both the copyright owner and the above publisher of this book.

FRANK'S INTRODUCTION

Over the decades, I became acutely aware of the lack of journalistic or historical accounts of what happened during May 1970 and understood that this had created a huge gap in the record of America's modern history. When I began looking for materials for this book, I was shocked to find that even though there were limited accounts, chapters and summaries of the rebellion in various books about the anti-Vietnam war movement of the Sixties and Seventies, not one book told more of the full story. I understood then that the book had to be written.

I was there - I was a participant in the Rebellion, being a college student at the University of California San Diego earning a degree in Sociology and living on campus in the married student housing. Truly, I thought of myself as a foot soldier for the "revolution" during that May and was never in leadership roles nor took part in the planning of actions or meetings. Yet, I personally felt the tensions and excitement, the anger, the hostilities, the comradery, the power of collective actions and the demoralizing attributes of factionalism. I witnessed confrontations and building take-overs and the frailties and vicissitudes of administrators and heard the exhortations of some of the greatest.

Upon retiring from my 20-year law practice – during which I honed my legal research skills – I became a citizen journalist, blogger and editor of an online news platform published in San Diego, the *OB Rag*. As the 50th anniversary of Kent State and the Rebellion approached, I felt compelled to research and begin writing about May 1970. In the end, the material for this report was researched, compiled and written during the Trump presidency years, through two impeachment trials, during the presidential election of 2020, through the pandemic (my partner, Patty Jones, and I both caught COVID during the summer of 2022) and completed in July 2024 during that year's turbulent and crucial election cycle.

Tragically, some of those I was writing for began to pass. Alan Canfora, wounded at Kent State in 1970 in the National Guard fusillade, more than anyone else stubbornly kept the memory of the KSU murders alive both on that campus and nationally. Alan passed away in the fall of 2021. Also,

John "Mike" Williams, who assisted me in the latter months of 2021 with his insightful editing, passed at the end of January in 2022.

ACKNOWLEDGEMENTS

The author will be forever indebted to the individuals who helped with the book: they include those who assisted in editing and submitted their own story from May 1970—John "Mike" Williams, Mel Freilicher, Peter Bohmer, and Steve Zivolich, for editing help Arlene Fink, to others who submitted their stories—Kate Bell, Doug Coffey, Anna Daniels, Byron King, William Maltz, Kris Schlech, Bruce Seifer, Ken Wachsberger and Steve Wimmers, to Shawn Drake for his material support, to Forrest Seguin for his cover art, and to Dickie Magidoff for his editing and book cover assistance.

INTRODUCTION TO THE MAY 1970 REBELLION

This is a story of an important but forgotten and buried chapter of modern American history. It's a story—and record—of the May 1970 Rebellion—a day-to-day narrative of the National Student Strike – the largest student strike in American history.

More chronology than narrative, this indepth review of one month recounts what happened when the President of the United States in late April of 1970 invaded a sovereign nation in Southeast Asia—Cambodia. The response by American college, university and high school students – who wisely saw the military incursion as an expansion of the Vietnam war – brought much of the nation's higher education system to a halt. And the ensuing repression – mostly notably the massacre of four students at Kent State University in Ohio – provoked America's students to such a degree that their response rocked the nation, creating a political crisis for the nation and for the Establishment.

The ensuing rebellion forever changed America and its politics. It's why the song "Ohio" by Crosby, Stills, Nash and Young still reverberates today with that generation of Americans who experienced and lived through the May Rebellion. And it's why then-Chief Justice of the US Supreme Court, Earl Warren, called it the worst American crisis since the Civil War, and it's why historian Howard Zinn confirmed it was indeed the largest student strike in history. The President's Commission on Campus Unrest in 1970 reported: "The crisis on American campuses has no parallel in the history of the nation. This crisis has roots in divisions of American society as deep as any since the Civil War."

Generally, the student-led upheaval of May 1970 is known in this country, with the main collective memory that of the Kent State murders, and to a much lesser extent the two deaths at Jackson State. Many have seen the iconic photo of Mary Ann Vecchio kneeling over the lifeless body of Jeff Miller laying in a river of his own blood, one of the four who died at Kent State.

But that's about it. Nothing else is really known about the tsunami of a rebellion that swept through the country during that fateful May. There is no book about it and certainly no movie or documentary. For over 50 years the real story of what happened, what came down, how young Americans were galvanized that month so many years ago has been hidden, interned, and forgotten - with the actions and voices of the rebels smothered by the dust of official avoidance and denial.

This half century of cover-up of a crucial chapter of our history has been enabled by academia and by the Establishment press, for no reporter nor journalist, nor writer nor historian, nor magazine, book, newspaper, cable television station, university, historical society, academic association has attempted to unearth what exactly happened across the nation during those weeks of protest and rebellion. Until now—until this report—the full story and record have never been told.

A major chapter in the nation's modern history, it's the story of the thousands, hundreds of thousands, of the one to four million college students who were involved in the national student strike, its demonstrations, mass meetings, marches, leafletting, lobbying, petitioning, letter-writing, sit-ins, building occupations and confrontations with law enforcement. Students were galvanized and mobilized across the country and the unprecedented movement they created impacted hundreds of campuses.

This story and record of May 1970 is based upon reports from over 700 specific college and university campuses, with the principal sources being the accounts contemporaneously written and published by campus newspapers and strike newsletters that sprang up – all written by participants and observers. This presentation of the record signals that the cover-up is over, and it is the author's hope that it will inspire others to dig even deeper into the stories of the Rebellion in their own locales and campuses.

The National Student Strike

Once the National Student Strike unfolded in response to President Nixon's invasion of Cambodia, and through the government's reactive repression, the human toll was stark. Eight deaths were directly attributed to the Rebellion: four at Kent State, two at Jackson State, and two self-immolations in protest of the war. Plus, over 1200 students were injured or wounded during the month.

The first week of the strike was the most intense. During each of the four days immediately following the Kent State massacre on Monday, May 4, there was a daily average of 200,000 students involved in protests, demonstrations, mass meetings and marches. And over a hundred colleges went out on strike each day during that four-day period. Then on Saturday May 9th, 100,000 to 120,000 demonstrators – mostly students – marched and protested in Washington DC alone.

Overall, during May 1970, 1,419 colleges and universities were involved in or affected by the National Student Strike with demonstrations, rallies and mass meetings. Student strikes, class boycotts or school shut-downs occurred at 637 campuses. (In 1970 there were between 7.4 and 8 million college students in the U.S. attending 2500 institutions.)

Over the course of the month, from Maine to California, from Florida to Washington State and many points in between, there was a minimum of 91 violent clashes between students and law enforcement and teargas was used to subdue protesters in 41 of them. 67 live rounds were fired at Kent State, hundreds were shot off at Jackson State, and National Guardsmen bayonetted nearly a dozen people at the University of New Mexico. Over two dozen people on four different campuses were wounded by police buckshot or birdshot. And overall, 1,228 to 1,307 people were wounded or injured—not including the many hundreds sickened by teargas and/or who didn't report their injuries—and 170 law enforcement officers were also reportedly injured. Between 4,454 and 4,608 students were arrested (including some non-students) during May, according to our record.

The book *SDS* reported, "Violent demonstrations occurred on at least 73 campuses ... and at 26 schools, demonstrations were serious, prolonged, and marked by clashes between students and police, with tear gas, broken windows."

National Guards

The National Guards of 16 states were activated on 24 occasions and deployed on 15 campuses.[1] and placed on alert near nine others.[2] The book *SDS* pointed out that it was "the first time such a massive response [by National Guards] had ever been used in a nonracial crisis."

ROTC, Sit-ins, Arson and States of Emergencies

During May, campus ROTC programs and facilities were targeted by protesters at 156 schools, including 31 sit-ins or take-overs, 24 fires from arson or attempts, and trashings at 18 schools. There were 83 sit-ins or occupations held in other campus buildings – mostly administrative centers – and most by far were non-violent with little property damage. Vandalism, trashings and arson in non-ROTC building did occur at 51 campuses – four buildings were totally demolished and windows broken and other minor damage at 37 schools. *SDS* claimed there were 95 incidents of bombings and arson associated with college campuses during May.

In direct response to the Rebellion, the governors of four states (Michigan, Ohio, Kentucky and South Carolina) declared campuses in a state of emergency, and the governor of California shut down the entire state system of public education for four days—19 colleges and 9 universities. Nation-wide, curfews were established and enforced on 14 colleges.

Street and Freeway Blockades, Newsletters and Memorials

Street blockades – the classic insurrectionist tactic – were erected at a minimum of 40 campuses where protesters shut down roads and blocked access by law enforcement and delivery trucks in efforts to bring "business as usual" to a halt. Human blockades in front of campus buildings occurred at another 17 schools.

Students were involved in 26 take-overs, sit-ins or human blockades of major roads – most of them close to campus. In a signal of a new militancy, on nine different occasions students ran out onto active freeways, blocked traffic and brought them to a halt. At some, students distributed flyers and talked to motorists about their strike and the war. In a dramatic twist in the Mid-west, demonstrators sat-down and blocked railroad tracks for hours. A "Honk Your Horn for Peace" protest outside a Virginia university disrupted traffic throughout the city.

Students used an array of tactics: (these are minimum numbers) informational picket lines at 83 campuses; teach-ins, seminars and workshops on the war and related issues at 119 schools; "Free Universities" or alternate courses at another 14; strike newsletters or sympathetic student newspapers on 81 campuses; and 12 schools sponsored regional strike conferences. Defense contractors on campuses were an issue at 25 schools—with 11 involving protests – half of which were sit-ins or building occupations. Also, students from four campuses led demonstrations at defense plants or factories over the month.

Strike newsletters that sprang up usually operated in conjunction with strike organizing committees and published announcements of protests, teach-in schedules, and sympathetic opinion pieces about the strike. Many carried reports and news of protests from across the country, keeping local strikers up-to-date with the progression of the nation-wide movement.

During May, 136 memorials were held in honor of the Kent State Four and 12 for those murdered at Jackson State College and one for George Winne's self-immolation at UC San Diego. Lowering the American flag to half-staff in honor of the Kent State students was an issue at 43 campuses, whereas the burning of the American flag in protest occurred at only four. Twenty-seven protest hunger strikes were staged, campus referendums on Cambodia, Nixon and related issues were held at 42 schools, and protest "tent cities" or student encampments were set up at 14. Twenty-eight protests at local draft or induction centers were held, mainly organized by students, and between 1600 to 2100 draft cards were either collected and sent to a national antiwar center or burned.

Door-to-Door Canvassing, Marches to Downtowns and State Capitols

Canvassing campaigns were organized by students at 49 campuses where people went door-to-door in local neighborhoods with peace petitions and information about their strikes. Students from at least 11 campuses leafletted local factories or joined picket lines at worksites, and a minimum of 13 schools sponsored leafletting at malls and shopping centers.

Students and their allies marched on 32 state capitols during May and organized another 79 protest marches to local downtowns—sit-ins and street occupations were held in 34 of them. Federal Buildings, courthouses and Post Offices were non-violently targeted in 39 demonstrations whereas in contrast, merchants' windows were broken in 22 incidents during protests; fires were set in businesses in seven towns or cities. Seven schools had boycott campaigns against local merchants to pressure them into supporting student antiwar and civil rights efforts.

Around Armed Forces Day in late May, there were 15 protests or rallies where students joined antiwar GIs at or near military facilities. Most were entirely peaceful, but military authorities used an array of tactics in efforts to decrease GI turn-out—from arrests of organizers to the wide distribution of weekend passes.

This detailed report of the responses during May 1970 by American students is a chronology organized geographically, telling the story day-to-day, week-by-week, campus-by-campus, and state-by-state, beginning with colleges and universities in the Northeast and ending with those in Southern California. Each chapter proceeds through the six regions of the nation: the Northeast, the Southeast, the Midwest, the Southwest, the Rocky Mountain region and the Pacific (the regions utilized by the US Post Office). Due to its length, the paperback version was made into two volumes. Volume 1 covers the first week of the Rebellion – up through Friday, May 8, and Volume 2 includes the rest of May, from Saturday, the 9th through May 31st.

Why "Rebellion"?

The protests of May 1970 were not simply "another student springtime outburst" but the high water mark of American students' resistance to the Vietnam war and the policies of the Nixon administration. (See Epilogue.) At the same time May was not a "revolution" as some wished or feared, not even an "insurrection" that others fantasized, but a rebellion – often defined as an act of violent or open formidable resistance to an established government or ruler, that is usually unsuccessful.

Establishing the record of what happened during the May 1970 Rebellion was my task. And now, the voices and actions of the young of yesteryear speak and act for themselves. And for the rest of us.

Organizations Referred to in the Text

Students for a Democratic Society was the key organization of the student New Left. Founded in 1960 under the Port Huron Statement, it called for participatory democracy in America, and by 1969 had grown to 304 chapters with a membership somewhere between 30,000 to 100,000—mostly at college campuses. SDS played a leading role in the growing anti-Vietnam War movement and was especially focused on challenging university complicity such as campus ROTC programs. It was also very active in movements against poverty and racism, on and off campus. With time, SDS became increasingly anti-imperialist, in support of "Third World" revolutions and the civil rights and Black Power movement within the US. However, due to major divisions among its factions and members, SDS fell apart after a 1969 convention in Chicago.

Progressive Labor (PL) a minor but national force within the anti-war movement, PL became active in SDS beginning in the mid 1960's, having broken from mainline American leftists to form a Maoist and pro-China organization. Socially conservative, PL focused more on class-based change and away from support for the Black Panthers and Black Studies departments. Working through its campus group, the Student Worker Alliance, it gained a growing influence within SDS and stacked the 1969 SDS convention with a majority of the delegates. When other factions broke off from SDS, PL was only too happy to take control of the disintegrating national organization for its own.

Weather Underground was a prominent faction of SDS and in 1969 most its leadership formed the Weathermen organization with a focus to engage in militant actions in support of the Vietnamese revolution and the Black liberation struggle in America. After the 1969 convention, they abandoned SDS to focus on building Weathermen and decided to become totally clandestine. In doing so, these veteran student activists and SDS leaders were not available nor involved in the May Rebellion. And for a number of years, they conducted a bombing campaign against imperialist targets—careful not to injure people in their actions. They disbanded in the mid 1970's although some members continued in clandestine work, and over the decades, many resurfaced.

Socialist Workers Party (SWP) became a major anti-Vietnam war group in forming the SMC (Student Mobilization Committee) in the mid 1960's and took a leadership role in many of the large anti-war demonstrations. They called for immediate U.S. withdrawal but did not support the National Liberation Front and North Vietnam. In the demonstrations they led, they believed that Vietnam should be the only issue, and did not ally with other struggles such as Black Liberation, and believed protests should be massive but without civil disobedience.

The Chicago 8 Conspiracy was a group of eight defendants involved in the anti-war and counterculture protests in Chicago during the 1968 Democratic National Convention, who were then charged by the U.S. Department of Justice with conspiracy, crossing state lines with intent to incite a riot and other related charges. The Chicago Eight were Rennie Davis, David Dellinger, John Froines, Tom Hayden, Abbie Hoffman, Jerry Rubin, Lee Weiner and Bobby Seale – the chair of the Black Panther Party. They became the Chicago Seven after the case against Bobby Seale was declared a mistrial. Eventually, all of the defendants were acquitted of conspiracy, and in the end, all other convictions were reversed on appeal, and the government declined to retry the case. For many young people the group became symbols of the youthful and rebellious counter-culture within the anti-Vietnam war movement. Members of the Conspiracy traveled the country, speaking mainly on college campuses to hugely receptive audiences.

The Black Panther Party was a left-wing Black power political organization founded by Bobby Seale and Huey P. Newton in October 1966 in Oakland, California. It gained an early militant reputation and following for its practice of cop-watching while armed which challenged the excessive force and misconduct of the Oakland Police Department. In the late 1960s, the Party created the Free Breakfast for Children Programs, education programs, community health clinics, and advocated for class struggle, rather than a racial struggle. FBI Director J. Edgar Hoover called the party "the greatest threat to the internal security of the country," and ordered the FBI to conduct campaigns of illegal sabotage and covert counterintelligence gathering under COINTELPRO, including surveillance, infiltration, police harassment and even assassinations. Two party leaders, Fred Hampton and Mark Clark were assassinated in 1969 with FBI assistance during a raid of the Chicago Police Department, while other members were involved in fatal firefights with police. Initially however, government persecution contributed to the party's growth among

African Americans and the political left. With a national newspaper and hundreds of chapters nation-wide, its membership peaked in 1970. The party gradually declined over the next decade, due to its vilification by the mainstream press and infighting—caused in part by COINTELPRO.

Chapter 5
SATURDAY MAY 9 – SUNDAY MAY 10

The March on Washington DC

Saturday, May 9 was the day of the big march – the day of the mass mobilization by Americans at the nation's capital in reaction to Nixon's Cambodian invasion and the murders of students at Kent State. Organized by the New Mobe—short for the New Mobilization Committee to End the War in Vietnam – it was the largest protest during May 1970 and an immense and historic outpouring of anti-war demonstrators who rallied and marched through Washington, DC and in front of the White House.

Crowds began to gather at the Ellipse, the protest site, and to their amazement, they found the White House completely surrounded by a ring of city buses parked bumper-to-bumper, insulating Nixon from the masses. And unbeknownst to them, Nixon had a contingent of the 82nd Airborne positioned in the basement of the executive office building—connected to the White House by an underground passageway. Counsel to Nixon, Charles Colson later recalled that he "went down just to talk to some of the guys and walk among them, and they're lying on the floor leaning on their packs and their helmets and their cartridge belts and their rifles cocked and you're thinking, 'This can't be the United States of America. This is not the greatest free democracy in the world. This is a nation at war with itself.'"

By the time the massive crowd had assembled at 1 pm, it was a blistering 90 degrees. Crowd estimates ranged from the official "60,000" to 75,000, 100,000—even 130,000. Thirty Congressmen and Senators participated including New York Senators Jacob Javits and Charles Goodell. Several hundred federal workers were there behind banners that read, "Federal Bums Against the War," and "Federal Employees for Peace." And for most of the young demonstrators this was their first ever Washington DC anti-war protest.

New Mobe leaders Fred Halstead and Brad Lyttle had flown to Washington early to prepare for the protest, and somehow had mobilized a force of 500 people trained in and prepared for nonviolent mass civil disobedience (CD)—along with an estimated 20,000 others also ready for CD. In addition, there was another corps of 3,000 "marshals" whose job was to keep order within the crowd.

Swamped by the logistical challenges of organizing such an event in such a short time, Mobe leaders had waited until they were up on the stage to decide what to do. And the direction of the rally fell to a small group of long-time male activists—Dave Dellinger, Rennie Davis, Arthur Waskow, and Robert Greenblatt – three of whom had not been at the April 29 planning meeting. Compounding their problems, the Mobe leadership hadn't invited many of the traditional peace activists to attend, speak, or get involved, nor did they bring to the stage the organic and local leaders of the campus rebellions.

Within segments of the crowd and among many activists, there was a high expectation of mass civil disobedience. A 4,000 watt sound system sat on the stage ready to reach everyone in the crowd. Marshals carried over a dozen bullhorns which could have broadcast any action. A whole range of prominent anti-war figures, politicians, entertainers, and academic figures were close by to give moral support to any action, and all the TV networks were on hand, ready for live coverage.

Speaker after speaker addressed the throng, but those behind them on the stage argued for over two hours on what to do. The sad reality was that no consensus had been planned and nothing came together on the stage—therefore, no coherent plan of action was announced by any of the speakers.

The speakers who did address the gigantic crowd were brilliant; many encouraged students to continue and spread the student strike, or to stay in Washington to pressure Congress to cut off war funding, or to return to their communities to organize against governmental policies. Doug Miranda, a leader of the New Haven Black Panther Party, lectured students that they didn't have to look around the globe for issues because African Americans and their leaders were being repressed right here in this country. John Froines of the Chicago 8 and Robert Scheer of *Ramparts* magazine spoke to the predominantly white crowd of the need for white activists to support the Black Panthers. One observer noted that there appeared to be more Black participants in the crowd than at previous anti-war mobilizations. Black Panther members led chants and thousands of people screamed, "Fuck Nixon!' within yards of the White House.

New Mobe Director Ron Young warned the youthful mass, "We realize mass protests won't end the war," but the nationwide student strike had to generate a more general strike, "and we'll end the war that way. We're here to back down the military. We're here to push them out of Vietnam!" Other speakers included actress-activist Jane Fonda, Benjamin Spock and Dave Dellinger. Dellinger told the crowd, "This is not a picnic on the lawn. This is no time for fun and games. This is the time to build up a head of steam." Abbie Hoffman yelled to the crowd, "The United States has lost its face in South Vietnam, and it will lose its ass in Cambodia!"

By 3:30 rally organizers on stage were still arguing over who should speak and what should be done, and with their attention divided between running the rally and figuring out what CD action to take, both failed. The rally lost focus and no call for militant action emanated from the podium. Out in the Ellipse, the scenario was becoming what Dellinger had warned against—a super-picnic on the lawn—and people drifted away due to the heat or disillusionment. Several thousand wandered over to watch a group of nude men and women wading in the cool waters of the Lincoln Memorial Reflecting Pool, and it was there that the first two arrests came. One young woman, mesmerized by the scene, said, "It's too beautiful a day for anything ugly to happen."

Three hours into the rally and out of frustration, individual Mobe leaders began making unilateral decisions. Organizer Stewart Meacham called CD activists over to the west side of the Ellipse for a march up 17th Street to the White House. Yet just moments later, Dellinger enacted a similar plan but for a march up 15th Street – which brought most of the demonstrators to the east side of the Ellipse. No clear instructions were given, however, on how and where the marchers should conduct a sit-down. Plus, this main group was without the activists trained in civil disobedience.

Tens of thousands flowed out of the Ellipse and followed a large number of black coffins to the streets, and around the White House and

Lafayette Park, still cordoned off by a wall of municipal buses. The coffins were labeled, "GIs," "Black Panthers," "Kent State," "Vietnamese," and "Cambodians."

Control of the immense event by the original coordinators evaporated once the masses of demonstrators moved away from the stage and the Ellipse. In the vacuum, control of its direction fell into the hands of the rally marshals who weren't trained in civil disobedience – quite the opposite. When the largest contingent of the march approached H Street there was an effort at civil disobedience. But without any leadership at the head of the march and with the breakdown of communication, the marshals actually discouraged people from CD and sitting in the streets; they kept the throng moving by pushing protesters away from H Street.

It wasn't until late afternoon that the first serious confrontation occurred. Demonstrators began rocking one of the city buses blocking the entrance to Lafayette Park, and police moved in and dispersed them using CS gas. Another confrontation occurred at the Justice Department where 500 militants threw bricks and bottles at police and at windows of the building, who were then forced back after a volley of tear gas.

As the main march disintegrated, peace marshals busied themselves with breaking up several spontaneous small-scale sit-downs, believing these actions would only lead to people being gassed and hurt. But as the afternoon darkened into evening, more clashes erupted and a force of the DC Civil Defense police showed up. They moved on scattered groups of protestors still sitting in at downtown intersections. Even the small crowd that had gathered for two days to give support to the former Peace Corps volunteers occupying a government building was cleared out.

Over at **George Washington University** and now that it was dark, hundreds of students who had been at the main protest filtered back to their campus. Fired up and feeling righteous, they went to work and set up barricades near the university and only a half mile from the White House. Around the same time, a "revolutionary" contingent of 400 militants marched from the university to Dupont Circle and smashed windows at banks, stock exchange offices and other large businesses along the way. Their main target was the International Association of Police Chiefs building but before they could find the building, police found them, and a major confrontation erupted at the Circle. The revolutionaries were driven back towards campus.

When police showed up at the barricades just outside campus, they were pelted with rocks and bottles, and in response unleashed a heavy tear gas attack. But reinforced with those driven from Dupont Circle and now nearly 1,000 strong, protesters set the barricades on fire and overturned a bus. Eventually all demonstrators were pushed back to the university but skirmishes continued until the prestigious school was so permeated with tear gas, that the student strike center had to be evacuated.

Students at nearby **Catholic University** stopped transporting injured students after their busses were gassed by Civil Defense police units. A New Mobe ambulance was also forced to turn back after trying to respond to a medic's call about 150 injured students. Around midnight, Washington Police Chief Jerry Wilson called off the teargas assault at George Washington and reported the campus was completely sealed off by two of his Civil Defense units. The clash at the university had been the most serious violence of the entire day in DC.

Over the course of the entire protest there had been a minimum of 350 arrested—mostly for misdemeanors—and according to city police, only two dozen people had been injured. There also had been more than one hundred windows broken in what police labeled "minor" violence. District of Columbia Mayor Walter Washington said the violence from Saturday night could not be attributed to the crowd at the main demonstration which he described as "peaceful."

Ray Price, one of Nixon's chief speechwriters, had a different view in recalling the Washington demonstration. "The city was an armed camp. The mobs were smashing windows, slashing tires, dragging parked cars into intersections, even throwing bedsprings off overpasses into the traffic down below. This was the quote, "student protest." That's not student protest, that's civil war."

In the end, many in the student strike movement were greatly disappointed. Both participants and those thousands across the country who watched the march unfold on live TV, had harbored expectations that something "heavy" would come down in DC. Despite a massive march at the seat of power, the lack of any organized civil disobedience resulted in the loss of a tremendous opportunity to bring Washington DC to a halt. Veteran anti-war activist Norma Becker remembered that it was "such a letdown ...The demonstration was like a picnic, which did not correspond to the mood or psychology. What happened ... was not commensurate either to the invasion of Cambodia or to Kent State. There was a deep and pervasive feeling of sellout." And many felt the massive DC action did little to transmute the "anguished cry of frustration from the American public" into an "effective response," and that "the voiceless army of students who had put themselves under the New Mobe banner for a day returned in sullen silence to their broken campuses."

On the other hand, others were gratified that the massive display of dissent was largely peaceful. Mobe leader Brad Lyttle saw a bright side. They had organized a giant rally close to the White House, where Nixon's Indochina policies had been denounced; people were called to strike against the war; and the rally had been widely and objectively covered by the mass media. The overwhelming peaceful, orderly and nonviolent nature of the demonstration stood in stark contrast to the government's war policies abroad and its violent repression of dissent at home, a violence so prevalent that Rennie Davis had predicted martial law coming to DC.

Activists had less than two weeks to promote and organize the demonstration – yet they organized it in less than one. Over 100,000 people had been mobilized to protest Cambodia, Kent State and the Black Panthers, it had taken place on the Ellipse—which the government had initially denied, and the New Mobe simply declared its intention to hold the rally and had not relied on a government permit to hold the event. This affirmed the people's right to peacefully assemble where they wished.

"Anger, hope and a renewed sense of commitment were there in the thousands of people who came," an editorial from the National Strike Information Center observed, "but the mood of the crowd failed to cohere in a comprehensive and politically meaningful program of action." The May 12 editorial, entitled "On Washington: Off Bullshit," continued: "From the speakers' platform there came the usual exhortations to 'keep working,' turn in draft cards, get involved in local politics, etc., but the main stream of potentially radical political energy was largely dissipated as Nixon predicted it would be the night before—through the 'safety valves' of dull speeches, tired rhetoric, exhausting heat, splash parties in the Reflecting Pool and aimless trashing."

The editorial advised, "In Washington we proved to ourselves once again that the movement is built at home, that effective political action can occur only after months and years of intensive local organizing. It's not through mass demonstrations organized by others but through day to day work we do ourselves that our political consciousness grows, and that a strong, united and politically meaningful movement is built."

Two weeks after the massive protest in Washington, its main organizer – the New Mobe—broke up. The organization divided on the very issue that had caused the DC leadership to fail at that crucial and historic moment: the question of civil disobedience. The SWP and its student adjunct, SMC, were not willing to be part of a coalition where civil disobedience was a possible tactic and were content to form their own "national coalition" focused singularly on getting US troops out of Vietnam. Fortunately, other groups and individuals within the Mobe pulled together a new national network called the People's Coalition for Peace and Justice, which led anti-war actions the next spring.

Northeast
Maine
Colby College, Waterville

Over the weekend, both of Maine's Senators, Margaret Chase Smith and Edmund Muskie, came to speak at Colby. On Saturday Smith spoke before a crowd of 2,000 and to the dismay of many, expressed support for President Nixon's war policy. During a Q and A, Smith was asked how she felt about the systematic oppression of the Black Panthers, and replied, well, she didn't like the Black Panthers, the Weathermen or similar organizations. At this, Charles Terrell, a Black Colby student, stood up and loudly retorted, "I don't like you or Nixon or any of you, but I have to deal with you because you are the establishment." Students broke out in enthusiastic cheers.

On Sunday, Senator Muskie fared somewhat better before a larger crowd of 3,000 to 4,000 students from around the state. Attacking Nixon's widening of the war into Cambodia, Muskie read a resolution that he planned to introduce in the Senate the very next day. It called for an immediate ceasefire in Indochina and a withdrawal of all US troops within 18 months. Muskie's position was that only history can judge the motives of American involvement in Vietnam—which he attributed to a US desire to "buy time" for the South Vietnamese to build a country. But then he proclaimed that Americans had bought enough time at too great a price and that the time had come to withdraw.

Muskie was asked about his own reversal of opinion on Vietnam in 1968. He replied that his change had not come about because of "political expediency," but because he genuinely believed the United States was following "a mistaken policy in continuing its military involvement within Southeast Asia." He could not justify American support to the right-wing regime in South Vietnam and stated he was against any continuation of that support. (Muskie had campaigned against Nixon in 1968 as Hubert Humphrey's vice-presidential running mate and would campaign in the 1972 Democratic Party presidential primary until he fell victim to Nixon's "dirty tricks.")

After Muskie spoke, part of the crowd left and the rally morphed into a mass meeting of 1200 Colby students – with some from other schools—to figure out where they were going to go from there. Several Colby professors took the mic and spoke in favor of ending the strike, saying it had served its purpose. Were Colby students truly wavering? Potentially, the entire future of the student strike in Maine hung in the balance.

Then Herb Coursen, a Bowdoin College English professor spoke. A fighter pilot in the USAF during the 1950s, a Shakespearian author and poet, he was an early opponent of the war in Vietnam, one of the original members of Veterans for Peace. Invoking Nixon, Cambodia and the Kent State students, Coursen said if Colby students continued their strike, it would push his campus at Bowdoin and the students at the University of Maine in likewise directions and help them maintain their strike momentums. After reading a passage from the Declaration of Independence, he received sustained applause, and when he concluded, a standing ovation. It was abundantly clear where the sentiment of the mass of Colby students lay. When the floor was opened for discussion, most who spoke were in favor of continuing the strike with slight variations of degree. When the assembly took a student-only vote on whether to continue the strike, the results were overwhelming in favor: 1,041 to 134, with 30 abstentions.

Despite the decisiveness of the students, the faculty took a different turn. During their meeting that night, they took a vote to end the strike and resume classes the following Monday. Many students were shocked by their vote and felt betrayed. The student newspaper, *The Echo*, leveled a blistering criticism at them. "This was extremely unfortunate in that it was a grievous setback to the student protest against President Nixon's policies in Southeast Asia and at home and in that it has undercut and effectively killed the sense of community that existed for only a few short days."

For astute students, the effort to resume classes and squash the strike was seen as a ploy by the college president and the academic council to get back to 'business as usual' as they had, it turned out, railroaded the motion through the faculty meeting. In response, the student government met the next day and passed a resolution that the strike would still continue in full effect.

Bowdoin College – Brunswick

While some of their compatriots were in DC, a large number of Bowdoin students on Saturday headed for Colby College to participate in something called the "Maine Coordinating Committee" and to hear Maine Senator Smith and anti-war actor Gary Merrill speak.

That night at Bowdoin's Strike Central, a call came in from Washington DC. Four Bowdoin men had been arrested and over the phone recounted the events leading to their arrests – they were quite jovial about it. The mass march in DC had been called "peaceful" by the press, but there had been sporadic incidents and arrests, and Bowdoin students Robert Loeb, John Rhodes, Ted Raabe and William Walbridge had been detained for violating a police line.

Authorities in Washington had mapped out certain public areas for overnight camping by demonstrators, and the Bowdoin men had chosen to sleep by one designated area near the Washington Monument. During the night, someone had broken one of the spotlights illuminating the Monument, and using this as an excuse, Capitol police began to clear out the area around the Monument – with tear gas.

The four fled but at every turn, they said, they were met with police who ordered them in different directions. Eventually, they were guided into one roped off area and found themselves trapped. When they tried to cross the rope barrier, they were immediately detained and charged with violating the police line—one was also charged with disorderly conduct. They all pled not guilty to the misdemeanor charges and bond was set at $10 each – paid for by New Mobe organizers. Later the next week, Raabe and Walbridge would go to trial and have their charges dropped when the judge ruled they had been forced into the restricted area. The misdemeanor trials for Rhodes and Loeb were set for later in May and early June.

On Sunday, while some Bowdoin students went to area churches and spoke with parishioners about the strike, more travelled to Colby College to hear Sen. Muskie. Upon their return, they spread the news that Colby students had voted to continue their strike by an overwhelming margin.

Also, over the weekend, a notice appeared around campus which stated: "The manager of the Moulton Union Book Store voted in favor of the preposterous resolution passed by the Brunswick Town Council." The Council had condemned Bowdoin students for disrupting a local high school and asked that the college keep all student activities on campus. The notice asked, "Should Bowdoin students continue to support a book store whose leadership holds such irrational beliefs? BOYCOTT THE BOOK STORE!"

By Sunday, to some, the strike began showing signs of fraying as disillusioned strikers and non-strikers bound for spring packed up and went home. Strike leaders, however, kept positive and assured themselves that enough students would remain on campus to continue the strike.

Bates College – Lewiston

On Sunday morning, over half a dozen Bates students gave talks at local congregations in the Lewiston Auburn area about why their school was on strike. And priests and ministers at other churches informed their assemblies about the activities at the campus. Canvassing outside churches was also permitted, and students encouraged people to write their congressmen. "The response to this was extremely encouraging," students reported.

During the first days of the strike, Bates students heard of an extreme blood shortage at local hospitals, and in response, the strike steering committee organized a campus blood drive, and by Sunday noon over one hundred students had signed up as donors.

New Hampshire
Dartmouth College – Hanover

Dartmouth faculty met over the weekend and hammered out a grading procedure for students on strike, and by a near-unanimous voice vote, approved a fairly liberal proposal. It read in part: "Students who do not complete courses in which they are presently enrolled for a grade will have these courses listed on their transcripts with the notation: The student participated in one- half of this course in the Spring of 1970. By action of the Faculty of Arts and Sciences this was accepted as satisfying distributive, major, and graduation requirements which would normally have been fulfilled by the course."

A staff member of *Strike Newsletter* explained the resolution. "Simply, that a student can do whatever he wants for the rest of the term without academic penalties. In other words, it is up to each student to decide what is the most valuable thing for him to do and DO IT." The grading proposal, came to be known as the "Dartmouth Plan" and one of the most sympathetic plans for striking students by a faculty body anywhere in the country during the May rebellion. Students at other colleges attempted to emulate it, but few were successful – mainly because administrators and professors resisted its liberality.

University of New Hampshire – Durham

Saturday's issue of *Strike Daily* provided a glimpse into the details of the Durham strike. First, there were plenty of actions to announce: Gibbs Hall dormitory had been "liberated" and its residents voted to implement their own rules; a memorial service was being held that morning at Cowell Stadium for the Kent State students "murdered last week"; a mass rally at Thompson Hall was scheduled Saturday; and another anti-war rally was planned for the parking lot of a local shopping mall on Sunday night.

Saturday and Sunday were also "Parent's Weekend" at the university and parents and families were invited to a series of panel talks, which included "Restructuring the University," "Racism and the Black Panther Party," "The War in Indochina," "Women and the Strike," and a slide show on "Population and Ecology."

It was also announced the Hotel Administration Department was suspending classes for two weeks prior to the national election in November to allow students to "become a viable force in changing the American political system…" And an ad hoc committee was formed "to deal with any conflict of interest that may arise between students and faculty," over grades and class requirements.

A local committee of UNDO (Union for National Draft Opposition) had formed as part of a national effort "to flood the draft boards with so much mail and confusion that the boards will shut down." It proposed that all men should apply for conscientious objector status and all women should also register for the draft and also apply for CO status.

A boycott of Coke was called for in another article. "Student strikers are conducting an economic boycott all across the nation against the Coca-Cola Company and the products it owns or controls. Therefore, the following junk should not be purchased: Tab, Sprite, Fresca, Miller Beer, Minute Maid products, Real Gold products, Hi-C, all Phillip Morris products- Marlboro, Parliament, Virginia Slims, Philip Morris, Alpine, and Paxton cigarettes. … By applying pressure to this conglomerate, we can force it to take a stand against the war." The boycott was to start at midnight, Saturday, May 9.

Lastly, one brief news item was about students at local Oyster River High School who were discussing how they could liberate their own school and hold workshops. The item reported, "Many pupils have been dismissed, so that they may join UNH liberation study groups."

Vermont
Vermont State Capital Building in Montpelier

A memorial service for the Kent State victims was held on Saturday, May 9, at the State Capitol Building in Montpelier and was sponsored by a regional conference of striking colleges – including **University of Vermont, Goddard, Middlebury, Champlain, Saint Michael's,** and

Lyndon. It was scheduled in solidarity with and at the same time as the Washington DC mass demonstration.

St. Michael's College – Winooski Park

Students at St. Michael's staged an 80-hour vigil at the chapel to mourn the deaths of the four slain at Kent State and were joined by students from **UVM, Trinity** and **Champlain**. Some came carrying candles and silently knelt at the altar. Others at the vestibule talked about what was going on—all the while, folk songs were being quietly song.

College President Bernard Boutin appeared at a strike rally outside the chapel and acknowledged his support for the strike. Students genuinely felt validated by his presence there and at seminars and other events. When the rally wrapped-up, four students shrouded in black carried white crosses to the chapel followed by a procession of dozens. The crosses were placed on the marble steps of the altar, songs were sung, and a service and consecration held. The chaplain invited students to gather around the altar for the Mass, and he concluded with a prayer, "Lord, make me an instrument of your peace."

Massachusetts

Boston

Early Saturday morning, James Shea, a Massachusetts State Representative and a leading critic of the war, took his own life at his Newton home in a Boston suburb. He had recently spearheaded a successful drive in passing legislation prohibiting Massachusetts citizens from being forced to serve in an undeclared war and had just days earlier given his support to the strike. He had said, "I enthusiastically endorse the National Student Strike as an effective means of making it unmistakably clear to those who set national war policy in the legislative and executive branches that the young in this country find the level of their setting of national war policy utterly unacceptable."

According to the Newton police chief, Mrs. Shea saw her husband raise the pistol to his head with both hands, pull the trigger and fall back on the floor. She said her husband committed suicide because of political pressures and over his despair about the war's escalation.

Northeastern University in Boston

The campus at Northeastern had been very peaceful – until Saturday night. Around 10 pm Boston police responded to citizen complaints about a loud dorm block party on Hemenway Street. Police ordered the crowd to disperse calling it an unlawful assembly and a disturbance of the peace with loud music being played in the middle of the street.

Roughly a hundred officers moved on the block party and using tear gas and police dogs encouraged everyone to disperse. But people who ran into dorms were chased by officers who literally broke down glass doors when they busted in. One group of students away from the party site were also targeted for not complying.

By 1 am, the streets had been cleared. Yet, police had left behind a scene of mayhem and wreckage. The reports then began coming in; students who cleared the streets were still chased by cops swinging billy-clubs; officers ransacked six private apartments and clubbed the occupants; an elderly man caught in the crowd was beaten and left in the street; a blind man and his wife were beaten in their apartment and held an hour before being allowed to seek medical attention.

These outrageous reports were corroborated by the proctor of Smith Hall, Barbara Hurts, and by the director of Northeastern housing, Mr. Robbins. Robbins along with two other resident directors had been clubbed and Robbins' child injured during a police sweep of the lobby of his residence. In the dorms, police broke through locked doors, beat students in their rooms, and some witnesses observed officers with drawn revolvers. There was one report that an officer shot his weapon in the air as a threat to students on the rooftops. And in one bizarre report, witnesses saw tactical police, once they "captured" the rooftops, throw rocks, bottles and bricks down at students, passing cars and neighbors below.

Student leaders through all of this had attempted to call the Governor's office – but with no success and communication with the mayor's office had broken down both between the tactical police force and student liaisons. Injured students, bystanders, and even police officers were driven to various hospitals for treatment. The Northeastern Health Services itself was overwhelmed, because in the end, and unbelievably, more officers were injured during the fracas than partying students—100 versus 85.

Smith College

On Sunday, students from the all-women's college and a few local schools canvassed Northampton townspeople with anti-war petitions and information about their strike. That night, a crowd of 300 people met in the Quad to hear Black Panther leader Doug Miranda speak – students had raised $1,000 for his expenses.

A speech by Syd Waller, a member of the Black Students Association, during May exemplified the consciousness of Women's Liberation at Smith. "This is a national Student Strike. Each campus is supposed to have its own version. Ours is a strike on the campus of a college for women, and although it is being by and large run by women, men from other campuses have been trying to take it over. We need the help of all, men and women, for this is a strike on behalf of all humanity. Smith is a women's college – run predominately by men just as the strike might give the impression of being directed by men – but still, a women's college."

"We need to run our own strike. We're capable of running our own strike. We as women have a particular vision of what war can mean to humanity. This is a strike to end the torture and massacre in Cambodia and at home, to end the usurpation of power by President Nixon. Students all over the country have been striking, and women students have only just begun to realize our political power, and our responsibility to make full use of it."

"Women in our culture are considered and trained to be more compassionate and sensitive than men, thus we may be able to sympathize more fully with the victims of atrocities. It is seldom pointed out that for every male soldier killed, nine women and babies die. We're women, we strike as women, and we unite on behalf of the entire human race, not in a neo-militaristic violent strike, but in a peaceful humanitarian way."

Connecticut
Wesleyan University – Middletown

On Sunday, May 10, Wesleyan hosted a regional conference of campuses with ongoing strike actions, and delegates from 33 schools attended. They reaffirmed their solidarity and overwhelmingly approved a resolution to continue the national student strike in support of the three demands enunciated at New Haven.

New York State
New York City

On Saturday—the day after the so-called "Hard-Hat Riot" when construction workers had violented attacked peaceful demonstrators at Wall Street—Mayor John V. Lindsay publicly apologized and conceded some officers had "failed to perform their duty." Both he and Police Chief Timothy Leary said Friday's riot was made possible by police dereliction, and that not enough policemen had been stationed in the area at the time of the demonstration.

Details later emerged about the riot on May 8th—known in some circles as "Bloody Friday." It definitely was not some spontaneous eruption by the proletariat, but a carefully orchestrated plan originating in the White House itself. The head of the New York Building and Construction Trades Council was Peter Brennan, a big supporter of President Nixon. So, when he got a call from Nixon's special counsel Chuck Colson to take the lead in organizing a counter-demonstration against student protesters, Brennan was all to happy to comply. When Nixon was re-elected in 1972, Brennan was appointed his Labor Secretary.

In more fallout from the hard-hat riot, hundreds of workers and students met and formed the City-Wide Work Stoppage Committee to promote a general labor strike against the war. A committee spokesperson said, "Everyone at the meeting was for a general strike to demand immediate withdrawal from Southeast Asia. The question," the rep said, "is when."

Generally, labor support for the national anti-war movement was visible in the metropolitan New York area, and union organizations had mobilized several protests in protest of the war. For instance, District 37 of the Wholesale and Retail Clerks union had pressed for a work stoppage and a campaign to impeach Nixon. During the strike at Columbia University the previous week, students won support from campus workers. There was a fear, however, that the hard-hat riot portended a dangerous turn by labor against the anti-war movement and that "Bloody Sunday" would be repeated elsewhere. Fortunately, as the strike wore on, the fear evaporated when no incidents of its scale broke out.

Over the weekend on Saturday night, the Strike Headquarters of the New York City Student Mobilization Committee was severely vandalized. All their equipment was stolen, their phones destroyed, mailing and contact lists pilfered and all money pouches emptied.

After a week of anti-war actions at **St. John's University**, five Army trucks parked at their school were set on fire Saturday night. On Sunday, the faculty at **Queens College** voted to suspend all classes and exams for the rest of the term. Students from Queens had marched to Wall Street on Friday, the same day peace demonstrators were attacked by a mob of hard-hats. The faculty and students at **Staten Island Community College** on Sunday voted to join the national strike and suspend classes for the rest of the term.

Syracuse University

At a Saturday press conference, Chancellor John Corbally announced that classes would begin on Monday, the 11th. He knew this was a controversial directive, so, surprisingly, he added that students had not been shortchanged educationally by the strike, but in fact the great majority had learned more in the past week than perhaps in the whole academic year.

Corbally responded to a number of questions. On the issue of the Black Panthers, he said he needed more information and planned to meet with students about them. 'What about grades?' He replied it wasn't his decision and punted the issue to the various deans. On the issue of the student-erected barricades, he did say they needed to be resolved, but denied there was any impasse of importance. On the issue of a court injunction, he said students were not in any violation and there wasn't any action to be taken against them. Corbally also praised Syracuse Police Chief Sardino for leading a competent and sympathetic police force during the strike.

Later that day Chief Sardino had the chance to prove the Chancellor's praise. When campus workers at the University Physical Plant began removing the barricade next to the Administration Building, immediately a crowd of a couple hundred students formed to block the effort. The chief was alerted to the situation and addressed the students. "You can put your barricades back up, as soon as they get out some dangerous explosive material." The Chief then asserted, "The only person who can order me to bring police onto this campus is a state Supreme Court Judge and I have not been told to do so at this time."

Moments later, Professor Fred Morgner emerged and confirmed Sardino's claims—the workers needed to remove propane gas tanks from the geology construction site but the barricade blocked the route. The barricades would remain, Morgner said, once the tanks came out. With this assurance, crews moved to clear the way and by mid-afternoon, the barricade was back up.

Saturday night, Hendrick's Chapel was the site of a mass meeting of the student body. Unlike past meetings, some felt this one was characterized by a sense of solidarity and unanimity. A strike committee representative, Bob Tembeckian, called for the cancellation of all formal classes and for students to remain non-violent. With no opposition, the audience immediately burst into a standing ovation. They also decided that construction workers on campus blocked by student barricades would be allowed back at their sites.

Sunday morning the strike committee responded to Chancellor Corbally's statement that classes would resume on Monday. Students had just recently voted overwhelmingly to cease all formal classroom instruction for the semester, which would allow them and faculty members to work in the Syracuse community and participate in workshops and seminars on strike issues. "We do not believe in closing the university and sending people home," the committee said in a statement published in *Shut Down*, the strike newsletter.

The only reason to halt classes, the committee argued, was to enable the entire university to commit itself to those strike issues. "Universities are founded upon the principle of human dignity and freedom. Yet these principles are greatly imperiled by US's actions in South East Asia, and by the repression of Black Panthers and other groups in this country." The university had to re-affirm those principles with the suspension of formal classes until the end of the semester. Then the strike committee made a puzzling claim—that the university was "precipitating violence" by opening the school because "groups on campus which the Strike

Committee does not represent ... are intent on visiting violence on the University." They hoped they could "cooperate with the Chancellor to avoid the disasters that have recently occurred on college campuses across the country." Later that morning, a memorial service was held at Hendricks Chapel for one of those disasters – the four dead students at Kent State.

SUNY Cortland

On Saturday, May 9, striking students marched from Corey Union on campus to the Court House Green and Cortland City Hall. A wide spectrum of the campus was involved in the protest including the "radical caucus" – the occupiers of the administration building. As students marched into town, others distributed strike literature to townspeople along the way on the Indochina war, inflation and political repression of the Panthers.

An important focus of the strike was the campaign to canvass the Cortland community, and it continued throughout Saturday. Canvassers went door-to-door and spoke with people about the strike, Kent State, asked them to sign petitions opposed to the war and to send letters or telegrams to their Congressional representatives. In just a few days, the campaign had instigated nearly 1,000 letters and telegrams.

An estimated 6,000 **Binghamton University** students, high school students, and local residents on Saturday marched from campus to the downtown courthouse in Binghamton. The huge column wound its way along the parkway, over a bridge, and culminated on Court Street, where picket lines were set up along both sides of the road.

Late Saturday evening, students at **Skidmore College** in Saratoga Springs mounted the steps of two buses, which then departed campus for Interstate 90. It was part of a coast-to-coast, mass protest along the highways from Boston to Seattle. As the *Skidmore News* announced, "People are asked to bring simple signs (big letters, simple message, so people don't run off road trying to read them.) A 50-cent donation is asked to pay for the bus drivers."

Southeast
University of Virginia -Charlottesville

On Saturday, the day after police arrested 68 people at a non-violent "Honk for Peace" protest, the Charlottesville Commonwealth Attorney criticized the arrests and confirmed that "ultimate responsibility for loosening the [police] forces on the grounds rested with the UV administration headed by President Edgar F. Shannon whom we recognized as the head."

For his part, President Shannon must have had a prick at his conscience and decided he had to do something to both bring the university community back together and enhance his standing with students, so he announced he was giving a major address on the Lawn. 4,000 students and faculty members showed up, many out of curiosity to see what the administration's next step would be, and they ended up listening to Shannon deliver a break-out, anti-war message to the large audience.

At first, Dr. Shannon asked his audience to "continue to help me to preserve the university as a place of learning and of free expression and ideas," but then veered into controversy and instantly changed his standing with students. He had been earlier denounced at one recent protest and was responsible for requesting the police presence last Friday—but this day was different. He told the crowd he wished to find "practical ways to advance the cause of peace in Vietnam and to bring about change on the national scene, beyond the university." Shannon charged Nixon with using military campaigns in Southeast Asia, especially the invasion of Cambodia, to reassure uneasy Americans that US troops were making progress, all to regain the public's support for the war. His message surprised many on the Lawn and Shannon was enthusiastically applauded.

He then presented a petition to the audience and requested support for an anti-war delegation of students and faculty to head to Washington to lobby for peace. Within 24 hours of the speech, over 5,000 signatures had been collected and Student Council President Jim Roebuck was on his way to Washington along with President Shannon.

Washington and Lee University – Lexington, Virginia

On Saturday, a moment of levity occurred for strikers at W&L, according to the campus press, when a contingent of four students from campus attended the graduation exercises of cadets at **Virginia Military Institute**, which was literally right next door. Dressed in bellbottoms, one in a judge's robe, the long-haired group was led by striker Dave Katz who carried a large bag of marshmallows. Two state troopers approached and warned them, "It's their graduation, so no disturbances or interference." Katz responded, "We're just going to watch the parade. We all love a parade. We're just going to eat these marshmallows."

For a second time, they were approached, this time by the grounds superintendent who informed them they were trespassing and had to leave immediately. The students responded that there were hundreds of other people there watching the parade, but were told, "They're not trespassing, just you." Then the state troopers returned and also ordered them to leave. To avoid arrest, the troupe got up and left the parade grounds. Later Katz said, "The only apparent reason for our ejection was that we were dressed funny, had long hair, and were carrying marshmallows. Maybe they thought the marshmallows were loaded."

Students at **James Madison University** went on strike but butted heads with the college president who refused to alter class and exam schedules. Working primarily on the campaign to support the Hatfield-McGovern amendment, students felt isolated, organized few seminars due to a lack of speakers, and desperately needed draft information.

Strike assistance was also needed on the campus of **Mary Baldwin College** in Staunton. Lacking organizational backing, a referendum on a strike failed, and the faculty refused to allow pass / fail grades. Lastly, it appeared the main focus of students was on lobbying in Washington and researching Congressional candidates.

North Carolina State University at Raleigh

Student Body President Cathy Sterling hoped to capitalize on the energy from Friday's large anti-war march on the Capitol in Raleigh and issued a call for a boycott of classes on Sunday, May 10. The boycott would not be a strike, she iterated, but a "Peace Retreat" that would explore issues related to the war. She and other organizers asked the administration for a moratorium for the remainder of the semester to allow them to hold the retreat. The student newspaper, the *Technician*, endorsed it and stated the boycott was to allow the campus community to discuss the war, and was "not a leave of absence for students to hit the beaches three weeks early."

Atlanta, Georgia

For a week **Emory University** students and other Atlanta residents of the Emory Mobilization Committee had been preparing to protest President Nixon's visit to the Atlanta area on Saturday, May 9. He was to dedicate the memorial to the Confederacy at Stone Mountain, about 15 miles outside Atlanta. But Nixon had to cancel—he was in DC being confronted by tens of thousands of demonstrators – and had to send Vice-President Agnew in his stead. When Agnew spoke, he said nothing at all about student unrest, but did lay out Nixon's plan for a national realignment of power—Nixon's "Southern Strategy"—and welcomed the South back into the country and into the GOP.

In the largest anti-Vietnam war demonstration in Atlanta's history, a large crowd of 5,000 people, mainly college and high school students, marched Sunday the 10th from Piedmont Park down Peachtree Street to the Georgia State Capitol. The procession that passed through downtown Atlanta was both solemn and festive—no incidents were reported.

Other colleges in Georgia held anti-racism or anti-war demonstrations, including both **Paine College** in Augusta and **Albany College** where protest actions were led by Black students. At **Columbus College** 150 students had a show-down with the president over his refusal to lower the American flag to half-staff in honor of the Kent State slain.

Augusta, Georgia

A series of events that played out tragically began when the body of Charles Oatman, a 16-year-old Black youth with a mental disability, was brought to a mortuary in the heart of the Black community. He had died at the local jail and police claimed he had been fatally injured in a fall from his bunk. Shocked at the conditions of Oatman's body, the mortician called Grady Abrams—the only Black member of the City Council. Abrams came to the mortuary and viewed the youth's 104-pound corpse. He described what he saw:

"There was this 16-year-old kid that had been brutally beaten. He had three gashes the length of his back maybe about an inch deep. The back of his skull was crushed in. He had cigarette burns from the tip of his fingers down to his toes. They were all over his body."

Immediately questions were raised. For one, why wasn't Oatman, a disabled youth, placed at the Youth Detention Center instead of at the over-crowded adult Richmond County Jail? And why were Oatman's injuries inconsistent with a fall from his bunk?

News of Oatman's death spread like wildfire through the community and rumors swirled that he had been beaten by police. With anger clearly mounting, that night a crowd of more than 200 residents gathered outside the Richmond County Jail demanding answers from the sheriff. Meanwhile, police officers with weapons drawn surrounded the jailhouse.

Inside, Councilmember Abrams and other city officials were meeting with Sheriff E.R. Atkins who told them an investigation into the incident was under way. Yet the official explanation still remained—Oatman was punched by another inmate while on his upper bunk and fell to the floor busting his skull, which caused his death.

Abrams reported back to the crowd and everyone moved to the Tabernacle Baptist Church to discuss the situation. No one was satisfied, many were upset and one man said he wanted to take the jail apart, brick by brick. Finally, the group decided to hold a demonstration the next day, Monday, in front of the municipal building on Greene Street, where they would demand a further and more satisfactory explanation.

Racial tensions in Augusta had simmered for decades, arguably for a century. In 1970, some Black neighborhoods still had dirt streets, and many were without sewers or the use of city water. And Grady Abrams, the city councilman, had for quite a long while tried to draw the attention of the white-dominated establishment to the social disparities, inequities and to threats of racial unrest. But to no avail – the white elites were in deep denial, at best.

More than 300 student demonstrators, mainly from the **University of Miami Coral Gables** campus, staged a protest rally on Saturday, May 9, in front of Federal Building in downtown Miami. When the rally broke up, squads of students hit the shopping centers and malls and handed out leaflets about their strike and the national crisis of Cambodia and Kent State,

At the **University of Alabama in Tuscaloosa** on Saturday evening, a student-faculty ad hoc coalition of 200-300 people met with President

Dave Mathews in an effort to find a compromise to restrictions he had placed on students—groups larger than six were not permitted on campus and state troopers were on standby ready to enforce the rule. A "compromise" of sorts was reached—students agreed to a 3-day moratorium on mass demonstrations and gatherings, and Mathews agreed on a hearing process to review future student grievances.

Jackson State College – Jackson, Mississippi
May 9, Saturday

On Saturday, a dozen Jackson State students joined over a hundred students from the mostly all-white Millsaps College in a downtown peace rally at the War Memorial. The rally had been sponsored by the Jackson Peace Coordinating Committee, whose rally flyer stated organizers wanted to find common cause with African-American residents. Two state patrolmen approached the demonstrators and told them it was illegal to hold a protest on state property, so they either had to leave or be arrested. The group then marched two blocks to city property where it was legal and then held their rally.

In 1970, African-Americans made up 40 percent of Jackson's population of 154,000, yet white elites dominated the political and economic arenas, holding legislative control in the city. The racial divide extended to poorer levels of education and limited earning potential among the city's Black residents. In 1970, the average Black family earned less than half of the median income of Jackson's white families.

Loyola University—New Orleans, Louisiana

By mid-day Saturday, the occupation and sleep-in at Danna Student Center had become a center for the campus anti-war movement. Beginning Friday, roughly 100 people had brought signs, sleeping bags, mattresses, posters – and books—and had occupied the student center. Books were everywhere – it was exam week.

That afternoon, a mass meeting attended by 400 students decided to respond to Father Jolley's refusal to endorse a grading policy approved by much of the campus. They began organizing a series of protests and declared they would continue the occupation until Jolley agreed to their demands. In good news for strikers, the list of faculty members who agreed to make final exams optional was growing, and over the weekend, more joined and expressed support for the plan.

That night, a candlelight vigil was held in front of Marquette Hall to protest the Cambodian invasion and the Kent State slayings. And at midnight, a student fast for peace began, in which students planned to fast for a nine day period in three-day shifts, taking only water and vitamins.

On Sunday morning, students set up a picket line in front of Holy Name Church on St. Charles Avenue which bordered Loyola. It was part of an effort to inform the community of their beliefs and of the university's refusal to take a stand on the crisis.

Midwest

Cleveland, Ohio Peace Rally

On Saturday, May 9, over 2,000 people congregated behind Severance Hall in Cleveland for a peace rally, including students from **Case Western Reserve**, **Hiram College** and **Cleveland State University**. Many middle aged people and grade schoolers were in attendance, and some of them had helped to distribute literature about the war and student strikes. After a memorable first-hand report of the Kent State massacre by KSU student Mike York, protest music was performed by members of the Cleveland Orchestra and students from the Cleveland Institute of Music. Workshops for members of the crowd on war and economic issues had been set up by organizers to be conducted by students and faculty members from the colleges.

Oberlin College, Ohio

Over the weekend, advertisements appeared in Ohio newspapers which read: "The Oberlin College community as a whole has agreed to accommodate Kent students not wishing to return home early, the purpose of this action is to provide Kent students with a base to continue working together rather than as scattered individuals." About 220 **Kent State** students and several professors did accept Oberlin's offer and moved to the campus to study and pursue antiwar efforts until their school reopened for the summer quarter in late June.

In light of campus unrest, students and administrators at **Hebrew Union College** in Cincinnati, agreed on Saturday that "business-as-usual" was out of the question for the next few days.

During the early hours on Saturday the last of the occupiers at the **University of Michigan Ann Arbor** left North Hall after a 33-hour occupation of ROTC quarters. There had been only a handful of arrests and no major damage to the building. (North Hall was later demolished in 2014 and ROTC and Navy ROTC offices were moved to other campus buildings.)

On Sunday, President Keast of **Wayne State University in Detroit** declared that normal class schedules would resume on Monday. Despite picket lines full of strikers, the administration on Monday would estimate that class attendance was at 75%.

Several thousand **Indiana University** students and antiwar activists from the community marched peacefully into downtown South Bend on Saturday, after rallying at Leeper Park. It was part of the South Bend campus "Cambodia Week" – an effort to unite students with community people.

University of Notre Dame – South Bend

By Sunday, students had collected 10,000 signatures on President Hesburgh's petition to President Nixon demanding immediate withdrawal of all American troops from Southeast Asia. Students would go on and eventually collect a total of 23,000 signatures within the South Bend community.

In a letter to President Nixon that accompanied the petition, Hesburgh wrote, "I have seen a moral rebirth on this campus during the past 10 days of May that is unparalleled in my lifetime, most of which has been spent at universities, mainly this one." Hesburgh never received a response from the White House, and he never knew whether Nixon saw his letter or the petition. Regardless, the nation's outcry – including the critical Hesburgh statement and petition—forced an early withdrawal of U.S. troops from Cambodia.

Purdue University – Lafayette, Indiana

Some Purdue students had left the state to attend the gigantic protest in Washington, D.C., while those on campus Saturday were involved in three separate actions. First, there was a pro-ROTC rally where speakers noted ROTC's long tradition on the campus and urged students to vote in favor of keeping the program at an upcoming Monday referendum.

The second was a Black Solidarity Rally organized by the Black Student Union with the goal of increasing communications between Purdue students and Lafayette's Black community. 150 students listened to Mark McCarty, a Black Panther from Gary, describe the persecution of the Panthers and the imprisonment of its chairman Bobby Seale.

Later in the afternoon, the third action was a first-hand account of the shootings at Kent State by history teaching assistant, Jackie Stewart. And lo and behold, the pro-ROTC rally members converged with the Black Solidarity ralliers to hear her experiences. Stewart said she was a mere ten feet from National Guardsmen, when "for no reason at all ... they turned and fired into the crowd." She blamed Ohio Governor James A. Rhodes, President Nixon, and Vice President Agnew for causing the tragedy. She then solicited financial help for some 200 Kent State students still in jail, and told the Purdue crowd that KSU students and faculty remained steadfast in getting firearms banished from campus and in eliminating ROTC.

Chicago Peace March, Saturday, May 9

On Saturday, May 9, the City of Chicago experienced the largest out-pouring of opposition to the Vietnam war during the entire month of May. Organized by the Chicago Peace Council in conjunction with area colleges, the march and rally in downtown Chicago included up to 25,000 people. **Northwestern University** activists estimated 1,000 students from their campus were involved and many from the **University of Chicago** and **Loyola University** were also in the crowds.

To get to the downtown Civic Center, 400 Northwestern students took buses from campus south to the Loop, while hundreds of others found their own way. By the time the NU delegation hit the Civic Center, massive throngs overflowed the plaza cramming adjoining streets. Knots of people handed out literature and pamphlets, covering everything from protesting servicemen to women's liberation, and NU students gave out copies of the *Daily Northwestern*. When a young kid climbed the famous Picasso statue in the plaza and tied a red flag with a white peace sign to one of its spokes, the crowd cheered.

Finally, the massive crowd moved out of the plaza—while blue-helmeted Chicago police officers lined Washington Street—and turned down Dearborn Avenue for the four blocks to the Federal Building. Anti-war chants and slogans ricocheted off the tall buildings, peace signs and clenched fists were thrown at people on the sidewalks and bystanders flashed smiles or peace signs back. When the throngs reached the Federal Building, they were joined by another group and the combined sea of people turned east towards Grant Park.

It was 1:30 when the first waves of people reached the southern end of the park, and it took another hour for the rest of the ten block-long column to pour in. The march itself was peaceful and without incident, as organizers had provided marshals and medics to assist the crowds.

At Grant Park, the scene of the 1968 Chicago police riots during the Democratic Convention, the statue of General Logan was completely taken over by protesters. He was decked out with anti-war banners, American flags, and flags of the National Liberation Front and North Vietnam. One of the speakers was vice-chair of the Chicago Peace Council, Jack Spiegel, who told the crowd, "The strike movement will not stop with the students," and urged them to "turn out in the community and organize a general consumers' and workers' strike." The crowd cheered.

NU favorite and student body president, Eva Jefferson, spoke and said one hopeful sign she saw was "the unions are beginning to join us." She said, "The best thing we can do next week is to shut America down. The only person who should be working next week is Richard Nixon." She added, "The beautiful thing that is happening in Evanston, is that people stop and listen to us. There's a lot of work yet to be done. Let's stop talking to each other" and get out into the community. The crowd gave her a standing ovation.

Northwestern University – Evanston, Illinois

Back at the Northwestern campus, a small cadre had guarded the Sheridan Road barricade all Friday night, some had even slept at the barricade, but by Saturday morning most were dog tired. The barricade—standing all of five feet in height and three-feet in width – was made of sawhorses, tree limbs, rocks, pieces of concrete, gate sections and other odds and ends students had picked up and thrown into the heap. Complaints by locals and attempts to dismantle it plagued the barricaders and it was even going to be an issue at an upcoming Evanston Aldermen meeting on Monday.

Also Saturday, National Guard units that had been called up for duty in Evanston rolled out of town. They were no longer needed as Evanston city officials on Friday night had declared "the threat to have passed."

City Manager Wayne Anderson was the official who had originally called Governor Ogilvie to request the Guard and had claimed the city expected more than 10,000 students at a rally at Dyche Stadium—and local Evanston police could not handle a crowd of that size. Then Ogilvie ordered the Guard to deploy to Evanston—but the governor for some reason ordered the Guard to be sent directly to Dyche Stadium, the site of the massive rally. Catching wind of a potential disaster, level-headed city officials met the Guard on the way into town and directed them to a local elementary school more than a mile from Northwestern, where they bedded down for their one night stand.

Kendall College in Chicago had gone on strike on Thursday for three days due to the strong anti-war sentiment on campus. But on Sunday, the College Council - composed of 7 students, 7 faculty members and 7 administrators - voted to end the strike and resume classes. The decision was taken despite an earlier vote by students to continue the strike by 260 to 165. (Kendall's enrollment was about 800.)

University of Illinois - Urbana and Champaign

On Saturday, workshops and teach-ins held on the campus Quadrangle included sessions on a wide range of issues: the controversial Pentagon Illiac IV super-computer, university complicity in the war, the campus ROTC, the "positive vibrations" of cooperatives and communal living, underground newspapers, women's liberation, self-defense and socialist Cuba. A rally – called an "Illiaction"—brought out a crowd of thousands who enjoyed the warm weather and were in a festive, even "riotous spirit."

After the rally, the campus mood dramatically changed when a long line of chanting demonstrators marched from the Quad to first, the construction site of the super-computer and then to the armory. Walking in the middle of the street, protesters blocked traffic and targeted a few storefront windows. Tension mounted at one intersection when the crowd halted and sat down in the street.

It didn't take long for dozens of Champaign police officers to arrive. Chief Harvey Shirley had also showed and with his megaphone, warned students to clear the streets or face arrest. When students didn't budge, the chief ordered his men to move in, which they did, arresting eight in the process.

During the rest of the afternoon large restless crowds milled about on the Quad and on campus streets. About 6 p.m. state police and National Guardsmen disembarked from their buses parked nearby. Days earlier—on Wednesday—city officials had asked for a deployment of the Guard to assist local police in enforcing an 8 pm to 6 am curfew, and Governor Ogilvy ordered up 2,100 National Guard troops for the Champaign-Urbana area.

It was close to 6:15 when police and Guard units formed up. They moved south in a large sweep of the campus, marching through and around the Illini Student Union, all the way pushing and shoving students toward the Quad. As more state troopers lined up on other sides of the Quad, students watched nervously as they realized they were being surrounded.

Without warning, squads of state troopers charged onto the Quad, and individual students were abruptly grabbed and hauled away to three buses parked close by. This dramatic escalation continued until over 100 people had been taken into custody—one of the largest, single mass arrests of peaceful students during the May rebellion.

The buses rolled to a site near Memorial Stadium being used as a detention center, and the arrestees were then transferred to police stations. Once the mass arrest was over, state troopers and the Guard departed campus, leaving in their wake thousands still on the Quad—shocked and angered. The arrests appeared to have been random. 102 people had been taken into custody including monitors, newspaper and TV reporters and a botanist taking pictures of plants and trees.

A little after 8 pm a fire alarm in the Illini Union was pulled and a university employee called police to quell a disturbance inside the building. State troopers returned to the student center and began pushing students out and onto the Quad, and a few reacted by smashing windows and setting fire to a sofa. Yet, once the "Staties" had cleared the building, they again moved off. About a half hour later, a crowd of 1,000 outraged students formed at the Quad and *en mass* marched to the stadium to demand the release of those arrested. Along the way, police cars were stoned and more windows smashed, and some of those who remained on the Quad vandalized Altgeld Hall, the administration building.

It seemed like a giant chess game was being played out on the campus, its Quad and crisscrossing streets. Around 10 pm, state police made their next move – and brought with them 750 National Guardsmen. Upon their arrival, both groups were initially met with a barrage of rocks, but after advancing, students fell back. Once again, the Quad was surrounded – this time by Guardsmen—who slowly swept through and cleared it. To control the entire area, state troopers marched up nearby streets and made more arrests.

The overwhelming combined force of local, state police and Guardsmen resulted in a deserted Quad by 11:30 pm, and a heavy downpour forced diehards to immediately seek shelter. Those arrested were held overnight and booked on numerous charges before being released.

The issue of the mass arrests became paramount on campus, and its decision came somewhere from within the chain of command between the Guard and state police. The "sweep" had even caught the administration off-guard. Vice-Chancellor for Campus Affairs George Frampton admitted he didn't know why students on the Quadrangle were arrested, and that even he had been denied entrance to the converted stadium by "the guard at the door." Dean of Students Hugh Satterlee was also totally surprised at the clamp-down. He had been in a special meeting of deans that very afternoon involved in the process of de-escalating the root causes of the strike.

Students and faculty took note of the total lack of university control of the situation, which further alienated the faculty from the administration. Faculty members criticized "the inability of Chancellor Peltason and his staff to maintain control of this campus after they had made the decision to allow it to be turned into an armed camp." Over the weekend, another 54 people were arrested, mostly for curfew violations.

Sunday, May 10

After the storms of the night had passed, 6,000 students rallied Sunday on the Main Quad, clearly upset over the mass arrests and the heavy-handed tactics of law enforcement. Campus administrators scrambled to put their Humpty-Dumpty back together. One official announced the National Guard would be demobilized and that the State Police would not intervene again on campus unless there was violence. Dean Satterlee even told striking students the administration would not take any punitive measures against them. Chancellor Peltason went so far as to release a statement that authorized so-called "liberation classes" for the following week.

Yet, after the sweep and mass arrests, many students and faculty gave up on having any confidence in Chancellor Peltason and his administration. Students ridiculed him for authorizing the liberation classes and mocked him by declaring themselves "liberated" from the campus. When a student government steering committee member, Ted Byers, made a motion to "secede from the United States and declare war on the country," students heartily applauded him.

Northern Illinois University – DeKalb

On Saturday, students initiated a new tactic and form of protest: a boycott of 17 local DeKalb merchants who were described as unfair to students due to their exploitative prices and inferior goods. Five businesses were called "friends" with "fair prices"—three food markets, a gas station and a discount store. A student boycott advocate, Gary Murphy, said, "The purpose isn't to drive merchants out of business but to give students a fair shake and to promote better selling practices." He added, "Merchants can recover from a broken window, but nothing says that people must buy from their stops." Those businesses boycotted needed to become "fair" in their pricing and selling practices, he said.

Southern Illinois University- Carbondale

Tensions on the Carbondale campus continued over the weekend, as National Guardsmen blocked all entrances to the university. Students had suffered the Guard deployed on their campus for days, a police tear gas attack the previous Friday, over 150 arrests and hundreds treated for tear gas. And incredibly, 322 more people were arrested over the weekend, 146 for curfew violations, with half of those arrested being non-students. By the end of the weekend, the 200 National Guardsmen stationed at Southern Illinois were the only Illinois guardsmen still on active duty.

University of Wisconsin in Madison

Chancellor Edwin Young on Sunday, May 10, announced that the next week on campus would be his "alternative week of involvement" and would consist of discussions, workshops and other programs related to the war and the national student strike. Immediately, activists saw this as one more effort by the chancellor to distract students from his stubborn refusal to close the campus.

At a night rally on Union Terrace attended by 1,000 people, strike leaders denounced Young's "alternative week" as an attempt to "co-opt the strike and obscure the real issues." At the conclusion of the rally, with rain pouring down, hundreds of strikers ran up Bascom Hill and initiated a half hour of trashing campus windows.

After administrators on Sunday announced **Marquette University in Milwaukee** would not be closed, students went on a brief rampage and broke several windows on campus and area storefronts.

St. Paul, Minnesota Peace March

Saturday, May 9, was the regional anti-war march to the St. Paul Capitol, and according to the local **Carleton College** student press, a "carnival spirit" prevailed as thousands of demonstrators converged on the city. Many Carleton and **St. Olaf College** students had driven north to attend the unprecedented demonstration and joined crowds from the **University of Minnesota Twin Cities** campus. A large, helium balloon with the word "Pax" and a peace sign floated about the massive throng, estimated to be over 20,000 people. Marchers carried signs identifying themselves as "Veterans for Peace," "Social Workers for Peace," and "Medics for Peace" carried by people wearing white coats. One sign read, "Department of Geography Volleyball Players for Peace."

People along the parade route hung out of windows and balconies and waved and smiled at the young protesters. In one stretch, the march went through an exclusive St. Paul residential neighborhood with fine old homes, including the Governor's mansion. One student newspaper reported, "Out of these homes poured fathers and grandfathers dressed in charcoal gray with tailored vests and matching cufflinks and tie clips, and grand-mothers and mothers in suits with fur-trimmed collars, and children dressed in party dresses with patent leather shoes. Out of other homes streamed teeny-boppers in knee-highs and surfer shirts or college students in jeans and bell-bottoms. But nearly everyone smiled, and many grinning grandmothers flashed the peace sign, causing the crowd to cheer, 'Join us!' And a few did."

The police presence was fairly lowkey. A few officers smiled and chatted with marchers, and when one officer raised his hand in a peace sign, he was immediately handed a marshmallow and received cheers from the marchers.

On Sunday, more than 200 students at the **University of Missouri – Columbia** met and endorsed a set of demands to present to the university administration. They included that either Chancellor John Schwada or President Weaver take a stand against the war in Indochina; that there would be no further penalties against striking students or faculty members; and that students may cease attendance on a class-by-class basis.

University of Iowa – Iowa City
Saturday, May 9

During Saturday's early hours, an old, framed multistory classroom building burned down in a huge fire blamed on arsonists. Affectionately known as "Big Pink," the Old Armory was considered a firetrap and scheduled to be torn down, but still contained a few offices for a writing lab. A much smaller fire was lit in a restroom in the East Hall Annex. As firemen poured water on the ruins of Big Pink, Iowa Gov. Robert Ray ordered up 400 National Guardsmen to deploy to Iowa City.

During the day, National Guard troops moved onto the Johnson County Fairgrounds just outside city and Guard helicopters monitored the area around the Pentacrest, the usual site of campus protests. Rain began falling and everything on the surface seemed clean and peaceful, but underneath, tension smoldered, just like Big Pink. Armed police were stationed in the Old Capitol and the Guard was very close by and on standby.

To add to the tension, over the weekend Iowa City police had fired their weapons at a group of African American students whom they claimed were attempting to break into a jewelry store. No one was injured but seven were arrested. Charges of burglary were denied by the Black students who claimed it was a case of blatant racism on the part of police.

Sunday, May 10

By Sunday morning President William Boyd was ready to lower the tension and compromise with strikers. He announced the university would remain open only until the end of the semester on May 26, and that students could leave and not be required to take classes or final exams. Boyd said students "fearing for their safety" could return home without academic sanctions. Those who chose not to go to class or take finals were given three options: complete all course work later; accept a pass grade or withdraw grade; or take a letter grade based on work already completed. Students were given two days in which to choose one of the options.

Strike leaders were incensed and called Boyd's "compromise" a "strike-breaking device." However, the options did allow students to continue the strike.

Sunday night, more than 800 students met inside King Chapel at **Cornell College** in Mt. Vernon to respond to the national crisis. After a lengthy discussion, an overwhelming majority decided to continue the regular academic and exam schedules—the school was a third of the way through the exam period—but also decided to organize student groups and discussion sessions on Cambodia, Kent State and other issues for that upcoming Tuesday, May 12.

University of Kansas – Lawrence

It was a beautiful spring Saturday in Lawrence, Kansas, and 600 students met in Woodrun Auditorium to organize a series of protest projects. They included Congressional lobbying, community canvassing in Lawrence, organizing a speakers' bureau and holding workshops on the war and related issues. Students also organized letter-writing campaigns, petition drives and talks at civic clubs. On campus about a quarter of the student body continued with "business as usual" while the vast majority were involved in the alternative activities, observed the strike newsletter. Each day, workshops were held on women's liberation, grassroots politics, and the most popular—the history of the Vietnam war.

In the town of Emporia, roughly 60 miles southwest of Lawrence, students from the **College of Emporia** on Sunday marched from campus to downtown in protest to the war and the killings at Kent State. They were joined by 200 students from nearby **Kansas State Teachers College**.

University of Nebraska, Lincoln
Saturday, May 9

A slew of speakers bent on raising consciousness took the mic at Saturday's peace rally at the women's PE field. It had been sponsored by the May 9 Coalition and had attracted 4,000 to 5,000 people. Nearly everyone who attended was handed a daisy at the gates, but David Rice from the Black Panther Omaha chapter, said, "No flower in the world will stop a bullet. The only way to get power to the people is to defend it, because flowers and talk of love won't do it. Love is fine, but when President Adolph Nixon says he won't be influenced by peaceful protest," anti-war activists would be "foolish" to not defend themselves from violence by the government. "Unorganized confrontation with the police will only get you four dead Kent students. Protestors must learn to deal with the government the same way the Vietnamese people are dealing with the American government."

John Swomley, a pacifist professor, addressed the large crowd. "The United States is trying to maintain imperialism by violence." The real reason behind Nixon's decision to move US troops 22.7 miles into Cambodia, he said, was not to destroy NLF headquarters and sanctuaries but to move them 23 miles inland. "Part-time demonstrations and occasional resistance to our Indochina policy" must end. What was needed, Swomley said, was a sustained effort to end the war. Students were tired of elected representatives and college administrators who protect the military-industrial complex. "Students can and should get rid of ROTC on campus – without violence," he said, by applying pressure on the administrations. "ROTC remains on campus only with your approval. You have allowed campuses to become little West Points." Swomley concluded by advocating for a boycott by students as an effective way of creating change—students needed to stop buying products from companies who "beat the war drums."

Another speaker, Dr. James Kavanaugh, author and former Roman Catholic priest, told the crowd that life was more important than education. "You can live without a degree. Hell. I've got three I never use." He claimed reform and revolution were more important than education, for the educated ultimately become the intellectual elite who don't do anything to affect change. "A human revolution proceeds from love," he told them.

Speaker John Green from Omaha cried out it was "beautiful!" to see "8,000 people show up to protest the war in Lincoln, Nebraska." Having just returned from Washington, he urged students to collect signatures on the Hatfield-McGovern bill which would cut all funds for military expenditures in Southeast Asia after December.

A delegation of Winnebago Native Americans attended the rally, and their speaker, Rueben Snake, explained the US was in Indochina to honor treaties. But, he said, the country had never flinched from breaking treaties with "your First Americans." The Winnebagos had come to spread the word and gain support among students about their conflict with the Army Corps of Engineers, who wanted to take over a piece of their historic land and turn it into a recreation area.

Another speaker, Rev. Tom Rehorn, a Sioux City minister, told the large crowd the North Vietnamese and Viet Cong were "little Davids up against American Goliaths. They have withstood us for nine years and they will do it for nine more." Change cannot come about without exerting pressure, Rehorn said, "because power has never moved voluntarily." If students got rid of their fear and expended some courage, "You'll be surprised what you can get away with." Anti-war activists had to use their intelligence and organize against "cold cash politics and rifles or else you'll be playing tiddlywinks like the church has been doing." Finally, he emphasized, "Radicals for peace and love" won't get far if they don't cultivate support from the community.

Another religious man, James Armstrong, a Methodist bishop, addressed the assembly and declared war was no longer a defensible strategy. "Unless people like us," he said, "call an end to war, war will put an end to people like us." The country was becoming more and more a military state, he said, and that since World War II more than one trillion dollars had been spent for the military.

Fred Stover, president of the U.S. Farmers' Association, also took the microphone. Focusing on the war's drain on resources, he said, "As long as the nation's resources are involved in the Asian quagmire, there is not enough money for assistance for the producers of the food." Stover said political courage was the ammunition that college students and Americans must use to convince the government to get out of Asia.

Meanwhile, 1200 miles away, the campus delegation of four students visiting Congressional offices in Washington DC experienced some progress. They had spoken with an aide to Sen. Frank Church (D-Idaho) about his boss' sponsorship of the amendment to withhold funds from US operations in Cambodia, and they had even spoken with an aide to President Nixon about the concerns of Mid-western students. Once their official business was over, they took part in the large, massive demonstration at the White House, and one later noted that DC had the same "party atmosphere" as the take-over of the ROTC building did back on campus. One group was skinny-dipping in the Tidal Basin, while others were playing "Dixie" on kazoos at the Lincoln Memorial. Later in the evening, two of them were caught in a tear-gas barrage on their way back to their hotel.

Sunday, May 10

On Sunday evening at a university-wide town hall meeting, conservative pro-war students and their professor allies used parliamentary procedures to try to have the strike voted down and out. One prominent pro-strike activist never had a chance to speak even though he was second-in-line at one of the floor mics. Yet, a vote by a show of hands was inconclusive, so anti-war activists successfully lobbied for the use of a secret ballot to decide the fate of the strike. The ballot was taken and results were to be announced at a meeting Monday morning.

Southwest

University of New Mexico – Albuquerque

The campus was still reeling over the weekend from Friday, the day when nearly a dozen people were wounded by National Guardsmen's bayonets and 130 non-violent demonstrators had been arrested. One female university teacher, among the 30 women arrested and placed in the drunk tank in the old county courthouse, found one of her students in tears. The student was one of those responsible for taking down the names of people arrested and the phone numbers of families and friends to contact, had been caught up in the sweep. The teacher spoke to officers in charge and explained that the female student shouldn't have been arrested and showed them the list of loved ones and phone numbers. The officers let her out.

On Saturday, James Toulouse, a prominent Albuquerque civil rights attorney showed up at the courthouse to represent the protesters pro bono. They were released on their own recognizance and a few weeks later, all civil charges were dismissed. Back on campus, those arrested were immediately placed on social probation by an unrepentant administration.

Rocky Mountains
Peace March in Denver, Colorado

Saturday, May 9, was the day of an historic antiwar march in Denver, one of the largest demonstrations ever staged in the city, and up to 12,000 demonstrators paraded the eight blocks from the Federal Building to the State Capitol. Hundreds of students from the University of Denver took part and joined students from universities and colleges from across the region, including the Boulder and Denver campuses of the **University of Colorado, Colorado State University** at Fort Collins, **Loretto Heights, University of Northern Colorado, Temple Buell College, Southern Colorado State College**, and **Metropolitan State College**.

The huge crowd assembled at the Federal Building at 19th and Stout around noon and marched to the steps of the State Capitol for a program of speakers. Nearly 100 students accompanied a musical band from their Fort Collins campus called the "Lexington Volunteers" which led from the front of the march. Following them were students from Boulder who carried 4-foot high white wooden crosses with the words "Kent State." Marchers sang, "All we are saying is give peace a chance," while others beseeched onlookers with chants, "Join us! Join us!" Once at the Capitol, people sat on a grassy slope as speakers denounced Nixon, the war, the Kent State murders and the Cambodia invasion. Details were non-existent but apparently there were some arrests.

University of Denver

By Sunday night on the University of Denver campus, steam was rising from Chancellor Maurice Mitchell's head. He had had enough. He had received reports, although unconfirmed, that 80 percent of the inhabitants of Woodstock West were nonstudents. At the very least, it appeared that the counter-cultural and anti-war encampment had grown beyond just his students. He decided to call in the Denver police, if he must, to handle the situation and that evening Mitchell addressed the students at the encampment and broke the news to them. In no uncertain terms, he said, Woodstock West was illegal, an improper use of university facilities and would have to be torn down and taken apart. If the students didn't dismantle it themselves, he warned, city and state police would arrive the next day to do it.

Colorado State University at Fort Collins

The Colorado Bureau of Investigation stepped in to assist campus security in their probe of the fire that destroyed Old Main on Friday night and the subsequent firebombing attempt at an ROTC building. The campus police chief believed the fire "was not caused by a CSU student" and his officers had a non-student suspect in custody, despite a witness' claims that police had the wrong guy. Damage from the Old Main fire was still being assessed but geology, art department and grad students had lost research, academic papers, art portfolios and personal items.

Meanwhile, two dozen students collected and cleaned bricks from the destroyed building with the hopes that they "might possibly be sold to CSU alumni" to raise money for the construction of a new building or a memorial. One student suggested money raised ought to go toward building a Center for Peace and Non-Violence.

Sunday, May 10

After the Old Main fire, enthusiasm for the student strike waned and strike leaders struggled to maintain its presence on campus. They told reporters for the *Collegian*, the campus newspaper, that one "senseless act" should not prevent them from voicing their peaceful opposition to the Southeast Asian wars. The canvassing of local communities in Fort Collins, they said, had turned up considerable support for the strike, and stopping at this point would be a "cop-out." The central issue was still there—the US expansion of the war.

University of Utah – Salt Lake City

A full page ad published in the Sunday Salt Lake City paper strongly criticized violence at campus demonstrations and had been paid for by some 450 university students, despite the absence of any violence on their own campus. The only campus disturbance had been a completely non-violent occupation of a campus building and the peaceful arrest of 80 protesters. Yet clearly a strong conservative sentiment still predominated on the campus. In student referendums, majorities had opposed Nixon's Cambodian action and the actions taken at Kent State, but most were against the strike and against abolishing ROTC.

Pacific

March in Spokane, Washington

On Saturday, May 9, 400 demonstrators marched in Spokane against the wars, many from **Eastern Washington State** in Cheney. Organizers knew that, coincidentally, both the Democratic and Republican County conventions were being held in Spokane that weekend, and they planned to present both with anti-war resolutions. Demonstrations began with the Democrats who were in the Davenport Hotel, and from there protesters circled the block several times, chanting "Peace now!" and singing "Give peace a chance." They then marched to the Republican convention at the Masonic Temple. They had no permit, but still police blocked intersections along the route for them.

The resolution presented to both conventions demanded the "immediate withdrawal of all US troops from Southeast Asia," a call to support the Senate defunding the troops, and a demand that Nixon apologize to the families of the students killed at Kent State. The resolutions ended with, "If you cannot accept this, if you cannot decide now, you will fail in your purpose as a political party."

At the end of the march, the crowd assembled in the Federal Building mall. One of the student organizers from **Fort Wright College**, Linda Moore, asked the crowd, "Who said policy isn't made in the streets? The president is beginning to listen; he will continue to listen." During the demonstration, several American flags had been displayed flown upside down, and Moore explained their symbology. It was an international sign of distress, she said, a symbol of the nation's troubles. But, she added, "We need more than symbols."

International Border Invasion

On Saturday, May 9th, a violent, international border incident occurred when hundreds of young Canadians "invaded" the United States as a protest of American aggression in Cambodia. The Canadians massed on their side and simply marched down Interstate 5, totally unimpeded by the US. Customs and Border Patrol. Originally, their plan was to march down the freeway for 22.1 miles, the same distance Nixon ordered US troops to march into Cambodia, but instead, they filed down the off-ramp into the small, border town of Blaine, Washington.

The invaders found the local post office and took the US flag down. But by this time, local kids from Blaine showed up. Rocks were thrown and several fist-fights broke out. The Canadians made a tactical retreat and withdrew to the grounds of the Peace Arch Historical Park just east of the freeway and continued to block all four lanes of I-5. About a hundred youth from town followed them, and fusillades of obscenities were exchanged. The obscenities gave way to more short-lived fist fights.

At this point, the Americans charged the invaders and an all-out, pitched battle erupted with rocks, bottles, cans and other objects being thrown by both sides. The Whatcom County Sheriff called for assistance from the Washington State Patrol and units from as far south as Seattle responded. But none wanted to get involved in the international incident.

At one point, 30 State Patrolmen stood some 300 yards away and watched the battle. The County Sheriff called the Royal Canadian Mounted Police for help, and a few Mounties showed up but they remained a discreet distance away from the fighting.

Finally, the young men from Blaine retreated, and were ushered 200 yards south by County Sheriffs. In the vacuum, the Canadians built a bonfire in the middle of the freeway right on the international boundary. Apparently, they had vandalized some monuments and floodlights in the park and had splashed paint on the Peace Arch.

Yet, the Canadians were not done. At that moment, a Canadian-bound Burlington Northern freight train came down the tracks just west of I-5. The Canadians rushed up to the train and behind a fence bombed it with rocks, smashing the windows and denting the sides of brand new cars on their way to Canada. During the bombardment, native Blaine kids pleaded with the State Patrol officers to intervene but in vain. The invaders retreated across the border to their own vehicles and took off. For four hours the freeway had been blocked and state troopers had rerouted traffic onto a nearby truck route. Several Canadians and Americans were seen bleeding as they retreated. One Blaine police officer was injured when something thrown struck him in the face. There had not been one arrest.

On Sunday, Canadians returned, but this time it was a whole different scene. Hundreds of Canadians massed on the international border and hosted a "be-in" on their side of Peace Arch. They sang folk songs, placed flowers inside the Arch and spoke of living in peace with their American neighbors. Meanwhile, about 200 yards away, between 150 and 200 young people from Blaine watched and waited for something to happen. Many were in their teens, or even younger, and carried baseball bats, golf clubs, pipes, and wood stakes "just in case."

University of Washington – Seattle

Over the weekend, a number of different student groups met, formed a strike committee and declared the student strike official—to last until their demands were met. They began making plans to send leafletting committees to go door to door in Seattle's working class neighborhoods to expand the movement. There was also serious talk among students and faculty members to launch an alternative New University that would hold classes on relevant issues but meet off campus.

On Saturday, May 9, Oregon Governor Tom McCall announced he had instructed university presidents to reopen the doors to their campuses—closed the previous week because of protest demonstrations over Cambodia and Kent State.

Portland State University – Portland, Oregon
Saturday, May 9

University President Gregory Wolfe held a press conference on Saturday to explain the events that had occurred at his campus. The day before, a memorial service for the Kent State four had been held in Washington Park, and he had been holding discussions with the strike committee "to bring people together" for "a peaceful solution" and to avoid "the potentially explosive situation on the campus." "Our main problem has been the security and safety of the property and personnel," Wolfe said, and praised students for keeping the buildings clean and free of violence. There had been few "broken bones and arrests," but conceded there had been some damage, such as the $200-$300 done to the student center alone.

As he wrapped up, Wolfe veered into dangerous territory by verbalizing misconceptions that could lead to arrests by law enforcement or violence by vigilantes. Some strike actions, he claimed, had been initiated by outsiders who were "mostly non-students [who] made an ugly joke out of a community crisis." He had spoken to student staff members who told him they'd never seen 95 percent of the people at a party in Smith Center. "I know that students have been coming in from all over – Vancouver, all around Portland, other institutions and even from California." Then the whooper. "It was probably the largest invasion of a student population that could be possibly imagined."

It wasn't a good day for Wolfe. Later, a crowd of strikers gathered below his office on Montgomery Street and chanted, "We want Wolfe! We want Wolfe!" It was ironic – some were there protesting the closure of campus buildings – not their opening, and some were there because Wolfe's closure prevented them from cleaning the building up after a week of protests. A couple of students found an extension ladder, leaned it against the building, and climbed to the second floor fire escape and got inside. They set off a fire alarm, ran down to the first floor and opened the doors for the others. A few ran inside and up to the third floor but were urged by faculty members and strike leaders to return because Wolfe was about to address the crowd.

Climbing up on a bandstand in front of Smith Memorial President Wolfe spoke to the students. "I don't know who represents you anymore," he said, and posed a question to the students: 'What meaning would the strike have, if the strikers lost the ability and faculties to work with the institutions as they were?' Pointing to the Smith Memorial Center, he said, "This building here became an area of diversion. There was no violence, and we are happy for it." He asserted the majority of students wanted the buildings reopened for classes. Shouts of disagreement rose from the assembly and arguments broke out. Wolfe continued, "Through the week, I have been meeting with faculty and students, and we have concluded this morning that we would close this building – primarily to get it open again."

Wolfe had just claimed he had to close the student union building in order to open it. In essence, the strike could continue, but classes must resume. Wolfe started to say, "Some of the barricades will remain up ..." but was interrupted by shouts of "All of them! All of them!" Wolfe pressed on, "We must get back to our business on Monday."

At this point, several from the crowd jumped up on the bandstand. A male student shouted, "We started with five demands, and they have nothing to do with the building!" He was immediately shouted down – but then there was a chorus of "Let him talk! Let him talk!" Someone grabbed the mic and asked the crowd, "Do we need to hear any more from President Wolfe?" People yelled back "Yes!" and Wolfe repeated his talking points.

A woman student took the mic and called on the crowd to "Take the building!" but her plea went unanswered. She handed the mic to Gary Waller, assistant professor of sociology. "I'm supposed to be radical," Waller said. "Let me be a moderate for a minute." The strike needed to continue, he said, until at least May 20 because the national strike had called for a halt to all business as usual across the country on that date. He criticized students for all their arguing and told them they ought to be out leafletting high schools and the community. Waller reminded strikers that the fourth floor of the student center – Smith—was still open, and, "We still have the park. Wolfe better understand that." By then President Wolfe had split, and the crowd began to thin out, leaving a few stragglers to argue.

Sunday, May 10

Over the weekend, the Chancellor of the Oregon state system of higher education, Roy Lieuallen, declared a "limited emergency" at Portland. This sent strikers into a brief panic as they thought it could open the door to repressive measures by law enforcement. President Wolfe, however, came to the Chancellor's defense, and publicly explained that Lieuallen had made the statement due to all the reactions and complaints he had received from the press, the public and other higher-ups about turmoil on the Portland campus. Staff personnel had even been sent home early and told to take their valuables.

The chief source of the complaints was the takeover by strikers of some of the Park Blocks, a dozen north-south blocks next to the campus often used for art shows and cultural events. After most of the campus had shut down, strikers had commandeered sections of the Park Blocks, setting up barricades throughout and on some cross streets. And as the campus protests evolved, the barricades in Park Blocks became the symbol of the strike. At first, only crude clusters of park benches, the barricades were enlarged to include park tables, tarps, tents, pieces of wood and garbage barrels. Fires in the garbage barrels at night not only warmed the strikers, but also reminded everyone the strike was still alive.

Moreover, the barricades brought cohesion to the strike and helped create an intangible substance called camaraderie among the barricade people. Their solidarity was what kept them at their "posts" for extended periods of time, with not much sleep, enduring cold and rainy nights, and importantly, giving inspiration to others. Over the days and nights, the blocks morphed into one extended community. Walkways through the barricades and shelters were given eccentric names, like Fort Tricia Nixon, Freedom Suite, Katanga Junction, Liberty Junction, and the Bobby Seale Memorial. The Bobby Seale Memorial had its name changed to Wipe Out Alley after a garbage truck plowed through it at 3 a.m. on Saturday.

Food was very much part of the scene. Food trucks would show up at mealtimes offering strikers a wide array of tasty options. The barricaders also received home-baked specials from sympathetic passers-by and friends and became the best fed "revolutionaries" on campus. During the life of the barricades, there had been no violence and few scuffles—except for the garbage truck incident and a drunk gunman who wandered in. The police wisely stayed away.

California
Humboldt State College—Humboldt

Over the weekend, a representative of the Humboldt strike committee, Mike Denaga, traveled to San Jose State to attend what was billed as the National Strike Congress. During the convention, Denaga handed in 460 draft cards from Humboldt students, which impressed everyone and especially the group the United Draft Organization that they designated Humboldt State as the northern headquarters for the network. During the rest of May, Humboldt sent another 600 draft cards to the main anti-draft center at Princeton University.

Mills College – Oakland

On Saturday, several dozen canvassers from the all-women's Mills College went door-to-door in three different Oakland communities to talk to residents about the wars and ask them to sign a petition in support of the McGovern-Hatfield amendment to cut off war funding.

A larger Bay Area campaign they were working with had assigned Mills students three communities to canvas: the white residential area next to the campus, the African American community below East 14 Street and the Chicano barrio by Foothill and Fruitvale. They carried leaflets in Spanish.

After three hours of canvassing, the women regrouped and shared their experiences about their encounters. One senior said, "A woman invited us in and we found that she was generally opposed to the war and specifically objected to Nixon's actions. Then her husband came in and gleefully launched into his tirade. He thought we must invade China and then Russia and meanwhile get all of the Commies out of the universities."

Two sophomores had visited some "very white, very conservative" homes near 66th Street and McArthur, and residents they met were scared of students. Some were angry and one shouted, "Student, damn right we should be in Cambodia and Vietnam, and you should be there too!" They also encountered one resident who said, "Honey, I used to write letters, but what good did it do?"

One canvasser had met a "career army man" who was "very open, very intelligent" and willing to listen, but asked many questions like whether SDS was behind all the protests. Another canvasser had a man ask her, "Since we're really talking about murder in Vietnam," would she sign his anti-abortion petition? Another person she talked with was positive the "communists" were out to convert all the kids, but first had to separate them from their parents.

San Francisco Area Colleges

President S.I. Hayakawa at **San Francisco State College** announced Sunday that he intended to keep the campus open. The once explosive campus had remained relatively quiet during the two weeks of national campus protests in May. Meanwhile, at **Golden Gate College**, a majority of law students voted to continue their strike for the remainder of the term.

[Author's note: Despite one account that a massive crowd of up to 150,000 anti-war protesters marched in the streets of San Francisco on Saturday, May 9, 1970—the same day as the massive demonstration in Washington DC—there is no corroborating evidence that an event of that magnitude took place.]

San Jose State College

The weekend's National Strike Congress at San Jose State concluded on Sunday, May 10. Delegates from schools across California had tried to nail together a framework for unified actions but by the end, there was more disunity than unity. The weekend had been crammed full of workshops on draft resistance, worker-student coalitions, national lobbying, and "communications."

Yet, many participants had felt it was a time for action, not talk about the past exploits of different colleges, and left dissatisfied that the "congress" had not achieved a substantial commitment to concerted action. Before the conference ended, it did pass a resolution that embodied the three national strike demands: an end to the Vietnam and Cambodia wars, amnesty for political prisoners, and an end to campus complicity with the war machine. A few other idealistic demands were tacked on—a demand to end racism and a call for draft resistance for all California males.

Los Angeles & UCLA

On Saturday, May 9, many **UCLA** students were part of large protest of 10,000 people that marched in Los Angeles against President Nixon's war policies in Cambodia and the killings at Kent State. They rallied in Exposition Park and listened to speeches and rock bands.

Southern California Colleges

On Sunday, at a noon rally and the day before **Cal State Los Angeles** was to reopen, several psychology professors pledged to suspend their classes to support efforts by students to close the school for the remainder of the academic year.

The student strike at **University of Southern California** had gone all week without incident, mainly due in all probability to the tactics strikers took. One, to educate the campus community about Vietnam – there were educational films on Vietnam shown daily; and two, a letter writing campaign to government officials calling for an end to the war. By the end of the week, USC students had delivered 50,000 letters to Los Angeles City Hall. On Saturday, President Topping announced his approval of a plan where students could use the rest of the semester to work against or protest the Indochina wars without academic penalty, coupled with several liberal options about grades and course work.

Campus administrators at **Loyola University** and **Marymount College** declared Sunday and Monday as "Peace Days," and sent Nixon a telegram advocating that he "use all the resources within your power to demonstrate clearly your intention to end our involvement in Southeast Asia." (In 1973, Loyola and Marymount officially merged and assumed the name Loyola Marymount University.)

Peace March in San Diego

By San Diego standards, it was a huge. On Saturday, May 9, between 10,000 to 12,000 people marched through downtown San Diego, the conservative, longtime Navy town labeled Nixon's "Lucky City." The city had only seen something like it once before, and that was in September 1969 during the Vietnam Moratorium. Now, eight months later, the massive crowd took a similar route and walked from Horton Plaza west on Broadway to the County Courthouse. Chants of "Peace now!" reverberated off the downtown high-rise buildings.

As the crowd of young people and students marched in the streets they were met by many people with somber faces. Some expressed sympathy while others stared in stony silence or yelled obscenities. On Fifth Avenue, in contrast, five or six laborers held signs in support. There were also families with young children. A parent was asked by a local campus newspaper reporter why they had brought their children to a protest where violence could break out, and she responded, "It was a risk we had to take ... we must have peace ...we couldn't protect them from violence in any better way."

When the front ranks moved past the courthouse, members of the group Movement for a Democratic Military (MDM) linked arms with fellow protesters and did a slow, exaggerated goose-step for half a block. As other marchers filed by the slim crowds in front of the courthouse, they sang the Christmas carol, "Silent Night," while an old white-haired man harangued them from the sidewalk. They marched past the U.S. Armed Forces Recruiting Office, and a cry went up, "Hell no, we won't go!"

The march turned, moved past the City Administration Building on C Street, then up Fifth Avenue to Bankers' Hill. At Juniper Street, it turned right and flowed into Balboa Park for a rally in a natural amphitheater. "Nixon said he would bring us together," one speaker told the crowd sitting down on the grassy slope. "We have not seen people come out for peace as they have today." Another speaker said the Nixon administration was "widening the credibility gap. Nixon uses troop withdrawal to hide the fact of … continuing the war indefinitely." Just that morning, the speaker said, Nixon had sent an additional 2500 troops into Cambodia. "The thing that is going to count now in Washington, for those senators ready to cut off funds for war is telegrams." A spokesman for MDM told protesters, "Sitting on the lawn talking to trees would not accomplish anything." He urged people to join a May 16 Armed Forces Day march to Camp Pendleton, a large Marine Corps base up the coast from San Diego.

More speakers and some music followed. By then, the thousands of antiwar protesters who had been mobilized began drifting away, many having to trek the few miles down the hill to downtown San Diego. For some, the rally was anticlimactic and a great disappointment. For others, it was a wonderful and massive show that even San Diego had a vibrant anti-war movement. Yet, organizers had brought out thousands only to have them succumb to sitting on soft grass listening to speakers, going from an energized mass to the participation level of an audience. Why, just the day before, 3,000 students had non-violently shut down the Naval Electronics Lab for hours.

UC San Diego

George Winne, Jr., 23, a history major, casually walked out to the middle of Revelle Plaza, the main rally site on the UC San Diego campus. It was about 4 o'clock on Sunday afternoon, the 10th of May. Winne carried a sign, "In God's name, end this war." He also carried rags saturated with gasoline. He sat down, covered himself with the rags and lit himself on fire. Immediately Winne went up in a blaze, and he leaped up and began to run around the plaza.

Student and antiwar leader Byron King was in a first floor lounge of Blake Hall planning a sit-in for the next day. Fifty years later, King recalled, "I saw a man ...walk to the center of the Revelle Plaza. He carried several items including a gas can. Suddenly the man jumped up and started running in flames."

Antiwar activist Bill Maltz was on Revelle Plaza that afternoon with a small group of other students. He recalled, "All of a sudden, I see this man on fire running and screaming. Several people reacted and tried to put out the flames. It was a horrific and graphic moment that left me feeling quite sickened. I think that almost everyone that day in the plaza was horrified by what they saw."

King remembered that fellow anti-war student Keith Stowe was also there. "Keith Stowe was the first to reach Winne, knocking him down and rolling him over to put out the flames. Both George and Keith were rushed to the hospital."

Keith Stowe recounted his experience in the Spring 2019 issue of UCSD's *Triton* magazine. "I didn't see George pour the gasoline on himself, but we all ran out once we saw him ablaze. I immediately tackled him and rolled over on him to put the flames out. He was taller and heavier than I thought so I'm glad I hit him hard to get him down. But the fire didn't go out easily. ... Many others helped with their jackets by then, and someone threw a blanket from a dorm window. A campus police car appeared on the plaza and took George and me to the hospital." They both sat in the backseat and Stowe later wrote, "George was clearly badly burned and I knew he would die soon. He tried to talk, but it came out as a harsh, loud whisper. He said I should have let him die."

Once at Scripps Hospital, Winne was treated for third and fourth degree burns over 95 percent of his body and at 2 a.m., succumbed to his injuries. Reportedly, Winne was conscious up until his death and had muttered to others that his act was "very personal and spiritual," and kept repeating there was an urgent need to end the Vietnam war. His parents, Capt. and Mrs. George Winne, were at the hospital that night and said it all "came as a total surprise and shock." His mother recounted that since Christmas he had been "very uncommunicative and wouldn't talk to me." She knew her son was becoming increasingly frustrated with the war, she told UCSD campus press, but thought he would have been "too bright and too sensitive" for such an act. Before he died, Winne asked his parents to write a letter to the President, and told them, "The world is in such a horrible mess and Nixon is part of it." Winne was also against guns, and had said, "get rid of guns. Guns just mean more guns." At the end and while being pumped with large doses of morphine, Winne kept repeating the Lord's Prayer and sections from the scriptures.

George Winne, Jr. a senior, was set to graduate the next month. Born April 2, 1947, in Detroit, Michigan, the son of a retired Navy captain, he had been raised in a military household. And for a while, had attended the Colorado School of Mines where he was considered an "outstanding ROTC cadet." Winne transferred to UCSD and attended Muir College as a major in history. Although he had not been involved in any campus protest actions, he was vehemently against the war. His friends described him as a "loner type" who had deep, sincere moral and political beliefs. His closest friend had said that he had become quieter and more withdrawn in recent months and had taken an interest in Oriental mysticism and organic foods. It was also known that Winne had recently received a draft notice.

Later that Sunday evening, Byron King was working on the layout for the next edition of a radical campus newspaper when a campus police officer stopped by. King recounted, "He had been in the ambulance with Winn and was deeply shaken by the experience. He claimed that Winne was begging the officer to shoot him. It was one of those moments when opponents shared a connection through common grief."

Literature grad student Mel Freilicher was also on campus Sunday night at a strike meeting in Revelle Cafeteria, and remembered, "the place was packed with crazed and desperate students. When a liberal professor got up to speak about sending a student lobby to D.C., students started throwing cafeteria chairs at him; several were lifting up a table when he fled." An organizer announced that anyone interested in the lobbying approach go to a separate meeting." Freilicher recalled, "The remaining majority — quite a large group — sat there basically trying to figure out an appropriate response to Winne's death. Of course, there was none."

Almost immediately, a circle of candles and flowers appeared on the burnt marks on the plaza and the next day campus minister Lesley

Atkinson and new left philosopher Professor Herbert Marcuse led a memorial for Winne. Students and faculty filed through Revelle Plaza paying their respects, trying to process the death of a fellow student.

Four decades later in 2010, a permanent memorial bench and bronze plaque were erected on Revelle Plaza in George Winne's honor just yards from where he had set himself on fire. The effort by UCSD professors and students was led by Niall Twohig, a lecturer and PhD in Literature and Cultural Studies, and several veterans of the 1970 May strike at UCSD attended the commemoration. The Peace Memorial commemorates not only Winne, but all those who protested that May. It reads: "For George Winne Jr., the student activists of May 1970, and all those who continue the struggle for a peaceful world."

Chapter 6
MONDAY, MAY 11 – SUNDAY, MAY 17

The Second Week of the Strike

When Monday, May 11, 1970, dawned in America, the nationwide student strike was still going on—with 268 colleges and universities on strike until the end of the academic term, and many of the 450 schools on strike the previous week extending their boycott of business as usual. Strikes at 167 high schools were also being held. Yet, at the same time, on Monday, many colleges and universities reopened after being closed down due to protests the previous week—including the entire California state system of 28 public institutions and 280,000 students.

But tragically, during this second week, the monstrous reality of America's institutionalized racism and system of white supremacy reared its ugly head with the killings by police of Black men in Augusta, Georgia, and at Jackson State in Mississippi.

Augusta, Georgia
Monday, May 11

On Monday, several leaders of the Black community met with white county and city officials inside the Augusta Municipal Building to get answers to the prison death of Charles Oatman. Oatman had been a 16-year-old Black youth with a mental disability whom police initially had claimed died in a fall from his jail bunk. But on Sunday when his body was brought to a mortuary in the Black community, the mortician found evidence of a brutal beating, torture and a crushed skull.

Meanwhile, several hundred people gathered outside the Municipal Building for a planned protest and it was announced two of Oatman's Black cellmates had been charged with his murder. Angered, the crowd pulled down the Georgia state flag, burned it and were going after the American flag when officials and the community leaders rushed outside from their meeting. Two ministers emerged and spoke to the throng of 300 to 500 angry residents, convincing them to move the protest to a different location.

The crowd began moving down the street when a rock was thrown through a bus window. This was the spark – and for the next few hours, the African-American community of Augusta rebelled. Fires were set in businesses, their windows smashed and some were looted. Black businesses were spared after "Soul brother" was painted on the outside. In the midst of the rioting, a few white people were attacked. In one incident, a white man was pulled from his truck and beaten, and then two Black men ran up and rescued him. The crowd rocked his truck until it tipped over. Looting and fires continued for three hours, as clouds of smoke billowed into the sky and hundreds of residents filled the streets.

Then, a wall of white policemen carrying shotguns appeared. Led by police Captain Beck – a notorious racist – the line advanced on the crowd. Beck yelled out, "Y'all have had your chance. Now, I'm taking over." The officers leveled their shotguns and began shooting directly into the crowds. No teargas, no birdshot, just live ammunition.

Once the smoke cleared and the crowds had dispersed, six Black men laid dead, four in their twenties or younger. Witnesses said three were innocent bystanders, and none were known militants. Later, Dr. Irvine Phinizy, medical examiner for the Richmond County Coroner's Office, concluded that all six had been shot in the back. One victim, 19-year-old John Stokes, had been shot nine times. Those killed were Mack Wilson, Jr., John (Johnnie) Stokes, William Wright, Jr., Charlie Mack Murphy, Sammie Larry McCullough and John Bennings. No weapons were found on any of them.

An additional 62 people were injured, and more than 300 arrested. Police claimed there were snipers, but not one police officer had been shot or wounded. At least 20 downtown buildings burned down with property damage estimated to be more than $1 million.

At the request of Augusta Mayor Millard Beckum, Georgia Governor Lester Maddox summoned the National Guard—as well as state police. The two thousand Guard members deployed to Augusta made a noisy arrival in the middle of the night as truck convoys and tanks rumbled down city streets with soldiers perched ready to fire their machine guns. The rebellion was over.

Tuesday, May 12

Tuesday morning, Augusta residents awoke to find their streets patrolled by Guardsmen carrying live ammunition with orders to shoot if necessary. That afternoon, Gov. Maddox himself inspected the riot-torn area while Black and white leaders sought a permanent end to the unrest.

The student body president of **Augusta College**, Henry Allen Green, an African American, told Atlanta's WSB-TV News that Augusta's white leaders had been willfully blind. He said, "The Black people of Augusta are tired of being told that there is no racial problem here. Whereas our local officials have not seen a problem now our nation knows that Augusta has a problem."

In Augusta, the problems were widespread. Data from the 1960 U.S. Census showed only 20% of Augusta's African American adults had high school diplomas, and several Black neighborhoods lacked sewerage and water. The white-dominated city had put off their demands for infrastructure for nearly 20 years, according to City Council meeting minutes.

On May 16, the Black Panther Party condemned the killings but also criticized "the racist luxury for white students to strike over the war in Viet-Nam and Cambodia and not voice scorn and condemnation against the war that is being waged against the Black Panther Party in particular and Black People in general." The statement said that when four white students at Kent State were murdered, students "poured into the streets and closed down schools throughout the country. Yet a little more than a week later six black people in Augusta, Ga. were shot in the back," and "once again racist indifference to the cold-blooded murder of Black People has failed to move the masses of white Amerika." The Party warned of a coming "race war," which America could not survive; the Party advocated a class war instead.

It wouldn't be until May 20 that the Guardsmen departed Augusta. The Justice Department did order an investigation to determine if the civil rights of the dead were violated, and eventually two Augusta officers were tried in federal court—but both were acquitted.

Fifty years later, the mayor and six of the ten city council members were African American.

Jackson State College in Mississippi
Wednesday, May 13

Jackson, Mississippi, the state capital is less than 500 miles from Augusta, Georgia. And late Wednesday night, a crowd congregated outside a women's dormitory at Jackson State College, an all-Black institution. It was a warm spring night, and some 300 students and locals—called "cornerboys"—gathered along Lynch Street, a major east-west road that literally split the campus in half. Cornerboys were young toughs, a little older than the students, who hung out and protected their turf. Some had jobs, some carried weapons and were known to commit petty crimes and vandalism.

As night closed in, an annual spring ritual began, and members of the crowd began throwing rocks and bottles at passing white motorists. However, on this particular evening, something different was in the air. There was the usual resentment of white people driving fancy cars through their campus, but there was a keener edge to the frustration among the young along Lynch Street—a new anger at the local racist police force and white power structure. It made it easy throwing rocks at passing cars. Not all the victims of the barrages were white and at least three Black motorists or passengers were injured by glass.

Around 10:30 pm the mood of the crowd changed. Egged on by cornerboys, the crowd of 150 took up chants against the Vietnam war and ROTC, chants heard on campus the previous week. Fairly spontaneously, the crowd surged across Lynch Street and down two blocks towards the ROTC offices. "Get the ROTC building!" and "Let's burn down Rotsy!" were heard when the crowd reached the two-story building. Rocks and bottles pelted the building, windows were smashed, and an ROTC car was dented. At long last, two campus security officers emerged and pulled their weapons – causing the students to scatter. It was only momentary. Within minutes, they returned and repeated the game with the guards. This went on for some time until the protesters withdrew to Lynch Street and the dorms.

The crowd, upon its return, ignited a small fire in the middle of Lynch Street, and fed it with benches and other wood. In response, Jackson City Police mobilized and accompanied by a platoon of state troopers formed up along Lynch Street and set up barricades and roadblocks on streets that ran into campus. A city armored van called "Thompson's Tank" brought up the rear as the columns of state and city police marched towards the ROTC buildings. When they passed the dorms, crowds emerged and yelled at them. "Pigs! Pigs!" and "You white sons-of-bitches!" A few rocks were thrown but police stayed in formation and closed in on the ROTC buildings.

At one point, students threatened to march to downtown Jackson but were blocked by a police skirmish line across Lynch Street. The stand-off lingered but things eventually quieted down and by 2:30 am, all was quiet. The state troopers left but the city cops stayed the night protecting sanitation workers who cleaned up the glass, bottles, and all the charred rubble, leaving little evidence of the "mini-riot." One student gave a local reporter reasons for the disruption, "It's a lot of things. The war, Cambodia, the draft, the governor, Mississippi. It's not just one thing."

Later that evening, two Molotov cocktails hit the ROTC building—one fizzled and the other temporarily lit a porch roof but was easily put out by security.

Thursday, May 14

Thursday morning, the president of Jackson State, John Peoples, was informed by the commanding general of the Mississippi National Guard that 600 troops had been deployed and would be stationed at a nearby armory. It wasn't until 3 pm that Peoples met with student leaders to find out what caused the firebombs at the ROTC buildings, telling them he wanted to prevent another occurrence. For two hours, they explained to Peoples that there wasn't one cause, not one single issue – there was Kent State, Cambodia but also a whole raft of local campus issues, such as strict curfews for women, complaints about the dining hall food, insufficient administrative actions on student issues.

Once that meeting was over, Peoples went to another and described Wednesday night's mini-riot to the faculty. Later that day, Peoples wrote a 2-page letter to the campus community in which he blamed everything on a "faceless, mindless mob of students and non-students bent on doing violence." He informed the campus about the hundreds of Guardsmen in Jackson and stated, "My understanding is that the guardsmen will be reluctant to use force, but if it is necessary to use force, to protect life and property, it will be used decisively."

Fearing a repeat of the night before, President Peoples called up Chief Pierce of the Jackson Police and requested that Lynch Street be closed after dark, but the Chief declined. White people in Jackson were not about to give up their right-of-way through the Black college.

Thursday night was another typical spring evening, hot and muggy. On campus, it was business as usual. Students were going to a campus concert, some had gone for beer at local bars, the choir was meeting, a big party for the school's basketball team was being held, fraternity pledges were walking around, students were studying for finals and typing papers. However, it wasn't a typical night at the ROTC building. Inside, military police and campus security were hunkering down – there had been rumors about another attempt to burn it down.

Around 9:30 pm a small group of students and locals formed on a darkened knoll next to one of the dorms along Lynch Street. It looked like it was going to be a repeat of the night before, and once again cars of white motorists were hit with rocks. This time, the rock-throwers were cheered on by another hundred students nearby. A Jackson city police officer witnessed what was going on and radioed dispatch. "Call that security guard out there at Jackson State and see if they can't scatter them niggers!"

Around this time, a handful of locals discovered an old dump truck near the football field, abandoned for the day by its driver. A cornerboy jumped into the cab, started it up and drove it over to Lynch Street—where the truck stalled. After it wouldn't start, the old truck was set on fire and the cab burst into flames.

It was 11 pm when Jackson city police got the alarm. Soon paddy wagons and Thompson's Tank – with 8 to 10 policemen inside with rifles – were on their way to Jackson State. Chief Pierce called up the highway patrol and requested their assistance. Once police arrived on campus, they set up barricades along Lynch Street and when the highway patrol showed up, there was a force of nearly 100 white law enforcement officers on the grounds of a Black college. The patrolmen were led by Officer Jones who was so notorious, his nickname was "Goon."

Police formed a column behind the armored van and advanced on the dormitories, and as the officers approached, they were met with howls and curses. Once they reached the burning truck in the middle of Lynch Street, police set up a skirmish line. Directly in front of them was a 5-story dormitory. Students yelled at them from windows in all five stories. "Pigs!" they shouted.

On the other side of the skirmish line, students began throwing rocks. A police commander heard a report of shots being fired but had no collaboration. A fire truck was requested, and a lower-ranking officer asked a superior if they should use tear gas. By midnight, the fire in the old truck was out and at one end of the skirmish line students had retreated to their dorms. Police assembled for a sweep up Lynch Street, forming up behind the Tank. At the moment, up to 200 students were still congregating in front of the west wing of Alexander Hall, a 5-story girls' dormitory.

The police column marched up Lynch and when they reached Alexander Hall, they stopped, turned and faced a chain-link fence directly in front of the dorm. Inside the dorm were nearly a thousand young women, many in their pajamas and nightgowns, reading, taking showers, listening to radios, doing their hair, already asleep, on phones in the dorm's booths. But downstairs and outside, a crowd of students yelled and jeered at dozens of white police officers with shotguns. The noise was so loud that individuals next to each other had to yell to be heard.

Roughly 12:05 a.m.

An officer with a bullhorn approached and tried to address the students. Just then a bottle flew through the air and exploded near the police line. Startled by what may have sounded like a gunshot, one whole line of patrolmen – took that moment to fire their weapons. At 12:05, there was a roar of gunfire. Other officers joined in. Police shot at the students in front of them, they shot up at the windows, they shot at the dorm stairwell door. And the officers kept firing; they knelt and fired, they stood and fired, they fired from the hip, from the shoulder – they kept shooting until their guns had emptied.

There had been no verbal warning of lethal weapons; there had been no tear gas. Police had opened fire with rifles, automatic weapons, a machine gun (in the Tank truck) and riot shotguns. They fired for a long 28 seconds.

Amidst the screams, a police sergeant radioed for ambulances. "How many do you need?" the dispatcher asked. He replied, "You better send all that you can get." Before anyone moved to assist the wounded, police officers picked up and pocketed their empty shells in the street. Finally, officers moved about the wounded, pointing them out to students so they could retrieve their bleeding friends. A white cop said, "You niggers over there, go check behind those bushes. There's a nigger over in them bushes - check him out."

Two bodies were found that weren't moving. One young man was found near a magnolia tree in front of one of the dorms. The body of another young man was found across the street near the dining hall. The dispatcher asked who the deceased were, and "Goons" answered, "They're nigger students." Fourteen people had been hit by gunfire. Two died and two were in critical condition.

James Green and Phil Gibbs died that night at Jackson State. Phil Gibbs was 21, a junior pre-law major with a wife, a child and a baby on the way, and was found 50 feet east of the dorm door. He had been hit four times. He had helped to integrate several businesses in Jackson over the last few years, but he was not a militant. He was in the vicinity of the dorms because he had dropped off a friend who had to be back for the midnight curfew.

James Earl Green was 17 and found sprawled in front of a dining hall. Green, a senior at Jim Hill High School, had stopped to watch the action on his walk home from work at a grocery store not far from campus. He always took Lynch Street as it was a main thoroughfare. He had been hit once in the chest.

Immediately police claimed there were snipers, that they had been in a crossfire with snipers. Yet, no snipers were ever found; no weapons were ever found; no police officers had been wounded; no witnesses who saw or heard snipers were found. Law enforcement had used the exact same excuse at Kent State and at Augusta—'there were snipers, that's why we had to shoot back.'

When campus security guards rushed into Alexander Hall in search of snipers, they found women students coming out from under their beds, screaming, crying. The guards had to step over pools of blood, climb up the bullet-ridden stairwells, walk down upstairs halls with blood splattered floors, saw students using towels to wipe blood off the arms and legs of their dorm mates. But no sniper was found. The lobby's huge glass windows had been blown out and blood streaks marred the floor. Women screamed as the wounded were carried out on stretchers. Out on Lynch in front of the dorm, male students cursed at the arriving white ambulance responders, grabbed the stretchers, and said no whites would carry their wounded.

About 10 minutes to 1 am, National Guard medics and a doctor arrived to assist the wounded. Near 1 am, a troop of National Guard soldiers with bayonets on display marched to the dorm area to relieve city and state police.

When the first ambulance that responded to the campus reached Baptist Hospital, its staff declined to take the wounded Black students. This meant that all the ambulances had to go an extra mile to the Medical Center including two students in critical condition.

Back at Jackson State, most of the students who lived on campus gathered in front of one dorm, anticipating an address by President Peoples. In the dark, emotions overflowed and students looked for friends to ensure they were all right, others wept; others were so angry they wanted to march downtown to show they would never submit to the "white pigs" and had to be reminded that National Guardsmen held the roads. Nobody wanted more bloodshed.

When President Peoples arrived, he smelled gun smoke and saw blood. Shocked and overwhelmed, he really didn't know what to do or say. At a student leader's suggestion, Peoples led the students in a prayer and then asked them all to return to their dorms. But they weren't going back – not tonight. Some went to go fetch blankets and they ended up staying all night on the lawn. Some prayed. Others sang freedom songs. "Ain' gonna let nobody turn me 'round ...turn me 'round, turn me 'round."

Friday, May 15

When students awoke Friday, they were able for the first time to view the amount of damage inflicted on the dorm – and on their fellow students.

Alexander Hall looked like it had been used for target practice; its walls riddled by buckshot; two six-foot windows were gone, shredded drapes flapped in the breeze, and bullet holes in the concrete walls were the size of silver dollars. Students found bullet holes in other dorms – including in one hall two blocks away. They found splats of blood everywhere.

Almost instinctively, students began collecting spent shells, took photos of bullet holes and found other spent material out in the street. They wanted to gather evidence for safekeeping—they feared a cover-up. Many of them the night before had witnessed patrolmen stuffing their pockets with spent shells immediately after the shootings while ignoring the wounded.

At a gathering with students that morning, President Peoples announced that the school was closing, and everyone had to leave the campus and go home. There would be no finals and diplomas would be mailed. He also told them the shootings would not go unavenged and said it had been a miracle that considering the hundreds of rounds fired indiscriminately, more students hadn't been killed.

Two miles north of Jackson State at Millsaps College, a predominantly white school, 150 students gathered at noon to protest the killings at Jackson State. Wearing black armbands and joined by a dozen faculty members, they solemnly and silently marched the mile to the Governor's Mansion in downtown Jackson. Two students led the procession carrying wooden crosses with the names of the slain - "Phillip Gibbs" and "James E. Green."

As they marched, they passed the Baptist Hospital that had denied treatment to the wounded Black students just the night before. When they approached the Governor's Mansion, they were joined by Black students from **Tougaloo College**. In front of the mansion, 50 highway patrolmen stood by with clubs and shotguns and glared at the students as they filed by. It was – sadly—the very first organized protest of the Jackson State killings by another campus in the nation.

Students from Jackson State and leaders of Mississippi NAACP held a press conference at 4 pm at the Masonic Temple on Lynch Street. They strongly refuted reports of snipers and called for an impartial investigation. The field secretary of the NAACP, Alex Waites, was angry but spoke firmly.

"The actions of the highway patrol, and other officers if so involved, constitutes murder. The bullet holes in the girls' dormitory show a deliberate pattern to the violence. All floors of the building were fired upon, with a concentration upon a ground-floor doorway where fleeing students were trying to enter. Students were shot both inside and outside the building. We cannot find justification for the shooting of fleeing students, regardless of the supposed provocation."

The discharge of guns showed, Waites said, "the highway patrol's hatred against Black people." It was significant that no tear gas was used and there was no evidence of a sniper. He had no faith, he poignantly added, in any investigation by "the white power structure" and called for a special biracial committee to investigate the shootings.

Mayor Charles Evers of Fayette, the brother of well-known slain civil rights activist, Medgar Evers, also spoke to reporters: "Police shot my folks down – it was simple as that. We don't have to explain nothin'. It is obvious that they shot the building up. It is obvious that there are two dead blacks." If the campus had been a white campus, he said, "no bullets would have been fired."

Evers continued, "Therefore, we say we have racism and hatred here. And we're sick and tired of it. If the mayor and the governor can't control their own policemen, they ought to be tried for malfeasance. They can't run their offices." Then Evers singled out the state patrol leader "Goon" Jones and wanted him arrested and held for murder or conspiring to murder. "He's the one who called us 'niggers.'" Just the year before, Charles Evers had become the first African American mayor of a city in Mississippi since Reconstruction days.

Robert Clark, the only Black representative in the Mississippi senate in 1970, spoke out against the "killing and indiscriminate firing upon black students." Clark declared that the gunfire "could under no conceivable circumstances have been justifiable or lawful."

Saturday, May 16

The first of several investigations into the shootings began Saturday morning with a meeting of the biracial committee Mayor Russel Davis had appointed. Davis had named two Black civil rights attorneys to the panel, an unprecedented act for the town was not used to its white police being scrutinized by its African American citizens. Immediately, five Jackson city police officers refused to speak to the committee—although the mayor ended up persuading several to testify. And on Sunday, Julian Bond – the famed civil rights activist – came to Jackson and spoke at a memorial service for the young men.

The biracial committee interviewed five Jackson police officers, including the top three in command. None of them had seen sniper fire and the only two officers who had claimed there had been snipers were inside Thompson's Tank at the time. 250 bullet holes were counted in the steel and concrete of the dorm building.

The FBI also began to conduct their own investigation, but the state highway patrol refused to cooperate with them. For the Jackson State murders, no officer was ever arrested. The President's Commission on Campus Unrest concluded, "the 28-second fusillade from police officers was an unreasonable, unjustified overreaction.... A broad barrage of gunfire in response to reported and unconfirmed sniper fire is never warranted."

Lynch Street was permanently closed on campus and renamed Gibbs-Green Plaza. No one was prosecuted for the shootings, but an attorney filed a $13.8 million civil lawsuit in 1970 against state and local officials and law enforcement officers. The case went to trial in February 1972 in Biloxi, and when an all-white male jury came back with a not guilty verdict, officers in the courtroom erupted in cheers.

Northeast
Maine
Colby College – Waterville

As the strike settled in for its second full week, the Colby campus was alive with meetings, workshops, panel discussions and a teach-in. One of the more important meetings was the coordination needed for the canvassing of Waterville residents on the strike and war issues.

Panels and workshops included, "Is the Environmental Movement detracting from anti-war efforts or do they both consider the same Problem?" and "America and the Third World – a discussion of American racism, the war, and the repression of Black people here and abroad." There was a panel on the draft and on an all-day teach-in for high school students.

On Wednesday, May 13, *Strike Notes* reported on problems Colby strikers were having in relation to local high schools. "As far as youth groups are concerned, we're still having problems getting into local high schools." There were successes. "The dance troupe from Colby presented their dance recital to several [local high] schools and were able to engage in extended 'raps' about contemporary issues of our military involvement, the draft and student expression."

Announcements in *Strike Notes* included a panel to cover "Scientist's Responsibilities in a Defense-Oriented Tech Society," a meeting of conscientious draft objectors on the steps of the library, and this apt note: "Free baby-sitting for children of those who wish to participate in workshops and discussions on the strike" along with a phone number and the admonition "to call at least one hour before you need the sitter, please."

On Friday, for some reason, the Colby student government conducted another poll on students' opinions on war-related issues. 533 students voted and the results were published the following Tuesday. The first question asked, "Do you agree with the government's moving ground troops into Cambodia?" Not surprisingly, 430 said no, and 60 replied yes. Another asked, "Do you think that ROTC at Colby College should be abolished?" 278 answered yes and 191 were opposed.

Augusta, Maine

In Augusta – the capital of Maine—on Friday, May 15, the Penobscot Indian tribe warned Maine Governor Kenneth Curtis that they may secede from the state if he did not honor an 1818 treaty in time for the upcoming 150th anniversary celebration of the City of Old Town, one of the oldest English settlements in Maine. The treaty had promised Native Americans an annual 500 bushels of corn, 100 pounds of gun powder, 400 pounds of shot, 50 pounds of tobacco, and 50 dollars in silver. A spokesperson for the Native Americans said that the treaty was never honored despite the tribes' ceding territory that amounted to half the state.

Bowdoin College – Brunswick
Monday, May 11

On Monday, the campus still simmered over insults by the Brunswick Town Council toward striking Bowdoin students. On May 8 the Council passed a resolution that condemned the Bowdoin "revolt" for a "disruption" at Brunswick High School. In response, strike headquarters issued a statement that slammed the council for its poor choice of the word "revolt," as it connoted violence, which was not being planned or expected. "In fact, the campus is entirely peaceful," and strikers hoped the wording of the resolution would be changed.

A new petition against ROTC circulated on campus, and proponents said they had collected 150 signatures in little more than two hours. Just that afternoon at a regular faculty meeting, a motion was made to terminate the ROTC program, but the issue was tabled until its next meeting.

Tuesday, May 12

Continuing the blow-back against the Brunswick Town Council, the Tuesday edition of the local newspaper, the *Bath-Brunswick Times-Record*, exclaimed, "All that was missing from this declaration was a warning to the Bowdoin students and faculty members to get out of town before sunset." It went on, "The resolution serves no useful purpose that we can think of. There is no 'revolt' at Bowdoin College and there has been no disruption at Brunswick High School. ... If there is unrest in the community and at the high school it doesn't originate on the Bowdoin campus but in the general atmosphere of the times. The Brunswick Town Council might usefully address itself to some of these issues."

In a Brunswick District Court on Tuesday, Judge Simon found a 21-year-old local man guilty of assault and battery on a Bowdoin student on strike. Sophomore Edwin Whitford had been wearing a black armband in support of the strike and standing on Maine Street when he was assaulted. Fining the assailant $100, the judge leaned forward and lectured him. "It is people like you who cause these riots and other difficulties that are going on around the country. It doesn't matter if you disagree with his views, or if I disagree with his views. There is absolutely no justification for beating him up — touching him, even — and that applies, of course, both ways." The judge said the student had "a perfect right" to wear the symbol and was breaking no law. "I'm not going to let anyone take the law into his own hands if I can help it. You pass that on because I mean it," he said forcefully to the defendant.

Wednesday, May 13

It was meant to be a different type of demonstration by college students. 50 Bowdoin students wanted to show Brunswick townspeople their goodwill and for over 8 hours, they picked up trash and junk from around local neighborhoods. They collected enough litter to fill a room ten feet square by eight feet high. When it was over, they were praised by a Public Works worker. "They're a nice bunch of guys," he said. "There wasn't one of them that wasn't working. They even bought my lunch for me."

During the day, Bath Memorial Hospital sent out an emergency request for blood donations. Bowdoin students responded quickly, Strike headquarters reported, and won praise from hospital staff.

That morning, College President Roger Howell received a visit from David Scarponi, the head of the Brunswick Town Council, who gave Howell a copy of the controversial Council resolution. There was no record of the meeting, but doubtless, Scarponi was there to press Howell on the resolution's conclusion, which stated: "We therefore request that Bowdoin College use every means within their power to keep all activity on the campus." President Howell publicly-released a letter to Scarponi where he politely thanked and assured the town council that he shared the concern that college members do not disrupt public schools. He also invited council members to visit the campus and attend some of the seminars and workshops. He concluded with a slight jab and said issues could be dealt with by understanding and talking openly and freely with each other.

Thursday, May 14

The main event Thursday evening was an All College meeting inside Morrell Gymnasium called by President Howell to discuss the issue of ROTC. It was a modest turn-out—only some 250 to 300 students showed up for Howell's meeting. Yet, there was a growing opposition to Strike Central's petition for the abolition of the ROTC program. Also muddying the waters was a competing petition that requested ROTC leave the campus for more individualized and apolitical reasons.

Serving as chair, Alan Kolod, a former editor of the student newspaper, introduced President Howell. Howell told students the presence or non-presence of ROTC was a fair question for discussion and claimed the current ROTC program was voluntary and academic credit was not granted.

Kolod then read off an astounding statement, signed by 14 current Bowdoin ROTC cadets. It requested that Bowdoin College sever all connections with ROTC. The cadets "insisted that their names not be revealed to the U.S. Army."

In the debate that followed, a student in favor of ROTC stated, "The ROTC program provides for one of the best ways to fulfill my military obligation," and "provides the means by which change can be accomplished." Another said, "Many of the opponents of ROTC on this campus are fond of quoting the Bill of Rights. I suggest they look to Article IX and ask themselves if they are not infringing upon my right to make my own decisions affecting my life... I support the 'machine' and deny that you have the right to prevent my doing so by joining ROTC. If dissent is not to be stifled, then neither should consent." He claimed if the faculty voted against the ROTC program, it would be "voting against freedom of choice, and ... individualism."

Two speakers then described their opposition to ROTC. Mike Noble, a graduate of the University of Rochester and an Army veteran, denounced the Army's basic training, and said atrocities were commonplace. As a common soldier, he said, "you're not worth shit." Colleges which allow ROTC were guilty of moral hypocrisy, and he urged Bowdoin to remove ROTC. "They have closed their last death contract on the life of a young man who came here to learn how to live," Noble said.

Professor Douglas McGee, the former chair of Bowdoin's Military Affairs Committee, said the separation of ROTC from Bowdoin involved only a small cost, "which in my judgment should be paid... As I figure it, ROTC ought to go." While people spoke, students had been leaving in twos and threes and by time it concluded, there was less than 70 still in the gym. Strike Headquarters issued an explanation for the level of enthusiasm. "Most students feel the issue has already been settled and ROTC will be removed from campus."

A competing event had also been held that night—a concert for the people of Brunswick sponsored by the Department of Music with performances by Bowdoin students and faculty members. Held at the First Parish Church, it was an effort to connect the campus with the community, to break down the divide between "town vs. gown."

Friday, May 15

On Friday, student David McCarthy announced that a charity softball game had been organized between the Bowdoin faculty and administration and the Brunswick High School faculty and administration. It was to be played at Pickard Field in the middle of the afternoon, and donations would be accepted at the gate with all proceeds going to a Vietnamese orphanage. All members of the Brunswick Town Council along with all members of the local school board had been invited. With tongue firmly in cheek, McCarthy added that Council chair David Scarponi was expected to toss out the first ball and the school board chairman was to be the honorary scorekeeper. Area clergymen would serve as umpires and, McCarthy's announcement said, "We anticipate that protests and bickering over close calls will be kept at a minimum." He added, "There was no immediate word on whether President Howell, reportedly still recovering from injuries suffered in a recent rugby scrimmage, would play for the Bowdoin team."

University of Maine – Portland

As students returned to class, strikers on the Portland campus struggled to maintain their visibility by wearing red armbands. They organized teach-ins and a training program for petitioners to go door-to-door in the city's neighborhoods. Their main focus, however, was a statewide effort to influence the Democratic State Convention being held over the weekend in Portland. Maine Students for Constructive Action had issued a call for students to "Create a Peace Congress and stop the War Machine" by attending the convention and its rallies. On Saturday, May 16, 3,000 delegates and a contingent of anti-war college students – many from the university – descended on Portland for the convention. Besides the Vietnam War, another key issue at the two-day convention was the state income tax.

Outside the convention hall, students from throughout Maine rallied – including many Bowdoin and University of Maine students—and marched to a local park for a demonstration. They then moved to a stadium behind the convention hall and listened to its proceedings over loudspeakers. One student said that regardless of what happened inside the convention hall, a "people's convention" would be held after the Democrats had theirs.

New Hampshire
University of New Hampshire – Durham

There seemed to be something different in the air when the week started. And Wednesday's *Strike Daily* declared, "Nothing happened in the national news, so there's no news." By Friday, there was a discernible atmospheric change, and it was clear the strike was collapsing. Students were leaving the campus in busloads.

"So Where Do We Go from Here?" was the title of an editorial in *Strike Daily*. "The 'academic year' is ending, the enthusiasm for the Strike has dwindled, and people are going home soon — if they haven't left already. There are still many valuable things going on that have grown out of our Strike to Shut It Down to Open It Up." The editorial claimed the university had been opened up with "community work," "the workshops," work in the dorms, and surmised "UNH will never be the same." It asked, "Will we all go away this summer and forgot about this, or will we continue to broaden and solidify the things that we have begun?"

The question hung in the air. Strikers had pledged to continue actions through the summer, but nothing had solidified organizationally to ensure it happened. *Strike Daily* continued to publish for another week, but whether there were any students still on campus outside the strike committees to read it was unknown.

On May 15, a large delegation from a group called the Committee for New Hampshire and Vermont Canvass—including 16 members from UNH—arrived in Washington DC, carrying an anti-war petition with 10,000 signatures gathered from the two-state region. They presented the petitions at meetings with New Hampshire Senators Norris Cotton and Thomas McIntyre.

Dartmouth College – Hanover

On Tuesday, classes resumed at Dartmouth and Wednesday's issue of *Strike Newsletter*, asked, "Back to the Old Routine?" The article surmised, "There is a good deal of confusion around the campus right now. We have started a strike and the problem is, it worked. We have earned a lot of time to work on the major problems of the day but have no clear way to act on them." It advised, "If answers are to come, they will have to come from us.

The time is past when we could wait for someone else to tell is what to do. Listening to somebody else is how we got into Vietnam in the first place. There are no experts."

Lastly, it encouraged students to get involved, talk to friends and dormmates, attend workshops. "We couldn't end the war and racism in one week," and concluded, "We can make sure that Dartmouth will continue to function to create wisdom and action, for the rest of this term and in the coming years."

At a mass meeting Wednesday night, Dartmouth students talked about their plans to attend an upcoming march in Manchester, by car—about 75 miles away. They were cautioned by a veteran activist, "Dartmouth is NOT running this march. This is supposedly a peaceful march but many conflicting rumors concerning it have been received. Manchester is a heavy city. Know where you are going."

On Friday, 25 students from Dartmouth arrived in Washington as part of the delegation of Vermont – New Hampshire students who presented an anti-war petition to the state's senators. Over the course of the week, Dartmouth students and faculty had collected several thousand signatures while canvassing neighborhoods in Hanover and other towns and cities, including a few in Vermont.

Saturday saw the lowering of flags at Dartmouth to half-staff in memory of the two Black men killed by police at Jackson State College. President Kemey ordered the lowering at a ceremony and spoke a few words drawing a parallel between their deaths and those at Kent State.

Plymouth State College – Plymouth, New Hampshire
Tuesday, May 12

At a mass meeting held Tuesday night, May 12, 750 students took a vote on two proposals that had been lumped together. One called for final exams and classes to be optional, and the other outlined a program of seminars and workshops on relevant issues open to the community, coupled with a campaign of canvassing townspeople for their opinions on the war and other issues. Nearly three-quarters voted for the proposals (542 to 214).

Afterwards, however, at a special meeting faculty responded negatively to the idea of optional finals. After listening to presentations by student leaders, they voted that classes would continue as usual and that final examinations were an option – not of the student but of the faculty member. Faculty members did pledge to assist in organizing seminars and discussion groups.

On Friday, May 15, students from **Saint Francis College** traveled to Biddeford, about 30 miles north, where they set up a picket line in front of Marimon, a company that manufactured military machine-guns. The company tested their weapons only 1800 feet from a local elementary school.

Vermont

Monday, May 11, the **Bennington College** faculty decided to re-affirm its academic obligations, in discussing actions taken by students in support of a strike. At the same time, however, they expressed support for students' political activities on campus including strike-related actions.

On Thursday, the UPI reported that members of the Vermont United Electrical and Machine Workers agreed with the strong anti-war sentiment of the union's executive board, which had demanded the immediate withdrawal of all U.S. troops from Cambodia. Headquartered in Montpelier, the union blamed Nixon administration policies for the killings of the four at Kent State University. UEW official Peter Palmer told the press that not one member of the Vermont Union had voiced opposition to the statement. The statement, he said, "has met very strong agreement from older members and some of the younger ones feel it wasn't strong enough."

Massachusetts
Boston Area
Northeastern University

In the aftermath of the "police riot" (*Boston Globe*) Saturday night, May 9th, Boston Mayor Kevin White on Monday established an 8:00 pm curfew for the Northeastern dorm area and surrounding streets. Saturday night, police had used clubs, tear gas and police dogs to disperse a crowd of student revelers, leaving 85 injured. Mayor White also announced the Boston Tactical Police Force would remain in the area from 8 pm to the following 9 am.

Angered about the gestapo tactics of police and fearing more violence, the faculty at Northeastern met all morning and into the afternoon. At around 7 pm – an hour before the curfew and after voting overwhelmingly for the action – the faculty marched in an orderly fashion over to the campus dorm section to protect students from the Boston police unit. Fortunately, no incidents were reported.

Harvard University

Monday the 11th witnessed picket lines once again in front of campus buildings, including the Main Administration building. One major issue for the hundred students picketing was the threat of administration reprisals against university employees who had participated in anti-war activities the week before. Tensions were high, and at one point a dean was denied entry to the administration building.

Later in the day, the university charged some 40 students with violating the right of free speech by their actions on the picket lines. Yet, picketers refused to quit despite even more threats from the administration if picketing continued. On Tuesday, students continued their militant picketing and university employees continued to honor them.

Also, teams from campus kept up efforts to leaflet local factories and nearby suburbs with information about the strike and what was happening at the university. An Ad Hoc Committee also formed on campus to organize the Boston area in a petition drive calling for Nixon's impeachment. Nixon had violated the constitutional system of separation of powers, the petition explained, and had accelerated the war in Southeast Asia without consulting the Senate. Agnew's name was added to the petition on the grounds of having crossed state lines to incite a riot.

On Friday the 15th, Harvard students organized a non-violent 300-person sit-in at the Boston Army base, aimed at stopping buses full of draft inductees. Police moved in and arrested 67 protesters, who offered no resistance. The action was part of the buildup for rallies at military posts across the nation that upcoming weekend.

Boston University

Some dorms on Monday were still open and about a third of the remaining students on campus were in strike mode. Knowing that all the dorms would be shut down by that Friday, students at Northeastern offered dorm space to BU students. Then on Sunday, the university reversed its policy—one that had made life unpleasant for strikers—and agreed to keep three floors in one dorm open during the summer for strikers, free of charge.

Also on Sunday, one of the last campus rallies of the strike was held to mourn the two young Black men slain by police at Jackson State.

MIT (Mass. Institute of Technology)

MIT students were responsible for creating an anti-war fund that went nation-wide that requested every college professor in the country to contribute at least one day's salary to a fund for peace candidates for the November 1970 election. Its sponsors – which included 6 Nobel Prize winners such as Harold C. Urey and James D. Watson—hoped to raise as much as $15 million. Other sponsors included Jerome B. Wiesner, Provost of MIT, and Mary I. Bunting, President of Radcliffe.

Students also organized a five-day program of discussions on key topics with workers at area plants and factories and distributed leaflets at different worksites to get the word out. Topics included how the domestic economy was affected by the war, Black and minority repression, and a critique of the Nixon administration.

Later during the strike, it was announced that MIT's radio station had sent 12,000 radiograms with messages about the strike movement to area Congressmen.

University of Massachusetts Boston

It was the beginning of the second week of the strike at UMass and the campus strike newsletter, *The Mass Media*, was full of announcements that offered a glimpse into the life of the strike. Students from UMass and Amherst were to "stage a mass bank withdrawal campaign" to attack the economic base of the war-profiteers on Tuesday. A student security group was meeting at 12 noon, with the primary purpose of preventing theft and destruction of university property.

A short blurb: "Women: Now is the time to unite, to fight against: war, racism, the oppression of women. Women's liberation at U Mass Boston has established a Center for Women – students and non-students. The center is located in the main lounge of the Sawyer Building." Meetings and workshops of the Women's Liberation group were listed: those interested in forming a woman's commune would meet on Thursday; workshops for Friday included "The myth of the vaginal orgasm," "Women and violence" and "Abortion, birth control and your body."

Students were urged to join faculty members to lobby in Washington DC on Wednesday; to take part in a non-violent direct action at the Boston Army Base on Friday; to leaflet and talk to GIs on Saturday; or join a radical street theater group that was forming up that week. Tuesday included a talk by a Peace Corps veteran, a workshop on "Imperialism, theory and practice," and a talk by Kent State English instructor Leonard Deutsch "about the Kent State incident."

Howard Zinn of Boston University and two other professors were giving a lecture on "How to Change America," with a discussion period to follow; Brookline High School students were on strike and holding an open meeting at their strike headquarters; there was an offer to do silk screening for shirts and jackets for only $5; poster printing at the Massachusetts College of Art was offered for "any design;" non-violent training sessions were being given at the Loeb Drama Center in Cambridge; the film "Huey"- a documentary on Huey Newton, a leader of the Black Panthers—was in the Auditorium; and tickets were still available for the May 19th Red Sox game with Cleveland - "Only $1 at student affairs office."

The strike newsletter—because the US Senate was about to vote on the Cooper-Church Amendment—advised that, "Everyone is asked to deluge the offices of the following uncommitted senators with telegrams and phone calls" with names and numbers listed. The bill - an amendment attached to a major funding bill – by Sen. John Cooper (R-Kentucky) and Frank Church (D-Idaho)—had been introduced in response to the Cambodian incursion.

Church and Cooper, some of the first senators to openly oppose the Vietnam War, sought to end funding for U.S. ground troops and military advisors in Cambodia and Laos after the end of June 1970. Eventually approved by the Senate, the measure failed in the House by a vote of 237 to 153. A revised version, although more limited, did pass Congress in December and was enacted in early January 1971.

Brandeis

Brandeis hosted two conferences during the second week of the strike – a tax resistance confab at the Heller School of Brandeis, and two days of the National Economic Action Committee. The Action Committee expressed solidarity with the economic boycott for peace initiated the previous week in Washington D.C., that urged consumers and especially students to stop purchases of Coca Cola products and Marlboro cigarettes (Philip Morris Co.). Then surprisingly, on Sunday, the National Strike Information Center (NSIC) at Brandeis announced the national campaign had called off the consumer boycott of Marlboro and other Phillip Morris products. Boycott organizers had been overly impressed by the "attitude" and "cooperation" by Phillip Morris.

On Tuesday, May 12, the strike information center counted 286 colleges with some level of continuing strike activity, despite the reopening of many campuses after the strike's tumultuous first week.

Also on Tuesday, the NSIC announced that *CBS* had refused to sell Senator George McGovern—a leading critic of the war—any airtime. The national strike newsletter was sent out to campuses across the nation on a daily basis and it urged readers to send letters of protest to CBS. And according to network officials, public response was "very heavy." Rival *NBC* did air a half-hour show with McGovern and four of his amendment co-sponsors to cut military funding, the McGovern-Hatfield amendment. (McGovern would go on and become the 1972 Democratic Party presidential candidate—and lose by a landslide to Nixon.)

A country-wide survey by NSIC on Thursday showed only 13 college-level campuses remained officially closed because of antiwar activities, but the academic routine at many continued to be interrupted by special antiwar programs. On Thursday, the strike information center counted 278 colleges with some level of student strike activity. They had counted 286 on Tuesday and 267 on Wednesday.

Wheaton College, Norton

The focus of a Monday workshop at the all-women's college was organizing what students felt was a different kind of anti-war tactic and strategy—an economic boycott. Various models and ideas were batted around; New York City Mayor John Lindsay's "Sick-of-the-War Day"; the 1969 Christmas campaign against buying war toys; and the "Pause for Peace" – a one-hour nationwide work stoppage. Other ideas included a Stock market boycott involving large-scale stock sales to pressure corporations to change their policies on war and discriminatory employment; the withdrawal of money from personal bank accounts to deplete banks' reserves; and a general boycott of Christmas spending in 1970.

The student newspaper, *The Gazette*, reported on how Wheaton students had carried out an extensive outreach and canvassing campaign during the week about US troops in Southeast Asia. They had canvassed workers at different area factories and residents in different neighborhoods and had set up information booths in shopping areas. They visited factories in the nearby small towns, like Taunton, Foxborough, Attleboro and Mansfield. They approached workers at the end of work shifts, in parking lots or at factory gates, and handed them fact sheets about the wars. They also handed out envelopes and letters addressed to members of Congress asking for the removal of troops from Southeast Asia, all ready to be signed, stamped and mailed.

Susie Tallman, a staff reporter for the *Gazette*, spoke to one group of Wheaton women stationed in front of Trucchi's Supermarket in Norton. They had been motivated by the crisis and wanted to involve themselves in the local community especially around Cambodia. This group had set up information booths every day during the week in different small towns, including Norton and Pawtucket in Rhode Island. As they stood in front of Trucchi's, they discussed America's problems with shoppers, working in shifts during day-light hours.

Lewis P. Trucchi, the store manager, expressed his appreciation. "The girls here are sincere people and I applaud what they are doing outside the store. They are trying to inform the people of this community about what's happening in America today and what each individual can do about the situation. They discuss their opinions and then the people they are talking with relate their views to the girls." For him personally, it was a big change. Wheaton College had finally joined the community. "For many,

many years," he remarked, "it was just a college in Norton and the girls there never took a stand on any issue. I certainly give them credit for coming out and talking to people the way they have."

Kent State had been the turning point for them, the women told reporter Tallman. It was time for them to become concerned, vocal citizens in the community. Student Lorin said, "We're here to inform people. We tell them our position and listen while they explain their views to us. We're not here to make people believe the way we believe about the Cambodian War. We're here to get them to think about the situation and—hopefully to form an opinion, take a stand and work towards changing current policy if they believe it should be."

"We have all types of people coming up to talk with us," Lorin said, "then there are some who say that they would rather not discuss the issue of Cambodia. People are usually impressed by the fact that we are well-dressed, clean-cut girls who are taking a stand on an issue of national importance. We're not hippie-looking. Not everyone agrees with us, but we don't ask them to. All we want the people to do is have an opinion and to voice that opinion."

Marcia Clay, a junior and English literature major, recounted to the reporter how one Saturday, they took a poll of shoppers' opinions at the booth at Trucchi's. Did they agree with President Nixon, or did they think the US should leave Cambodia and Vietnam or could the United States win? "The majority of the people polled said that they thought the United States should leave Vietnam and Cambodia now," Marica said. "We're not being dogmatic when we talk with people here. We're only concerned, and we want other people to be aware of the situation. Personally, I question the government of the United States with their policies about Vietnam. We need more facts and what is happening here is political repression in the United States today."

A junior history major, Lalla Dodge, told Tallman, "I realized that democracy is just a myth and now I'd like to work towards a better society, a more truthful country. I believe we're doing a lot for Wheaton College by being here and they have done a lot for us by allowing us to have this week to strike." She went further, "Actually, this isn't a strike. The school year was over last Friday, and exams don't end until May 23, so we're having teach-ins and workshops to discuss current problems in America."

"There are still girls who are writing papers," noted student Italia, "and we all have to take final exams if we want a letter grade. We can take an incomplete in a course if we want to and then make it up next fall, but we haven't stopped school because of the national strike." Marcia added, "The consensus of the students at Wheaton are moderate, just as they are across the United States. We represent a majority of the college students today. We're not violent and we're not radicals, we just want the people to think."

A junior government major, Gigi Coyle, pointed out, "We're asking people to write their Congressmen about Cambodia and the situation of our country. Nixon will have to eventually go to his Congress, and they can then say that they have received such and such amount of telegrams and letters stating their people want such and action." Coyle added, that incredulously, "One woman I talked to today asked if she would get into trouble writing her Congressman."

These women students agreed that the majority of Wheaton students felt the way student Betty Robbins did, as she had expressed in the strike newsletter: "I realize that many of my ideas are revolutionary in the light of our present society. But I reject and resent the implication that, in order to attain my goals, I must be a revolutionary socialist. I denounce this violence just as I denounce the violence in Southeast Asia, in our cities, in our minds."

Fitchburg State College

Students had been out on strike for the whole first week, beginning on May 4, the day of Kent State. The entire edition of the May 14 *Cycle*, the campus strike newspaper, was dedicated to the memory of the four students and strikers hoped the edition would move their fellow students "to help put an end to the Southeast Asian war and to all political repression here in America." The front cover had large photos of the two women killed at Kent State, Allison Krause and Sandy Scheuer, next to Carl Sandburg's poem, "Pile the bodies high …. I am the grass. Let me work."

Worcester State College

On Monday, students from **Worcester** joined others from **Holy Cross College** and **Clark College** and returned to the Worcester Massachusetts

Draft Board, the site of a sit-in on Friday. But this time, there were five times as many. 400 protesters sat down outside the building and occupied part of the seventh floor. Police showed up and warned them they were trespassing. Most refused to leave and officers began making arrests. People gave no resistance, and no incidents nor injuries were reported. By the end, 287 people had been arrested—mostly from Holy Cross and Clark, making it one of the nation's largest mass arrests during the May rebellion. Less than a week later on May 17, Worcester area students linked up with Boston students and demonstrated against the war at Fort Devens as part of a national antiwar presence on Armed Forces Day.

Student anti-war activities also occurred at **Hampshire College** in western Massachusetts during the first two weeks of May, including the circulation of a petition for the impeachment of President Nixon signed by numerous faculty members.

It was on Tuesday when students from **University of Massachusetts Amherst** aligned with students from **Amherst College** and **UMass Boston** and staged a mass bank withdrawal in an effort to undercut the reserves of the "corporate war machine."

During the week, the White House announced that Julie (Nixon) Eisenhower and hubby David Eisenhower had decided not to attend their graduation exercises at **Smith** and **Amherst** colleges in fear of provoking protests.

Williams College

Students at Williams believed their strike was going so well that many of them traveled to at least a dozen other colleges to lend guidance and assistance in their strikes, including **Cape Cod Community College, Amherst, Vassar, Skidmore**, and even **Albany State**. Williams students viewed their role as mostly an organizational one, talking to as many different people as they could, offering help, distributing fact and information sheets, and suppling silk-screened fists for shirts—symbols of the strike. Once students at the different campuses "caught-up," the Williams students would back off. That was the idea. However, at a few of the campuses, such as **Skidmore, Smith**, and **Mt. Holyoke**, Women's Liberation group members charged the Williams men with "male chauvinism," and resented how they appeared to be running their strikes for them.

The "Special Edition" of the campus newspaper, the *Williams Record*, for May 14th reported the campaign "Pause for Peace" had disbanded. The movement's leaders had decided to disengage the group, the article said, "because of a lack of support for a nation-wide work stoppage and a lack of financial support." Despite numerous endorsements and general statements of cooperation, "no major corporation or union leaders have been actively willing to take the lead," it stated.

Rhode Island
Brown University – Providence

Bernard Miller, father of Jeffrey Miller, one of the students killed at Kent State, on Friday, May 15, addressed an audience at Brown University and said he believed his son's death could be a turning point for the nation—to either disaster or peace. The KSU deaths, Miller said, "could well touch off a cycle of violence and repression which will bring America crashing down, or we can convert this moment into a shining hour which can jolt the conscience of this sleepwalking nation into redemptive action."

Connecticut
University of Connecticut – Storrs
Monday, May 11

On Monday, hundreds of students jammed into an old, World War II-era Bay hangar that served as part of the ROTC facilities and began turning it into a daycare center. Dissatisfied with University President Homer Babbidge's response to demands presented him on Friday by leaders of the strike committee, they began their occupation by decorating it, painting the walls with flowers, cartoons, and peace symbols.

The occupation continued and hours passed without a response from the administration. Finally, word came that Babbidge would speak at the hangar, and hundreds of other students joined the occupiers. It wasn't until almost 1 am that the president appeared and spoke to the 500 people now crowded inside. Babbidge started with a concession—the university would no longer apply for Department of Defense contracts and the ROTC program would be modified. Conceding that a day care center was important, he questioned students' tactics and choice of location. At the end of his spiel, Babbidge warned occupiers they would be in jeopardy if they didn't leave the building. When he left, it was around 2 am and he was followed by the 300 students who came just to hear him. Over the next two hours, most of those who remained filtered out of the hangar.

Wednesday, May 13

Administration officials arrived at the hangar at 7 am and found only six occupiers. And when the Provost and Dean of Students requested they leave, they immediately complied. So ended the first of several occupations.

More disruptions were to occur during the day. Later that morning, about 40 white students disrupted classes in the Von der Menden Recital Hall and the Social Sciences Building. In response, the Dean of Students identified nine of them, and by the afternoon had taken steps to suspend them. In the afternoon, another group of African-American students disrupted an Engineering School exam. But this time, the Dean notched up his response; he interviewed faculty members and students in seeking their identities and threatened them with more than suspensions – but with criminal charges.

The Dean's disproportionate response angered Black students. Why, just a week earlier the administration had held a campus-wide program about racial sensitivities and respect.

Just coincidentally, there was a Black issues rally held on the mall at the Student Union and 600 people were in attendance. A speaker alleged racism in the disproportionate actions by the Dean and this triggered a march on the administration building. When the large contingent of demonstrators converged on the building, Babbidge came outside and attempted to speak, but at that moment 150 protesters skirted past him and entered the building. It was another occupation – the second for the campus.

Strikers continued the occupation for four hours, but it started at the end of a workday – and little actual disruption of business as usual occurred. A small group of about 20 occupiers broke off from the main group and went on a rampage, causing damage to telephone lines, windows and plastic signs—later estimated at $1,500. Around 7 pm, a local TV cameraman covering the occupation was approached by a student who demanded he give up his film. When the cameraman refused, he was assaulted – which, of course, also made the news.

By 8:30 pm, all occupiers had left the building. Soon after students – including some of the original occupiers – returned to clean up the building. Yet, the back-to-back building take-overs had jarred the administration, and campus security began an immediate investigation into the latest one. At midnight, President Babbidge held an emergency meeting with the University Senate Executive Committee to consider options. The only public statement from him was broadcast over the campus radio station and expressed the seriousness of the crisis, and that deep considerations were being taken to close down the university.

Thursday, May 14

By Thursday, cracks appeared in the strike coalition. The most recent occupation and its damage hadn't set well with some strikers. The McMahon Coed Council, representing 580 students, announced it was withdrawing from the coalition because of an "unwillingness or inability of the Coalition to take a public stand on willful destruction of public property." The next day, the Intra-Fraternity Council also pulled out. Things got worse. The Dean of Students suspended eight students identified in the first disruption incident, plus took steps to suspend another 15 for the Engineering exam brouhaha. Their cases were all to be heard by the University Committee on Student Conduct.

Friday, May 15

On Friday, classes ended for the spring term. Campus security announced they had arrested the cameraman's alleged assailant and had charged him with breach of peace by assault. The cameraman was reported to be in good condition, having undergone facial surgery. Three of the Black students involved in the Engineering School disruption were suspended. And 300 students signed up to repaint the ROTC hangar, where idealistic strikers had wanted a day care center.

Eastern Connecticut State College - Windham

On Monday, *Strike News* published the complete schedule for the day. It consisted of a talk at 2 pm on the Union steps by a Kent State student about the killings; a "big" general meeting at 3:30 pm at the Union; a 7 pm meeting at the gym for marshals – 50 were needed—in preparation for a large rally on Saturday; at 7:15 pm the guerrilla theater workshop was to meet for a rehearsal with plans for a presentation on Thursday.

Seminars for the day included "Social factors of the War," a workshop for community work over the summer and the "History of Southeast Asia since 1954." Lastly, *Strike News* encouraged students to patronize local Windham merchants who supported the strike – eight were listed, and boycott those not supporting the strike – only three.

Yale

Students at Yale organized what they called the Peace Commencement fund, a campaign to convince graduating seniors to donate money they saved by not wearing caps and gowns to the campaigns of peace candidate in the upcoming congressional elections. The campaign was supported by well-known anti-war activists, including William Sloan Coffin and Sam Brown.

For two days, May 13 and 14, Yale hosted a National Strike Conference with representatives from 250 to 300 striking colleges, universities and high schools. Under the banner of "Toward a Summer of Resistance and Liberation," tactics, strategies, and ideas on the strike were exchanged based on students' experiences from the last couple of weeks. Organizers viewed the national strike as a political event of great historic importance and tried to maintain the conference's main focus on how to continue the strike without faltering or losing momentum.

Obvious enthusiasm and optimism buoyed the student delegates through plenary sessions and workshops, and the conference heard speeches and reports from well-known activists and from different corners of the strike. Yale's Assistant Professor Ken Mills gave the opening speech in which he stressed the importance of the strike in holding the line against fascism and repression and called for a massive "summer of resistance." He emphasized that the struggles of whites, Blacks and "third world peoples" were all related because they were all against the systematic repression inherent in American society.

Bill Farley of the Yale Strike Committee spoke on the necessity of preventing the government from exterminating the entire radical left. Ron Weisenberger from Kent State proposed a new Declaration of Independence. Sybil Leferts, a representative of the National Strike

Information Center at Brandeis, explained the history and present functioning of the information coordinating hub.

Tom Breslin, a University of Virginia student, said that in the south the strike was still gaining momentum. Other speakers included Doug Miranda of the Black Panthers, Rennie Davis of the Conspiracy, Lee Webb—*Ramparts* magazine's Washington editor, and Peter Strauss of the American Servicemen's Union—who spoke of the vital and increasingly successful attempts being made to organize GIs.

Solidarity statements were made and condemnations issued, particularly of "the murder of our brothers and sisters at Jackson, Augusta and Kent State." The optimism was contagious to everyone at the conference. Unfortunately, a good number of the conference attendees could not carry that optimism back to their respective campuses, because strikes at some campuses were faltering and losing momentum, and at some schools, students were returning to their homes in troves.

On Tuesday, May 12, 150 students at **Fairfield University** barricaded themselves inside a campus building after recommendations from the pro-strike student council on academic regulations were ignored by the administration. After a two-day occupation, students were served with a court order which motivated them to evacuate. A religious school by nature, 15 students also undertook a two-day fast in mourning for the Kent State dead.

New York State

Skidmore College - Saratoga Springs

After women students had massed for a strike meeting on the Green on Monday, a workshop entitled "Bringing it home" was held for them in how they—"Skiddies"—could continue anti-war efforts within their home towns.

Later in the day, enough interest was shown at a meeting of the Union for National Draft Opposition (UNDO) to form a Skidmore chapter and raise money for the group. Campus organizers explained their role was to "educate the Skidmore student body about UNDO and what we, as women, could do to 'aid, abet and council' those men who have handed their draft cards in, those who wish to avoid induction and therefore would need legal counsel." Information on UNDO was taped to mirrors in every bathroom on campus. (Skidmore College became co-ed in 1971.)

Skiddies had organized a panel discussion about the war and what was going on at Skidmore for the Saratoga Springs community for that evening, scheduled at 7 pm. Three faculty members and four students were to debate the issues with recently-elected Mayor Sarto Smaldone, owner of a local drive-in. Smaldone had accepted an official invitation to the event and a local judge was to moderate.

Perhaps because the local newspaper, *the Saratogian*, had headlined the event, Skidmore organizers received an anxious call from Mayor Smaldone. He told them it was his understanding that he was going to address Skidmore students – not be part of an open debate between the community and Skidmore. Students tried to reassure him, but in the end, none of it mattered, for townspeople failed to show up at the anointed hour. One faculty organizer officially closed the meeting, saying another could be held whenever the community requested it. Panel members got up and adjourned into another room—and then surprisingly, a number of residents actually did show – and civil discourse broke out and prevailed. Participants later described it as a "valuable discussion" in breaking down barriers between the college and Saratoga Springs.

Union College – Schenectady
Monday, May 11

The *Union Press* campus newspaper on Monday, May 11, published an editorial that exclaimed universities had become "a central influence" in American society and could be used as important bases for spreading the goals of the strike. Nixon had said that the next two months were crucial, it went on, and therefore the national strike should be focused on that same time period. In addition, the editorial laid out complaints that strike organizers had—the distortion the mass media gave as the aims of the strike, only demands about the Indochina war were reported, whereas demands about the repression of the Black Panthers and university complicity in government war policies did not receive sufficient coverage.

Tuesday, May 12

A small contingent from Union College on Tuesday, May 12, hooked up with several thousand other students from local colleges and blocked entrances to all federal buildings in downtown Albany, the state capitol. Not one arrest was made during the six-hour non-violent protest.

Wednesday, May 13

Again, on Wednesday, downtown Albany felt the impact of the national student strike. Union students joined thousands of others from some 40 campus communities in a march and rally of 5,000 to 10,000 people at the Capitol Building.

The march began with a rally at **Albany State**, and around 1:30 a huge column formed up and proceeded all the way into downtown Albany, with nary an expression of hostility along the route - even as they passed several construction sites. A recent attack on peace marchers by construction workers in downtown New York City was on the minds of some.

However, once the crowd reached their destination, they were harangued by a few hardhat workers standing on the other side of a police line. But another group of construction workers walked up and actually joined the rally and listened to speeches. Police officers stationed around the Capitol were restrained and mainly out of sight.

One of the high points of the rally came when Ron Young of the New Mobe exhorted the crowd to burn or get rid of their draft cards, and immediately, a lone figure stood up, took out his draft card and set it on fire. He received a huge ovation – the largest of the afternoon. Young urged everyone to attend an open house at Fort Dix the following weekend on Armed Forces Day as part of a nation-wide protest at military bases.

Spencer Jackson of **Albany State**'s Third World Liberation – a group that supported the National Student Strike – was next. He expressed his ire that the Black Panthers and Bobby Seale's trial in New Haven were not getting the media coverage they deserved. Then pointing to an American flag and a banner that read, "God Bless the U.S.A." that had been raised to the top of a nearby building by construction workers, Jackson condemned those who hid behind the symbol of the American flag. At his conclusion, he received one of the best receptions from the crowd. A member of the Black Panther Party also spoke and talked of the repression on Black people. He was also warmly received and many raised clenched fists.

John Froines of Chicago 8 fame addressed the throng and linked the repression of the Panthers, the killings at Kent State with the war in

Indochina. They were all symptoms of the same disorder in American society and government, he said. Rather than "Vietnamizing" the war, Nixon was trying to Americanize the world. If that happened, "then we are going to Vietnamize America, and the youth of America are going to become the Vietcong." He also foresaw vast demonstrations in New Haven during the upcoming summer, and then shouted, "If they convict Bobby Seale and the Panthers, the protestors will pick up New Haven and send it to the moon!"

The *Union Press* reported that for some students, the event had been a peaceful, happy rally and march on a pleasant afternoon, where bystanders had been invited to participate and marchers hadn't alienated anyone. Others had mixed feelings; the speakers weren't up to what they expected – there had been rumors about appearances by William Kunstler, Mrs. Bobby Seale, and entertainers from Pete Seeger to Joni Mitchell and even the Grateful Dead.

May 14, Thursday

In Thursday's *Union Press*, an editorial entitled "The Second Movement" described the moment striking students across the country had come to. "Warm red blood of our brothers and sisters, both Black and white, has seeped through the cracks, crevasses, and fault lines of our campuses. Their blood, along with many others, has unnecessarily fertilized the earth. The students of America have been educated to think, not to fight. Fortunately for the vast majority, we have not found it necessary to prostitute our souls and consciences to the military in order to finance a college education. Our inadequacies in the area of self-defense have resulted in death. Frankly," it stated, "we have neither the training nor the arms to take on the armor and tactics of the military machine."

"It logically follows that at this point we must learn a lesson from our martyred fellow students. We must not allow them to die in vain. The Second Movement, in which we are actively involved, is built upon a foundation of peace. The First Movement ... has died. Its death can be directly attributed to passive participation. The Second Movement, if it is to succeed, must be centered around constructive community work. The information and ideas collected on the campuses must be disseminated to Middle America. The only way this can be carried out is by a constructive crusade, one that utilizes effective and rational means to attain our outlined national objectives."

The editorial exclaimed, "...WE are the 'vanguards' of this Second Movement. Much of the work will seem uninteresting and unproductive only because the results of our efforts will not be immediately recognized. But we must never lose sight of our goals, peace in Indochina and an end to political and domestic oppression." It concluded, "If we are sincere in our determination to change a country that most certainly merits innumerable changes, then we must constructively focus our enormous supply of energy, intelligence and manpower. No longer can our potential be wasted in passive participation. Onlookers must become workers."

Also Thursday came the pronouncement that according to the National Strike Information Center 11,023 draft cards had been turned in across the nation to protest US involvement in Indochina. The report listed the number of draft cards turned in from various campuses and regions: 2,083 draft cards came from UC Berkeley, 2,050 from Southern California, 603 from Stony Brook in Long Island, 350 turned in at Harvard, 350 from Chicago University, 360 from Princeton, 600 from Humboldt State College in northern California, and four from women at Swarthmore.

State University of New York (SUNY) – Albany
Tuesday, May 12

Under the slogan, "stop business as usual," 2000 to 3,000 students rallied early Tuesday morning on the SUNY campus before marching to downtown Albany. They'd been joined by students from at least ten area colleges – including **Williams, St. Lawrence** and a small contingent from **Union**. Once marchers left the campus, they proceeded to the Federal Building and Post Office, surrounding them with picket lines and bodies. All entrances were blocked and at some places protesters stood six deep. They refused to let any workers inside and mail trucks were allowed out but no new mail was allowed in, virtually halting mail service in the city of 130,000. Some Postal workers had reportedly stayed in the building overnight.

By 12 noon, the sidewalks were packed with 600 supporters and onlookers—police had made no effort to halt or constrain the protest. There were occasional harsh verbal exchanges and a few minor scuffles broke out between protesters and construction workers. And at least one hardhat was taken away by police after assaulting a photographer. At one point, a dozen men carrying an American flag charged into student lines and punched their way to the main entrance of the Federal Building. But they were forced back and dispersed due to coordinated efforts of student marshals and police. There were friendly encounters between students and construction workers who expressed genuine interest in the recent storms of student protest. A few discovered that students' feelings about government oppression matched their own.

One of the more difficult challenges for blockaders during the 6-hour protest was holding the mail entrance on the left side of the Federal building. Taunted by shouts and threats from hardhats, protesters—most of whom were from State University—refused to budge – and later perceived this as a major victory. They remained outside the buildings for nearly an entire work day, they chanted "Peace Now!' and sang patriotic songs. Marshals persuaded one group not to display a Vietcong flag they had brought.

During the entire civil disobedience, no arrests were made. The goal had been to stop normal business and mail service at the Federal Building – which had been achieved. Participants gave credit to John Kaufman, Albany State strike leader, and his marshals for coordinating the blockade. Some students felt the perseverance of the blockaders in their resolve to conduct a peaceful protest won respect in the eyes of the community, and they hoped that the next day's rally at the Capitol would be met with equal success.

Wednesday, May 13

Wednesday's massive march on the Albany State Capitol appeared to be a repeat of the day before when it began with a 1 pm rally at SUNY. But after the crowd finally assembled, its size was more than double that of Tuesday's—at least 5,000 strong. Chants and slogans dominated the air as marchers trekked the four-plus miles to downtown, walking five abreast along the length of Washington Avenue. The huge throng attracted supporters and gawkers. Residents came out of their houses, construction workers halted work to gape, high schoolers streamed out of their schools, businesspeople stood in their doors or leaned out of their windows. "Peace now!" the crowd demanded, and "One-two-three-four, Free Bobby and stop the war!", or "1,2,3,4 - Free the Panthers, end the war!"

Tensions mounted whenever marchers passed a construction site because SUNY students the week before had been injured by plaster deliberately thrown at them by workers during a demonstration in downtown Albany. As they marched by, students glared at the hardhats.

The crowd reached the rally site and poured into the park that surrounded the Capitol. Estimates of the crowd size ranged from more than 5,000 (*The Carillon, Union Press*) to 9,000 (National Strike Information Center) to the *Skidmore News* which reported, "approximately 8,000 students marched from Albany State to the State Capitol where they were met with an already assembled group."

Back at SUNY Albany, details of the costs and expenses caused by the strike came out. For one, the strike had forced the cancellation of Alumni Weekend, Parents Weekend, the State Fair, and a concert by the University-Community Symphony Orchestra. For another, monetary support for strike-related activities had come from the Student Association, which included financing the Strike Committee itself, the strike newspaper, $5,000 to continue the day care center begun by the Women's Liberation Front, and $15,000 to establish a "Free University" that was to begin on July 1. And finally, damages on campus from May 4 through the 13th were estimated by the administration to be from $80,000 to $100,000. $3,000 alone was spent on removing slogans and signs from the walls. Other costs, undoubtedly, had to do with repairs from firebombs and other arson on campus.

New York City & Region—Day By Day Chronicle
Monday, May 11

On Monday, Peter J. Brennan, president of the 200,000-member Building and Construction Trades Council of Greater New York, announced a rally in support of the war at City Hall for noon on Wednesday, May 20. The rally had the backing of Joint Council 16 of the Teamsters, the long shoremen's union and sections of the Communication Workers of America. Brennan, a long-time Nixon supporter, had been instrumental – along with the White House—in organizing the violent

Hardhat Riot against peace demonstrators at Wall Street just that previous Friday, May 8.

Picket lines were gone from the all-women's **Barnard College** by Monday, yet strikers were working on a variety of projects, both on and off the campus, although many students had simply returned home. Three members of the strike coalition summarized their views in a public statement. They wrote that even though the strike had ended, "the crisis which precipitated the strike has not." The crisis endured, they said, "in the deaths of the Kent State 4, the Jackson 2, and the Augusta 6," and by the spread of the war. "The crisis is with us in the continuance of racism in the United States and in the conflict between the executive and legislative bodies of our government. The crisis which afflicts our nation has been with us many years; it will exist for many years to come." They concluded, "It is only by our affirmation of human freedom, dignity, and justice for all people, our affirmation by our lives and work, that the struggle will be ended." It was signed by June Mee, Margo Sullivan, and Julie Rosenblum.

By Monday, classroom activity at **Columbia University** had virtually grounded to a halt. "Militant" picket lines blocked campus buildings while other students were out canvassing New York City neighborhoods. Whole tiers of university departments were involved in strike actions, including the graduate schools of teachers, architecture, law, engineering, business, social work, library services, international affairs and education. During the strike, the campus School of Library Service distributed various treatises on the history of US involvement in Vietnam and the history of the Geneva Accords. A strike publication, *Seize the Time*, reported that the Columbia strike had gained support from campus employees—cafeteria workers had closed down the school's three dining halls and maintenance workers had walked off their jobs.

At a raucous rally in the **Baruch College** auditorium on Monday, close to 2,000 students were forced to face the issue of final exams. Many were too anxious and angry to act as if it was all 'business as usual' yet were worried about what course material would be covered by finals. Any time someone mentioned "finals" it was met with yells, jeers and "ribald instructions how finals should be treated," one observer noted. Students were not receptive even to a report from the Baruch Committee of 26

– formed to find compromises on the issue of tuition which had been prominent before the national crisis.

When the faculty went into session to discuss grade policy, between 100 and 200 students jammed the 14th and 15th floors in a temporary take-over of the building, which displaced several accounting classes. However, at 5 pm, they all peacefully departed the building, and in response, the administration cancelled classes for the next day so the faculty could meet on the grades issue without classroom commitments.

The Baruch College *Bum!* newsletter for Monday had a headline, "Remember Orangeburg!" over a list of American students killed by law enforcement since 1962. "1962 – 2 men, University of Mississippi; Feb 8, 1968—3 Black students shot down at South Carolina State College, Orangeburg, SC; May 15, 1969 [James Rector] bystander killed by buckshot near People's Park, Berkeley; May 23, 1969—Black student found shot to death at North Carolina A&T Univ., Greensboro, NC; April 18, 1970 - student [Kevin Moran] killed by single bullet at UC Santa Barbara; May 4: Kent state 4." It summarized: "12 Dead, so far." Sadly, within a few days, there will be two more names to add to the list – from Jackson State on May 15.

Later Monday, hundreds of Baruch students attended a huge convocation on the campus of the **City College of New York** in Lewisohn Stadium, and estimates of the crowd ranged from 3,000 to 10,000. Shouts of "Peace now!" opened the event, joined by chants of "Strike! Strike!", "Power to the People!" and "Impeach Nixon!" Charles Rivers, of the Iron Workers Union, addressed the massive throng. "We're not going to surrender the flag to bigots, and it means a hell of a lot more to us than them," he said, referring to the "Hardhat Riot."

A speaker who exemplified the general tone of the assembly was Prof. Paul Minkoff of the Faculty Action Coordinating Committee who declared, "We want a strike that is directed at organizing ... CCNY as a base for the liberation struggle. We don't want the school shut down, we want it opened up." David McReynolds, leader of the War Resistance League, also spoke. And amazingly, 1,000 of the usually conservative engineering students joined in on the vote to strike until American troops were withdrawn from Cambodia.

Tuesday, May 12

Tuesday's Issue No. 3 of the **Columbia University Teachers College** "Newsletter" reported that many college departments had organized their own separate anti-war activities, including Special Ed., Guidance, School Psychology, Speech Pathology and Audiology. They had canvassed their own students, contacted professional organizations, wrote alumni, held meetings and set up anti-war tables in their offices "to coordinate activities within that department." The newsletter also made an appeal for contributions for a quarter page ad in the *New York Times* with an anti-war message that faculty planned to publish. $1500 of the $2000 had been raised and the balance was due by noon that day.

The newsletter also published a demand statement by a campus group called the Black Representation Organization with "the full support of the Black Community at Teachers College, Columbia University."

"That Black people for hundreds of years have been subjected to racist oppression both institutional and individua. That in particular, Teachers College has been the direct financial beneficiary of racism in the past. That Teachers College has displayed massive insensitivity to the plight and situation of Black People. In light of these facts and particularly in light of the recent lynching of 6 Black men in Augusta, Georgia, we make the following demands," which included that Teachers College President John Fischer declare Monday, May 18th, as a day of mourning and close the institution.

Other demands included: a bail fund for Black Panthers, to recruit and hire more Black people in all capacities, to open up university facilities to Black and Puerto Rican employees and the community at large, establish a program of financial assistance for Black students, and to ensure Black faculty and students were represented "on all Admission Committees." One demand of local interest asked to "support our efforts to obtain a visa of entry to the U.S. for Mrs. Shirley Dubois, wife of the great Black educator and humanist [W.E.B. Du Bois]."

At **CW Post College**, the Tuesday edition of *Grok,* a leftwing student newspaper, listed the day's political education classes at the renamed "Bobby Seale University": "Women's Liberation," "Personal Liberation,"

"Latin America and Cuba," and "Military- Industrial- Educational complex," plus discussion sessions on guerilla theater, the Black Panther organization, and on "Socialism and Capitalism."

Wednesday, May 13

On Wednesday, 400 engineering students held a unique protest against the war when they demonstrated in front of the International Engineering Building in the UN Plaza. They came from prestigious engineering schools and had one message: they would refuse to work for companies involved in war materials or war research. The engineering students were from **Columbia University School of Engineering, CUNY, NYU, Pratt Institute, Cooper Union, Brooklyn Poly. Tech** and **Stevens Institute** and presented their pledges to officials in the building. They then marched to Rockefeller Center where they split up to cover the different engineering businesses—General Electric, Sylvania, Dow Chemicals and AVCO—and present them with requests to cease their war interests.

At **Baruch College** over 1,000 students met on Wednesday to hear the faculty's response to their demands about grades – the main ones were no finals and more flexibility for strikers. At first, they booed when word that finals would be given, but after a detailed, patient explanation of the entire faculty resolution – finals based on material up to early May— most students were convinced that the faculty response was reasonably fair, even though they hadn't achieved what they had wanted.

Thursday, May 14

On Thursday, **Teachers College** President Fischer responded to the first demand made by African American students and announced the campus would be closed that day "to express the anguish of the members of this institution at the murder of six black Americans in Augusta, Georgia." He also agreed to close down the school on Monday, also demanded.

In his statement, Fischer directly referred to the Augusta, Georgia, police killing of six Blacks on May 11. "That such an incident could occur even once would be enough to revolt and shame every civilized person. The Augusta murders are not an isolated incident; they are but the latest consequence of the violence that curses our whole society and the cruel repression that has afflicted our black brothers for centuries." He added, "There sometimes occur events of such over-riding importance that we can attend to them properly only by calling a halt to normal activities in order to consider the depth of their significance and the breadth of their implications for the future."

73 cadets, on Thursday, at the **U.S. Merchant Marine Academy** located at Kings Point on Long Island signed a petition refusing to march in Saturday's Armed Forces Day Parade as an anti-war protest. Late that night, Rear Adm. Gordon McClintock, superintendent at the academy, announced that all the cadets had changed their mind. Apparently, the action was quieted after the dissident cadets were threatened with expulsion.

Friday, May 15

Militant students at **City College of New York** on Friday disrupted ROTC classes in Townsend Harris Hall. But when they tried to enter the dean of student's office, campus policemen stopped them and in the resulting scuffle, three students were arrested.

Saturday, May 16

In a celebration of Armed Forces Day, 10,000 military personnel marched down Fifth Avenue on Saturday in a light drizzle without incident. The participants in the 21st annual parade were received with applause, cheers and flag-waving by spectators lining the avenue. A number of bystanders held placards such as, "We Love Our Country," and "Support the President."

Also on Saturday, a *Business Week* editorial warned: "If the events of the past two weeks have done nothing else, they should have convinced the U.S. that the student protest movement has to be taken seriously...The invasion of Cambodia and the senseless shooting of four students at Kent State ... have consolidated the academic community against the war, against business, and against government. This is a dangerous situation. It threatens the whole economic and social structure of the nation."

Central New York State
SUNY Potsdam –
A week after dozens of students from campus had attended the huge march in Washington, DC, a group on Saturday drove north to Montreal, a little over 100 miles, to meet and talk with young American men who had fled to Canada to avoid the draft. Called "deserters" and "draft dodgers"

by some, they had organized themselves into the American Deserters Committee to provide information, material assistance and counseling for those who crossed the border for political reasons.

The Potsdam students listened to the ex-pats as they covered a range of topics. On the possibility of amnesty? Most would refuse it. Morale? Generally high. Job opportunities? Generally good in Canada, although poor in Montreal with a 9% unemployment rate. Sympathy from Canadians? French Canadians were very sympathetic, but English Canadians in Montreal were indifferent to hostile. The future role of the deserter in Canadian life? Most said they plan on living in Canada "forever," although perhaps not in Montreal.

After their visit, one Potsdam student wrote in the campus press, "One interesting observation that the American exiles made concerned the increasing use of repressive measures by the U.S. government. These actions are becoming especially obvious to people outside the country." In the eyes of the Potsdam students, the deserters were the "victims of apple-pie democracy and the American way: do it or be damned!"

Other schools in the Potsdam area on strike included **Canton Technological Institute** where students boycotted classes through the first week of the strike; classes at **Potsdam State College** were cancelled from May 4 to May 11; classes were also cancelled for most of the week at **Clarkson College of Technology**, and many classes were suspended at **St. Lawrence University**.

On Monday, 400 to 500 **Colgate University** students and faculty members were in Washington DC to confront Secretary of State William Rogers, a Colgate Trustee. They staged a protest outside the State Department and a delegation of 10 students met with Rogers to urge him to either resign his cabinet post or resign from the Colgate Board of Trustees.

Syracuse University

Even though "business as usual" officially resumed on Monday, only one quarter of the institution's 17,000 students were in attendance. The administration reported that the campus had suffered close to a million dollars in damage over the course of the strike, yet despite that, there had not been a single arrest.

On Tuesday, a 24-hour dance marathon was held on campus to raise money for the strike fund, under the title, "They Shoot Students, Don't They?" (a reference to the 1969 movie "They Shoot Horses, Don't They?") When it ended on Wednesday, it had raised more than $1,000.

On Friday, the office of local Syracuse Democratic Congressman James Hanley announced over the previous two weeks it had been flooded with mail about the Cambodia situation. Out of 866 letters received, 807 were written to protest the war's expansion, while only 59 supported Nixon's action.

By the end of the week, however, Syracuse strikers began to despair. "Students are slowly but surely beginning to leave this campus," bemoaned an article in the strike newsletter, *Shut-Down 21*. Only two to three hundred were left, "but many others are planning to leave soon. Parties are springing up as rapidly as classes are emptying out." Strikers had planned to protest the Syracuse University Research Center, a military research facility, but an organizing meeting brought out only 20 students and faculty. Strike organizers were having trouble getting students to sign up as marshals and staff at Strike HQ were disappearing. The article asked, "What has happened? Are the issues no longer relevant? Are people too lazy to continue the protest? Does anyone give a damn? ... What happened to the five thousand students who voted to strike on May 4 ....? We have our chance - we are throwing it away."

At **Cornell University** on Wednesday, a group of strikers constructed a fake "peace tank" and laid "siege" to the ROTC building by firing candy and flowers at the campus military headquarters.

Rochester Institute of Technology RIT

The strike movement at the Rochester campus was slow to galvanize but finally on Thursday evening nearly 2,500 students, faculty, and staff met in the spirit of a traditional "New England town meeting." (One lone student did smash $5,500 worth of plate glass windows a week earlier.) The main focus of the meeting was to discuss a recommendation by two RIT students to set up an "Alternate University"—whose premise was the establishment of a regular college atmosphere but with classes and courses relevant to current political and educational changes inspired by the national campus unrest.

One proponent said the purpose of the Alternative University would be "to offer not necessarily an alternative to attend regular classes, but an opportunity to learn even more." It would be an "academic buffet" of varied courses and methods of instruction by RIT professors and qualified outside speakers. Some suggested courses were philosophies of government, policies of military control, student education, and on other relevant and current issues. A consensus among advocates was this different kind of university rejected the traditional ways of education – which had brought the country to where it was. By mid-May, a hundred students and instructors were working on it.

On another front, the Student Association achieved a victory when the campus Policy Committee unanimously voted to dramatically increase its student representation, from only three students on the 35-member body to up to one-third of its members.

One national campaign that circulated among RIT students was an effort to get everybody across the country to do nothing on Friday, May 15th—a boycott of business as usual. A leaflet appeared on campus: "Don't Do Anything on May 15, 1970. Stay home – don't be a part of the war making society. Don't march – don't demonstrate publicly. Don't do anything. Let's see if the war-makers can make this country go without us. – Bet they can't." However, this campaign appeared to suffer a similar fate as the "National Pause Day" and fizzled for a variety of factors – mainly, insufficient sponsorship.

New Jersey
Livingston College – Piscataway

In the late hours of Monday night, a firebomb exploded in the police science building and completely destroyed the old wooden structure, formerly used for military barracks. Police suspected a link between the firebombing and student anti-war unrest on campus.

Later in the week, New Jersey Governor William Cahill sent out a request that all state colleges send representatives to meet with him in the capital in Trenton that Friday. He wanted representatives of student governments, editors of student newspapers, as well as strike leaders.

Livingston College sent Jim Greenman, Wayne Johnson, and Margret Rosario.

Livingston hosted an incoming freshman orientation on Saturday, and Dean Ernest Lynton made such an eloquent statement against the Vietnam war, that he won praise in one of the last issues of *Strike News*. "He came out very strongly against the direction of American society, he blasted the Indo Chinese war and the government's reactions and inactions regarding dissent from Nixon's foreign aid and domestic policies." Incoming students were also given the background of the student strike, its history, basic structure and an outline of strike activities by a representative of the strike committee, Scott Siegel. Copies of *Strike News* were also handed to them and their parents, to give as accurate a picture as possible as to what the strike was all about.

Another article in *Strike News* reported on former US Supreme Court Justice Earl Warren's public statement that, "The country is in its greatest crisis in living memory." The crisis, Warren said, was attributed to war, inflation, unemployment, poverty, and repression, but above all "to our failure to enforce the due process and equal protection section of the 14th amendment." Section 1 of the 14th amendment states: "No State shall make or enforce any law which shall abridge the privileges or immunities of citizens of the United States; nor shall any State deprive any person of life, liberty, or property, without due process of law; nor deny to any person within its jurisdiction the equal protection of the laws."

Rutgers University – New Brunswick

On Tuesday, May 12, 1,500 students crammed into the Rutgers gym to hear New Jersey elected politicians give their positions on the wars. Democratic Senator Harrison Williams referred to Rutgers President Mason Gross as "one of our heroes" for his public opposition to the Cambodia invasion and his criticism of Nixon. It was ironic, Williams said, that Nixon's actions in Cambodia had brought the nation together – in opposition. No issue, he said, in his fifteen years of public life, had brought forth this much concern from the nation. Favoring the Cooper-Church Amendment, he joined calls for an immediate withdrawal from southeast Asia.

New Jersey Congressman Frank Thompson, also a Democrat, described his pessimism in the passage of the McGovern-Hatfield bill. The current bill, he said, had little or no chance at all of being adopted, unless there was a change in the composition of Congress itself. If 50 or more seats in Congress were against the war, the bill would pass. Thompson did acknowledge that the current student activism had been responsible for the renewal of the political process in America, that the activism had been called for and was a necessary part of political change.

At **Princeton University** on Wednesday, it was reported that a 20-year-old freshman had been arrested and charged in connection with a fire in a basement at Nassau Hall and an attempted fire bombing at the Institute for Defense Analysis. Police said the suspect was being held pending an arson investigation.

Rutgers University – Newark
Friday, May 15

On Friday, May 15, dozens of students and a few faculty members staged a sit-in on campus to protest the war and the recent police killings of young Black men at Jackson State. When police arrived, most of the protesters were detained, taken downtown to a police station where some were beaten and injured when thrown down stairs, yet only five were formerly arrested. That Saturday, a demonstration at Military Park in Newark was held in protest of the police beatings of the students and faculty.

Miles away in Washington, DC, 50 students from the small **Westminster Choir College** then in Princeton, held aloft a banner, "Singers for Peace," and sang their recently composed "Peace Anthem" in Lafayette Park across from the White House. They also sang in the rotunda of the Capitol and at the Washington Monument.

Ft Dix

On Saturday at US Army post Fort Dix—16 miles from Trenton—3,000 anti-war demonstrators joined a handful of servicemen at a rally and attempted to march onto the base. Fifty military police officers with bayonets at the ready blocked them. Demonstrators were then corralled when the MPs rolled out a barbed wire blockade and sprayed pepper fog to break up the protest. A few students tried to outflank the troops by running through nearby woods but were stopped by state police. A half-dozen demonstrators were clubbed but not arrested. Earlier, all GIs had been restricted to the base and normal operations were cancelled because of the "potential of disturbances."

Pennsylvania
Lafayette College – Easton
May 11, Monday

On Monday, many students were involved in strike-related actions which included telephone campaigning at 9 am, canvassing in the community at mid-day, then a local neighborhood playground clean-up in the afternoon, plus the writing of letters and postcards. *Strike Bulletin* published a schedule of workshops and seminars for the upcoming week, which included "Confrontation Politics," "the Role of the College in Modern Society," a workshop on women's liberation, a seminar on "Imperialism in US Foreign Policy" with a speech by Tran Van Dinh, the former South Vietnam ambassador to the US; and lastly, a speaker on "the Revolutionary Aspects of the Concept of Ecology."

The *Strike Bulletin* for Tuesday reprinted part of a May 8 *New York Times* editorial on Saturday's protest in Washington. "The nation's children are in the streets today because their parents have remained for too long deaf, blind and mute in the false security of comfortable homes. It is not our sons and daughters who should be laying their bodies on the line in the streets of the nation's capital tomorrow in a great – and one fervently hopes – nonviolent plea for a reveille in Washington. It is their parents who should be there, in the corridors of Congress, demanding of their elected representatives a forthright return to the principles of peace and justice that are being trampled."

Muhlenberg College – Allentown

Many Allentown campus students were still straggling back from Saturday's massive march in Washington on Monday. What little strike activity there was directed toward specific peace candidate work and legislative action.

The *Muhlenberg Weekly* for Thursday printed a report about the nationwide protests. "The nation's strongest wave of campus dissent in a single week culminated in Saturday's peace rally in Washington," with a crowd of "some 75,000." It continued, "Strikes were evident on many college campuses. More than 230 schools were affected for varying periods of time. The campus protest movement may never have erupted in all its abundant energy were it not for the tragic deaths of four students at Kent State." It quoted Bucknell College student Don Bowen who spoke at the Washington rally, "The shooting of the students at Kent State brought us together on extremely short notice. I think the Woodstock nation is beginning to get through to the country."

Pennsylvania State University – University Park

In the Monday, May 11, *On Campus* newsletter, the student chairperson of the annual Spring Week event explained why it had been cancelled. "There were a lot of people on campus who felt it wouldn't be appropriate for them to go out and have fun in a carnival atmosphere while so many serious things are happening around the nation and on campus," stated Floyd McKeag. He added that many students and student groups who had helped with Spring Week in the past were not interested this year.

University faculty senate chairman Arthur Lewis, Jr, called for a special senate meeting on Tuesday in response to an anti-war petition signed by 55 members of the faculty. When it was time to vote on a resolution based on the petition, all but a handful of faculty in Schwab Auditorium endorsed the statement. Immediately, however, Lewis declared the vote was void because it needed a unanimous vote. The 800 students in attendance could not believe their ears and their boos reverberated off the walls of the large auditorium.

By the middle of the week, it was clear that class attendance at Penn State had plummeted below 50% in classes with liberal subjects. The student government sponsored a student referendum over Tuesday and Wednesday, and more than 11,000 out of a student body of 18,000 voted to substitute regular classes with antiwar teach-ins. This vote and Lewis' procedural maneuver intensified the growing polarization between students and the administration.

Other Pennsylvania Colleges

President John Stauffer of **Randolph-Macon College** in Huntingdon decided to reopen the campus on Friday after all classes had been closed the first week of May. His decision to reopen, he said, was in part because the mass demonstrations in Washington DC "had been orderly." In the far southeast corner of the state, students at **Lincoln University** began a campaign to create a national moratorium and nation-wide strike by Black students in protest of the killings of Black men by police in Augusta, Georgia.

At **North Hampton Community College** nearly 200 students decided they were going on strike despite the student government vote not to strike. On Wednesday night at **Cedar Crest College** in Allentown, there was an 11 pm sing-in of peace songs in front of the president's house. On Thursday the campus focused on the oppression of African-Americans. There was a "reparations day" for Black Panthers, a film "What Is Prejudice?" and a rally with speeches by a local Black Panther member and a local Black minister. Ten miles southwest of Allentown at **Kutztown State College** students went out on strike—but only on the Kent State issue.

Maryland
University of Maryland – College Park
Monday May 11

On Monday, members of the Wilson Elkins administration met with the Board of Regents to resolve the issues of class and grading policies. Two proposals were being considered – one by an ad hoc student-faculty committee headed by Professor Thomas Aylward, and one named after Ernest Chaples, an assistant professor who proposed it with a different ad hoc group of faculty. The key difference was that the Chaples Plan supported the strike and the Strike Steering Committee,

Both plans were opposed to any academic penalty to students for striking, but students believed the Aylward Plan gave too much leeway and discretion to teachers who could penalize students for political reasons. The Chaples Plan contained safeguards to protect students – and had widespread support among striking students and the moribund Student Government Association. At the end of the meeting, the Aylward Plan was adopted by the Regents and the administration—but had yet to be approved by the full faculty.

In the early afternoon, a huge assemblage of nearly 3,000 striking students was held in Cole Field House to consider the question of further action against ROTC. A motion was made to take over the Reckord Armory building which housed the ROTC offices—but lost by about 1800 to 1200 votes. Still, many strikers believed they still needed to act against ROTC, and a good-sized crowd of close to 500 left the meeting and marched on the armory. It was close to 2 pm.

At the armory, protesters moved into and occupied the building – but it was very brief. Leaders of the action switched gears and decided to march down to Route One—other students had already gathered there. It would be the fifth blockade of the roadway since May 1, but it wasn't near the scale and intensity of earlier take-overs. Police did not appear and peace was largely maintained by marshals with green armbands who ushered demonstrators to the roadsides. What some considered a "block party" finally ended at 2:30 am without any substantive disorder.

Tuesday, May 12

On Tuesday, the campus appeared calm—almost normal. Things were so quiet that Chancellor Charles Bishop showed up on the College Park campus to give his "State of the University" speech. A reporter from *The Washington Post* was on hand and from the grassy mall reported, "Hundreds of students were busying themselves studying, playing with Frisbees, or sleeping in the sun."

Yet the calm was deceptive. Just off campus 1,100 National Guardsmen were poised to return if protests rekindled. There was so much tension at a faculty assembly held to consider the competing grading plans, it was decided the issue was too important to be resolved with a voice vote and required a faculty referendum.

Wednesday, May 13

On Wednesday, a memorial service was held on the mall in honor of the dead from Kent State, Jackson State, and Augusta, Georgia. Hundreds listened to speakers, including the Rev. Channing Phillips, John Clark from the Baltimore Black Panthers, and Woody Farrar, a member of the University Black Student Union.

Elsewhere on campus, there were several instances of repressive crackdowns by the administration—a physical plant worker had been fired for strike activity, and two athlete brothers, Charlie and Jim Schrader, had been kicked off the track team for participating in strike rallies.

The Student Government Association finally shook off its lethargy and at a meeting during the day, endorsed the Chaples Plan on grading policy. And when it looked like the administration was intent on supporting the rival plan, the student government threatened that they themselves would lead the next action if the Chaples Plan was not accepted. They gave the administration one day to respond, or they would "actively lead the student body to the liberation of Route 1."

Thursday, May 14

President Elkins had called an emergency meeting of the Board of Regents for early Thursday evening, and it was there he claimed those instigating violence on his campus were "a highly radical element partially inside and partially outside the university." One Regent then asked, "Have you ever heard of counter-intelligence? That's what you have to use on the campus. You've got to use the same tactics against the sons-of-bitches as they use against the university." In the end, Elkins and the Board agreed strong measures were needed to end the disruptions once and for all.

Meanwhile, two other events of importance were going on simultaneously—a nighttime student strike rally and a faculty meeting in Cole Field House on grading policies. The faculty by referendum chose the more conservative Aylward Plan in a lobsided vote of 1,583 to 696. They had ignored the endorsements and overwhelming student and strikers' support of the Chaples proposal, which had received 10,000 signatures in support. When students at the rally heard of the faculty vote, they exploded in anger and immediately marched over to Route One and "liberated" it. This was the sixth take-over of the roadway and this time the "liberated zone" included a five-block adjacent area.

By the time the flood of students swamped Route One, there were 5,000 to 6,000 people – the largest ever blockade during the two and half weeks of protests at the College Park campus.

This time, protesters built barricades with trash cans filled with firewood and fortified with doors, sawhorses and no-parking signs ripped from the pavement. They dragged construction equipment into the middle of the road and lit it on fire - a dark plume of dark smoke billowed into the night air. Police intelligence agents were spotted on storefront rooftops, and students pelted them with rocks.

Inevitably, police arrived in force brandishing nightsticks and accompanied by growling and snapping K-9s. They advanced down Route One and cleared it of demonstrators, who retreated behind barricades and onto the surrounding streets. But students had the numbers on their side, and they refused to disperse. To convince them otherwise, police began firing tear gas at the crowds but they held their ground.

At 10 pm, the National Guard showed up and advanced on the barricades, hurling a barrage of tear gas canisters toward the demonstrators. It was estimated that within their first ten minutes, Guardsmen had shot off 50 rounds of tear gas and pepper gas. Students chanted, "Pigs off campus!" and "1-2-3-4, we don't want your fucking war!" Brave ones picked up the tear gas canisters and threw them back at the Guard. Yet, Guardsmen continued their advance—General Warfield had ordered them to clear the area and proceed onto campus.

Across campus, another situation was developing. A couple dozen students had a different plan—to go into the administration building for a sit-in. One strike leader told his fellow activists, "We shouldn't go to Route One, we should go to the administration building, because that's the only place that these problems can be solved. People driving on Route One, they don't deserve to be held up for an hour on their way home." When they reached the offices, however, the students were surprised to find them empty. They milled about in the lobby, walked through some of the offices, chanted some slogans, and took the felt directory board down and switched the letters to read: "End the war in Vietnam now." Suddenly, Lt. Downs of the campus police appeared. Warning the students they faced arrest if they stayed, he assigned a couple of officers to remain. Yet, nothing happened—no damage was done, no arrests were made, and the students left around 9:30. The sit-in had lasted just over an hour and the only ones remaining in the building were campus police officers.

Out at Route One, Guardsmen were in the process of chasing thousands from the roadway back onto the sprawling university grounds. Pitched skirmishes raged between the two sides as clouds of stinging teargas enveloped the campus. Protesters broke into small groups, smashed windows, tore down light poles – at one point all lights on campus were knocked out—and continued to pelt soldiers with rocks and other objects.

At one point, General Warfield realized his advance onto the campus had stalled despite over a 100 rounds of tear gas being fired off. His troops were unable to push through the large campus with all its wide-open fields and building complexes. Warfield needed reinforcements and he ordered another contingent of National Guard to be brought in.

It was around 10:30 pm over at the administration building, the site of the earlier brief sit-in, when roving bands of students took out several windows. Feeling vulnerable, the handful of campus police inside evacuated the building, and in the vacuum, over 100 people swooped in. They immediately ransacked the lobby, threw furniture out the windows and lit some of it on fire, also setting a fire on the lobby floor. Soon, the trashers vanished and minutes later a small group of students accompanied firefighters in putting out the flames, while outside, hundreds milled about. Twice in one night, the old administration building had been occupied and thoroughly trashed the second time. Guardsmen arrived and dispersed the crowd outside.

It was midnight before order was restored. An additional 700 National Guardsmen were trucked in, bringing the Guard contingent up to 1,200. Over 100 demonstrators had been arrested, and two dozen students had been ordered off campus. Governor Mandel issued a "state of emergency"—again. And again, the campus was placed under martial law where gatherings of 100 or more were banned, an 11 pm to 6 am curfew was imposed and once more, Guardsmen patrolled the campus. Thursday, May 14, was the most explosive, violent day in the history of the University of Maryland. And Route One was again the focus, having been occupied for the sixth time.

Friday, May 15

On Friday, the campus was under martial law and under a state of emergency, and Guardsmen patrolled its grounds. The university administration and Governor Marvin Mandel used the moment to take swift and drastic action against the strike leadership. Governor Mandel – "Marshmallow Marvin" – turned over control of the university to the National Guard commander, General Warfield, with full cooperation from President Elkin and his administration. Warfield was given carte blanche to enforce the campus curfew, the ban of large rallies and the authority to evict anyone from campus involved in protests.

Warfield wasted no time and quickly went into action. Twenty-five students were identified and immediately banned from the university with formal evictions for breaking and entering, and destruction of state property; felony warrants were issued for another ten. Most of those targeted by Warfield were well-known leaders of the campus strike and anti-war movement, whose names had been supplied by the administration. In addition, Warfield cancelled scheduled meetings of the faculty assembly and the University Senate. One student critic called it. "National Guard General Edwin Warfield—the military dictator of the University of Maryland."

The *Baltimore Sun* reported that "many pictures and thousands of feet of television tape were made by authorities" during the actions in the administration building and the various occupations of Route One, and invariably, were used to identify protesters. It didn't take long for suspicions to rise among students and attentive faculty members that President Elkin was attempting to use the accusations to remove the strike leadership—without knowing who did the actual trashing.

In June, a month later, the felonies were dropped by the grand jury for insufficient evidence and made into misdemeanors. Those ultimately arrested became known as the "Maryland Nine" (a tenth member was subsequently added).

Saturday, May 16

With their campus under siege, the Strike Steering Committee met off-campus on Saturday at the Catholic University Law School. The committee decided to defy the ban on rallies and made plans for a demonstration at the mall for the next Tuesday, May 19.

Morgan State in Baltimore

What began peacefully as a protest by students on Friday against the Jackson State killings, turned violent when a platoon of 30 police officers arrived. Met with a volley of rocks, police responded by lobbing teargas grenades at students on a dorm lawn. More students joined in and at one point, there were at least 1,000 people blocking traffic on busy Baltimore streets. The confrontation gained steam when 300 additional police sent in threw more teargas at the crowds. After two hours of clashes, peace was restored around 8 pm. Two women students were injured, and nine people arrested on disorderly conduct charges.

Also, on Friday at **Bowie State College**, students held a rally and memorial service for the Kent State dead, the three Black students killed in 1968 at Orangeburg, South Carolina, and for those recently killed in Augusta and at Jackson State.

At **Fort Meade**, headquarters of the First Army, official ceremonies for Armed Forces Day were canceled, and instead 300 antiwar youths, perhaps 30 of them off-duty G.I.'s in civilian clothes, marched and rallied near the post. After a two-mile march that skirted the base, demonstrators sat in a grassy field about a mile from the Fort Meade gate and listened to speeches, including one by Abbie Hoffman. Hoffman, the Yippie leader, called for a "war of liberation" by young people in the United States to force an end to the fighting in Vietnam. Other speeches were given by Susan Schnall, an Army nurse jailed for her antiwar efforts, a member of the Black Panther Party, GIs and gray-haired revolutionaries from Spain.

Washington, D.C

Most of the people who had come to DC to demonstrate on Saturday left immediately after the rally and march. Many, however, stayed to lobby Congressional members and joined hundreds of other students who crammed the halls of Congress over Monday and Tuesday. Their singular demand: Congress must put an end to the Cambodian invasion and authorize an immediate withdrawal from Vietnam. The lobbyists from academia included about 1,000 students and 75 faculty members from

Yale—with President Kingman Brewster leading the contingent, 600 from Brandeis and 400 from Colgate.

Also Monday in Washington, the states' fifty governors met with President Nixon to discuss Southeast Asia and the turmoil on college campuses. Afterwards, a handful spoke to the press. New Hampshire Republican Governor Walter Peterson said the meeting was "a very useful discussion of events leading to the President's decision to send troops into Cambodia. There was also a very fine and lengthy discussion of the problem of dissent on campuses and how the administration approach might better be presented to students." Democratic Connecticut Governor John Dempsey also spoke favorably. "It was a most constructive meeting, very informative," and Nixon "listened to us" and called for a dialogue with the establishment.

Democratic Governor Frank Licht of Rhode Island had a different view but denied that he had had a heated exchange with Vice-President Agnew over the situation on college campuses. Maine Governor Kenneth Curtis remarked, "There's got to be a lot more restrained talk from the National Administration. If we tell the students not to react violently, we have to practice what we preach."

Students who supported the war also mobilized and were in the capital doing their own lobbying. About 100 young people from the "Youth Committee for Peace with Freedom" pushed against Senate amendments that would put restraints on U.S. military operations in Indochina and mandate an American pullout. They called the amendments "a formula for betrayal and capitulation," and described the Cambodian operation as headed for success.

It was rush-hour on Monday when a large group of **American University** students non-violently blocked traffic at key intersections near campus in Washington's Northwest. When police arrived, they confronted the demonstrators with clubs and teargas – and once again - blanketed the campus with the disabling irritant. Many students were hospitalized and reports of the clash described it as more violent than the one the previous Wednesday night, May 6, when 15 students and two policemen had been injured. On Tuesday, May 12, students, faculty and the administration publicly charged that the DC police had "overreacted" in dealing with the protest.

At the DC office of the New Mobe, several days after the large march, the G.I. Task Force announced that antiwar organizations with military members would hold demonstrations to protest Armed Forces Day at 43 military installations across the country over the upcoming weekend. Also, the Pentagon announced it was canceling Armed Forces Day ceremonies at 23 military bases due to threats of peace demonstrations.

Over on Capitol Hill on Tuesday, Secretary of Defense Melvin R. Laird testified before the Senate Armed Services Committee that the withdrawal of American troops from Cambodia had already begun. He said several thousand U.S. troops had left Cambodia after completing their missions and more were to come out during the current week. He insisted major operations against the "Communist sanctuaries" would be completed by June 15 but added that if future operations are required in Cambodia, they would be carried out by the South Vietnamese army.

On Wednesday, an *ABC* radio news broadcast reported that two unnamed top officials of the White House administration had argued to President Nixon that a majority of the country's 7 million college and university students were in sympathy with the protests and adverse reaction by academia to the Cambodian escalation, and that sympathizers with the strikers were increasing in significant numbers. They had warned Nixon that he needed to be much more understanding of the youth of the nation then he had been in the last two weeks.

During the week, House Republican leader Gerald Ford came out against Nixon's proposal to end student deferments for men subject to the draft. However, the chair of the House Armed Services Committee, Mendel Rivers, countered that he was becoming "disenchanted" with students because "seeing 350 colleges closed down" by those, as he put it, "dedicated students who have been deferred" had changed his mind. Student deferments did end in September 1971 and the Vietnam war draft itself ended in January 1973.

African-American students at **Federal City College** in DC made a public statement at the end of the week in response to the deaths in Augusta, Georgia, and at Jackson State. They viewed "these atrocities as a continuation and expansion of genocide that has been perpetrated against Black people since the beginning of the fourteenth century." They issued a call for Black students to commit to organize and educate the Black community, and stated, "The school as a functional unit of the community shall no longer cater to the interests of the white people, nor serve as a center for Americanization." It ended: "What we understand is that our goal is to be totally free, not totally integrated. We must organize to mobilize our people to control all these political institutions in our communities, for the future is ours!"

Southeast

Virginia

Randolph-Macon Women's College – Ashland

Following a student assembly on Monday night, many of the 650 who attended expressed a willingness to get involved in antiwar work. Then the next day, Tuesday, May 12, a campus-wide referendum was conducted involving an astounding 93 percent of the student body and an overwhelming majority - 584 to 105 - voted in favor of instituting some form of class stoppage. More than 450 of those who voted endorsed allowing students to be involved in anti-war work without academic penalty.

Earlier in the day, nearly a dozen faculty members signed a statement deploring the enlargement of the war in Indochina and that the Cambodia "invasion is a direct violation of the balance of power established by the Constitution and thus threatens civil liberties at home while foreshadowing even larger calamities abroad."

That night, 600 students and faculty members gathered in Blackwell Auditorium to hear a new faculty policy announced which allowed students to postpone all examinations and miss the remainder of their classes without academic penalty but required to complete all course work by the end of September.

Students on the Ashland campus on Friday organized their very first campus-wide protest against US aggression in Cambodia. A special strike office was set up, seminars were organized, and students and faculty began the groundwork for a Free University on campus. That afternoon, a memorial service for the Kent State slain was held.

University of Virginia - Charlottesville

University President Edgar Shannon's antiwar speech before a large campus crowd on Saturday, May 9, resulted in a rush of negative feedback from state politicians. Virginia Senator Harry Byrd, the same Democratic senator Shannon had arranged to meet with students, told the press that Shannon had been too lenient in dealing with campus demonstrators, and that he was wrong to criticize Nixon's expansion of the Vietnam War. Virginia Governor Linwood Holton declared that he would never allow the University of Virginia to be closed. Lt. Gov. Sargent Reynolds piled on and cautioned students against going to extremes and said the banner of individual freedom was being desecrated by "a militant and radical few." Yet, immediate support also flowed in, and more than 2,500 signatures were collected from the campus community on a petition backing Shannon.

During the week, a campus referendum on the student strike was taken and two-thirds of the student body who voted—4,909 to 2,266—favored the strike. In contrast, the faculty voted to keep ROTC with academic credits.

By Wednesday, many students had returned to classrooms despite the earlier vote in favor of a strike. Still, six of the strikers' nine demands had been accepted, charges from the big bust of some 60 people the week before had been greatly reduced or dropped, and President Shannon was publicly calling on Virginia's senators to oppose the war. The strike committee no longer set up its daily presence on the Lawn, and it appeared that life as usual was being restored.

Sweet Briar College

A lengthy teach-in on Monday, May 11, on the Vietnam-Cambodia crisis was held in various locations around the all-women's college. At an evening community meeting, strike steering committee members argued that a strike, the suspension of classes and cancellation of exams would enable the college to organize a movement of protest against Nixon's Southeast Asia policy. Others wanted to focus on domestic problems, such as campaigning for city council candidates in Lynchburg. Most, however, recognized the gravity of the national crisis, and by a two-thirds majority, 517 to 198, voted to strike and for a voluntary suspension of classes. The strike was to begin that night and the college would "reconvene on September 21, 1970, on its pre-May 11, 1970, basis." Yet, the vote had no binding force as the informal community meeting had no authority to suspend classes.

During the remainder of the week, students continued a variety of strike-related activities, including organizing a chapter of the Committee for a New Congress. All week, strikers had been holding meetings in the Refectory Quadrangle using amplifiers, but the noise disturbed students in their rooms studying for finals—and as a result on Friday, the strike steering committee was told their events had to be moved over to a more remote area near the Gymnasium.

Also on Friday, most of the staff at the campus newspaper, *Sweet Briar News,* decided to discontinue the paper for the academic season, although some staff continued to publish a dittoed sheet called the *Sweet Briar Free Press* in coordination with the strike steering committee. Yet, after classes ended, Friday May 15, attendance at strike events tapered off. Finals were held as scheduled, but of the 3,000 individual examinations scheduled, only 57% were actually taken.

Over the summer, Sweet Briar Dean Catherine Sims in a speech to alumnae on campus for reunions, gave a summary of the pros and cons of the student strike, something she called "the Happening." Dean Sim's cons: people's time was wasted because many speeches were on the same topic by people not specialists, largely repeating what they had read – there was "a sameness about the speeches and seminars." Some students took advantage and just simply left the campus for the summer. Others, she said, oversimplified the problems and didn't advance their understanding "of some of the stubborn issues in Vietnam" which had been "a major problem for presidents of the United States." She was critical of what she called "the theory of 'instant expertise,'" didn't like the intolerance of some, and felt distain for the "emotionalism of the large community meetings" where speeches didn't emphasize a rational approach.

On the pros side, the main one – which she said could not be understated – was that "the 'Happening' was a genuine educational experience for all of us. It woke up some students who had never before thought of themselves as citizens." Students found out where Cambodia was and, "they found out the Congressional district they live in. They found out the names of the Congressmen and their Senators. They perhaps wrote their first letter to their congressman or Senator." Students learned facts of life about themselves. "Some found that they had the ability to speak, that they could organize."

One of the main lessons students learned, Dean Sims said, was that they could participate in strike activities, inform themselves and at the same time, go to class, complete their course work, and take their exams. "They found they could do both, and this is a lesson worth learning for life." They also "learned a little humility and that is a very valuable lesson to learn early."

The Dean recounted an interaction she had had with a student. "One girl, bright, a good student, but never before interested in public matters, attended a few seminars, read some material handed out to her, and then went to the shopping center ... one Saturday to 'educate' the people there." But, the Dean recounted, "It was she who got the education. She talked with a couple of men who had been in Vietnam. She discovered that other people, people in overalls or cotton house dresses, weren't as uninformed as she thought they were." When she returned to campus that afternoon, "she was indeed humble, even somewhat embarrassed. She said, 'I couldn't answer their questions. They knew more than I did.'"

Sims said there exists a kind of arrogance in the academic world which assumes that people who have not gone to college and don't have advanced degrees were therefore ignorant, waiting to be educated. "At best," she said, "the experience enhanced respect for freedom, for the society in which we live, with its many imperfections but also a tradition of freedom." She added, "On the whole, the 'happening' was worth the price we paid for it; that is, it was worth it - if there is a carry over."

"If we turn out a few lawyers concerned not merely to practice law but to make themselves experts in some aspect of the law, so as to reform antiquated procedures; if we turn out a few writers willing to work hard, to get up facts, to follow up stories; if we turn out, that is, some competent specialists, and a much larger number of active, interested, public-spirited citizens, willing to work through democratic procedures to improve our society, then," she finished with a flourish, "it will have been worthwhile!"

Washington and Lee University – Lexington
Monday, May 11

The turnout for a strike vote on Monday was momentous with 96.5% of the student body participating and then voting overwhelmingly to join the national student strike and to cancel classes for the remainder of the term. In comparison, there was a 71.2% turn out that spring for student council elections, and a 79% turnout for spring elections in 1969 which included curriculum changes.

That night, however, the elation students felt quickly evaporated when the faculty failed to either endorse pass / fail options or close the university. Many students felt betrayed, not only because of their huge vote for a strike but because the Monday faculty vote conflicted with their earlier vote just four days earlier to allow students to skip class and make up course work before the end of September.

Tuesday, May 12

On Tuesday, students held an 11 am news conference and struck back. Student body vice-president Joe Tompkins condemned the faculty votes as "ill-advised and disrespectful," and called for students to boycott classes, work on antiwar activities, and – in a unique protest tactic – to not register for the fall classes.

Washington and Lee President Robert Huntley rushed to mollify students, and in front of a crowd of 1,000, gave the faculty's perspective. He described them as sincere and called their decision an "unintentional betrayal of head and not of heart." A number of student speakers got up and criticized their decision and expressed their sense of betrayal, eliciting applause from the audience.

May 13, Wednesday

The "Campus Newsletter" for Wednesday published a brief report on talks at the Free University Forum. One was titled "Patterns of Aggression: Individual, Social, and National," and assistant professor of psychology Dr. David Elmes, explained, "One of the major factors leading to aggressive behavior is frustration," and "we in fact often reward aggressive behavior in our society. We reward our political leaders by being silent. When we don't raise havoc about an aggressive foreign policy, we increase the likelihood of its being repeated in the future."

In "Civil Disobedience," Assistant Law Professor Andrew McThenia explained it as an act of protest by a person who says, "This is a valid law you have enacted, but there is a higher law — my conscience — that tells me I cannot obey it." Civil disobedience requires "an acceptance of the penalty for breaking a law." Philosophy Instructor Robert Steck added, "The civil disobedient recognizes and affirms the legality of the existing structure, while the revolutionary does not."

During the first weeks of May, the Free University held 50 forums on a wide range of subjects, from facts about Vietnam to poetry readings—everybody had been welcomed as there was no political litmus test to attend. On Wednesday, a large crowd attended a seminar called "Towards Utopia," and the discussion spanned everything from Plato's *Republic* to communal living, from individual happiness to the ideal state, and on the conflict between talk and action, between discussion and practical application. For those first few weeks, forum attendance ranged from 50 to 150 people, but with the arrival of exams, it dropped by half.

In the regular classes themselves, by the end of the second week, attendance had dropped from the normal 80 percent to between 50 and 60 percent. Strikers sent a telegram to the National Center of Strike Information and optimistically declared the class boycott at W&L was 90 percent effective. Partially in response to that assertion, in mid-May, Washington and Lee was designated by the National Strike Committee as the headquarters for the South-Central Strike region. (Other regional strike headquarters included Brandeis for the northeastern region, Northwestern University for the midwestern region, and Berkeley for the western region.)

On Sunday, the new strike HQ held its first news conference and issued a blistering critique on the American Establishment, the justice system, mainstream media and on student and citizen complacency.

Virginia Polytechnic Institute and State University – Blacksburg
Tuesday, May 12 -

Students at the Blacksburg campus, commonly known as Virginia Tech, finally joined the nationwide student strike and on Tuesday, May 12, 150 students, in protest of the national crisis, took over Williams Hall—an academic building.

Wednesday, May 13

At 6 am on Wednesday, 100 Montgomery County Sheriff's Deputies showed up at Williams Hall and arrested the occupiers—who offered no resistance. University President T. Marshall Hahn promptly suspended the 107 students who had been arrested for trespass.

During the week, a strike referendum clearly showed a divided campus. More than half the student body participated with 2,888 voting to strike and 2,400 against. Of those who voted to strike, the vast majority of 2,160 voted only for a voluntary strike.

Friday, May 15

On Friday, 3,000 students rallied to protest how the students arrested Wednesday were being treated and demanded amnesty for the "Blacksburg 107." A petition also circulated on campus for the recall of President Hahn. 57 Tech students began a hunger strike in protest of the arrested students and declared that Hahn had violated the rights of students, as outlined in the campus rule and policy manual, and had acted in such a manner as to usurp his administrative powers.

Saturday, May 16

On Saturday, several hundred students met at the War Memorial on campus to continue their protests of the administration's handling of the Blacksburg 107. When more showed up, the rally morphed into a march to Squires Student Center as a protest not only of Hahn's recalcitrance but of Cambodia and Kent State. By the time the crowd reached the center, it had swollen to 2,500 people.

In comparison with other university presidents, Hahn took some extremely hardline positions. He not only refused to recognize recommendations offered by both the student government and the faculty but had also refused to even negotiate with students. His administration had acquiesced to the quartering of hundreds of state police in Blacksburg in case of campus turmoil. Yet, it got worse. In the face of the majority of students who voted to strike, Hahn took the incredible position that all strikers should simply resign from school. It was an unprecedented stance among administrations across the country during May 1970.

Tensions on campus ratchetted up even more when it became known that threats had been made against the hunger strikers—as well as retaliatory counter- threats if they were harmed. One state trooper quoted in the local press claimed enough explosives had been stolen from local construction sites to level the entire stone and brick Virginia Tech campus. Over the next few days, there were reports of scattered violence and fire bombings on campus, but student militants still felt apathy was a huge problem at Tech, and the campus remained divided. The suspended students – the Blacksburg 107 – were ordered to face trial in mid-June.

Other Virginia Colleges

Students at the **College of William and Mary** in Williamsburg occupied a hallway in an administration building overnight on Sunday, but administrators paid little attention and called it "innocuous." The next day, Monday, May 11th, they decided to remain in the building and expand the sit-in. Their action eventually forced the faculty to vote on antiwar issues students had raised. Campus polls showed this action and other campus demonstrations were supported by over half the student population. Expecting the faculty to show them support, the 75 occupiers left the building in an act of good faith.

At the Petersburg campus of **Virginia State College**, Dean Elwood Boone's response in a meeting to students' concerns over protest, strike and grades issues was so unsatisfactory they rebelled. Two hundred students stormed the Dean's house, surrounded it and laid siege with barrages of bricks, forcing the Dean and his spouse to flee. Damage to the house was later estimated at $1,000.

A contingent of students from **Virginia Commonwealth** joined several thousand anti-war protesters on Friday for a peace march and rally in Richmond. After gathering in Monroe Park, the crowd marched down the main street to Capitol Square less than a mile away. At the rally, the keynote speaker was an assistant to Interior Secretary Walter Hickel—who had been the most outspoken and sympathetic member of Nixon's cabinet for America's youth. At **Virginia Union University** in Richmond on Sunday, a fire was set in the Colburn Hall Chapel.

North Carolina

North Carolina State University at Raleigh
Tuesday, May 12

On Tuesday, Student Body President Cathy Sterling made a presentation at a Faculty Senate meeting on what she called the "Peace Retreat," a program of antiwar events and alternative classes for the remainder of the semester. Her presentation called for no academic penalties for participating students and outlined recommendations for classes, grades, and incompletes. Then, the senate went into over three hours of debate, and ended up approving their own program recommendations, never taking the Peace Retreat up for a vote. They treated the Peace Retreat as any other authorized extra-curricular activity—students are excused from class but had to still make up any course work missed. It would be the same for a football player, they explained, who missed classes because of a game or a student who missed classes because of a university-sponsored trip. It was a blow to students. The Senate had failed to pass any of their recommendations for letter grades or pass/fail grades.

After the senate had taken their vote, Sterling stood before them and announced their decision was not satisfactory and that she would take the Peace Retreat proposal to the full General Faculty, meeting the next day. Angered, her student government colleagues called for an early evening meeting to decide on what to do next, and when word got out, 500 students showed up in the Union Ballroom. A consensus formed to hold a rally that night at 11 and stage an all-night vigil on the University Plaza and library lawn as a visible form of pressure on the faculty. Hundreds took off, marched through the campus, chanting antiwar slogans and canvassed the dorms. At 11pm a thousand students rallied and heard the update about the faculty vote. Clearly incensed, many took part in the all-night vigil.

Wednesday, May 13

The general faculty meeting was scheduled for 4 pm and the war-related workshops and vigil on University Plaza ended in time for students to attend. As soon as they entered Nelson Auditorium, everyone was reminded that its air-conditioning had not been fixed. Faculty members debated the students' proposal in the sweltering 100 degree heat over the course of two and half hours, as students brought in cokes for thirsty professors and instructors. Chancellor Caldwell presided and at the podium, Cathy Sterling read the student proposal on the Peace Retreat. It had been endorsed by Chancellor Caldwell, she said, and added that 4,650 signatures had been collected on a petition supporting it.

Meanwhile, several hundred students waited for the results outside on the lawn at D.H. Hill Library. Inside, the auditorium was tense and the heat stifling when the first vote on the student proposal was taken by a show of hands. It was so close, the "ayes" had to be recounted. Finally, the Chancellor declared, "The motion carries 265 to 233." Cheers rang out. The faculty had endorsed the entire student proposal. News of the faculty vote instantly flooded the campus, and students yelled, "We won! We won!" and hugged each other. Faculty members exited the building and were greeted by cheering students. Some faculty raised their fingers in the peace sign or victory sign. Others walked past the students with looks of disgust. Sterling got up before the crowd and said that this vote showed faculty members were placing their trust in students and students couldn't let them down. The position adopted called for students, after consulting with their instructor, to choose one of four grade alternatives: (1) continue as usual; (2) receive a letter grade for the course based on work presently completed; (3) receive a pass/fail grade for the course, based on work presently completed; or (4) receive an incomplete as a grade for the course and make the work up later.

Attached to the faculty resolution was a statement: "We ... feel that the university, by virtue of its preoccupation with the human condition, is not isolated from the life of the society in which it exists. Due to the extraordinary situation facing our nation at this time, created by the high degree of polarization, we feel that it is necessary for students to be able to participate in expressions of genuine concern."

Thursday, May 14

Thursday was a day full of antiwar related activities from workshops to a student-called convocation, and hundreds – even thousands—of students were engaged, even though class attendance and campus operations were normal. Workshops held were entitled, "Sociological Effects of the Indochinese War upon Americans and Southeast Asians," "The Effect of the Indochinese War on Black Americans," and "Racism in America and techniques for community action."

Up to 3,000 people from the campus community attended the 4 pm convocation in Reynolds Coliseum to hear explanations of the Peace Retreat and the grading rules, and both Student President Sterling and Chancellor Caldwell spoke. The Chancellor praised the past two weeks and said students and faculty members had become engaged in campus activism and that overall, the campus was showing more collective thinking. "The demand for relevance in education at all levels is absolutely sound," he said. "The idea that students ought to be concerned and involved in the social and political issues of their time is entirely valid. The concept of academic freedom for teachers as well as the right to act as individual citizens is indispensable." The Chancellor received a standing ovation – as did Cathy Sterling – the first woman student body president of NCSU.

Thursday afternoon, a unique Peace Retreat event was held with nine local barbers. Called the "Fleece for Peace" drive, the barbers had volunteered to cut the hair of a few hundred male students so the "straight community" could relate to them as they canvassed Raleigh neighborhoods The collected hair was sewn into a dove-shaped pillow and sent to President Nixon. A few radical students, though, refused to "stand for any sort of rape of the locks."

Friday, May 15

The Black Action Committee had formed on campus to "bring the issues behind the Indochinese War to Black communities of Raleigh," and on Friday and Saturday, they canvassed local neighborhoods with the message that the "war is of special concern to Black people" and "relates to the oppression of Black people at home." They also informed people of an antiwar rally in Fayetteville on May 16 near the Army post Ft. Bragg and invited the community to participate in activities at the Raleigh campus.

About 500 people, including students from other campuses attended a 10 pm candlelight march held in memory of the two African-American men killed by police at Jackson State. The service was led by Rev. Taylor Scott.

Saturday, May 16

On Saturday antiwar students on the Raleigh campus held a Counter-Armed Forces Day "to display opposition to a military that encouraged genocide, destruction, and continued fighting in Vietnam and

Cambodia." The day was also a display of solidarity with G.I.s opposed to the war.

Sunday, May 17

On Sunday, in response to the Jackson State shootings, the campus Black Action Committee renamed itself the Ghetto. Its leader, Toni Foxwell, complained that few white NCSU students had expressed concerns about the recent killings and he called for a "brief retreat from the Peace Retreat." "Since our liberal white counterparts refuse to treat the larger issue that has caused their goddamn war, we as Black people have a responsibility to ourselves, to our dead brothers, and to our unborn children to stop, evaluate, and practice." After attending services at Black churches on Sunday, members of the Ghetto mourned the Jackson State deaths with a vigil that lasted until Tuesday morning. They continued to refuse to engage in Peace Retreat activities.

At the **University of North Carolina** in Chapel Hill strike actions over the week included 400 students traveling to DC to meet up with North Carolina Congressional representatives, three days of workshops led by the Law School called "The War and Dissent on Campus" and a blood drive which collected 400 pints of blood for local hospitals, symbolizing the loss of blood in the war. And on Saturday, Chapel Hill students were involved in a motorcade down to the Army post at Ft. Bragg for a protest against Armed Forces Day.

Many students at **Duke University** on Monday jumped into a campaign dubbed the Peace Offensive and attempted to get Durham citizens to apply pressure on their congressmen to take stands against the war. Another campus group, the Political Action Committee, pushed the campus community to contact their congressional representatives with specific support for the McGovern-Hatfield Amendment. A local chapter of the Union for National Draft Opposition emerged on campus, and a group of seniors distributed white armbands to wear as an antiwar protest during graduation ceremonies on June 1.

On Saturday just outside Fayetteville, antiwar protesters conducted a demonstration at the **Fort Bragg** army post. An estimated 750 to 1,000 GIs and between 2,500 and 3,000 student protesters moved onto the post and heard speeches by Mark Lane, a Warren Commission critic, Jane Fonda,

Rennie Davis and GIs John Vail and Hal Noyes. Davis was arrested for obscenity for using the word "motherfucker" (later thrown out of court) and both Jane Fonda and Mark Lane were escorted off the base. Command had given out huge numbers of passes the day before in hopes of getting GIs out of the area. (Ft. Bragg, named for a Confederate general, was renamed Ft. Liberty in 2023.)

South Carolina
University of South Carolina – Columbia
Monday, May 11

On Monday, a special meeting of the Board of Trustees convened in the administration building to discuss disciplinary actions against some 40 students arrested at a sit-in the previous Thursday inside the student center. Outside, a crowd began gathering while Colombia City police patrolled the campus. By 3 pm, the crowd had expanded to about 300 people—many upset with the police presence and a fear that the arrested students would be railroaded without fair trials. Students sent demands to those running the inquiry that the accused should be reinstated until their trials were over and that the hearing ought to be held in a more open format. Both demands were rejected.

Angered even more, the crowd continued to grow. About 4 pm, part of the crowd, about 250 students, stormed into the building and engaged in a frenetic but nonviolent sit-in on the first floor, while a small group vandalized offices on the upper floors. Freaked out, administrators locked themselves inside a second-floor conference room guarded by several security officers. One account reported that "the president and several trustees were stranded on upper floors."

On the first floor, confusion reigned and outside tension mounted because no one knew what was going on inside. Details are sketchy, but it's probable the local police commander relayed a message to the governor that the situation was volatile, that they were outnumbered, and he feared a full-scale riot. We do know that Democratic Governor Robert McNair was notified of the turmoil, and once again he ordered the National Guard to subdue the university campus. Still, up to then, there had been no injuries or arrests.

It was about 8 pm, when 150 Guardsmen finally showed up on campus, and they were met with a throng of 1,000 to 2,000 screaming, hooting insurrectionists ready to rumble. (The UPI reported "1,000".) It's unclear how it started, but by 9 pm, rocks, bottles and firecrackers were being exchanged with tear gas canisters. When tear gas seeped into the ventilation systems of several dorms, a near panic ensued and streets were flooded with students streaming out of the halls. The chaotic situation grew worse and in the confusion Guardsmen and police clubbed and arrested a handful of students trying to evacuate.

The liberal use of tear gas and a sweep of the campus by the Guard and state highway patrolmen convinced the initial crowd to break up. Students scattered onto downtown Columbia streets and continued to jeer and throw objects at Guardsmen. Throughout the night, small groups staged hit and run attacks on the part-time soldiers who had been ordered by Gov. McNair to arrest any student found outside the dorms.

Sometime during the hours of the early morning, order was restored. And when students awoke Tuesday, they found themselves under a 6 am to 9 pm curfew by order of the governor. Reports of injuries and arrests from the night were actually light—several students were injured from clubbing and two Guardsmen had minor injuries.

Tuesday, May 12

Tuesday on campus passed relatively quietly, but it was a different story that night. Minutes before 9, more than 300 students gathered at an intersection one block from campus and three blocks south of the South Carolina statehouse. It was a rally of sorts, but by 9:30 pm, it constituted a violation of the 9 pm curfew.

Students started pelting passing police and National Guard vehicles with volleys of rocks and bottles, and a nearby contingent of 200 National Guardsmen moved into position a block away. Soon, tear gas canisters were being fired at the crowd, and in a definitive show of force, Guardsmen marched down the street with fixed bayonets. But protesters refused to give ground and more rocks were thrown. For the second night in a row, Guardsmen and police fought pitched skirmishes with rock-throwing USC students, and tear gas choked the darkened streets. This night, however, police were more aggressive and chased down and arrested 100 people.

Under a constant barrage of tear gas, demonstrators finally melted away into the night.

Wednesday, May 13

On Wednesday, the relative calm on campus was enforced by police and National Guardsmen. And it was during this "eye" of the storm that Dr. Tom Jones, university president, finally took some leadership. He and numerous faculty members held dorm meetings during the week to hear out the concerns of students, and in response, Jones convinced Gov. McNair to remove state police from the student center at Russel House. Jones also agreed to empower the student government to regulate activities in certain university buildings. These moves helped maintain the calm.

At the end of the week, Jane Fonda hosted an antiwar rally on the steps of the State Capitol building, next to campus, and dozens, if not hundreds, from the Columbia campus attended.

It wouldn't be until Monday, May 19, however, that the governor would end the state of emergency on campus and lift the curfew.

Sunday, May 17

As part of the nationwide campaign of anti-war actions at military bases, 1,000 protesters rallied outside the **Charleston Naval Base** on Sunday, May 17, the very first anti-war action at the base. The 200 GIs at the rally had to endure the brass's intimidation tactics, and uniformed members were chased away by the Shore Patrol. A similar protest had been planned for Fort Jackson – about a mile from the USC campus – but had to be cancelled due to the repressive measures taken against organizers. The main GI organizer himself was jailed under trumped up charges of larceny and trespass.

Florida

University of South Florida – Tampa

Wednesday, May 13

The Wednesday issue of the campus paper, *The Oracle*, published a retrospective by student Rod Brooker, titled, "Bias and Indirection Killed the Student Strike." He asked why the strike failed and shrank "from thousands Tuesday [May 5] to a few hundred Friday, and to only a memory Monday." Brooker outlined a number of factors and explained, "The strike started in a wave of honest emotion. None but the most calloused or inhuman could fail to be both grief-stricken and horrified by the slaughter of four fellow members of the nationwide university community...."

The "major cause" of how the strike "killed itself", he wrote, "was lack of support from moderate people," due to a "bias against 'hippies' who formed a major nucleus of strikers." The bias was even held by those sympathetic to the cause, which prevented their participation and blocked "useful dialogue." Brooker recounted one "straight male student" who asked, "Why should I support the strike when all it seems to be is a bunch of hippies grooving to music ...?" Bias was also seen in "an anti-strike backlash from the Colleges of Business and Engineering, whose members claimed they were not really represented in Student Government."

On the flip side, Brooker wrote, the rhetoric of some protest speakers "became more and more inflammatory while old values began to reassert themselves upon strike supporters as the shock of Monday [Kent State] wore off." He added, "The radical element of strikers, who should have tried to moderate their words to hold moderate followers, succeeded in alienating them." The strike committed suicide because it "was plagued from the start by lack of unified and coherent leadership that could successfully sell new concepts to moderate and conservative people."

On the positive side, workshops were organized for those boycotting classes, and at least one day was spent taking the strikers' message to the community. Yet, Brooker said, "there were never even enough volunteers to maintain pickets at the entrances to the university," and strikers came to question the leadership's effective use of their time and energy. Finally, he concluded, "A great failing of the strike was that there were no satisfactory actions. And that's why there was no sign of strike Monday morning."

Kentucky

Western Kentucky University – Bowling Green

Protests on the Bowling Green campus against Cambodia and Kent continued into their second week, but President Dero Downing had had enough. There had been just too many disruptions on his campus. He called up the university's lawyers and they went to court mid-week and received a temporary restraining order – not on anyone specific – but, incredibly, for "each and every member of the university community." Clearly over-broad and unconstitutional, students reacted angrily to the administrative move, and more than one hundred signed up to test the restraining order by staging a mass meeting to openly defy the ban.

Buffeted by the push-back on his overly-broad restraining order, President Downing on Friday had it modified to include only five specific student leaders. Once named, the five were served with restraining orders and prohibited from participating in protest activity on campus.

Tennessee

Vanderbilt University – Nashville

Vanderbilt Chancellor George Heard accepted an appointment from President Nixon to lead a national committee on campus views and communications. In reaction, 50 students staged a sit-in Monday in Kirkland Hall in protest. In addition, a petition was circulated requesting the chancellor resign the appointment. Students genuinely believed Nixon's appointment of Heard was a ploy to sidetrack opposition to the White House, and understood that even with ideal communications, there was a huge yawning canyon between campuses and the White House. Chancellor Heard was seen as well-meaning, but ineffectual - a "crutch" for Nixon. Heard, by then in Washington, responded two days later saying his intention was to carry out his goals to the best of his ability.

A new group, the pro-war Concerned Students, held their own rally on campus Thursday, May 14, and speakers from the student body and faculty spoke in support of Nixon's policy in Cambodia. One speaker said, "We believe in achieving peace through policy, not peace through appeasement." Dr. Phillip Rollinson of the English department told the crowd of a few hundred, "If a house has termites, you shouldn't burn the whole house down." Wounded Vietnam veteran Tom Martin, sitting in a wheelchair, told fellow students, "Now at last the majority of Americans are recognizing the need to speak out [in support of the war]."

On the other side of the political spectrum, students opposed to ROTC's "favored position" at the school had received an influx of activism and energy with the Cambodian invasion. University administrators were spooked about the intensified interest in ROTC and posted campus police at ROTC buildings round-the-clock.

Antiwar students, however, directed their focus not on ROTC buildings but on organizing a demonstration at the annual Spring Naval ROTC Review. During the review, 100 or so demonstrators chanted antiwar slogans while several stood on the west side of Neely lawn draped in grim-reaper costumes and holding a coffin marked "ROTC." Later the coffin was carried over to Kirkland Hall, where Chaplain Beverly Asbury led students in prayer.

Knoxville College students held a strike after the shooting deaths of the two young Black men, Phillip Gibbs and James E. Green, at **Jackson State** in Mississippi. Officials said the school would be closed for some time.

Alabama
University of Alabama, Tuscaloosa

On Tuesday, President David Mathews issued a statement in which he rejected all the demands submitted to him by Black and women students. They had requested a Black history studies, the recruitment of more Black professors and students and a women's studies course. Frustrated, 800 students peacefully rallied that evening in protest of Mathews' stance.

Due to numerous sit-ins, the occupations of campus buildings and the destruction of Dressler Hall, state troopers patrolled the campus and National Guardsmen had been deployed nearby. Alabama Governor Lester Brewer had taken over governance of the university, had imposed a 9 pm campus curfew and had banned all demonstrations. After two attempts to hold "illegal" teach-ins resulted in arrests. Brewer went further – he threatened to expel any student or faculty member from UA if they were involved in any demonstration.

These tough rules incensed many. The University Fraternity Council was outraged called for a boycott of local merchants to excerpt pressure on Brewer. Even President Mathews was upset at the governor's over-reach. Mathews, who at the age of 35, was the university's youngest president and probably one of the youngest in the nation, pulled his connections and obtained equal TV time for students to publicly answer the governor.

The small city of Anniston, just outside **Fort McClellan**, was the site of a GI protest on Saturday – the city's very first anti-war demonstration. Roughly 250 people, including 50 GIs, rallied in the city's auditorium for music and speakers, including Flo Kennedy, Howard Levy and Richard Boone, the actor. Many of the post's units were given extra duty to discourage their participation at the event, and a key organizer had his water suspiciously turned off by the landlord.

At the **University of Southern Mississippi**, in response to the Jackson State murders, students enacted a general strike for two days.

Louisiana
Loyola University New Orleans
Tuesday, May 12

In a "Special Edition" Tuesday of the *Loyola Maroon*, the student newspaper announced: "Exams will continue as scheduled this week, along with the demonstrations and fast planned by the student protest movement. The protest movement is currently voicing opposition to refusal by the Very Rev. President Homer R. Jolley, SJ., to make a university statement in support of peace. Other protests concern Father Jolley's rejection of the Student Council's plan of optional exams, which had been proposed because of student concern over Cambodia and the killing of four students at Kent State University."

Armed Forces Day – May 16

Over the weekend, outside **Barksdale Air Force Base** near Shreveport, LA, GIs organized a festival of life and a series of antiwar workshops. Reportedly 600-700 people attended, including some 150-175 GIs. Authorities on base had at first attempted to deny organizers a permit which forced activists to go to court and obtain a federal injunction against the base.

Midwest
Ohio University – Athens
Monday, May 11

Weeks before the national student strike, students on the Athens campus had scheduled an assembly in Grover Center for May 11 with three political activist speakers—John Froines of the Chicago 8 Conspiracy, and speakers from the Ohio American Civil Liberties Union and the Youth

International Party. But on the eve of the event, Dean of Student Activities Thomas O'Keefe announced that only Froines would be allowed to speak, claiming this was campus speaker policy. There was an immediate an uproar among students. And just hours before the event, President Claude Sowle reversed O'Keefe's order, explaining he had not been consulted.

That night 3,500 students packed Grover Center to hear Froines, clearly the most well-known. Addressing the huge crowd, Froines pointed out the "striking similarities" between the American Revolution and the "revolution of today"—both were caused because the government "refused to listen to the people." Froines spoke of the Black Panther Party, and said they were "created by the repression of America." They have to be revolutionary he said, "not because they want to, but because they must survive." Political power must be "brought back to the people," he told his young crowd. "I think it's a beautiful thing to be in a revolution. America tells us that everything has been done and we should sit back home and watch the results on TV. That's not so," he said, "you have to continue the fight." He added, "Sometimes it is necessary that you throw a rock, but you only do it when you have to." Wrapping up, he declared, "We will survive, we will create a new order for we are the future. We will be peaceful as long as possible."

When the assembly broke up around 11 pm, 300 students moved and gathered outside the Chubb building, a former library scheduled to be remodeled into a student services building. A hundred forced their way in, breaking the glass door, and declared to the few surprised officials on hand they wanted to use Chubb as a "free university," and would, in the meantime, occupy it.

About midnight, Provost Robert Savage interrupted a group of 75 occupiers meeting on an upper floor and emphatically stated, "You are illegally occupying university property, and we're asking you to leave." The students responded they needed more time to talk but Savage insisted that if they remained, they would be violating university rules. This convinced many to move downstairs where small groups of administrators and students were in their own discussions. One official moved from one group to another, repeating the mantra that they were illegally in the building and had to leave. At one point, administrators announced to members of the press and faculty that they needed to leave because tear gas might be used to rout the students. The tear gas never came. Not that night.

It was around 1:30 am, when John Froines made a brief appearance and told the occupiers, "It looks like you've got a good building here. It looked dark when I first walked by but now it's yours." He suggested, "This building can become the headquarters of the Panther Defense fund in this area." A hundred voices cheered Froines as he left the building.

The occupiers got paper and pen out and formulated a set of demands—Chubb was to become a free university and a site for a "radical studies institute." Students viewed that Chubb as "our building" and that they be allowed to use it before it closed for remodeling. The occupiers were then visited by Dean of Faculties Taylor Culbert who urged, "If you wish to comply with us, you will leave." But hardly anyone left and they milled about and continued their talks.

About that time, occupiers heard the news that a fire had been discovered in the kitchen of a new residential annex and heavy smoke had damaged an adjoining cafeteria—both scheduled to open in the fall. It took nearly an hour for Athens fire fighters to put it out with damage later estimated at $125,000.

Sometime after 2 am Dean Culbert returned and made the protesters an offer. The university was willing to compromise and make alternative offices and rooms available in another building—Baker Center. Also, the university was "interested" in the free university concept and would even put their commitment in writing. Culbert ticked off a list of the spaces and offices available, including the Alumni Lounge. Yet, when occupiers took a vote on the compromise proposal, they turned it down nearly unanimously.

By 4 am, only 60 students remained in Chubb – and negotiations continued. At 4:45 am, editors at the student newspaper received a terse call from Provost Savage. He told them, "Based on the events of the evening there are serious questions of whether the university can remain open." The administration was mostly concerned about the fire bombings—not so much about the Chubb occupation. "Obviously, we are more concerned for the safety of the students," Savage said. It was "simply unpredictable" whether the school would remain open.

At 6 am Tuesday, when police surrounded Chubb and entered the building, no one was there – all occupiers had left. There had been no arrests and no property damage. Meanwhile, Athens police in riot gear continued to patrol neighboring streets and with security unusually tight, few students were allowed into the area.

Wednesday, May 13

On Wednesday, President Sowle announced he was suspending seven students he considered serious troublemakers and claimed – without elaboration – they were "a clear and present danger to the university." The two men and five women students ("coeds" in the parlance of the day) had been visible and active in demonstrations on campus throughout the year. When the faculty senate later recommended that the suspensions be lifted, Sowle refused.

That evening, a large crowd of a 1,000 students gathered near the edge of campus, and their anger from numerous issues had an easy target—Logan's, the town's only bookstore. For years, students claimed it had profited from its monopoly by charging outrageous prices. Its window was taken out by rocks. Over the next half hour, other storefront windows were smashed and small fires appeared in both commercial and campus buildings. Police showed up in force and advanced on the mass of students but were met with a fusillade of rocks. Police responded with tear gas shot directly at the students—the very first time tear gas had ever been used on the Athens campus. After two hours of skirmishes and ten arrests, the crowd dispersed.

Thursday, May 14

A tension-filled calm permeated campus on Thursday, but it wasn't until after dusk that hundreds of students began congregating on the College Green near Baker Center. In a short amount of time, the crowd grew to over a 1,000, and half of them began moving towards downtown Athens. City police, clad in riot helmets and dungaree coveralls, were not about to let that happen again and blocked their way. The mass of students were ordered to disperse by a patrol car loudspeaker, but they ignored the command and continued to cluster on the road just inside campus.

Just after 11 pm, police began lobbing tear gas canisters at that part of the crowd near the old Campus Gate. Yet, students scooped up many and hurled them back towards police lines, and each time a canister was returned, a cheer went up. Again, insurgents tried to advance towards downtown and let loose a heavy barrage of rocks, firecrackers and bricks – which rained down on the cops. More CS and CN gas projectiles were fired in response – and each time there was a teargas volley, cries for "water, water!" rang out and young men and women rushed out with buckets of water and rags. This went on for more than two hours. Dozens of windows in nearby shops and campus buildings were taken out and at least one building fire was set – which was quickly extinguished.

Every now and then, a police cruiser would roar down a street and gas canisters tossed from inside, and each time, the cruiser would be met with a volley of rocks. Tear gas was also shot at the crowd from the roof of Beckley's furniture store, where police had set up spotlights. A *New York Times* reporter, John Kifner, was on the scene that night and had also covered Kent State. Kifner reported that the barrage of rocks, bricks and bottles thrown at police at OU was much worse than at Kent State.

In the midst of all the skirmishing, several conflicts arose among students. For one, during the confrontations the role of student marshals had become quite controversial. Recruited to help keep order, the marshals included many athletes who attempted to restrain protesters and blocked them from retrieving bricks and actually got into fights with protestors. They were even seen hauling protesters over to the police to be arrested. One former star football player had told police he and his buddies were among the marshals and they'd "take care" of the protesters. Another hitch for the marshals was that earlier in the day, 500 marshal armbands had been stolen out of Baker Center – and presumably distributed to protestors. The university then had to issue "authorization" forms to the 'real' marshals.

There were also conflicts between protesters and some fraternities who closed their doors to people sickened by the teargas, although a few sororities provided water and refuge. There were also racial tensions. In one incident, Black students threw rocks and bricks at an all-white frat house, and in another, Black male students took over a women's dormitory, saying they were there to "protect our Black sisters against any violence." There was also compassion on display. At the height of the clashes, uniformed nurses from the Health Center were out in the streets assisting the injured.

Near 11:30 pm, a campus-owned automobile was destroyed by a firebomb, at least two more fires were started - both were quickly put out, and around midnight, there were reports of students on Union Street breaking the glass in parking meters and yanking them out of the sidewalk.

Campus security recorded details of the confrontation: "12:10 a.m. Chubb is getting pounded. Group is 250 strong. 12:15 a.m. Situation is totally out of hand. 12:30 a.m. Car still reported smoldering. A student has a bottle of gas found in that area instructed to hold and turn into the Security Office Friday." At one point, police were reporting a new incident every 10 minutes. One brief report stated: "Bomb under south bridge." Another had more detail: "Three hippie subjects coming down (Rt.) 33 on motorcycle, gas can in one hand and the other a gas mask."

One report from the night later grew into a campus legend. In the midst of all the chaos and clashes, a small group of students crept up to a Civil War statue of four Union soldiers holding rifles and removed the firearms. According to the legend, once the vandals stole the firearms, they buried them somewhere on university grounds. And despite various attempts, to this day, none of the rifles have ever been found.

Just before 1 am, Athens police, reinforced with officers from other towns and campus security, moved in on the college green and surrounded the demonstrators. A volley of teargas flooded the entire area and students scattered. Some found refuge at the bottom of Jefferson Hill, just east of the old campus gate, and it took police an hour of firing tear gas before they were dislodged. More gas was thrown to disperse small crowds on the West Green.

The streets of Athens near the campus were littered with brick and spent canisters when Dr. Sowle and Athens Mayor Raymond Shepard met to discuss the deteriorating situation. Shepard pushed to call in the National Guard and Sowle – who had vowed to "stand alone"—finally relented and allowed the mayor to make the formal request. At that moment, ironically, the streets surrounding the campus were actually quiet and clearing out.

Ohio Gov. James Rhodes gave the order—and up to 1,500 Guardsmen, 3 battalions, were deployed to Athens. Trucked to a staging area at the Athens Fair Grounds on the edge of town, the troops immediately began installing telephone lines. They had come from Athens and surrounding towns, but also from Newark, nearly 70 miles away, and Portsmouth, nearly 90 miles by vehicle. A Guard spokesman said units deployed to Athens were carrying live ammunition similar to the what the Guard had at Kent State. By early morning, they began entering Athens itself.

Then reports from the night's turmoil came in. Hudson Health Center reported 26 students treated for injuries and released, and another seven serious enough to be hospitalized. Over the two nights, a total of 48 students had been arrested. Damage was extensive. $65,000 in windows at Logan's, the notorious bookstore, and most nearby stores suffered similar fates, including Beckley's, the furniture store where police had set up search lights and fired tear gas. In total, storefront windows had been smashed over a two block area of downtown. Windows were also taken out on campus buildings including Chubb, Cutler Hall, Galbreath Chapel and a few others vandalized when students were forced to retreat from teargas.

A few hours after the National Guard had been ordered to Athens, President Sowle made the decision to close the campus, something he had resisted doing for nearly two weeks. At 3:10 am, the University Public Affairs Office released the official statement: "The university was to be closed effective immediately until the beginning of the summer quarter. Students would receive information by mail about options available with respect to grades and academic credit." Apparently, it was just for students. Sowle ordered, "All university personnel, faculty, staff and non-academic workers ... to report to work as usual on Friday."

Staff at the student newspaper, *The Post,* received word of the closure with a 3 am phone call from a Public Affairs official. No deadline had been set for students to leave campus, the official said, but final exams had been cancelled. Instructors and teaching assistants would still be paid their entire salary, but no decision was reached about pay for resident assistants. Plus, no decision about commencement had been made. It usually takes from 24 to 32 hours to completely clear the campus, the official stated. And luckily for students, National Guardsmen would be on hand to aid in any traffic problems created by the closure.

One student later recalled the night of closure, and students in his dorm were showering and getting ready to go uptown. He remembered why students had rebelled. "In all honesty, motivations could probably be attributed to a wide spectrum of things. Part war protest, anger about Kent State, part typical spring college revelry (alcohol-fueled), part anti-police/authority figure feelings, part anti-college bookstore sentiments (which captured a lot of student money), and so on."

That night, when he returned to his dorm room, everybody was listening to the student radio. "No one was sleeping. President Sowle delivered a message at approximately 2 a.m. that the university was closing and all students needed to be off campus within a day or two. The National Guard was coming into town later that morning. Students were restricted to campus until they could find transportation to leave town." He added, "Most students, I believe, were as relieved as I was that the campus was closing. Things had become so disruptive that attempts at studying or class work were futile. It was bittersweet because there was little time to say goodbye. I don't believe I got much sleep that night. Since my parents were in town, I could leave ASAP. So I packed up my stuff and left."

Friday, May 15

It was near chaos Friday morning when 17,000 students discovered they had been ordered from campus. At dawn, National Guardsmen, with bullets in their M-1 rifles moved onto university grounds and cordoned it off from Athens. Guardsmen lined downtown streets, and as one student recalled, "There was a national guardsman standing in every parking place." The Student Activities Office released information about transportation arrangements, but for those who lived in the dorms the circuits were totally jammed, and nobody could get a long-distance phone line out to call home. There was also confusion about the 1 to 6 a.m. curfew. Out on the streets, Athens cops said there was a curfew, yet at headquarters in the Athens City Building, Police Chief Fred James said he knew nothing about it.

Roadblocks at the entrances to Athens had been set up by the State Highway Patrol that previous midnight. A spokesman said, "We're just trying to keep people out of town, so no one gets hurt, but if they insist on going in we don't stop them." However, a spokesman for the Athens Police said no vehicles were being allowed into the city until morning.

By late in the afternoon most students had left campus. Yet, there was even confusion when it was to re-open. One announcement said May 19, another said not until the start of the summer quarter on June 22.

Saturday, May 16

Saturday morning, uptown Athens resembled a war zone. Broken windows, glass and spent canisters covered sidewalks and streets, and the putrid stench of tear gas still hung in the air. Elements of the National Guard continued to arrive – some via helicopter to Peden Stadium – the rest in dark green Army trucks. Yet, by the end of the weekend, it was over and the last battalion of National Guard had been dismissed.

Some observers – after viewing the aftermath – believed Athens and the university had suffered more damage than any other campus and town in Ohio during the May rebellion. Over the next year or so, the State of Ohio passed some very tough anti-rioting laws—specifically aimed at college students. Yet, things also became liberalized on campus. Hours for women students were eliminated and the university opened some of its governing committees to student representatives. Due to the closing of the university, the class of 1970 never officially graduated, so in 2010, over 125 former students of the class returned to the Athens campus for a belated commencement.

Antioch College – Yellow Springs
Wednesday, May 13

During a Wednesday morning meeting of the student body, a majority decided to have classes resumed on an "informal basis." However, there was an altogether different mood on display at an evening meeting. Student anger surfaced at the failure of the Administrative Council to follow through or support any of the campus community's demands to set aside monies for a Black Panther defense fund.

An easy consensus was reached that it was time to apply pressure on the administration of President James Dixon. "The time for action is now," said Al Steinberg, a research associate in biochemistry. Everyone seemed to agree with Steinberg but disagreed over what course of action to take. Some suggested a takeover of a major campus building, but Mike Melnick, of the Young Socialist Alliance, didn't think the community was ready for that. Psychology professor Lonnis Supnick advised, "You have to consider whether your action will have the effect of increasing or decreasing the number of people who will join with you." Another voice for action came from Fred Cox, minister of education for the Dayton chapter of the Black Panther Party. "Until you decide to get off your butts," he said, "you are going to do nothing. What you have here is a failure to activate."

Suddenly, someone yelled out, "All those who want to take over the building meet downstairs!" This brought some laughter, but it also caused more than 30 people to immediately jump up and scramble out the door. Some chanted, "Join us!" as they clamored downstairs. When those who went downstairs assembled, they moved to a hallway right outside President Dixon's office and came to a quick agreement to occupy the Bursar's office – the financial services office. At about 8:30 pm they moved in and physically took it over. They held a decision-making session and tasks were divided up. Some would work on their specific demands; others were dispersed to do "dorm work" – go to the dorms and recruit supporters; some departed to gather blankets and sleeping bags; door monitors were assigned; and somebody used bicycle chains to seal up all but one of the main doors.

When people tried to enter the building, monitors asked them whether they supported the action or not – and those who didn't were turned away. The acting bursar tried to get in but was rebuffed and then had to try a second time and told the door brigade he had to work on future payrolls, and they let him in. Around midnight, strikers who had gone out to do dorm work and gather supplies returned. A huge coffee maker started gurgling, sleeping bags were arranged on the floor, and the evening's third meeting began. Protesters stayed all night with some sleeping in the faculty lounge, guarding the only unlocked room in the building.

Thursday, May 14

Exactly 12 hours after it began, the occupation of the Bursar's Office ended at 8:40 am Thursday. The occupiers had planned to stay until noon but left early in response to complaints by financial office workers and other staff. Originally, students had agreed to allow Bursar personnel into the building to work on the day's payroll. Planned or not, students were invited to a meeting set up by a dean and were immediately confronted by secretaries with complaints. They didn't want to be the only employees in the building and accused students of taking actions "concerning our lives and our work" without consulting them. "We don't like being locked out," one secretary said. They were also upset that to get paid, they had to work, whereas other building workers were getting a paid holiday. They angrily demanded that students sign a pledge "promising not to take over the building again." The secretaries then stormed out of the meeting, leaving many of the students wide-eyed and open-jawed.

This pushback convinced the occupiers to end the take-over early, but they vowed to return to the Bursar's office if their demand for the Black Panther Defense Fund was not met by midnight Sunday. During the afternoon, the Administrative Council failed to locate funds for the Panther defense, and partially in response, a group of about 300 students and faculty decided to hold a teach-in on the Panthers the following Monday.

Friday, May 15

A reporter from the campus paper, *Antioch Record,* visited the nearby small town of Yellow Springs and reported how the student strike was affecting the community in Friday's issue. The Antioch Inn suffered numerous problems. It had to close and cancel two planned dinner parties. It was closed for Mother's Day for the first time in 35 years and visitors were forced to find other motel accommodations. Since the campus cafeteria was locked up, there was a run by students on doughnuts at the Village Bakery and students were also seen filling large bags of strike provisions at a local market. Business was so brisk at Gabby's restaurant that management had to lock the doors for an hour between lunch and dinner. Yellow Springs police chief James McKee commented, "I think it was fine if it helped accomplish a point. It hasn't affected us at all." However, his officers were keeping a close watch on the school during the strike, he said, watching for trouble from "the outside."

May 16

On Saturday, the Antioch Administrative Council endorsed a resolution that supported the students' demand for the Black Panthers defense fund. Also, the faculty voted for a 1% self-imposed salary tax, a "substantial portion of which" would go to the Panther fund.

Wilmington College – Wilmington

On Thursday afternoon, seven Wilmington women students attempted to register for the draft, as one of them said, "to throw a cog in the wheel of the war-machine." At 2:30, the women entered the Wilmington post office, walked up the stairs to the local Selective Service Board and approached the registrar, Mrs. Mary Lewis. The women included Susan Reid, Linda Robbins, Karen Thomas, Beth Stone, Jacqueline Toth, Meg Makransky, and Susanne McNeal. Once in the office, the women told Mrs. Lewis, "We want to register." And Mrs. Lewis replied, "No, we don't register girls." Reid asked, "How do you know we are girls? You need a birth certificate or search warrant to prove we are girls." Robbins added, "We are citizens of this society, and we feel we have the right to register."

Mrs. Lewis said, "Goodbye girls. Goodbye." Reid tried to engage her. "What are your feelings on girls being drafted?" Mrs. Lewis—"I wish you girls would leave." The students continued. Why couldn't she register the girls? "Because I am the registrar, and I am not going to register girls." One student said, "We will stay here until we see the law that says we can't be registered." Mrs. Lewis announced, "I'm sorry, but I'm not going to answer any questions."

Appearing nervous, Lewis reached for her phone. "Would you send a patrolman down." The Acting Postmaster, Mr. Davidson, then entered and told the women, "I would assume you could talk to your legislator," and said that controversial matters could not be discussed on the property. Getting no cooperation, the women left the building, and as they did, Mrs. Lewis told the *Witness* student reporter, "I advised them to go back to the college and finish their education." Later, Robbins explained their action. "We want equality for men. We want to see the draft abolished. The society that forces men to be violent while it allows women to be gentle is corrupt and corrupting. The draft is a manifestation of our sick, war-oriented society."

Friday, May 15

By Friday, May 15, it was clear strike activities and anti-war actions had peaked and were at a noticeable lower pitch than the week earlier. Yet, for some, the strike was still very much alive. One very optimistic member of the Strike Committee told the student newspaper "dozens" were working on strike activities full time and "another hundred" were assisting. They were making plans for a march in downtown Wilmington; they were organizing films, speakers and daily workshops on the war, the draft and the national crisis; some planned to work on dove Senate and Congressional candidates over the summer and into the fall; and plans were in the works for a Free University for high school students and community members. One positive thing that did happen over the summer was a vote by Wilmington students to approve a "co-ed" dorm – the first for the campus.

Case Western Reserve University

A group of strikers picketed the campus Union Club on Wednesday where trustees were having their closed meeting. Students had wanted their own meeting with the trustees to discuss the university's complicity with the war and had sent invitation letters to all of them. The letters requested the elimination of military training on campus and the election of a representative body made up of students, faculty and staff workers to direct and control university-owned stocks and bonds. They also requested the resignations of trustees linked with corporations who had war contracts and replaced by elected members who would work to end the war, racism and repression. It's not surprising, then, that only seven trustees responded to the letter – and none attended the student meeting.

Other Ohio Colleges

University of Akron President Auburn reopened the school on Monday, May 11, but stated, "while classes will be resumed, it will not be business as usual." All extra-curricular activities were cancelled or rescheduled. The Stark County Branch of **Kent State University** re-opened on Tuesday, after being closed since May 4, although no classes were held until the following day. Nearly 600 students and other members of the campus community attended two convocations held during the day in memory of the Kent State Four. Also on Tuesday, the **Oberlin College** faculty and administration announced the suspension of organized class activity for the remainder of the semester but added campus facilities would be available to outside students from closed Ohio campuses.

After the deaths of the two Black youth at Jackson State, the Black Student Union at **University of Toledo** handed the administration four resolutions: (1) A $200,000 endowment for Black students, (2) increased number of Black faculty and graduate students, (3) more scholarships for Black students, and (4) a three-day moratorium for the Jackson Two. After Jackson State, classes at the **University of Cincinnati** were initially cancelled just for Friday, May 15, but the administration decided the main campus would be closed for the remaining two weeks of the quarter.

Michigan
Eastern Michigan University – Ypsilanti
Monday, May 11

A calm had settled in on the campus because the previous week, President Harold Sponberg had cancelled classes—and strikers felt they had achieved a victory of sorts. But beginning Monday, everything changed and the calm evaporated. In the early afternoon, a protest rally was held in protest of Cambodia, Kent State and the suspension of six members of the strike leadership. At one point, some 60 people left the rally, moved to the middle of a campus road and staged a sit-in, forcing traffic to be re-routed by campus police. The commotion brought out hundreds from nearby dorms.

Wanting to be more visible, protesters moved to an intersection near Starkweather Hall and continued their sit-in. This was around 2 pm. The sit-in continued for another three hours, and by the time city police arrived, an estimated 1,000 students were congregating in the immediate vicinity, mostly as on-lookers. Police formed up in lines, and by now included local Ypsilanti cops, Michigan State Police and the Washtenaw County Sheriffs Tactical Unit.

A man in a white shirt and tie approached the sit-in from the police line, and yelled out, "Alright we've let you sit here for two hours!"—which was the cue for police to move in and make arrests. Half of the arrests in the intersection went without resistance, but the arrests of those who refused to leave was another matter. They locked arms and tried to kick police with their legs when they were grabbed. This gave police the excuse to get tough. Onlookers watched in horror as demonstrators were grabbed by their hair and heads and lifted off the ground—others were clubbed until they submitted. In all 39 protesters were arrested, then dragged over to waiting buses, taken downtown and charged with creating a disturbance.

Within minutes of the police departure, however, another 30 protesters reoccupied the street, and continued the human blockade of a major campus road—Forest Avenue. The arrests and the reoccupation brought out even more students and by 6 pm, there were 3,000 people mingling about. After the dinner hour, even more students poured out of the residence halls to check out what was happening.

Police did return. It was 8:15 pm when two university buses filled with officers arrived and ordered the crowd of 4,000 to disperse. People moved off the street, but not before singing a quick chorus of "America." Again, police withdrew, and again students returned and resumed the sit-in. As night fell, tensions were high; the crowd was restless. A few veteran student activists briefed them on tear gas tactics.

By 9:30 p.m., long lines of students crowded both sides of Forest Avenue—from McKenny Union to College Place. The few strike leaders who were left pleaded with people to get back into the street and sit down. The crowd became increasingly unruly, but suddenly a new idea seized many. They would erect a barricade across the road. Spontaneously, street signs were uprooted, resident hall signs torn down, other random debris grabbed – and added to the barricade. Signs and other wood in the barricade were set on fire, and a university van was pushed onto the street and used as part of the blockade. A traffic barricade was rammed through the van's windshield and then set on fire; an unlucky school truck was also pushed up and added to the blaze. No one noticed, but a few nearby windows were broken.

As night follows day, a bus full of county riot officers arrived. They formed up on one end of Forest Avenue and unleashed a canine patrol from the opposite end. A prominent protest leader was singled out for arrest, and after he put up a fight, was thrown into one of the buses. He ran to the back of the bus, kicked out the emergency window and escaped. Many of the others on the bus followed.

At 12:10 am, columns of police with clubs deliberately and slowly marched down Forest in formation, followed by two buses and additional officers. When the police got within distance, the crowd let loose a barrage of rocks. Seemingly within seconds, police responded with volleys – not of teargas—but of the much more dangerous birdshot—and masses of students scattered in all directions.

More streetlamps were broken and windows in the library and Pray-Harrold Hall were taken out. More arrests were made, which brought the total for the day to 76. School administrators set up a campus curfew effective at 10 pm for the area north of Forest Avenue.

Tuesday, May 12

The Eastern Echo, the student newspaper, on Tuesday headlined an article, "Sponberg Curtails Deliberations" which detailed how President Sponberg was ending deliberations with student activists. Sponberg had accused strike leaders of SLAM – the Student Liberation Action Movement—of not negotiating in good faith, and had just a week earlier, obtained restraining orders against some of the very same students he was negotiating with.

It was around 7 pm when a large crowd gathered at Pierce Hall to continue protests, because for them, nothing had been resolved. None of their issues had been addressed and the administration was taking a hardline approach to dissent. The crowd marched through several residence halls to pick-up supporters. Flushed with more people, they headed back to Forest Avenue and again blocked traffic. This went on for a couple of hours. Protest leaders urged people to leave the streets when police arrived, but the crowd was of a different mind. Most lined the sidewalks and watched with a mixture of curiosity and tension.

As the 10 pm curfew approached, faculty members, administrators and a few students tried to cajole the crowd into returning to their homes, but many were still just getting there. At 10 on the nose, Student Body President Barry Simon warned the crowd that the curfew would be enforced by police and that students who didn't wish to get hurt should leave the area. Within minutes, the crowd of 1,500 narrowed down to about 600.

It was a half hour later that many in the crowd formed the idea they could avoid the curfew if they left the curfew area, so, the crowd moved away and regrouped outside Welch Hall and blocked off an adjoining street. At the same time, other students milled about the famous Ypsilanti Water Tower – which looks like the keep of a medieval castle. More disorder was to follow. Welch Hall windows were broken, a plate glass window at McKenny Hall was damaged, and a fire started in the middle of a nearby street.

When police were bussed in this time, they were a force to contend with. 250 officers formed a line near the Water Tower, and when the order came, they charged students still milling about. This attack caused the entire stretch of blocks and open fields to become a battleground. Students hurled rocks and bottles and were then chased by officers. The doors at Welch Hall were ripped off but campus security prevented fleeing students from entering. Sometime after midnight, Washtenaw County sheriffs fired bird-shot into a group of students and wounded four.

By 1:30, the last lingering protesters had been cleared off the streets. Eighteen people had been arrested and windows broken at a half dozen campus buildings and several commercial establishments including a cleaners, a bank, a barber shop and an apartment complex suffered vandalism. According to the school's vice president of business and finance, property damage to the campus over the two nights was estimated at $35,000, plus another $10,000 in damage to burned university vehicles.

Wednesday, May 13

Michigan Governor William G. Milliken on Wednesday declared the city of Ypsilanti in a state of emergency and authorized police to enforce a 10 p.m. to 5:30 a.m. curfew in the campus area.

At noon 200 students demonstrated briefly outside Pray-Harrold Hall and vowed to return at 6 p.m. to the Pierce Mall. A student newspaper reporter observed that there didn't appear to be any veteran student leaders, as most if not all had been arrested or suspended. Unexpectedly, President Sponberg did make an appearance at the rally, and for the first time, met with students – those at the rally. He had no qualms, he told them, about expelling students who were "menaces" to the university. Sponberg's office, he claimed, had been deluged with angry calls from Ypsilanti residents upset the curfew had been imposed because of "stupid hippies."

Later that afternoon, Sponberg released a statement to the campus community in which he made three points: he pledged the school would not be forced to close; the university would appoint a student representative to the Board of Regents – one of the students' demands;

and he slammed SLAM and its members for 'not wanting progress for the students at EMU.' Soon after, newly-elected student body president, Barry Simon, made his own announcement that, as president, he would be filling the position for a "student representative with full-speaking rights on the Board of Regents."

That afternoon, a Faculty Senate meeting failed to take a stand on the closure of the school, one of the students' demands. This clearly disappointed those who gathered for a 6 pm rally. A half hour later, the crowd's numbers had risen to more than 2,000 but it had no clear direction. Many walked the short distance to Forest Avenue where they milled about while down the street, another 1,000 gathered in front of President Sponberg's residence. A few rocks were thrown at his car, but no serious damage was caused.

Over on Forest Avenue, a motorist being blocked panicked and drove in reverse striking at least four people behind him, carrying one person on his trunk for 30 feet. Angry students surrounded the car, smashed the windshield but the motorist sped away. A student on a motorcycle attempted to chase him but accidentally struck another student. Both injured students were taken to a local hospital—and later released. Over the course of the next hour, protesters' numbers dwindled down to roughly 60 people, who then dispersed just after 8 pm and just before Michigan State Police marched down Forest Avenue.

Governor Milliken's strict curfew regulations had changed the police-student battle plans. Instead of taking over and remaining in the streets, students retreated to residence halls, apartment buildings and houses, and then pelted police cars with bottles when they would pass by. Students also smashed hundreds of bottles on the streets in a tactic to slow down or prevent police cars from driving through. Around 9 pm this new type of confrontation played out. Squads of police cars raced through the campus only to be met with jeers and bottles from the buildings. When students on Forest Avenue were chased into campus buildings by club-wielding officers, they threw furniture and other items out the windows at them.

Police changed their tactics as well. For the first time during the rebellious student strike at EMU, police used tear gas. They had already used birdshot and had wounded four. Now police fired tear gas directly and indiscriminately into apartment buildings, dormitories, and fraternity houses. Residence halls filled with tear gas, and hundreds were forced to flee – many ended up camped out overnight in the dining commons. Buell Hall student residents claimed at least six canisters of tear gas had been fired directly into their hall through the main entrance.

In response to the indiscriminate use of teargas, residents built at least two large street fires, and one burned off and on for hours. Another blaze was set on the bridge over the Huron River in the northern area of the campus, which for a while prevented police from converging on a large group throwing bottles at other officers. During these tense moments, Washtenaw County Sheriff Douglas Harvey flew above the campus in a helicopter, and actually took it upon himself to throw tear gas bombs onto the crowds below. When Wednesday night's clashes finally subsided, 45 students had been arrested for curfew violations.

Sometime late Wednesday night, campus police informed the Student Activities Board that due to the unrest, all evening functions would be cancelled until May 21 or later. All meetings, films, and concerts were cancelled, including the Jefferson Airplane concert scheduled for campus that Saturday.

Barry Simon, student body president, heavily criticized the administration and the police. He charged, "It's stupidity on the part of the authorities that called the police in Monday afternoon. The brutal police tactics perpetuated the violence. If the authorities had any sense," he said, "they would have allowed the 30-40 kids to just sit in the street. The entire week snowballed from Monday afternoon." Finally, Simon claimed, "There were at least 1,000 more radicals today than last Friday."

Thursday, May 14

On Thursday, President Sponberg announced that the 113 to 120 students arrested over the three-day period of unrest were all suspended or placed on probation. Police estimated the total of arrests since Monday at 164. Most of those arrested were still in jail, as no bonds had been set until arraignment.

Friday, May 15

With dozens of student activists and leaders in jail or suspended, the campus appeared relatively quiet on Friday. Then out of the blue, President Sponberg announced university officials were setting up a commission to investigate students' complaints of police brutality as well as "all circumstances of the disturbances" that had plagued the campus for the past two weeks.

Sponberg listed the complaints to be investigated: unnecessary force used by police in the arrest of 39 students in a sit-in on Forest Avenue Monday afternoon; the use by Washtenaw County sheriff's deputies of bird-shot fired into a group of student demonstrators early Tuesday morning, wounding four students; police firing tear gas into apartment buildings, dormitories, and fraternity houses indiscriminately Wednesday night; and the excessive force used by Ypsilanti city police in arresting two Black students Thursday night.

On Friday, a leaflet on campus pleaded with students in large hand-written letters, "Don't Go Home." It read, "For three nights EMU has been a battle ground. We burned an EMU bus, we built barricades, we fought the pigs. We made the University pay $60,000 for carrying on business as usual, including ROTC, in the face of the invasion of Cambodia, and the attempted extermination of Bobby Seale and the Black Panther Party." It went on, "Sponberg, our very own little Nixon, ordered the use of EMU buses to carry our brothers and sisters off to Jail. We've been fighting at night, but during the day the university is a university." Finally, "We cannot stop fighting now." Another flyer called for a rally and march through campus and added a new demand—the immediate resignation of President Sponberg.

Yet, the fighting and protests at EMU were over. And although protests died down at EMU for the season, reforms were on their way. Nearly a year after the May strike, Eastern established two ad hoc committees to implement activists' demands, the Faculty Senate approved the creation of a Black Studies program, and two full-time recruiters with a team of part-timers were hired to increase minority enrollment.

Michigan State University – East Lansing
Thursday, May 14

Thursday was the day of the big antiwar march to the Michigan State Capitol in Lansing, and MSU students hosted a pre-march rally. Thousands of them then joined the huge procession that marched the four miles to the State Capitol, estimated at 10,000 people. Students from **Central Michigan University, Western Michigan University**, and **Lansing Community College** also participated.

In the morning, Michigan Governor William Milliken met with his legal advisor, a few university officials, and state police officers to figure out security measures and how to deal with tourists trying to enter the Capitol during the demonstration. In the end, they decided to block all entrances, allowing no one in who didn't have business in the building.

The massive throng reached the Capitol building and listened to a half hour of speeches, including from state representatives, Jack E. Vaughn (D-Detroit) and Daniel Cooper (D-Oak Park) who stressed their opposition to US involvement in Southeast Asia. Vaughn had introduced a bill preventing any Michigan resident from being compelled to serve in an undeclared war. After the speeches, demonstrators were allowed into the building to speak to their elected state representatives, 25 at a time. Most representatives were in session and students ended up speaking to only about a handful. The only incident during the otherwise peaceful demonstration occurred when an apparent drunk driver plowed into a line of marchers, injuring 5 to 10 people.

Friday, May 15

Friday's action on campus stood in stark contrast to Thursday's large peaceful march on the State Capitol. The Committee to Abolish ROTC had called a demonstration and sit-in for Friday morning at the building which housed ROTC facilities on campus, named Demonstration or "Dem" Hall. When protesters first reached the building, they found the doors locked and chained, guarded by a small squad of ROTC cadets. After a brief scuffle, protesters overpowered the cadets, unlocked the chains, and rushed into the building to take it over. The occupation by some 200 protesters effectively shut down ROTC operations for the entire day. Occupiers took over offices and engaged military personnel in rap sessions on the Indochina war and ROTC. They gave tours of the building to other students and held discussions on how to put the building to a more constructive use, such as a Strike Headquarters or a daycare center.

After eight hours of occupation, administration officials came in accompanied by plainclothes police officers and issued an ultimatum to the students to leave the building. But they ardently refused. Moments later, they watched through windows as a busload of State Police in riot gear pull up, disembark and enter the building. The students then quickly evacuated the building from a different door as a group and stood outside. As a light rain began to fall, they could see inside that officers were beginning to don gas masks. Spontaneously, they rushed the doors and tried to barricade the police inside—but there just wasn't enough of them. The officers emerged and the lights inside Dem Hall were suddenly extinguished. Without warning or orders to disperse, police attacked the students, hurling tear gas and the more "persuasive" pepper gas into the crowd. Initially shocked by the action, people scattered.

It was about a half hour later that many reassembled at the Student Union to talk over what had just happened and what to do next. Some dashed off to go confront President Wharton over the use of pepper gas and state cops. Others returned to Dem Hall – only to be repulsed again by teargas. For the rest, the night was over.

Northern Michigan University

In Wednesday's early hours a series of molotov cocktails were thrown through windows in a half dozen rooms at Kaye Hall. A few hours later, University President John Jamrich was awakened at home and confronted by 50 Black students on his lawn. They demanded that he cancel classes to mourn the deaths of the six African American men fatally shot by police in Augusta, Georgia, on Monday. Fairly quickly, Jamrich agreed to set aside a day for class discussions of the incident. Later in the day, Jamrich made a unique announcement for a university president, and ordered that students would have to store their guns in official facilities, and not in campus dorms or on their person in classrooms.

Thursday the Black Students Association presented a list of formal demands to the university administration which included an increase in Black faculty and student body, a Black studies program and library, and a $5,000 appropriation for Black cultural events each year. Jamrich responded that he would consider the demands, "...but I will initiate no crash program."

Students on Wednesday at **Macomb County Community College** put on a guerilla theater production as part of a week of antiwar activities. Actors played jury members with ear-muffs connected by string to judges, themselves strung puppet-fashion to an actor called "Wixon." The juries declared a guilty verdict for a Black, a hippie, and a student all found to be "un-American." The three were taken out and then "crucified."

At **Michigan Technological University** in the Upper Peninsula on Tuesday, roughly 200 ROTC cadets joined another 1,000 students in a one-day class boycott. Instead of class, the students and cadets began building a one-acre park near campus, in what was termed a symbolic protest against the war and the Kent State deaths.

Indiana

Indiana University – Bloomington
Monday, May 11

A campus-wide referendum held Monday on student opinion about the war and related issues demonstrated wide opposition to the war, support for the student strike, but also displayed a swarth of campus conservatism and latent racism. A total of 17,450 students voted and 12,345—nearly 71%—opposed Nixon's decision to invade Cambodia. Close to 10,000 voted to cancel classes to protest the war and another 12,000 or so supported a Congressional cutoff of funds for the war. However, on the issue of abolishing ROTC programs, 9,481 were in favor of keeping them, while 7,361 were opposed.

On other issues, student opinion was very mixed. Asked if the university should admit African-American students in direct proportion to their percentage of the state's population, students were split nearly 50-50. Plus, students were not in favor of university contributions to Black Panther Bobby Seale's defense fund (13,170 against and 3,356 for). Finally, on the matter of the Indiana University Foundation making its records and accounts public, 70% were in favor.

Pro-war sentiment and latent white supremacy on campus found encouragement in the town of Bloomington. Several right-wing and racist organizations were active, including Citizens for War Group—created by a university track coach, a racist vigilante outfit called the Concerned Citizens Group, as well as the Ku Klux Klan. On top of these sources of reaction, the local press was pro-war and its dismal coverage of strike activities consistently vilified students.

Wednesday, May 13

Even though 10,000 students had voted to cancel classes in Monday's referendum, President Joseph Sutton refused to go along. And in response, hundreds of angry students on Wednesday formed human blockades at the entrances to the administration building, Bryan Hall, with their chief demand being the suspension of classes for the remainder of the week. Tensions on campus rose dramatically when Bloomington police arrived and assembled nearby. Outraged at the escalation, blockaders threw rocks at the police line and lobbed a few at campus cops. Within minutes, police charged the crowd, scattered everyone and arrested eight students.

At a later mass meeting called by strike leaders to discuss future tactics, some wanted to continue the blockade of Bryan Hall, but others felt their aggressive militancy would cause Indiana Governor Edgar Whitcomb, known for his hostility toward student protests, to call in the National Guard. A consensus was formed to de-escalate the situation and strikers arranged a negotiation meeting with university officials. A deal was struck. Students agreed not to blockade the administration building if the president and chancellor met with students that day in the auditorium.

4,000 students packed themselves into the auditorium, while closed-circuit television cameras relayed the meeting to large classrooms in the school of journalism and other halls. Both President Sutton and Chancellor Carter spoke; they expressed sympathy with the students' concerns over the war and praised the peaceful nature of the demonstrations. Yet, while they acknowledged the thousands who voted to cancel classes, they disagreed with the closing of the university. The issue for them, they said, was their responsibility to the 55,000 students on all the campuses to keep classes open if any wanted to attend. Sutton and Carter did make two concessions. They agreed to work with the faculty council to find ways to include student participation in the governance of the university and agreed to declare a campus "Political Mobilization Day" to allow students "to express and organize their political leanings."

Purdue University – Lafayette
Tuesday, May 12

Even while the administration of President Frederick Hovde hosted a wide-open forum to discuss America's foreign policy and Purdue's response on Tuesday, May 12, the administration continued its process of suspending students for a May 1 incident in which 30 to 40 protesters disrupted ROTC exercises. And for some unexplained reason, the results of a student referendum on the status of ROTC had not been publicized.

The forum allowed an array of diverse opinions, and a Young Americans for Freedom type spoke and strongly supported ROTC on campus and the right of professors to engage in any type of research they chose. One speaker was the Executive Assistant to President Hovde, John Hicks – who back on May 1 had rejected student demands – said he favored Nixon's move into Cambodia.

On the other side, SDS leader Bob Rose criticized a university whose contracts and connections with the military rendered it "far from neutral." He challenged the university to broaden its research topics, finding cures for cancer instead of developing munitions for war.

Father Leo Piguet of St. Thomas Aquinas Center in West Lafayette urged students to use their considerable power "to prick the conscience of other people," and warned that "a stupid war overseas" will cause "a stupid war at home." Student body president Stan Jones said Purdue "must accept a moral responsibility to work against war," and drew a standing ovation when he called on students to become activists, "foot-soldiers" in joining the second American revolution that began at Kent State.

At **Indiana State University** in Terra Haute on Tuesday, a minor scuffle broke out between students and campus police over lowering the American flag to half-staff in honor of the Kent State students. 150 strikers had gathered at the flag pole and when the crowd attempted to lower the flag, university security officers moved in, and gave demonstrators 15 minutes to raise the flag back up. At that point a student tackled a policeman which resulted in a short scuffle. Three students were arrested, with one charged with assaulting an officer. ISU President Allan Rankin resolved the problem and had the flag lowered the next day.

A week of "liberation classes" began Monday at **Manchester College** with topics and material covered chosen by those students who participated. College officials announced that by the end of the week roughly half of the student population of 1,400 had attended the sessions.

Anti-war servicemen and their supporters tried to hold a rally at **Grissom Air Force Base** on Sunday, as part of the nationwide movement. Leafletting reportedly went well Saturday on base, but by Sunday, tight restrictions were placed on GIs and the local press urged locals "to come and break up the commie rally." Only 50 people showed and very few servicemen. Right-wingers with clubs arrived and physically broke up the gathering.

Illinois

Chicago Region

Roosevelt University – Chicago

On Monday, May 11, 2,000 students, faculty, and administrators jammed Altgeld Hall to decide whether to continue the strike. Faculty member Les Friedman, in favor of the strike, pointed out that for the first time universities and colleges were being effectively used to spread the anti-war campaign. Obed Lopez from the Latin American Defense Organization supported the strike, but cautioned, "None of my people can go to your school." When residents were killed in the barrio, he said, there was just silence—this brought sustained applause. No strike was called when Chicago Panther leader Fred Hampton was killed by police, he said. "There is no such thing as democracy for welfare recipients." Chicago jails are filled with Latinos and Blacks because they have no bond money – which again drew an ovation. Continue the strike, he implored. "Going back to school will show you are hypocrites."

One student against the strike warned that its leaders were "fascist." "You will be judged by your leaders," he warned, but jeers drowned out whatever else he had to say. Another male student opposed the strike because strikers used "scare tactics" such as starting false fire alarms and banging on walls while classes were in session. He called for the school to remain open, and shouted, "If you're with me, then make yourself heard!" That drew enthusiastic applause.

Speaking in support of the strike, Student Senate President Mark Podolner noted the massive crowd was the largest ever seen on campus. With a nod to the business students in the crowd, Podolner recalled the countless times business majors had sought his assistance as a draft counselor to stay out of the war. He said it was too late for individual action and that business students must join the anti-war movement, as "we're all in the same boat now."

Podolner conceded the strike was a reaction to whites being killed and acknowledged the objections to joining by Black students. But the issue at hand was "where do we go from here?" and commented that the university treated everyone like lowly peasants.

The speeches concluded and a consensus developed to hold a two-day poll of the campus community on whether to continue the strike. An election committee was formed which would organize the polling for Tuesday and Wednesday.

Two days later on Wednesday, 400 students and faculty attended a 10 am meeting in Altgeld Hall to hear the results of the poll on whether to continue the strike. For antiwar activists, the news was grim. Only 971 students voted for continuing the strike with 2,295 opposed. This vote placed the campus and the future of the strike at a critical juncture.

Podolner took the podium. Neither the faculty nor the administration recognized the legitimacy of the vote, he said, and in fact, two days earlier, a special faculty meeting had determined there was no such thing as a "strike" and that instructors had to return to their classrooms. Plus, faculty members working on the strike committee had received "ominous letters" stating that they should return to work and that there would be no "blanket credit" for striking students. Podolner recounted that he had confronted University President Rolf Weil about the possibility of the strike continuing, but Weil said no compromise would be offered or taken. Pololner asked the crowd to "think seriously" of the administration's stand, which he considered "pretty incredible." The administration had never said that they would accept the outcome of the vote and he asked how students could accept it either. Addressing those who supported a strike, he cried,

"This strike is on!" and pledged efforts would be made to demand the university's stock portfolio, to "find out where the money goes."

Just north of Roosevelt University at **Kendall College**, the administration suspended two students who had taken over a campus gym and machine shop and set up a type of "new university." Occupying the building since the weekend, they called it "Our School" and had planned to work with community groups for social change and to implement the national strike demands. Yet, they had acted against the College Council decision to end the strike. Plus, both were already on probationary suspension for participating in sit-ins protesting the college's limits on nighttime use of a campus recreation center.

At the predominantly Black **Southeast Junior College** in Chicago, a school boycott began on Wednesday, but it was not called to protest Cambodia nor any of the student deaths. Rather students vowed to keep the school closed until their demands were met, which included the reinstatement of a fired Black Studies Director, renaming the school after slain local Black Panther leaders Fred Hampton and Mark Clark, and replacing the acting president of the college, Doyle Bonjour, with an African-American. The next day, after the second straight day of disturbances over the demands, 50 police officers were called in to quell the turmoil, arresting six students in the process. Afterwards, classes were suspended indefinitely.

At **North Park College**, a private Christian school, 400 of the 1,200 students on campus met on Monday night, May 11 and voted to strike through the weekend. Students decided that the Christian institution had stood-by too long and had to take a stand immediately, including demanding a public condemnation of the war's expansion and the National Guard killings by the college administration.

Loyola University

At **Loyola University** a referendum was held Monday in which students voted overwhelmingly to allow those who wished to return to classes. The day before, a general faculty meeting had also voted for a return to class. Yet, it took the Dean of Faculty to remind the campus that the university had authorized faculty members to let students waive classes for the remainder of the school year and receive grades based on their work completed.

Sometime before 5 am on Tuesday, a molotov cocktail was thrown through a window of the ROTC facility in the Armory, and an office sustained minor damage from the fire and the water. In a public statement the Loyola strike steering committee condemned the action. "We state unequivocally again that this committee is dedicated to the principle of non-violent resistance as a means of overcoming the violence which permeates this society. We shall not resort to the path of violence which this society's governmental bodies are so quick to follow."

During the strike at **Mundelein College** – just east of Loyola—administrators established an "alternate college" for students and faculty members to use beyond Monday, the official end of the strike. The alternate classes would cover political issues and dissent, and about one-third of the faculty and student body signed up. (Mundelein was the last private Catholic women's college in Illinois and in 1991, became affiliated with Loyola.)

The **University of Chicago** officially reopened on Monday, but according to a university official, 80 to 90 per cent of students continued to boycott classes.

Northwestern University – Evanston
Monday, May 11
Early Monday, 50 students from the Evanston campus took off to make the 200-plus mile trip to the state capital in Springfield to witness the Illinois House debate Rep. Robert Mann's bill – a bill that would prevent Illinois men from being drafted into an undeclared war – such as Vietnam. Mann had spoken at a campus rally Friday night.

However, Northwestern's main focus during the day was a sit-in and take-over of the Medical School dean's office by as many as 30 medical and nursing students. At 9 am, the dissidents moved into the office of Assistant Dean Dr. Edward S. Petersen to protest the medical school's role in perpetuating the war in Vietnam and Cambodia. Petersen's office was chosen according to student organizer Lee Weiss because "He is one of many administrators who haven't lived up to their responsibilities."

Protesters said they wanted to set up a "People's Free Health University" and hold seminars with radical historian Staughton Lynd, the Black Panther Party, and the Young Lords Organization—a militant Puerto Rican organization. When asked to leave the premises by university officials, the group refused.

A spokesperson for the occupiers, many of whom were in their freshman or sophomore years, issued a critique of the medical school and its dean, Dr. Peterson, and included a litany of issues. They charged the medical school with providing low-quality care to poor people who used the school's clinics, for having a discriminatory admission policy against women, Blacks, Latino Americans and low-income white students – which perpetuated institutional racism. The school was also accused of grading medical and nursing students on nonacademic matters, subjecting them to unethical psychiatric exams and denying them access to their professional evaluations. Finally, the spokesperson bashed the school for exploiting hospital workers through low pay and the absence of grievance procedures. Naturally, medical school officials denied all the charges.

When occupiers announced they would hold a continuous 24-hour sit-in and teach-in in the dean's office, they were threatened with arrest by Asst. Security Director John Shackelford if they didn't depart by 5 pm. To head off any kind of confrontation, the School of Medicine faculty held an emergency session and voted to forego penalties against the students. They also voted to allow the sit-in to continue as a 24 hour teach-in, and elected faculty delegates to a student-faculty committee to consider the students' grievances. This averted any clash.

Back on the main campus that evening, in the midst of cold weather, fog and intermittent drizzle, 1,000 Northwestern student strikers began a 5-mile candlelit march for peace. It wove through Evanston residential neighborhoods and around 8:30 ended up at City Hall on Oak Street. As the five-block long column slowly filed by City Hall, marchers sang, "All we are saying is, give peace a chance." They then returned to the campus meadow, candles were placed on four mock graves, and for ten minutes, hundreds fell silent in tribute to the Kent State Four.

Yet, it was inside City Hall where things got lively. It was a meeting of the city's aldermen and on their agenda was Northwestern and the

Sheridan Road barricade and the call-up of the National Guard. There was also an anti-war proposal on the agenda that had been tabled a week earlier which caused the Municipal Building room to be jam packed with an audience waiting for the aldermen to act.

The Sheridan Road barricades were on the agenda because they had been a lingering issue for city officials. For days, residents had been complaining about the inconvenience and the constant rerouting of traffic. Alderman Frank Hoover asked the city manager to, "Take what steps he deems appropriate to return to the citizens of Evanston the use of Sheridan Road." The mayor, John Emery, confirmed that the chief of the highway division had made the same request, but then quipped, "With the condition of the street as it is, it was perhaps better off being closed."

Alderman Hoover – trying to keep it lighthearted – said, "Perhaps having the highway away from the lakefront would be a blessing." At least the city had been able to study traffic re-routing problems, he added, and could potentially close the road permanently. This was exactly what three NU grad students at the meeting were trying to get the council to do—tamp down vehicular traffic on Sheridan, making it safer and more pedestrian-oriented for the campus. After more discussion, nothing was decided (again) about Sheridan Road, but everyone in the room witnessed the ironic spectacle—some aldermen complained the barricade was an inconvenience, while others stressed that the barricade might have been a blessing in disguise.

Much more contentious was the issue of the city's call-up of the National Guard. Some aldermen had been rankled for not being consulted. Alderman Roosevelt Alexander complained, "I was appalled that the Guard was called to Evanston. I resent not being consulted or at least informed." He went on, "If the situation in Indochina is not resolved quickly, the issues about which I feel most strongly will be lost in revolution." He then rose, turned toward the audience and read a prepared statement. He agreed with the Northwestern strike and didn't think any action on the campus had warranted such a crisis response by city officials. He then read a statement from student body president Eva Jefferson, in which she denied a report that City Manager Wayne Anderson had consulted her before calling in the National Guard. "Mr. Anderson was not even in sporadic communication with me," her statement read. Jefferson said they spoke only after she had heard that the Guard was coming.

Anderson, the city manager, was present at the meeting and in response claimed he had obtained certain information from student and law enforcement sources that between 10,000 and 17,000 demonstrators were expected at Friday's rally at Northwestern. He had heard that members of five different groups with "recognized violence" would be attending – but he couldn't divulge their names. He explained, "We weighed that against 130 tired local police and 115 to 155 more which other agencies could commit. At 4 p.m., we asked for up to 1,000 troops. Friday, about 1 or 2 pm we evaluated all the information at our disposal. We knew students from the following schools were going to assembly ..."—he ticked off the names of a dozen colleges and high schools. He then said, "Student leaders had not told us they invited all those schools, nor that the rally was moved to Dyche Stadium." Then Anderson claimed he didn't have enough time to call each of the 18 aldermen beforehand because the timing of his call to the governor at 4 pm for the Guard call-up was critical. Messages had been sent to the aldermen's homes by 5 pm – afterwards.

Others on the council disagreed. Alderwoman Edna W. Summers cried, "I'm horrified that all you have to do is pick up the phone and you get a thousand troops." Her colleague Craig Cain saw it differently. "The fact that there was no trouble shows there was no over-reaction." Cain quickly added that the council had not passed the mayor's emergency powers which they had blocked for months. Alderman William Nott asked his fellow council members to put themselves in the mayor and city manager's positions of having to protect the city.

Representing the 8th District, Alderman Michael Schiltz raised another issue. "We should examine the degree to which we can maintain control once we call the militia in." Another council member, Shel Newberger, said, "We have heard that the Guard is poorly trained for riot duty. My question is whether they were prepared to do the job we might have wanted done Friday?" City Manager Anderson replied that the battalion of Guard sent was "the most experienced in the U.S." and had not fired one gun in its nine call-ups.

Another alderman, James P. McCourt, snorted, "Save your dime. It is nice to feel we are being advised, but if you smell smoke and need help, call the neighboring fire department, not me."

Then Quaife Ward of the 4th District, brought it all home when he said, "Much has been said tonight, but nothing about the major cause and reason for all this. These young people are saying something. They are saying it to what they consider their responsible leaders. If we can't respond, we don't belong here. I don't know how I'd vote now, but I feel it deserves discussion." (Ward would later become city manager for Evanston.) Mayor Emery then felt compelled to cite the legal authority used for calling the Guard. Illinois law states, he read, "Subject to the authority of the governor as commander in chief, the mayor may call out the militia to aid in suppressing riots and other disorderly conduct...."

Outside the meeting, Eva Jefferson maintained her criticism of Anderson, the city manager. She had sat through the meeting for at least an hour and had not been called to speak – and repeated that there had been no direct communication between her and the city manager from Wednesday to Friday afternoon—when she heard of the Guard call-up. She was certain someone at the student government office had been in contact with city hall. "I suppose I should apologize for not calling about the change in rally plans. I did not call because we did not expect trouble — the student marshals had it under control." She had been in contact with one of the deans and had assumed he was talking to the city. She added, "I was disturbed that he (Anderson) would make such a crucial decision without talking to us. Knowing the Guard was out there made the kids really uptight and nervous."

Tuesday, May 12

The next morning, an incident at one of the Sheridan Road barricades gave strikers a cause for concern. An angry motorist had tried to take a barricade down himself. Upset at the interruption of traffic, he drove his car right up to the edge of one barricade, got out and began dismantling it. Students told him to leave it alone, and a crowd gathered. Plainclothes police arrived and talked to the guy, who engaged in a brief shouting match with the dozen young men behind the barrier. Finally, he returned to his car, backed it away and drove off. It turned out that he had been arrested earlier for obstructing traffic on a nearby avenue, and had said, "If they can do it, why can't I?" The incident heightened fears that the city would use an incident like that as an excuse to use force to clear the street. Others were more concerned about an invasion of the campus by construction workers ala New York City.

A rally was held Tuesday on Deering Meadow to gear up for a campus-wide vote on strike options later in the day, and 600 people had gathered by the time speakers faced the crowd. The co-chair of the Evanston Black Caucus, Ronald Scott Lee, a student at the University of Illinois Circle Campus, spoke about the barricades. "My personal sympathies are entirely with the students," but traffic diverted by the barricades into the Black community was "fast becoming intolerable" and the chance of an incident involving children had increased. He said he was "neutral" on whether to tear them down but wanted to "explain the ramifications" of keeping them up. If they really wanted to improve Evanston, he told them, they needed to volunteer to help townspeople, to form block groups, to talk with residents and convince them that, "White is not always right and Black is not wrong."

Lee also pointedly spoke about the idea of holding a campus memorial for the six Black men killed by police in Augustus, Georgia. The killings had just occurred and there had been discussions of a memorial. Lee said memorial services only served "to get people off the hook. If the [Martin Luther] King memorial had been effective, then Augusta never would have happened."

Student President Jefferson also spoke and addressed the issue head on. She flatly rejected the idea of any memorial as a substitute for effective action, and challenged the crowd that if they were serious, they would do something to make a real change. Supporting Jefferson, Black Panther member "Gypsy" took students to task for not creating interaction with individuals outside the Northwestern community. "In the time that you took to put up those four graves, you weren't out in the community," he said, and lobbed a common Sixties quote at the crowd, "If you're not part of the solution, then you're part of the problem."

Other options for the school to take were offered up. Math Prof. Robert Welland proposed "restocking legislators" with peace candidates. "Unless you change the men in the system," he said, "you will not effect change in the system. You must eliminate those men who groove on destruction." He called for a nationwide coalition to vote out hawks and to form an effort on campus. Another option was to form a student-labor coalition and organize workers at defense plants. Another called for a boycott of banks and a civil disobedient shut down of Chicago's induction center. At one point, seven students got up and tore their draft cards in half, and said they planned to send them to Washington in protest of the war. A good number of speakers endorsed the formation of the New University, an alternative to the school structure. One told the rally that students ought to return to class and continue their anti-war activities, whereas yet another called for an all-out strike.

When the campus community finally took part in the balloting on the different options, over 5,000 people voted. The counting of votes resulted in the New University taking 80% or 4,078 votes; 604 voted to continue the strike and 410 voted to end the strike and return to "business as usual." The New University held the promise of an alternative to the normal school structure, where classes would give students the option of continuing to work on strike goals or return to class.

In the end, Northwestern students voted to return to classes – but to classes that promised to be wholly different than the ones they had prior to the strike. In fact, faculty members in some university departments had already made plans for the alternative structure. But not everyone was happy. Two dozen strikers were dissatisfied with what they called an inherent anti-strike bias in the language on the ballot because it had been written solely by faculty members and wanted a new vote. No one took up their complaint. Plus, 29 professors signed a statement calling for the barricades to be removed "to avoid confrontation with the community."

In terms of outreach to the community, striking students continued their distribution of anti-war leaflets at several shopping centers and at O'Hare Airport. They also estimated they had mobilized 100 volunteers for door-to-door canvassing and had contacted half of Evanston's residences with strike information.

Another outreach effort involved placing full page ads in Chicago's newspapers explaining strike goals. Funding was a major hurdle, as a full-page ad in the *Chicago Tribune* cost $5,000, and more like $1,800 in smaller papers. At a meeting Tuesday afternoon, students also considered placing ads on billboards. In either case, they needed money and planned to solicit funds from Evanston service clubs, like Kiwanis, local businesses, and NU faculty.

That evening, Northwestern's Board of Trustees met in special session and voted to open up the university's stock portfolio, one of the strike demands. University officials pledged to publish the list of the university's stock holding "immediately" as an addendum to the annual report of the university Business Manager. The University Controller said copies of the portfolio would be made available over the next few days.

Wednesday, May 13

Wednesday witnessed the full resumption of classes, and there was an expected calm on the Evanston campus, a normalcy administrators and faculty had hoped would return. But it didn't last long. At a meeting in the Speech Building, members of SDS and some militant allies decided to march on the Naval ROTC facility in Lunt Hall and forcefully remove classified material. They wanted to disrupt "business as usual" of the "living presence of the military" on campus and numbering around 100, marched to Lunt Hall.

One SDS member spoke to the campus newspaper about how all the rallies and speeches had failed. "Our impatience was getting to an explosive point. We decided to disregard the vote to end the strike and go to the basement of Lunt Hall to remove the ROTC." Another said they only wanted to "remove war research and war study materials" which they believed was in the office. And a third said, "The alternate university is a sham. It won't do much to end the war."

Once inside Lunt Hall, protesters began the search for the classified material but it was disrupted when a handful of their compatriots began to overturn desks and smash windows. Others took up a chant, "No trashing! No trashing!" and a type of standoff developed. But it was brief. Any conflict among the radicals evaporated when NROTC instructors barged in to stop the removal of materials and scuffles broke out. One NROTC official yelled out, "If it's a fight you want, it's a fight you'll get!" During the melee, people were pulled out of offices, others were thrown to the floor, some kicked in the head – but in the end, the instructors retreated, some through a window.

By the time campus security officers arrived at Lunt Hall, many protesters had left, but 45 were still in a basement corridor. After briefly resisting police, they were all detained, including seven non-students. Campus security had called Evanston police for assistance and they backed up their paddy wagon to the rear basement door of Lunt Hall and opened its doors – they were going to arrest everyone detained. Student Body President Jefferson arrived and pleaded with officials that the students should be tried by the university and not Cook County. Visibly shaken by the display of student disunity, Jefferson said, "If this university system is real, it should be able to handle things like this." By now, a crowd had gathered outside Lunt Hall.

Minutes later, seven demonstrators walked out the door, yelled "All power to the people!" and willingly got into the paddy wagon. People in the crowd chanted "Let them go! Let them go!" and began to close in on the vehicle. To avoid more conflict, Jefferson approached vice-president Franklin Kreml and the two of them conferred with the Evanston police captain and the campus security police chief. Not too soon after, Jefferson and Kreml announced that charges against NU students would stay within the university, but the six non-students detained would be charged in state court. This wasn't acceptable to some, and for a moment, the idea of trapping police officers inside Lunt Hall until charges were dropped ripped through the crowd. Yelling

"All or none!" students linked arms and pressed up against the doors of the building. Individual officers in the crowd seemed stunned and paralyzed. Students crowded around police cars and two got up on the hoods and yelled, "All or none!" Minutes into the standoff, the chief of campus security, McHugh, warned the crowd, "We have no prisoners, we're coming through." At that, police formed a V-wedge and pushed through the crowd making a path wide enough for themselves and their vehicles, including the paddy wagon and the 6 non-students.

Once police and security departed Lunt Hall, many in the crowd formed up into a spontaneous march to the administrative offices in Rebecca Crown Center. On the way, they ran into Vice-president Roland J Hinz and demanded the university refrain from pressing criminal charges against the non-students. By then, a crowd of some 350 students, non-students and faculty members had reached the squabble. Hinz wouldn't budge and claimed the non-students had come on campus to "trash" the NROTC office, and that if was up to him, he would press trespassing charges against all of them. He said when he arrived at Lunt after the disturbance, he found "substantial damage." Later, the university estimated there had been $5,000 in damage.

While police cleared demonstrators from Lunt Hall, university workers were clearing barricades off of Sheridan Road. Vice-president William Kerr had given instructions to the Buildings and Grounds department to remove the three barricades still remaining and haul all of it to the lakefill. Kerr had received a call from a math professor who told him strikers had concluded that the barricade "no longer served its original tactical or political purpose," and the professor suggested it was a good time for the school to remove them.

Student Tom Hayes told the campus press, "Most students have wanted the barricade to come down." He'd noticed that most of the students had left the barricades and even the red flags had been removed. "The people who lived with it, thought there was no use in defending it anymore." He added the barricades were "not removed to screw the left," and in fact, Hayes had asked Kerr to save the main barricade as "a symbol of the strike." "It means a lot to a lot of people, that some strikers may want to make it a monument." Kerr agreed to save it and have it taken to the lake fill south of the library.

It took university workers 45 minutes to remove the last barricade with a tractor and an acetylene torch but not before several hundred students tried to prevent its removal by staging a curb-to-curb sit-in across Sheridan. The barricades had been up for a week and were part of what students called "Northwestern's People's Park." Vice-president Kerr said it was simply a coincidence that the barricades were removed at the same time that Evanston police were clearing demonstrators from Lunt Hall.

Later, Kerr changed his story. Yes, he had given the order to clear the barricades but only after city officials had claimed that "outside forces might be coming to remove the barricade." To Kerr, that meant state highway cops, Cook County law enforcement or city police – as Sheridan Road was a state highway. Or it could have meant extreme right-wingers such as the group "Loyal Americans Against College Bums" who earlier had threatened to tear down the barricades.

Thursday, May 14

On Thursday, Chancellor J. Roscoe Miller released a statement about the Lunt Hall incident. He stated, "40 people ... attacked and injured NROTC personnel, broke windows, damaged furniture and generally ransacked the premises. On the basis of the evidence, charges against those participating in the destruction at Lunt Hall must be brought. Prompt hearings will be requested." Charges against the students, he said, would be "filed by the university. . .before the University Hearing and Appeals Board." He had been "advised that charges of trespass against non-students would be made in state court." Students' demands that no charges be brought and no suspensions ordered prior to any campus hearings "cannot be accepted," he said, in "a community dedicated to non-violence and due process....," without an inkling of its hypocrisy. He vowed to carry out suspensions if necessary.

Also, within a 12-hour period on Thursday, the university received seven bomb scares resulting in a number of buildings being closed down and temporarily evacuated, including the University Library, a computer center and the Technological Institute. A few phone calls alleging bombs were also made to Chicago newspapers. But no explosives were ever found.

The Daily Northwestern published a report from campus security on the vandalism and property destruction on campus during the strike. Windows had been broken at four buildings, locks had been filled with glue in doors all over school, the walls of Scott Grill – the student eatery and site of many strike meetings – had been redecorated with paintings and quotes, a wrought-iron fence had been removed and used for a barricade, and a number of unoccupied security cars had been vandalized. Reports of theft included a lamp, a chair, drapes and ping-pong tables from Scott Hall, and the repeated pilfering of food from the grill. The report also listed minor damage to landscaping from cars and motorcycles being driven indiscriminately over campus grounds. Then there was all the over-time required for security to work 16 to 20 hours a day, plus the costs of 20 extra men hired through a "rent-a-cop" agency.

Saturday - Sunday

At the Great Lakes Training Center in the Chicago area, all Armed Forces Day activities were canceled. Rear Admiral H. S. Ronkin said it was due to "dissident elements" posing a threat to visitors, although no demonstrators ever materialized. Elsewhere in Chicago at Fort Sheridan, an Armed Forces Day parade and ceremonies were held without incident. There were no politicians in view at the parade, apparently because an appearance would be construed as taking a position on the war. There were only two signs of dissent along the route — a youth waving a skull-and-crossbones flag and another with a placard reading "Are You a Fascist? Think About It."

University of Illinois – Urbana and Champaign

Monday, May 11

In the wee hours of Monday, three fire-bombings were reported—two hit a garage, and a third hit an administration building. Making administrators happy, a non-student was arrested.

The issue of the mass arrest of 100 people on Saturday had churned the campus and the display of heavy-handed police tactics during the arrest added to the pressure from students and some faculty for the resignation of the head of campus security, Paul Doebel. Doebel told the campus press that just before the arrests, he had called for reinforcements because they were under siege from a rock attack. He claimed the head of State Police, a Capt. Moser, had been in charge.

That night, 700 students marched to the Champaign police station and demanded to see the head of the Police Department, Chief Harvey Shirley. Surprising them, Shirley agreed to join the students in marching back to campus and hold a discussion with university officials about the arrests and events of the past week. Once back on campus, the large crowd was addressed by Vice-Chancellor George Frampton who called the mass arrests of 105 people "unjustified." He claimed he didn't know who ordered the arrests but pledged he would do whatever it took to prevent the arrest report of any innocent student being listed on their university record. Frampton urged the crowd to "Rise up and tell Nixon to bring the troops home or resign and take Agnew with him!"

Tuesday, May 12

By Tuesday, strike activism had dropped to about half of what it was, and strike leaders felt it didn't make sense to continue because of concessions made by the administration (demobilizing the National Guard, dropping punitive sanctions against strikers, allowing "liberation classes"). The student government-sponsored strike steering committee called for an end to the picketing of campus buildings "because of lack of participation and to allow picketers to attend liberation classes."

Wednesday, May 13

On Wednesday, the Defense Department's Advance Research Projects Agency announced that they were reviewing their decision to install the controversial $24 million computer at the Illinois campus, known as the Illiac IV super-computer. The super-computer had been targeted by campus anti-war activists because of its DoD funding. In the end, it was never delivered to the University of Illinois but in 1972 was shipped to NASA instead.

Illinois State University – Normal

Monday, May 11

Issues that continued to simmer on the Normal campus at the start of the second strike week were having the American flag lowered to half-staff in honor of the Kent State students and a rising tide of vandalism both on campus and in the nearby town of Normal. President Samuel Braden had made an agreement with antiwar students to have flags lowered during the previous week, but to have all flags raised back up on Monday.

Between Monday afternoon and early Tuesday, there had been a rash of incidents on campus: cherry bombs had been set off in Hovey Hall, the Union and the campus bookstore, red paint had been splattered all over, and there had been an attempted firebombing of the Normal police station. Some officials felt the incidents were meant to pressure the school to keep the flags at half-staff.

Tuesday, May 12

Tuesday morning, a small band of activists tried to lower the flag at the Quad but President Braden personally intervened and told them he refused to break his agreement with strikers and warned the students away. That evening a vacant house owned by the university was severely damaged by a fire of mysterious origins. More vandalism occurred in the local business district and a number of store windows were taken out.

Wednesday, May 13

President Braden on Wednesday morning met with his vice presidents about the increased vandalism. The only solution they came up with was a campus curfew where students would be required to stay in their rooms from midnight Wednesday to 6 am on Friday. When the curfew was announced, faculty and students were shocked by the news and by late afternoon, students were threatening to flaunt the new regulation.

When Normal town officials were informed of the curfew, they placed the entire town under a similar restriction as their solution to the growing number of attacks on businesses and town buildings. Officials from town and the university then set up joint patrols that would patrol the campus and the nearby business district, to be accompanied by police units.

Still, the curfew was a bitter pill and the Academic Senate's Executive Committee met with Braden and eventually persuaded him that faculty-student patrols were a more effective method to prevent vandalism and property destruction than a curfew. In response, Branden made a new arrangement with town officials—the town curfew would remain, but students could move about freely within campus boundaries. Patrols organized by the Academic Senate would guard against incidents on campus and were to be supplemented by 17 Illinois State troopers as a reserve force.

Students were very concerned about any new arrangements for the curfew and an overflow crowd gathered in the Union to learn the outcome of the meeting between Brandon and the Faculty Senate members. After a dean, a professor and the student body president tried to explain the new arrangement, the crowd demanded that Braden speak to them himself that night on why the curfew was necessary. Near 11 pm, 4,000 students assembled on the Quad to hear President Braden. When he spoke, Branden explained that due to the rise in vandalism, there was a likelihood the situation would get worse, and he wanted to prevent anything that would bring in the National Guard and force the university to close. He urged students to stay off the Quad and town streets that night.

After Branden's speech, some students remained in the Union student center to sit out the curfew, while others milled about in nervous anticipation. The campus patrols began at midnight, and faculty leaders and administrators were out in force to keep students calm. Meanwhile, Normal city police patrolled streets close to the campus.

Yet in an indication of the level of tension, around 1 am, a minor incident exploded into a violent confrontation between students and police. Several students returning to their dorms had to cross a city street but were stopped by police and threatened with arrest. Immediately a crowd of 300 rushed to the site and police reinforcements were also brought in. Administrators including President Braden and George Taylor, assistant dean of students, tried to intervene between students and officers, and eventually, Braden convinced the Normal police officers that the university's boundary was actually a block from where the students had been threatened with arrest. With that, a mixed group of city and campus police formed a line at the nearest intersection.

Most of the crowd that had poured out for the incident remained in front of the administration building, while a group of militants used verbal taunts and rocks in an effort to break up the police line. After one volley of rocks, the police line charged the larger group in front of the building, and suddenly there was a mad scramble of students running and police chasing them with batons swinging. Taylor, the assistant dean, was caught in the police rush, knocked to the ground, suffering a head wound that required treatment. Several students also received bruises and minor injuries, as well. The main body of students were persuaded to disperse by the police charge.

After the clash, Normal Mayor Charles Baugh met with university officials in the Union center, and it appeared that the main issue with students was the town curfew. As long as it remained, violent confrontations were a distinct possibility. At everyone's urging, Mayor Baugh gave in and at 4:15 am, Thursday, he ended the town curfew. The mayor, however, made it clear that he would not hesitate to ask for the National Guard if the university could not maintain order. Within an hour the streets around the university were empty, and except for the campus and police patrols, the Quad was quiet.

Thursday, May 14

The calm Thursday morning was a brief respite for the campus. The student-police clash the night before and the resultant lifting of the town curfew had perhaps left many exhausted. But not everyone—during a 30-minute spree around 4 pm, eight fires were started in various halls and buildings on campus. Most were in bathroom wastebaskets and were easily extinguished, but one in a classroom was more serious. Later that evening, well-known civil rights activist Julian Bond spoke to an overflow crowd in Capen Auditorium, and during his speech, another blaze was discovered – this one in Edwards Hall. The administration believed the university was under attack by a conspiracy to disrupt and injure the school.

Friday, May 15

On Friday, a vacuum created by the left-wing's exhaustion from non-stop actions over the previous ten days was filled by the right-wing on campus that saw fit to flex its muscles. A new group called "concerned students within the ISU community" held a noontime rally in McCormick Gym as a counterprotest to those wanting to close the university. Speakers included Normal's Mayor Baugh, conservative Republican State Senator Harber Hall, and the commanding general of the Illinois National Guard. Speakers lashed out at the antiwar movement and at those students and faculty who disrupted the campus. One speaker claimed there would have been more order on campus if the administration had more "backbone" in dealing with SDS and the Black Students Association – this was greeted with enthusiastic applause. A student speaker demanded that the SDS faculty advisor be fired due to his political activities and received an ovation.

Southern Illinois University- Carbondale
Monday, May 11

The campus calm on Monday was reinforced by the withdrawal of the National Guard that had been deployed to the campus and the surrounding town of Carbondale during the previous week to assist police in enforcing a curfew. Since Friday and over the weekend, an astonishing number of people had been arrested – 470 – nearly a third for curfew violations. Many of those detained were not students.

Tuesday, May 12

What observers called "an historic night" at the Carbondale campus began with a 6 pm rally of 700 in front of Morris Library. Rev. Matt Garrett told the crowd that President Delyte Morris had recently been making public pronouncements that the campus was not closing. "Morris was on TV today, and said this place is not going to shut down. I think we can change his mind. We've done our thing, but this university doesn't believe it needs to be shut down. We're going to show them. We're going to burn it to the ground if we have to, but don't get caught."

Bill Moffett of the New Student Mobilization also spoke and called for a march to the president's house to demand he close the school. "How many want to march now?" he asked and the crowd roared its approval. "I'm for it," Moffett said, "but we want an orderly, peaceful, militant anti-war demonstration. We don't want a physical confrontation." It was just past 7:30 when the crowd moved and as they marched past University City, they picked up more students. They chanted, "Come on people, it's your school too!" The curfew had begun but no police were in sight.

By the time the massive throng assembled on the lawn and grounds outside President Morris' home and office, they were between 4,000 and 6,000 strong. Most sat down on the grass and chanted, "On Strike — Shut It Down!" A few rocks were thrown through office windows and some in the crowd left in disgust. Morris and his wife had been evacuated earlier, so Chancellor Robert MacVicar met with demonstrators.

Protest organizers told MacVicar that the campus needed to be closed in protest of the war in Indochina. MacVicar – impressed with the size and attitude of the crowd – left momentarily to consult by phone with both President Morris and Illinois Gov. Richard B. Ogilvie. And here history was made. MacVicar returned and addressed the massive crowd. "We have done the only thing that is appropriate," he declared. "The president has given me permission to announce that the university will be closed." Immediately, thousands leaped to their feet and roared. People embraced, pounded each other's shoulders, shook hands. MacVicar added that students enrolled for spring quarter would receive credit and grades to date. There were more cheers and another round of applause.

"I am going back to the telephone," MacVicar said, "to advise the president to convene the board (of trustees) tonight. I am going to recommend that it is no longer possible for this university to operate on a normal schedule." He told the students, while adding a jab, "You have achieved your victory, now don't lose it with the activities of a few." People in the crowd began chanting "Peace! Peace! Peace!"

In downtown Carbondale, pandemonium broke out when word of MacVicar's announcement was heard. Students joyously ran into the streets and many chanted, "Close it now! Close it now!" It was reported that 10,000 students took over downtown Carbondale that night and held a victory carnival that lasted well into the morning.

Wednesday, May 13

The day after Chancellor MacVicar's historic announcement, the administration tried to walk it back. Officials announced a vote would be taken on Thursday by students, faculty, and staff to determine whether the majority wanted the campus to remain closed. Clearly, some in the administration hoped the campus community as a whole would step back from the precipice of closure. Meanwhile, the National Guard, which had just been withdrawn from Carbondale two days earlier, was recalled to the campus.

Thursday, May 14

On Thursday, nearly 12,000 people from the campus community voted on whether to keep the campus closed the rest of the semester. 8,224 voted for closure, two-thirds, while 3,675 were opposed.

Friday, May 15

The Board of Trustees met Friday and fearing "imminent danger to life and property" decided to follow the will of the majority and close the campus for the remainder of the semester. SIU was to be officially closed and dorms were to be shuttered come May 18, the following Monday.

Saturday, May 16

Two disturbing incidents occurred on Saturday. In the morning, an explosion rocked the residence of three SIU students on the eastern side of Carbondale causing the amputation of one man's leg and damaging a woman's eardrums. Reportedly, dozens of dynamite caps and several weapons were found inside. All three were arrested and held on $4500 bail. The FBI was brought in to investigate the incident.

Then that evening, 15 students were arrested after they were tear gassed inside their house on Bridge Street. They were in their living room when a platoon of Guardsmen appeared in the backyard and twenty police officers showed up on the front porch. More than a dozen tear gas canisters were lobbed through windows, and police blocked doors as people tried to fight their way out. The six women and nine men arrested were charged with illegal assembly. Police had no search warrants, had not knocked first and failed to warn those being arrested of their rights. The incident began popularly known as the "Bridge Street Massacre," and the students became a local *cause celebre*.

At **Lindenwood College** on Monday, the faculty sponsored a moratorium on "business as usual" with workshops on American foreign policy.

At **Illinois Wesleyan University**, in what officials termed "definite arson," fires broke out on Tuesday at opposite ends of the music building. Damage was extensive and estimated at $100,000. It was not known if there was any connection between recent anti-war protests and the fires.

At noon on Saturday, May 16, Black students at **Northern Illinois University** DeKalb staged a protest against the killings of the Black men at Jackson State College and in Augusta, Georgia. In response to demands by Black students and faculty, President Rhoten Smith announced a two-day moratorium of classes. A group of white students, 15 of whom were dorm reps, and two faculty members met and agreed to support all the demands or proposed actions of the Black students. One demand was for President Smith to write a formal letter to Mississippi Governor Lester Maddox condemning the Jackson State killings.

Wisconsin

University of Wisconsin – Milwaukee
Tuesday, May 12

For a week, strike headquarters had been run out of the Student Union building, but Chancellor Martin Klotsche had other ideas. Having already declared a "state of emergency" for the campus the previous Thursday, Klotshce made the announcement on Tuesday that he was ordering the entire building shut down. Campus police moved in and pushed 200 angry students out of the student center. Strikers viewed this as a naked effort to decapitate the strike.

People pushed out of the building regrouped in front of Mitchell Hall and began a protest of the chancellor's action. Within an hour, another 300 students joined them, and the large crowd then marched to the library, through the campus and swung back and returned to the Union building, now empty. Hundreds streamed in through a side door left open and began the re-occupation of the student union building. Students cleaned the building with brooms and mops, while others set up a first aid station and a "people's kitchen." Replenished with food, several hundred strikers spent the night in the liberated building.

Later Tuesday, the faculty held an historic and remarkable meeting. First, they condemned the Chancellor's use of police to clear out and close down the Union. They then moved their meeting over to the Union building to ensure occupying students were safe from police if there was another attempt to close the building. The faculty session went way into the night.

Wednesday, May 13

In response to the faculty's condemnation, Chancellor Klotsche on Wednesday declared the faculty meeting had been "unofficial" and any decisions made non-binding. Despite the chancellor's statement, the faculty reconvened their meeting in the Union. Meanwhile, strikers tried to take over the student campus newspaper, but were forced by the administration to issue their own publication.

Thursday, May 14

The focus for strikers on Thursday was to keep the Union Building open and its occupation going. Workshops were set up in various rooms, the faculty continued to meet inside, strikers worked on the new "strike" newspaper, music students gave a free concert in the "People's Hilton" and wild frisbee games were played in the ballroom. All the while there was the suspense that police would move in and close the building again.

On another front, students from campus had joined picket lines over the past week with members of the United Electrical Workers, Local 1111, who were on strike at Allen-Bradley, an electronics plant. The students had been warmly received by the workers, and on Thursday, they successfully turned away a small group of their fellow UWM students who appeared at the plant as strike-breakers.

Friday, May 15

Friday was the fourth day of the occupation of the Student Union. The first issue of "*Strike*" was published, numerous cultural activities were held in the ballroom, including performances of Bertolt Brecht's "The Measures Taken" and a W.C. Fields flick. And members of the Women's Liberation group involved in the occupation declared they were boycotting the kitchen.

Saturday, May 16

On Saturday, students from UWM joined a crowd in front of the House of Corrections in Milwaukee to support the "Milwaukee Three," local Black Panthers facing attempted murder charges of a police officer. Panthers Booker Collins, Jessie White and Earl Levrettes contended they all had been brutally beaten on six separate occasions within 24 hours after their arrest. All were found guilty; Collins and White were given 30-year sentences and Levrettes was eventually given ten after initially skipping bail.

University of Wisconsin in Madison

Monday, May 11

In its second week, the student strike on the Madison campus was beset with indecision and a lack of direction, reflecting exhaustion and problems with the strike's leadership. The previous week had been chaotic and had witnessed five nights of clashes between protesters and police. So, on Monday night at a rally on Union Terrace of 2,000 people, it was no surprise that the crowd reached a consensus against another night of violence. Instead, they decided to hold a Tuesday morning rally and make one final push to close down the school. In an effort to get everyone to attend, people went out to canvass the dorm complexes and neighborhoods.

Tuesday, May 12

The Tuesday morning rally had a very disappointing turnout – only some 300 people showed up. The plan was to march up Bascom Hill and form picket lines at the buildings, but when protesters arrived near the top, they were outnumbered by police and Guardsmen. Two dozen Guard jeeps and a score of patrol cars that arrived added to the intimidating show of force. Police verbally harassed protesters and few were arrested for failure to show student IDs. Students did set up picket lines but discontinued them after less than two hours after most of the crowd had dispersed.

A much larger crowd of 2,000 did show up at a 1 pm rally. From the rally, demonstrators moved from building to building, blocked doorways and rang hallways with strike chants. A scuffle at the Social Science building resulted in three arrests, but the vast majority kept the momentum going through the tense campus. Around 3:30 the crowd broke up. In total, 11 people had been arrested, mostly for failure to possess student ID's. Later, campus security reported the discovery of five to 10 Molotov cocktails in the Humanities, Commerce and Bascom buildings.

That night's rally of 1,000 people in the Union's Great Hall showed the strike leadership's inability to continue the strike. Amidst the confusion, two main proposals on tactics emerged. One, open up the university and turn it into an "Anti-war University" by using its facilities for strike activities. Or two, build a campaign to end counterinsurgency research at the university. Other tactics proposed ran the gamut—picketing, noise-making to interrupt classes, disruption of classes from "the inside" or street-fighting. After two hours of arguments, polemics and shouting, the meeting finally adjourned without a consensus. No one would admit it, but the student strike was collapsing. This was due to a number of factors, one probably just the pure exhaustion from multiple nights of running battles with police and National Guard.

Thursday, May 14

A relative calm descended on the Madison campus Thursday. Peaceful strike activities continued and there were no incidents of violence or confrontations between students and Guardsmen. In fact, National Guard commanders issued orders prohibiting any guardsman from fraternizing with students or getting involved in the campus antiwar movement.

Other Wisconsin Colleges

Early Monday at **Marquette University**, 500 residents of a men's dorm had to evacuate when it was firebombed—damage was estimated at $600. On Thursday, university president Father John Raynor declared in a statement to the campus community just before finals, if professors agreed, students could take their finals in the fall or accept final grades based on course work already completed. According to a university spokesperson, roughly 700 of the 3,000 students who resided in the dormitories soon left the campus.

On Wednesday, at **Wisconsin State College**, the Student Association executive board voted to seek a court injunction against President Roger E. Guiles' decision to temporarily suspend two students. They had been arrested on charges of possession of Molotov cocktails during the Algoma Road disturbance the week previous. Vice-president Mike Mullen moved to allocate up to $75 to get an injunction, which passed 3 to 1. Mullen said he would travel to Madison himself to seek the injunction. The two freshmen charged had been temporarily suspended pending the outcome of a formal hearing the upcoming week.

On Tuesday 400 students and faculty members at **Wisconsin State University** in Whitewater rallied against ROTC, and 70 demonstrators marched through the ROTC building without incident.

Minnesota

University of Minnesota – Twin Cities

Monday, May 11

On Monday, the first issue of "Strike Action" announced that the Strike Steering Committee had met on Sunday and voted to continue the strike. It also announced that the economic boycott committee was part of an effort at organizing a massive descent on American banks when people would withdraw funds from their accounts. It editorialized, "Massive national boycotts of selected 'soft' targets and massive national withdrawals from the banks will both test the power of the strike constituency and move rapidly toward an end to the debacle in SE Asia."

"Strike Action" also published a glowing report about an outreach project called "Community Action Center" which had brought students and community people together to conduct outreach about the war and the strike. Twenty-five "contact centers" had been established in churches, synagogues, neighborhood centers, and homes to facilitate the outreach. The centers in turn coordinated the many volunteers who had "poured out from the community and area colleges" to do door-to-door work, go into high schools, set up booths at shopping malls and talk with local groups. Some contact centers had been so successful they evolved into viable organizations themselves, coordinating dozens of people, organizing teach-ins and get-togethers with small church groups.

Overall, organizers of the project said it involved 500 to 1,000 people working in the community with students. The report claimed the outreach teams received "favorable response from most homes covered," because "the overwhelming majority of citizens are concerned about the crisis in the country today." The project had a few difficulties, including when canvassers in a neighborhood called Columbia Heights had to obtain a permit from police before they could go door-to-door.

"Strike Action" also covered anti-war work in local high schools and reported that at the end of the previous week, "over 65 high schools were mobilized." There had been a successful student walkout at St. Louis Park High School, one at Highland Park High with afternoon seminars, and a dismissal of classes for a full day at Edina High.

Wednesday, May 13

On Wednesday, there was a ploy by administrators and conservative students to cut off support for the strike by the Union student center, but a Board of Governors vote on discontinuing support of the strike failed by a vote of 6 to 4. A motion to extend an additional $500 for the Union center facilities and services was approved by a vote of 9 to 1.

Thursday, May 14

More than 2,000 students participated in a May 14 joint anti-war protest and mock "graduation." Most wore white headbands with peace symbols and grooved to the music of a local rock band. During a brief invocation by the Reverend Vincent Hawkinson, he prayed, "God, thank you for a few religious people who care more about life after birth than life after death." During the ceremony, 99 men turned in their draft cards, which were collected and forwarded to Princeton University, which in turn would mail them to the Selective Service along with thousands of other cards from colleges across the country.

Friday, May 15

On Friday, numerous UM students attended a concert by the Jefferson Airplane in Bloomington, a small town about ten minutes south. Afterwards, one of the singers, Marty Balin, along with two stagehands were busted for grass by Bloomington police. The three were reportedly held without charge in jail over the weekend in order to appear in court on Monday the 18th.

St. Olaf College – Northfield

"Hear ye! Hear ye! The United States District Court, District of Minnesota, is now in session, Commissioner Renfred presiding," rang out at the first formal hearing on Wednesday, May 13, for the 88 St. Olaf and Carleton students arrested a week earlier. The student defendants were in the new federal building, directly across the street from the old one where they had been arrested.

One defendant pled guilty, explaining that she was at the protest "to make a point and we made it." The other 87 decided to plead not guilty and go to trial. Their attorneys planned to argue that their right to free speech justified the sit-in, and that they were not actually breaking the law they were charged with, as the federal building doors were locked, hence they were not actually blocking the entrance.

Carleton College – Northfield

On Thursday, there was a revival of interest on campus in women's liberation when a well-publicized meeting drew about 40 students and faculty, whereas earlier efforts had only generated a handful. An organizer, Carol Blair, said, "We hope to involve more people, including men, than we had at our small discussions earlier this term." One positive development to come out of the meeting was the formation of several women's rap groups for the dorms, with plans to continue them through the term. Another organizer, Joann H. told the campus press, "The purpose of the rap groups is to increase our awareness of our own attitudes and the cultural patterns we were brought up to follow. Talking about it helps us discover what these patterns are and how they affect us. Once women are aware of these patterns and attitudes, each woman must relate it to her own life."

One participant said, "For me, the goal of women's lib is to get rid of the terms 'men's roles' and 'women's roles' and have each person considered as an individual." Another added this would lead to a fuller existence for both men and women. Other issues discussed included how relationships between women were perverted by competition for men, how women perceived other women's ideas as "silly" or "gossipy" and not along intellectual lines. Joann pointed out, "Evidence of this can be seen by looking at the leadership of the strike on this campus — it's almost entirely male. Women are hesitant to speak out when men are around."

Student Ellen recounted her efforts to organize a course next year in the history of women in society. It would begin with an anthropological background, tracing women's development through the ages, she said. She had researched the Equal Opportunity Commission in Washington and legal remedies to sexual discrimination. There was also talk at the meeting about forming an action group next year that would work on abortion reform, discrimination against women, and other women's issues.

The Carleton College Board of Trustees met on Saturday, May 16, and faced two historic items of business on their agenda. President John Nason called it a "milestone" in the school's history, a proposal that would allow students, faculty, administrators and trustees to have representation on the highest decision-making body of the college. After a short discussion, it was approved with only one dissenting vote.

The second item, much more problematic, proposed that the entire college community vote in a referendum on Carleton's General Motors stocks. Alternatives were offered by students and a faculty member which were identical to proposals by consumer advocate Ralph Nader and his "Campaign GM." Issues of GM's failures on pollution control, on safety issues, and on minority hiring were raised, but in the end, the trustees insisted the college should not take "a political stand," and voted down any referendum. Once they made this decision, the trustees decided unilaterally to vote for Carleton's 8,414 GM shares in favor of management and against Ralph Nader's proposals.

Students and faculty at **University of Minnesota Morris** organized a campaign in mid-May in support of the McGovern-Hatfield amendment. A campus assembly paid a silent tribute to the two young Black men killed by police at Jackson State in Mississippi.

At **Moorhead State College** (renamed **Minnesota State University at Moorhead**) students on Thursday voted 1,616 to 484 to have "liberated" classes for the remaining three weeks of the year in order to discuss the national crisis. Also, for two days Moorhead students hosted a series of all-day workshops at a "Movement Conference"—a prelude to regional demonstrations over the weekend against anti-ballistic missiles.

Iowa

University of Iowa – Iowa City

As picket lines circulated in front of several campus buildings on Tuesday, the administration announced that nearly 12,000 students – two-thirds of the student body – had signed up for one of President William Boyd's grading options and were preparing to leave campus. The previous Sunday, Boyd had made a compromise with students: the university would remain open until the end of the semester, and students could leave and not be required to take any more classes or finals. He had outlined several options for students, including returning home without academic sanctions.

The student press queried students on their reasons in choosing the options. Some said they did it to protect high grades they already had. Others wanted to avoid failing in classes they weren't doing well in, and some undoubtedly simply wanted to get off campus – especially, perhaps, after their school had witnessed one of the largest mass arrests in the state's history. A few students admitted their parents were fearful, while many said they didn't feel endangered at all. In essence, the university was still open, and classes were still being held, but by Tuesday two out of three students were in the process of leaving campus.

Only 40 students attended a Wednesday night meeting on May 13 to discuss further strike action, and it was clear it was over. The student base had evaporated. National Guardsmen and Highway Patrol officers had withdrawn and for the next two weeks, there would only be a skeleton of classes continuing.

On Tuesday at **Cornell College**, President Samuel Enoch Stumpf announced that college trustees had added a graduating senior to their board and had pledged to meet more often with students and faculty. After commencement, a study workshop was organized with 35 students and faculty members who met and discussed curriculum innovation, the governance of the college and the quality of student life.

At **Grinnell College**, 50 miles or so due west from Iowa City, antiwar protests were so intense that by mid-month, the administration closed the school down and ordered all students to leave immediately.

Missouri

University of Missouri, St Louis
Monday, May 11

The campus press, *The Current*, ran an article Monday on how Black students viewed the strike. Only a few Black students had been seen participating, so reporters sought out their opinions. They spoke with Rod McLean, who was involved in strike efforts and had helped organize the Miss Black contest on campus. McLean said the strike definitely had an impact outside the university. "Whites have shown that they can turn out to gain the support of others." Yet, he contrasted what had happened at UMSL with **Saint Louis University** where Black students "used the occasion to gain support from those whites who are becoming more conscious of Black problems. I wish that Black students at UMSL could have come together in a similar fashion, not necessarily to strike, but to bring attention to injustices against Blacks."

Michael Lewis, a director of the Association of Black Collegians (ABC), said the strike was effective nationally and had brought public attention to the presence of American troops in Cambodia and the death of four students at Kent State University. However, the strike had "not much effect at UMSL." The ways Black students participated at UMSL, he said, like his group, were in counseling Black high school students and working for deferred tuition payments.

Mike Jones, Executive Director of ABC, had a different take. Jones said Blacks have learned that "as a means of instituting change, strikes are not effective. A strike at a university doesn't mean anything to most people, Black or white." The strike would have little effect on policy on Southeast Asia, except to "tone down Nixon." Jones also doubted whether whites were aware of the injustices Blacks faced and contrasted the strikes following the deaths at Kent State to the lack of white response following the deaths of three Black students at South Carolina State College in February 1968. Forty students had also been injured in an Orangeburg, S. C., incident when Black students attempted to integrate a movie theater.

Reporters also spoke with Pat Boone, Miss Black UMSL. Boone told them that "closer bonds" between Black students at Saint Louis University allowed them to organize more successfully than Black students at UMSL. In sum, the reporters found that three of the four Black students interviewed sympathized with the strike effort.

Wednesday, May 13

By Wednesday, strikers felt a victory of sorts for the strike when 129 faculty members ended up signing a petition supporting the McGovern—Hatfield- Hughes- Goodell amendment in the US Senate. If passed, it would cut off funds for military actions in Cambodia, Laos, and Vietnam at various dates over the year and require the withdrawal of all military personnel from Vietnam by June 30, 1971.

Over the course of the week, groups of faculty and students formed to carry out an ambitious strike agenda – they set up a speaker's bureau, scheduled teach-ins, mobilized their fellow students at protest actions and organized political canvassing in local neighborhoods of St Louis.

University of Missouri – Columbia

Monday, May 11

On Monday, May 11, the largest demonstrations in the university's history took place when 3,000 protesters rallied on the Francis Quadrangle. The massive crowd sent delegates to Chancellor John Schwada's office to call on him to make an official statement condemning the Vietnam war. The administration's response? They locked the chancellor's office. Angry, dozens spontaneously sat down outside the office. Within minutes, campus police moved in and detained 32 people for trespassing—but shortly afterwards, all were released without charges.

Chancellor Schwada not only continued his refusal to speak out about the war or Kent State and continue his crack-down on campus dissent but upped the ante. Immediately following the huge demonstration, he enacted a set of strict "emergency regulations" which banned groups of three or more from congregating and banned the use of loudspeakers or bullhorns on campus.

Tuesday, May 12

A number of faculty members had canceled classes to enable students to participate in antiwar demonstrations and memorials for Kent State. On Tuesday, a group of faculty, students and administrators came to an agreement over how students who missed classes would be treated and how grades would be determined. Students were to be given a variety of options for taking finals and receiving grades, similar to other schools.

That seemed to be the end of the matter. But, when the Board of Curators met later in the week, they repudiated the agreement. They insisted faculty members and students needed to be disciplined, that grades and degrees needed to be withheld for those who had missed classes. They went further—they suspended the head of the Sociology Department, Daryl Hobbs, for not complying with the administration's "requests" to submit the names of faculty who had dismissed classes and who had given grades to students for work completed.

Yet, when the curators dismissed another professor for similar reasons, this was too much for the American Association of University Professors, who stepped in and formally censured the university. The censure lasted until 1981.

Saint Louis University

Beginning Monday, May 11, the campus experienced a wave of protests, sparked by Black students who had issues with the administration over racism at the school. Their main accusation had been against a white security guard for his racist behavior toward an African-American counselor. Because of the tension, President Paul Reinert obtained a temporary restraining order prohibiting campus disruptions.

A negotiating meeting was held Tuesday between school officials and trustees with a Black student delegation to rescind the restraining order, but officials refused. In response, the Black delegation walked out—they and their colleagues then initiated their own strike. They picketed classroom buildings and distributed leaflets that denounced the university's refusal to meet their demands.

However, there were several ugly incidents between striking African-American students and white students – and these led to renewed talks on Thursday. Finally, the administration agreed to a temporary suspension of the security guard, pending an investigation. On their part, Black students agreed to participate in further discussions with the administration.

Students at **Lincoln University** in Jefferson City pressured the president of the school to hold a memorium over the deaths at Kent State. On Tuesday, May 12, President Walter Daniel responded and announced that on May 20 the university family could "express its deep concerns for recent social occurrences" and because "a university should not and cannot remain aloof from events in its surroundings, Lincoln University places aside its normal academic routine on this day in order to focus upon these concerns." The school was an historic-Black public university, founded in 1866 by African-American veterans of the Civil War.

A day of protest on the **University of Missouri Kansas City** campus Monday included a rally and discussion groups on the Southeast Asian war, campus turmoil, and "minority group problems" in American society.

An anti-war rally on Monday at the campus of **Penn Valley Community College** began with a guerilla theater skit satirizing President Nixon as a puppet of the military-industrial complex.

Kansas

Over 2,000 students from the **University of Kansas** in Lawrence and other state schools gathered on the steps of the statehouse in Topeka on Wednesday, May 13, for a silent, motionless vigil against the war. After 15 minutes of silence, the entire crowd raised their clasped hands over their heads in a symbolic gesture of militant unity. Earlier, students had presented petitions to Kansas Governor Robert Docking urging him to call a special session of the state legislature to pass a law to prohibit young Kansan men from serving in the Vietnam war.

On Thursday, the 14th, at **Kansas State University** in Manhattan, a small explosive device went off and shattered several windows in the Mechanical Arts Building, which housed Army ROTC offices and classrooms. Dellinger Hall, a men's dormitory, was evacuated about 30 minutes later when a bomb threat was called in to the dorm switchboard. Both incidents were believed related to anti- war protests.

That weekend at the **Fort Riley** Army base, servicemen and their supporters held an antiwar rally attended by 1300 people, including an estimated 400 GIs. John Froines of the Chicago 8 and an editor of the *AWOL Press* spoke. Organizers were so encouraged with the response, that they began plans to start a local GI coffeehouse project.

Nebraska
University of Nebraska, Lincoln
Monday, May 11

On Monday morning, several thousand students filled the Coliseum to hear the results of a vote on the future of the strike that had been taken Sunday night at a university town hall meeting. When the numbers were announced – 1,357 opposed to the strike and 1,030 in favor—several hundred students walked out and later vowed to continue strike activities for the remainder of the week.

Wednesday, May 13

About 4 in the morning on Wednesday, campus police saw flames shooting out of a ground floor window of the Nebraska Student Union. When firemen arrived, they found two firebombs that had been tossed inside burning in a dining room. Two wooden chairs and some carpet were damaged. And later, two students were charged with arson.

That morning, despite a defeat by a close vote on Monday, students sympathetic to the strike tried a different tactic. They erected several tents on the north lawn of Love Library and called the settlement "the College of Life – a vehicle for educational reform." They organized discussions on cultural alternatives and educational reforms which involved dozens of students. The "happening" was so successful, that on two different occasions, administration officials ordered the tents removed. And after strikers appealed to President Joseph Soshnik, he countermanded the removal orders but only allowed one large tent for daytime discussions. The College of Life lasted until the last week of classes but perished in a heavy rainstorm. Soshnik refused to allow its resurrection.

Friday, May 15

In response to the murders of the two African-American men at Jackson State, two memorial services were held on the Lincoln campus. At the first, about 40 people—mostly Black—gathered at Memorial Stadium to lower the flag. The president of the African-American Concerned Students, Al Lewis, asked, "Where were all the artificial white liberals?" Then a candlelight memorial was held that evening on the north lawn of Love Library, attended by roughly 150 people including President and Mrs. Soshnik. After Soshnik spoke, there were prayers, more remarks, an eulogy, and then a speaker read a poem by a Black Lincoln sixth-grader:

> "Black kids are black and play in the ghetto,
> White kids are white and play in the meadow,
> Some black people like it and some people don't,
> Some white people don't care, and some never learn."

Friday's campus paper, *Lincoln Star*, published an editorial directed at three state senators who had been critical of Nebraska anti-war demonstrations. After congratulating NU students for their non-violent protests, it ended, "It's too bad the senators couldn't see fit to commend the University for the generally peaceful and responsible protest activities by students and faculty and the near-perfect manner in which the administration responded."

Hiram Scott College - Scottsbluff

On Monday, the Scottsbluff campus in the Nebraska panhandle experienced its very first anti-Vietnam war demonstration. An estimated 450 students assembled on the south lawn of the Library Science building and listened to speakers denounce the Vietnam war, the Cambodian invasion and Kent State. Dr. Joseph Meeker of the English department said Nixon's move into Cambodia was illegal and those who supported it were the ones against the law—rather than those who opposed the war. Student Gus Scully called on students to be more than just against the war, but to be leaders in what they believed in.

A sociology instructor, Dr. Nagin Sheth, accused Nixon of being responsible for the deaths at Kent State and countless more in South Vietnam. He proposed a program that called for draft evasion, a boycott of weapon producing corporations and a refusal to pay income taxes. Students gave him a standing ovation. The campus American flag had already been lowered to half-staff following Kent State on the administration's initiative and students responded by keeping protests peaceful. (In December 1970, the trustees of Hiram Scott College declared bankruptcy, and in 1974 the buildings and grounds were acquired by the University of Nebraska.)

At **South Dakota State University** about 50 students splintered off from the crowd of 400 after an uneventful May 15th anti-war rally to confront the university president, Hilton Briggs, about an official campus response to the national crisis. The group met Briggs in his office, and later witnesses claimed one student had knocked Briggs to the floor after he had tried to force the student out of a chair. (The main library was later named after Briggs.)

About 100 students gathered mid-week at the **Dakota State College** administration building to discuss Cambodia and Kent State with the college president, Dr. Harry Pitkin Bowes, and to request the campus flag be lowered to half-staff. Demonstrators chanted and clapped their hands in unison but Bowes refused to respond. Immediately, students staged a sit-in outside his office and vowed to remain until he agreed to hold a conference the next day on the issues.

Strike activities also occurred on the campus of **Northern State College** in Aberdeen according to the National Strike Center at Brandeis University.

University of North Dakota - Grand Forks
Monday, May 11

The big campus news on Monday was the cancellation of the annual Military Governor's Day scheduled for that Friday by President George Starcher, "because of tensions and concerns nationwide, and on our campus in recent weeks." Strikers hailed it as a victory—it had been one of their demands.

400 students mobilized for a 10 am march to downtown Grand Forks, hiked the 20 blocks to the county courthouse, and held a brief rally on the lawn. Speakers spoke against the war and explored the dimensions of effective dissent. Later back on campus, 1,000 people at 4 pm attended an all-campus meeting to vote on proposals over academic credit and whether to call on Nixon to immediately withdraw all troops from Southeast Asia. Both proposals passed and were sent on to the University Senate. The

academic proposal included one option that allowed students to drop classes to work on the strike without sanction.

Tuesday, May 12

Tuesday was the day students "bombed the ROTC." They attached messages of peace and love to paper airplanes they made, gathered in front of the campus ROTC building and threw their planes at the military facility. Since "the military solves its problems with bombs, we thought we might try that solution," their leaflet stated.

Friday, May 15

Friday's campus "Strike Newsletter" attempted a brief evaluation of the 12-day campus strike. Among victories, it counted the cancellation of the Military Governors Day, "the campus police have been disarmed" and "some kind of academic amnesty – not as broad as we had hoped but more than we had expected – has been granted." Crucial issues had been raised and a new student awareness had developed. "The university's failure to react to the central issues of the strike – the war and exploitation - has brought UND students to a realization of the unresponsive and undemocratic nature of this institution. This is a partial victory." The evaluation failed to mention the three bomb scares and the firebombing at Oxford Hall, where damage was minimal.

Scores of UND students attended a "Movement Conference" at **Moorhead State College** in Minnesota and took part in a series of all-day workshops on Thursday and Friday. The conference was the jumping-off point for a weekend of anti-nuclear missile protests called the "Festival of Love and Life." Workshops included, "The Urban Guerilla," American Imperialism, the Relevancy of Education, Women's Liberation, draft counseling, economic oppression, the Mexican-American Migrant workers, ABM (the anti- ballistic missile system), and the military-industrial complex.

The focus of anti-nuke activists shifted to the UND Grand Forks campus for a nighttime rally that included Dave Dellinger and John Froines along with folksinger Phil Ochs. Dellinger, Froines and Ochs had earlier participated at a coffeehouse event near the Grand Forks Air Force Base sponsored by GIs and GI Wives for Peace, attended by about 50 GIs.

Saturday, May 16

At 9 am Saturday morning, buses left the UND Student Union bound for Nekoma, nearly 100 miles northwest and the site of the regional demonstration against nuclear missile sites. 1,000 protesters, including active duty GI's, assembled at Nekoma for a short rally and then trekked the one mile to the missile site. They held a series of symbolic acts, including a kite-flying contest, the planting of durum wheat and the digging and filling up of holes.

In mid-May, the Governor of North Dakota, William Guy, met with about 2,000 students, and afterwards, he informed President Nixon that there would be no National Guard troops from North Dakota to counter anti-war protesters. Gov. Guy also arranged a plan giving all state construction workers a day off with pay in early November, presumably to engage in political activities.

Southwest

University of Oklahoma – Norman

Antiwar students on Tuesday peacefully demonstrated during an Armed Forces Day annual awards ceremony for ROTC cadets held inside the campus stadium. Over the week, pickets appeared outside campus buildings and during a demonstration a few students publicly burned their draft cards. In response, a small group of counterdemonstrators on the sidelines harassed and spat at them. Also, during the week, the university singled out seven students for disciplining for their role in a campus protest on May 5 that had resulted in an ugly clash between students and police, where three had been arrested. By mid-May, an uneasy calm had settled over the campus and administrators breathed a sigh of relief.

At **North Texas State University**, morning classes on Monday were cancelled to allow students to participate in a memorial for the Kent State students.

On Saturday, Armed Forces Day, two GI-sponsored protests occurred in Texas. Outside **Fort Hood**, GIs and their supporters held a rally and then marched through the town of Killeen. Between 800 and 900 service people marched in the street and another 500-600 followed on the sidewalks. Local police harassed the rally by surrounding the site, making it difficult for people to get in. (In 2023, the fort's name was changed to **Fort Cavazos**.)

In El Paso, near **Fort Bliss**, GIs held an anti-war folk and rock music festival with up to 2,000 participants – many of them GIs. Six months earlier, repression against anti-war soldiers had been so intense that GIs had sent over 100 letters with local newspaper accounts to Congressional representatives. Strangely, to a great degree, the repression at Ft Bliss stopped.

University of New Mexico – Albuquerque

On Saturday, the 130 or so people arrested at the University of New Mexico the previous day were released on their own recognizance. They had been arrested during a sit-in that occurred just prior to the bayoneting of 11 people by National Guardsmen. On Monday, May 11, the Albuquerque District Attorney filed criminal trespass complaints against all of them, but the judge disagreed and dismissed all the charges. Still, university administrators placed them on "social probation," which meant that if they committed other campus violations, they would be suspended.

On Tuesday, two-thirds of the campus custodians went on strike for higher wages and an end to the war. Of the 98 custodians, 66 went on strike but only the student members of the custodian crew raised peace as a demand.

University of Arizona – Tucson

On Monday, a flyer appeared on the Tucson campus and announced the school was "On Strike" and that the strike was a "show of solidarity with universities, colleges, and high schools all over the nation" to force Nixon and his military advisors to end the war. Included was a schedule of the day's events: picketing at all university entrances at 8 am, a rally on the mall at 10 am, and at noon, a Show of Solidarity – a strike meeting on the Student Union steps.

Faculty members had fastened together what they called the Experimental Studies Program, an alternative to the standard fare found in classrooms. And by the beginning of the week, the program was offering 14 seminars in which students could attend for credit if they had a faculty member's authorization. Some of the courses offered included, "The Perpetual University," "The University in the 1970's," "Crisis in the Community," "Left and Right Wing Revolutions," "Revolution in the Third World," and "Why Nixon Did What He Did."

Rocky Mountains
University of Denver

"Woodstock West" – the counter-cultural and anti-war encampment of tents and wood structures—remained over the weekend. But by 7 am on Monday, it faced a combined force of law enforcement including 200 to 250 Denver police and some 40 state troopers. Without warning, officers swept through the encampment and evicted most of the occupiers—one report estimated up to 1,000 people were on site. The vast majority left peacefully but 20 to 30 people refused and they were arrested, including two faculty members, and charged with violations of a 1969 campus disorder law. Police then formed a line around the perimeter of Woodstock West while maintenance crews dismantled it.

Once police departed, however, a funny thing happened. Within minutes, up to 600 students returned to the site and began building "Woodstock West II." Several teepees near the library had been ignored and were dragged over to the main encampment and what was left of Woodstock West I was retrieved from the dump. This time, students used "heavier nails and bigger beams and boards."

In response to the resurrection of Woodstock West, that afternoon Chancellor Maurice Mitchell held a press conference and emphatically repeated the police chief's threat that the National Guard would be called up to prevent the rebuilding of the tent town. Meanwhile the Faculty Steering Committee met and voted to extend the strike until Wednesday to give them more time to establish curriculum options. They also wanted to open up the university with more democratic governance policies, part of a national wave of reform in academia.

Tuesday, May 12

On Tuesday, the governor of Colorado himself, John Love, came on campus to try to reason with the residents of the encampment, and told them, "If we are to settle our differences in the streets, I fear not only for all of you, but for all our nation." During the rest of the day, there was a back-and-forth between administration officials with strikers and representatives of the tent-city. Strikers did submit a list of demands to the administration, which included the construction of a permanent outdoor forum, measures for academic reform and the establishment of a legal

Woodstock West residential area. But by the end of the day, the sides had hardened, and no consensus was reached. That night, Chancellor Mitchell contacted Gov. Love and told him he no longer had control of the campus. As soon as Love hung up with the chancellor, he called his National Guard commander and ordered a contingent of 700 troops to the Denver campus.

During the night, the 200 residents of Woodstock West II were warned that the National Guard were on their way to campus. They gathered together – it was probably their last meeting – they had a decision to make. Most wanted to avoid any confrontation and to "show the world we are really dedicated to peace." A consensus was reached—they would abandon the camp and evacuate before the arrival of the troops.

Wednesday, May 13

When the Colorado National Guard arrived early Wednesday morning at Woodstock West II, they only found a stray dog and one sleeping student. However, when students across campus awoke to the presence of the Guard on university grounds, they rushed over to the encampment. But by then, platoons of Guardsmen and squads of the 200 Denver police officers had already secured the site and the surrounding grove of trees. Even though there was no confrontation or "trouble," at least 10 students and non-students were arrested, and another ten detained pending the confirmation of their student status. Most were charged with curfew violations, which brought the number of people arrested since Monday to 85.

In a replay of the events from Monday, Guardsmen cordoned off the Woodstock area, including both sides of the road it straddled. They stood guard while workmen tore down the tent city for the second time in three days, using dump trucks and a front-end loader. Once the destruction was complete, the vast majority of the Guard and police units departed, leaving an 18-man force behind to prevent any rebuilding. Guardsmen remained on campus for another 2 1/2 hours.

Pamela Walker, then a junior, recalled the moment bitterly years later. "I really wanted to make my statement rather than have someone with power who wouldn't even listen to us come in and move us." When the cops and troopers arrived, she initially refused to leave, and her friends had to forcibly carry her away from the camp.

Probably unbeknownst to students, the National Guardsman who marched onto campus carried live ammunition. One member of the 220th military police unit that had taken part in the action disapproved of the live ammo. He told the *Denver Post*, "I thought that was crazy after Kent State," given that the atmosphere on campus was serious but not hostile. Another Guardsman wasn't happy and said, "It was a show of force, a power-play. We felt like we'd been misused."

That afternoon and evening, students did return – not with the idea of creating another Woodstock—but to communicate with the police officers left guarding the area. For hours, small groups of students went from officer to officer and "discussed, argued, agreed and laughed together," *The Denver Post* reported. One student said, "We're trying to love them to death. We want them to understand, and we don't want trouble." *The Post* reported, "Several times during the afternoon and evening command officers reminded patrolmen, relaxed in conversation, that their helmets were supposed to be on their heads, not under their arms. The patrolmen responded quickly, but by nightfall the formality had been destroyed and not one of the night force was wearing his helmet."

By Friday, the 15th, all the Guard units and police officers had been withdrawn, although, the campus was continually monitored by Denver police to ensure that Woodstock West III didn't materialize. Also Friday, 400 of the university's 430 faculty members held a special meeting and voted to support "the spirit of Woodstock."

At commencement later in the month, nearly two-thirds of the senior class wore either armbands with peace insignias or chose not to wear caps and gowns at all. To avoid any incidents, Chancellor Mitchell did not shake hands with graduates or personally sign their diplomas. The next fall, students did win a victory of sorts in convincing the administration and faculty to close the university down for two weeks before the November elections to allow students to work for peace candidates and campaigns.

Colorado State University at Fort Collins

As if to lay to rest claims the student strike had disappeared on the Fort Collins campus, 1,000 people rallied on the Student Center Plaza Monday afternoon and heard speakers call for a continuation of the strike and for alternative methods of action. After a street theatre performance by the Lexington Volunteers, student government president Don Weber extolled students to respect each other's rights, the right to strike, the right not to strike, and called for constructive dialogue and understanding, not personal confrontations.

An assistant professor of history, Dr. Meyer Nathan, told students he hoped the burning of Old Main the previous Friday night would not end the school's peace movement, and urged students to keep an open mind about the fire because no one really knew at that point who was responsible. The fire could have been started by someone on the radical right, he theorized, someone attempting to destroy the peace movement. Another history professor, Loren Crabtree, lectured how the United States was aiding one side of a civil war and was not containing China by fighting in Vietnam and Cambodia. This was a huge mistake, Crabtree said, and asked the students to make the moral choice and stick by it.

Student Jim Oliver advocated the use of an economic boycott to put pressure on the White House to withdraw troops from Southeast Asia. Don't make long distance telephone calls, he said, withdraw your money from the banks, and buy groceries from small stores instead of supermarkets. The rally ended with a call by a former student government president, Doug Phelps, for strikers to continue their work, and for non-strikers to work for peace through other methods.

On Monday, strike activities were still in full swing at the **University of Colorado Boulder** campus, and antiwar students continued their economic boycott of corporate products. On Tuesday faculty members approved an extension of course deadlines for withdrawals in order to provide another option to strikers. Picketing of campus buildings continued on Thursday and a host of professors conducted classes as part of the newly-created Experimental Studies Program, which offered alternatives to normal classroom subjects. Veterans for Peace staged an event and peace candidates came to campus soliciting support for their fall campaigns. And before the end of the week, students were out in the community canvassing and spreading the word about their strike and their opposition to the war.

On Friday, a group of students from **Metropolitan State College in Denver** showed up at the offices of the conservative *Rocky Mountain News* and demanded the paper publish a front page story about the deaths at Jackson State. Editors had originally published the story on page 14, but then promised to comply with the students' request for the Saturday edition, and to also print their statement arguing the action was genocide.

At Colorado Springs, just north of the US Army base at **Fort Carson**, 500 anti-war protesters joined 30 GIs in a "festival of life" on Friday. Organizers reported that leftist media pundit Paul Krassner spoke as did representatives from Movement for a Democratic Military. They also reported that repression against organizers included bomb threats and threats of arrest.

University of Wyoming – Laramie
Wednesday, May 13

On Wednesday, *Flagpole*— the campus publication of the student "Government in Exile"—announced that Governor's Day, scheduled for the very next day, would be a "university wide day of protest" with a student strike and a march on the ROTC ceremonies. "The protest will be non-violent and non-destructive," the article stated. "It is not directed against the university but is rather intended to express our indignation at the invasion of Cambodia and the expansion of US military action in Southeast Asia." It ended with a list of five demands and a call to "protest last week's dispatching of troops to this campus and the general lack of communication with the students by the administration and the governor."

Thursday, May 14

On Thursday, anti-war students and faculty members gathered in Prexy's Pasture for a major speech about non-violence, and then staged a militant but non-violent march on the ROTC ceremonies.

Over the next few days, representatives of the exiled student government met with President William Carlson over a variety of issues and afterwards felt the talks were a "fantastic success." They reported that Carlson conceded there was little likelihood state police would ever return to the campus with loaded riot guns and told them he hadn't come out to speak to students during the flagpole incident because the situation was so tense his presence wouldn't have served any useful purpose. But on the issue of a vacancy on the Board of Trustees, Carlson refused to recommend that it be filled by a student, and he would not consider working on lowering the rents and prices in Laramie as they were out of the university's jurisdiction.

As the campus approached the end of the semester, the government in exile sent out a flyer under the authority of its chairperson, W.R. Adler, which pledged the group would have a presence in the future and listed a series of proposals to be presented to the Board of Trustees over the summer. These included working with the administration "to assure fair housing for all students," the formation of a cooperative campus bookstore, and a program to make birth control and information available at the Student Health Service. The flyer also urged the university to do more "to clean up Laramie's air and water," to allow students to take time off to work on political campaigns, and to appoint students to fill vacancies on the Board of Trustees.

University of Montana – Missoula
Monday, May 11
Competing flyers flooded the campus on Monday in anticipation of the campus-wide vote on whether to maintain ROTC planned for Wednesday. One advocated keeping ROTC and accused anti-war students of being a "small vociferous minority of students and non-students" who dictated their will onto the rest of the campus. "The time has come for all students to stand up for their rights and express themselves," it stated.

A competing flyer stated, "The removal of ROTC is merely a curriculum change, not the denial of anyone's rights. Many things are not taught at the university which some people would like to take, such as police investigation taught by the FBI, and auto sales taught by GM." It went on, "Credit should be removed from all ROTC courses not to cripple the ROTC program, but to improve the academic status of the university. The military does not respond to moral questions; it acts on orders from the upper echelon. By necessity military training is authoritarian and anti-academic. The university acts to develop free thought. The military acts to stifle free thought."

Wednesday, May 13
Wednesday was the day of polling on the future of ROTC, and 58% of all students and 93% of all faculty cast ballots. Despite all the flyers

and pronouncements, a majority of students voted to retain the program by a margin of over 2 to 1, 2,844 versus 1,243 students; the faculty vote was in line, 288 versus 115. On the question of whether ROTC should be continued off-campus, the votes were similar, but not as lopsided. The polling settled the issue.

Thursday, May 14

Somewhat ironically, the day after the vote against ROTC failed, Herbert Marcuse, professor of political philosophy at the University of California at San Diego, spoke on "Radical Sensibility." A capacity crowd packed the campus ballroom to hear Marcuse, considered a leading spokesperson for the New Left and whose libertarian socialist views had heralded the hippie movement. Marcuse told the crowd that "Man" must change his sensibility in order to be liberated from a repressive society. Tina Torgrimson, a writer for the campus newspaper, the *Montana Kaimin*, reported on his talk for its May 15 edition.

Young radicals are confronted with a system of power immune to change, Marcuse said, and are being persecuted by people who should be defending them. "The young militants may well be those who save the goals of the American Revolution from being curdled into a bloodbath." The existing society has been reproduced by the older generation which forces its old values and old standards upon the young. Thus, this society has been reproduced not only in the minds of people, but in their reason.

Torgrimson, the reporter, recounted Marcuse's words, "Since man is also a rational animal, the 'emancipation of the senses' will also depend on a new rationality, he said. This is attainable only through long, painful processes of political education, both in and out of the classroom, Mr. Marcuse said. ... Sensibility is the most shifting quality of a human being and a 'new type of man and woman are emerging' because of the realization of their sensibilities through new goals and new experiences.... Man must overcome both physical and mental pollution to free himself from an environment of violence and deception, Mr. Marcuse said. The 'more or less gradual suffocation' of our life and our freedom ... can only be overcome by this new sensibility. The need for a beautiful and peaceful life and environment is one of the most liberating impulses of man .... He said the liberation of man involves the liberation of nature."

Classes at the **University of Idaho** were cancelled Monday to allow a campus-wide discussion of war-related issues, as was announced by the administration of President Ernest Hartung. Faculty members and students met on the Administration Building lawn and recounted the events of the last ten days. Many students had gone on strike over the past week, but Monday was the only day that was officially cancelled. Surprisingly, Mayor Handel of Moscow, the college town adjacent to campus, came out publicly in support of the student strike.

University of Nevada – Reno

Across the street from two large student residential buildings, Juniper and Manzanita Halls, sat the Hobbit Hole, an old two-story house that was used as a student hang-out. People lived there but it was also considered a hippie and counter-cultural center, a meeting place for student politicos, and a place where hitchhikers could stay for the night. In the early morning hours on Tuesday, May 12, Hobbit Hole was firebombed.

At the time, four young men lived there but only two were present when the bombs exploded. Witnesses reported seeing a man run from the house and jump into a late model, two-toned Mercury Cougar before it sped off. Extensive damage was done to the porch and to one end of the front of the house. Within minutes, Reno firemen extinguished the flames.

Occupants of Hobbit Hole had received anonymous threats before the firebombing. And one of the residents, a campus police officer, was visibly shaken after the incident. "Four people could have died," he said. Another resident wryly commented that he didn't think the student government would "pay for this one," referring to the student government's offer to pay for the damage at the ROTC offices caused by firebombs on May 7. At least one campus event was cancelled due to the firebombing. The old building on North Virginia Street has since been torn down and replaced with the university's continuing education center.

Tuesday's edition of *Sagebrush*, the campus newspaper, carried a disturbing article about two faculty members and seven students being investigated by the Board of Regents for their roles in the Governor's Day protest held the week earlier. Two faculty members from the English Department, Dr. Paul S. Adamian and teaching assistant Fred Maher, were ordered to appear before the Faculty Senate to answer for their actions during the protest. The Senate hearing was to decide whether, according to the University Code, the two should be fired.

The chairman of the Board of Regents, Proctor Hug, had been riding in the governor's car on the day of the protest when it was halted by student protesters. Hug claimed he witnessed both faculty members encourage students to block the motorcade and later lead protest actions at the stadium. In addition, Maher was asked to explain his alleged use of vulgar language in his English class regarding the governor, the university president and the administration.

Not too long after and critical of the Regents' decision to investigate two faculty members, the American Association of University Professors began their own investigation. At the time, the exact nature of the charges against Adamian and Maher were not known.

Eventually, the charges were dropped against the assistant Maher, but Dr. Adamian was fired. It was never clear why of all the professors present at the protest, Adamian was singled out. In fact, one of the regents who voted to fire him had raised this. Some professors, in hopes of sharing the blame and saving Adamian, signed a statement of complicity – but it fell on deaf ears. Adamian ended up taking the case to court and was represented by former Nevada Attorney General Charles Springer, later a Nevada supreme court justice. A U.S. District Court overturned the firing, but the ruling was later reversed by the U.S. Court of Appeals for the Ninth Circuit and the U.S. Supreme Court declined to take up the case. The firing of Prof. Adamian stood.

A leaflet distributed on campus on Friday, May 15, called for "Cowboys and longhairs unite behind a real cause. Let's get out of Cambodia and Vietnam," and announced a campus rally at the Manzanita Bowl for that day at noon. "Maintain a peaceful campus," it said, "and still protest an unjust war."

Pacific

Washington

Eastern Washington State College – Cheney

On Wednesday, May 13, a teach-in on Southeast Asia was held on the Cheney campus where President Emerson Shuck read his prepared remarks. "I personally join with those who believe that as a nation and a people we must remove ourselves as quickly as possible from a tragic disaster of inhumane involvement. The war in Southeast Asia has far exceeded its moral defensibility as a shield between the violent and nonviolent." When he finished, Shuck was met with a standing ovation. He continued extemporaneously. "The problems of our society and our nation are serious ones. The way we meet these problems is just as serious." The lowering of the flag was not in disrespect but was an "expression of the seriousness and concern" over the problems evident in the country, he said. "This especially is no time for fun and games in mob activity. Acts of disruption and violence are at this tense time deeply dangerous."

David Bell, a professor of political science and Southeast Asian specialist, gave a brief history of Cambodia, its war and revolution, from ancient times through the French colonial period to Nixon's invasion. He said Prince Sihounak, Cambodia's chief-of-state until he was ousted by the US-supported military coup in March 1970, was "kept in power by the unsurpassed loyalty from the peasants." The US had a chance to work with Cambodia but blew a "golden opportunity" with the recent invasion. He feared Cambodia would be drawn into a widening war. "The prospects are frightening..." he said, prophetically.

Joseph Schuster, an expert on the Constitution, told the crowd, "The Constitution is more than a legal document. It is a matter of spirit and intent," and Nixon's involvement in Cambodia was a violation of the spirit "if not a violation of the legality" of the Constitution. The administration had misled the country, Schuster said, and quoted from a *UPI* news release that four days prior to Nixon's announcement of US troops moving into Cambodia, Secretary of State William P. Rogers had given secret testimony to a House subcommittee that the administration had "no incentive to escalate." Schuster surmised, either Rogers intentionally misled Congress or he had been misinformed by Nixon.

University of Washington – Seattle
Monday, May 11

On Monday, classes officially resumed and early morning picket lines tried to block school entrances. However, picketers were persuaded to step aside by the tactical squad of the Seattle Police Department still on campus due to the turmoil from the previous week. Despite the tension and intimidation from law enforcement, 4,000 students attended an afternoon rally and voted to continue the strike "indefinitely." Yet, by mid-week, participation in strike activities had dropped off noticeably and the enormous crowds seen the week before had faded. One of the only strike-related "actions" during the week was the burning of an American flag on Tuesday in a small, spontaneous outburst of protest.

Friday, May 15

On Friday, a delegation of students from UW were in Washington DC to speak with Nixon and present him with a petition with over 9,000 signatures to stop the war. Meanwhile, back on campus on Friday, Black students – angry that there had been no official response or any protest to the killings at Jackson State—charged into the campus library and created havoc by pushing thousands of books off their shelves.

Elsewhere on the campus with the approach of final exams, students were returning to their studies and classes, crossing thinner and thinner picket lines. By the weekend, the strike was effectively over. Yet its demise had had some help. The administration of President Charles Odegaar had clamped down on the strike by both pressuring the student government not to fund it and the student media not to cover it—specifically KUOW-FM, the student-run radio station, and the *Daily* student newspaper.

The editor of the *Daily*, Bruce Olson, was progressive and did not bend to Odegaar's will. Olson had previously supported various campaigns by student radicals, with stories about SDS, BSU, the Seattle Liberation Front and supportive editorials. The events of May and the unprecedented numbers of students joining the strike had pushed Olson into dedicating the entire newspaper to covering the strike. During the last two weeks every issue of the *Daily* covered news from the previous day and upcoming strike events, with its announcements, editorials, and progress.

The Odegaar administration did go after the funds spent on strike activities by the student government and its strike-supporting president, Rick Silverman. Odegaar even eventually took the students to court and in June, persuaded a court to order the student government to stop funding the strike coalition. But by then, of course, the strike was over. Yet the New University had a life of its own, and importantly, a climate of student activism had been established on campus for the upcoming fall term.

At **Seattle University** events took a dramatic turn during the second week of strike protests. Students had used a liberated ROTC building for their strike headquarters and had taken over another hall for a day care center. When Seattle tactical police showed up, they used heavy-handed methods to evict the non-violent strikers and roughed up a good number of them in the process. In response, students called for the dismissal of the local police commissioner.

Western Washington State College – Bellingham
Tuesday, May 12

Delegates from Western State had attended a national student congress in San Jose, California, over the weekend and returned to Bellingham on Tuesday, energized and full of enthusiasm. Greg Baker from the associated students, two student legislators and the managing editor of the campus paper, the *Western Front* had joined delegates from 69 California colleges and 30 from out-of-state, including even a few from the East Coast.

The conference had pledged to back the New Haven national strike demands—the immediate withdrawal of U.S. forces in Southeast Asia, freedom for all political prisoners including the Black Panthers, and an end to colleges' complicity with the Pentagon, including research and recruiting. It also had voted to allow colleges complete autonomy as to how and to what extent they would carry out the demands. In addition, delegations from Washington and Oregon had met separately one night in a regional caucus and had pledged to halt the shipment of nerve gas through the Pacific Northwest. However, little did the Bellingham delegates suspect upon their return that the campus strike was in its last week.

Saturday, May 16

On Saturday night, 400 pro-war supporters from Bellingham and Whatcom County showed their grassroots strength with their own rally at the Federal Building. Carrying American flags and signs, they marched from a mall parking lot to the federal target. Mostly made up of adults and high school kids, the crowd had very few college students. Speakers called for an end of violence on college campuses and for a "renewal of good ol-fashioned patriotism." Warning college students, State Representative Dick Kink said, "Let them beware and let them be aware, violence will only mean an end of democracy." He threatened that "the silent majority would refuse to be silent any longer" and "will get involved to end violence."

A speaker from the American Legion waxed nostalgically for a time when "children didn't talk back to their parents, students didn't argue with professors, and Black and white people didn't fight each other." He respected the youth of Bellingham who participated in the rally, and claimed that "for every degenerate smoking marijuana and for every radical hippie who burns buildings, there are 1,000 good college kids sitting at home studying."

There was one speaker who tried to heroically counter the main narrative of the rally. Lee Cowen from Western Washington State told the crowd, "We of Western didn't want violence, and there has never been any violence in any Western demonstrations." Someone in the crowd yelled out "Yeah but let them try to close that freeway again!" Cowen answered, "Many strikes by unions are illegal, and often violent." The freeway was closed to make people listen just as illegal union walkouts are attempts to make people listen, he said.

"Students are frustrated in their attempts to seek peace," and after five years of marching to no avail, they are looking for a stronger way to show their beliefs. Cowen said many Western students wanted to talk to Bellingham people and wanted community understanding and communication. "If violence occurs as a result of misunderstanding, no one will be to blame except the leaders of Bellingham, students and citizens."

Back on campus, there was a move to honor the deaths of James E. Green and Phillip L. Gibbs at Jackson State just the day before. President Jerry Flora ordered all campus flags to be flown at half-staff on the upcoming Monday. Western's Black Student Union, however, wanted more and requested that classes be suspended for one day to mourn their deaths – like Kent State. Flora expressed concern, "It is a further extension of the tragedy at Kent State. We all should join the Black segments of our campus in concern over this very serious incident," but "could not grant" the one-day request.

Washington State Univesity – Pullman

Friday, May 15, was the annual end-of-year ROTC ceremonies and anti-war demonstrators showed up and attempted to disrupt the ceremony.

They threw raw meat onto the parade ground, ran among the student cadets, and attempted to drown out the loudspeakers during the award ceremonies with chants, heckling, and yells of "Sieg Heil!"

The campus newspaper, the *Daily Evergreen*, on Friday reported the outcome of a poll of graduate students on President Glenn Terrell's cancellation of classes and his sending Nixon a telegram on Cambodia. Thirty-one departments out of 38 responded and the results showed a definitive majority supported Terrell's actions. In contrast, a petition presented to the student government by a group called the Rational Alternative had 2,000 student signatures "in favor of President Terrell taking no stand on Southeast Asia for the students of WSU," and "opposed to the closure of classes."

At the Army post **Fort Lewis** in southern Tacoma, on Saturday—Armed Forces Day—200 antiwar supporters gathered with roughly 60 GIs for an all-day festival and picnic. Organizers later complained that Seattle students didn't turn out because it was not billed as a demonstration and there weren't any featured speakers.

Oregon
Portland State University
Monday, May 11

Early Monday morning, Portland city police arrived just off campus to ensure the removal of barricades that had been erected by student strikers in the Park Blocks. The barricades, shanties and tents within the string of contiguous park-like blocks had come to symbolize the strike at Portland State.

Portland Mayor Terry Schrunk and City Hall had been under mounting pressure by outraged local residents to do something about the student take-over of the Park Blocks and the seemingly endless demonstrations. Even some students wanted the campus to return to normal, and the city park bureau was angry about the use of park benches for barricades.

Finally, having had enough, Schrunk ordered in the Portland police and city crews began removing the barriers. At first, some students even voluntarily aided the city sanitation workers. And by the time crews approached the blockade near Cramer Hall – dubbed "Fort Tricia Nixon"

– hundreds of students had come out to observe the dismantling of the symbols of the strike.

It was slow going for city workers, and as more and more students showed up, Mayor Schrunk grew worried and ordered in more police. Just before 5 pm, scores of blue-helmeted officers massed at the southern end of the Parks Block and then lines of officers in formation began moving northward. City crews continued the dirty work of taking apart the plastic and wood shanties. Hundreds of students watched police as they slowly swept up the first two blocks of the wooded and grassy areas, with their mood changing from one of curiosity to one of anger.

At Harrison Street, police stopped – before them stood a make-shift field hospital – and they waited for instructions. Tensions soared because strikers anticipated what was about to happen. A handful of students and faculty members approached the police commander and informed him that the hospital was protected by a permit issued by the City Parks Commission that didn't expire until noon the next day. However, city park commissioner Francis Ivancie was contacted and said the permit had expired over the weekend. Police radioed for more instructions. By this point, up to four hundred demonstrators and on-lookers had gathered.

At about 5:40 pm, 20 members of the tactical squad all wearing white helmets advanced their way through police lines towards the field hospital. They formed a wedge and moved across the street just in front of it. Students and faculty members were freaking out and yelling at police. About 100 people locked arms and surrounded the hospital, chanting, "Peace. Peace. Peace," over and over. For them, the hospital tent was the last remaining symbol of the strike, and they were not about to let it go without an act of civil disobedience. Many sat down around the tent, prepared to be arrested. But they weren't prepared for what happened next.

An officer approached the demonstrators and yelled through a bullhorn, "I hereby command that you all leave the area. If you do not leave, you will be considered under arrest!" Loud yells of "Seig Heil! Seig Heil!" were the response. A small group of faculty members made their way to the front end of the police wedge and yelled at them not to advance. But the tac squad had their orders from Lt. James Brouilette—to charge in-wedge formation.

Seconds later, the wedge moved forward, and with grunts and growls, officers stomped and thrusted their way into the crowd around the tent, beating people with their 4-foot long riot batons. There were screams and many jumped up and scattered in a retreat across the street. But others weren't so lucky and in less than two minutes, police had laid waste to the civil disobedient protest. By 5:45 the hospital tent was in shreds and dozens of wounded students laid about the park.

Kevin Mulligan, student government senator and a strike leader, had been on the front line. He described what had happened to the campus press. "The Tactical Squad moved forward with riot sticks thrust forward. They moved forward on us and several people were hit. I moved away. In doing so, I was hit from behind and slipped in the mud, falling at the base of the tent. I was hit twice before I could right myself. I stayed on the streets trying to cool tempers and stop the rock and bottle throwing and helping people to the aid station."

The press reported that other witnesses to the mass beating had very emotional responses. One elderly grandmother said she couldn't believe her eyes. A woman student was seen running away with tears streaming down her cheeks. One male student on a roof that overlooked the park stared in disbelief as cops acted like "soldiers swarming, jabbing and smashing, butting their adversaries to the ground."

In just a few minutes, police had commandeered the entire block. Protesters too injured to walk were carried to a campus parking lot across the street, and the sound of ambulance sirens soon filled the air. Those students who had retreated began to answer with rocks, bottles, and clods of dirt. Cops pushed onto the next block and the remaining shanties were destroyed. For another half hour, police stood guard while city crews finished up. The tac squad then departed, followed by the blue helmets. Police who remained regrouped at a nearby parking lot but soon became targets of rock barrages.

Finally, by 7:15 pm, all law enforcement had pulled back and were nowhere in sight. They left behind 27 people who were admitted to four Portland hospitals, many with head injuries from being clubbed, although none serious enough to be life-threatening. One newspaper reporter on the scene said many of the injured had refused treatment. Another report listed

32 people beaten, one with his own crutch. Police reported that 15 cops had been injured. Six people were arrested, four for disorderly conduct, one for assaulting an officer, and one for resisting arrest and carrying a concealed weapon.

Dazed by the attack and still in shock, students assembled back in the student union ballroom, right off the park zone. Many of them wanted to make emergency strike plans while others wandered about the center angry and bitter. Kevin Mulligan told the *Vanguard*, "Now instead of a few militants striking with 2,000 sympathizers, we have 2,000 militants." An Op-ed in the *Vanguard* said, "The uncommitted are committed."

Over the course of the day, administrators who had been genuinely sickened by what had gone down met with students and faculty in efforts to piece together the events. President Gregory Wolfe was aghast. Later that night, he told students, "The university did not call the police," and that he had tried to persuade City Hall "to postpone their actions when the order to move was given to the police tactical squad." Afterwards, Wolfe got a hold of Mayor Schrunk and told him, "The circumstances did probably more to create a sense of bitter reaction among students who had been hitherto uninvolved, than anything else that could have happened." Schrunk later said he "regretted" the incident, but it was necessary to clear out the Park Blocks and close the encampment down.

When students finally gathered hours later to make sense of it all, one of the first issues raised was a call for an investigation of the police attack. Talk went into the night about what direction the strike should take and what its future would be. Some wanted to rebuild the barricades, while others claimed that would alienate the very people they wanted to join the strike.

For his part, President Wolfe called for students and faculty to "join together with new vigor and concern, — with a unity of purpose and resolve — to find the answers to these tormenting problems which face our university, our city, state and nation." Yet once again, Wolfe missed the gravity of the situation and how deeply students felt about what had just happened on his campus. After the demise of the hospital tent, a "memorial" was set up where it had been. A cross made up of flowers was placed on it encircled by more flowers, with a sign that read, "search your heart."

Tuesday, May 12

By Tuesday, the police attack had united the campus. Six hundred members of the faculty met and passed a resolution that condemned Portland police "for attacking people instead of arresting them." And it helped unite two opposing social and political factions—the "long hairs" and the "jocks." Miles apart philosophically, both factions came together in opposition to the violence by police and the routing of peaceful students.

The newly-found unity produced a large march that day of 3,500 students, faculty, and townspeople who converged on City Hall to protest the city's actions. The crowd presented a list of demands to Mayor Schrunk and other city officials, which included a full investigation of the Monday clash and the conditions leading up to it; charging any policeman who had committed an "abuse of public power"; the resignation of any public official implicated in the action; and the abolishment of the police Tactical Operations Platoon. Two more demands were tacked on during the march—the resignation of Mayor Schrunk and of City Commissioner Francis Ivancie. Not surprisingly, no immediate action on the demands were taken.

Wednesday, May 13

On Wednesday, *the Vanguard* ran a report by the director of Smith Memorial Center on the damage from students' three-day takeover. It ran up to $3,000 in repairs and cleaning costs; a lounge used as a bedroom had soiled carpet and furniture; paint had damaged walls and floors; other vandalism included burnt furniture, a ripped ballroom curtain, damage to a cash register and a typewriter, a half dozen broken windows, and $200 worth of food lost or taken from the cafeteria.

"Somebody has got to pay," the director said. "Who's going to pay? The great Silent Majority who stayed away?" He estimated that up to 2,000 people had marauded through the center for three days—students, "teeny-boppers" and "street people," and roughly 50 to 75 people had stayed overnight. "They essentially took over the Center in one way or another," he said.

For the remainder of the week, students continued the strike and boycott of classes. They circulated petitions calling for the recall of Portland Mayor Schrunk and City Commissioner Francis Ivancie. In general, however, the campus remained fairly calm and it appeared the majority of students had resumed their normal class schedules.

University of Oregon – Eugene

On Wednesday, three faculty members reported their classes had been disrupted by "guerilla skits" performed by students dressed in military and police garb. All true—members of the Radical Arts Troop, RAT, had visited classrooms and acted out a short, one minute play where actors would fall to the floor and others would beat them with paper tubes and shoot cap pistols at them, while yelling about the war, police and the military. The university administration took swift action. Once students were identified by the instructors, they were charged in student court.

A small demonstration on Thursday, May 14, had 50 people carrying red flags and chanting anti-ROTC slogans march out onto the open field next to the ROTC building. They staged mock attacks on the building, and at one point a window was accidentally broken. Because of the disturbance, both Army and Air Force ROTC drill classes were cancelled. The student who broke the window was identified and charged in student court for minor destruction of property and for the "overt interference with the operation of the institution, ie. cancellation of drill classes to avoid confrontation."

California

Humboldt State College
Monday, May 11

Monday was the first day of a five-day strike on the Humboldt campus, and the Community Action Committee organized daily picket lines, rallies, community canvassing and teach-ins. A staff was selected to publish the strike bulletin, which came out every day of the strike, listing its schedule and progress locally and around the country. Smaller groups, "sub-affinity" or caucuses, formed inside the Community Action Committee, such as the women's caucus which held its own meetings and the music caucus which provided booklets of strike songs at rallies.

The strike committee wanted to ensure student canvassers had a clear understanding of the Vietnam war and the Cambodia invasion, so canvassers were asked to attend teach-ins and training sessions. Teach-in coordinator, Wayne Dodge, was taken aback at how little students knew about Vietnam, so he set up a series of teach-ins specifically for canvassers and picketers. Students' attitudes – as well as their appearance—were stressed during the training sessions as being an important part of their effectiveness. They were to be respectful, have good listening skills, and be able to communicate with straight people.

Canvassers were encouraged to follow a formula of telling townspeople the history and the facts in order to engage them. After a few canvassers had tried this, they came to feel it was more effective to have an honest conversation with people using facts and their own personal opinions. The goal of canvassing was not only to educate residents but to get them involved, or at least get them to sign petitions and write letters to Congress. Student Pam Himelhock, the head coordinator for the canvassing campaign, had organized 55 "affinity groups" with 7 people each with the hope of reaching 16,000 homes throughout Humboldt County.

Tuesday, May 12

On the second day of the strike, college president Cornelius Siemens publicly expressed his sympathies with the strike movement. The students' conduct and message of peace was "nothing short of admirable," he said, and the strike had become a milestone in the county's history. Siemens viewed the US involvement in Vietnam as "tragic" and "further expansion utterly wrong." Like many college presidents, he wrote Nixon advocating for an end to the war and to express students' "widespread, deep-seated desire for peace." Dr. Siemens also said that the more colleges that became active in non-violent protests, the more their positive influence on the nation was inevitable.

However, Siemens was not thrilled Tuesday when the Vietnam Veterans Against the War created a mock bomb crater right outside the administration building. The vets dug an enormous hole similar to the thousands left across the Vietnamese landscape by US bombers. A sign next to it explained the vets were not out to destroy university property but to make a statement. They had carefully separated the topsoil from the subsoil so they could later restore the lawn when the strike was over. But a group of pro-war jocks came by and angrily refilled the hole, shoveling the topsoil in first with the subsoil on top.

Many Humboldt professors supported the strike movement despite efforts by administrators to keep them "professional" and apolitical. Facing threats of discipline and loss of salaries for violating school rules and cancelling classes, professors took a major step to protect themselves. They formed a campus chapter of the Union of Associated Professors, and defended striking students, pushing their colleagues not to penalize strikers. One professor of psychology, Andrew Karoly, wanted to open the campus to the public for the remainder of the school term and to be dedicated to "bringing the wars in Southeast Asia to an end."

Praise for the strikers and their faculty supporters came from the president of the faculty, Katheryn Corbett, and from the mayor of the nearby town of Arcata, Ward Falor, who commended students for their "lawful and orderly protest."

Of course, not everyone on campus or in Humboldt County supported the strike. Those in the community who agreed with Nixon's move into Cambodia saw anti-war protesters as unpatriotic. Yet even residents who disagreed with the student canvassers welcomed them into their homes to talk about the war. And students on campus critical of the strike complained of a new "breed of student" from the urban areas that was changing the school that was once a "sleepy, county school that served local students."

According to the campus press, many non-striking students generally supported the strike's cause, but did not participate for two main reasons: The strike would not have an impact on changing things, and missing class to participate was not worth disrupting their education.

Friday, May 15

By Friday, the last day of the strike, it was clear that the 5-day protest had been the largest, most sustained demonstration to date in the history of Humboldt County. An estimated 3,000 students and faculty had been involved in protesting the Cambodian invasion, Kent State and the draft. One account reported that nearly 50 percent of students were attending class, while the rest were out on Arcata Plaza, doing "college community peace activities." Sixty faculty members had pledged to strike, which left a good many classrooms completely empty.

Not one arrest had been made throughout the protest – which remained completely non-violent. Through the door-to-door canvassing, strikers met their goal of reaching 16,000 Humboldt County homes, and students did get residents to talk about the war. Students from the local Institute of Social Research performed a survey of residents and found that half of those who had student canvassers at their door felt their opinions on the war had been affected by the canvassers.

Yet, by the end of the week, the strike movement appeared to be in decline. And until the war ended in 1975, anti-war activism on campus never again reached the height of the May 1970 strike for peace. Still, Humboldt State and the town of Arcata were forever changed by the strike. The campus – once obscure – became afterwards an alternative haven for artists, lefties, potheads and Deadheads. For the school itself, the new notoriety found admission applications soaring.

Over time, Arcata discovered a new civic pride and experienced a cultural birth with restaurants, nightclubs, two repertory cinemas and a city council dominated not by the pro-lumber, anti-hippie old guard but by progressives. Led by ecology-minded councilmembers, Arcata opened one of the nation's first municipal recycling centers and converted a solid-waste dump on Humboldt Bay into a network of freshwater and saltwater ponds, tidal sloughs, mudflats and walking paths. And it all began with the May 1970 rebellion.

Sacramento

Students from all over California arrived in Sacramento Tuesday, May 12, to lobby their state legislators about the war. An organized group of 200 law students visited Assemblyman John Vasconcellos and appealed to him to create a bill prohibiting California servicemen from being required to fight in an undeclared war, similar to legislative efforts in other states.

California Governor Reagan just could not or would not control his tongue. At his weekly press conference on Wednesday, he was asked what he thought about the roving crowd of construction workers who had attacked peaceful demonstrators in New York City. He said it was as "understandable as the violence the other way." He was then asked whether he would characterize the hundreds of hardhats as "bums," the term he had used for campus demonstrators. "They haven't burned down any schools yet," he replied.

During the conference, Reagan pledged to keep all California public schools open—the very schools he had closed the week earlier. He denounced those campuses who had plans to excuse students so they could protest the war. The governor said "overreaction" to President Nixon's Cambodian strategy would "kill American soldiers by encouraging the enemy."

At the beginning of the week at **San Francisco State** picket lines greeted returning students and faculty members as anti-war activists pushed to extend the strike for the rest of the year. Also, on Tuesday at the **University of San Francisco**, a hundred law students made an appeal to their professors to abolish final exams for that year to allow them to join the protests against the Cambodian invasion. Students from the all-women's **Mills College** joined other women students from the East Bay on Thursday, and dressed in leotards and long flowing robes, approached young men on their way into the Oakland induction center and invited them to have tea and talk about refusing induction.

University of California – Berkeley
Monday, May 11

When UC Berkeley reconvened on Monday the 11th – as did all the other campuses closed by Gov. Reagan the week before – momentum for the student strike was affirmed when a near unanimous vote to continue it was taken by 8,000 to 10,000 people who rallied in Harmon Gym. The resolution that passed also called for an end to regular courses for the rest of the quarter, guaranteed pass grades to all registered students, and no financial loss by any university employee due to the strike.

The huge conclave also adopted demands from the Black Student Union and the Women's Liberation organization. The BSU wanted the "restructuring of education, in particular, open enrollment, increased funds for ethnic studies departments, and EOP [Equal Opportunity Program]." Women's Liberation demands included the immediate establishment of childcare centers to enable women to contribute to the antiwar effort, a women's studies department, and an end to the inferior status of non-academic staff, the majority of whom were women.

Debates about the direction of the strike inside the stuffy gym revolved around language that Professor Sheldon Wolin had used the week earlier at a huge assembly—the "post-bureaucratic man" and the coming "revolution." At one point, Wolin himself rose and cautioned, "Our greatest danger is any attempt to impose rigid, centralized control. Let us not escape from one stifling structure to establish another."

Tom Hayden addressed the huge crowd and reported on strike actions on the East Coast. At Yale, protesters continued to challenge the federal government's prosecution of Panther leader Bobby Seale. Groups were demanding United Nations intervention on behalf of oppressed ethnic groups in America, and others were working on a Continental Congress planned for the summer. Hayden called upon older students and veteran lefties to have patience with the new, coming-of-age recruits, who were green but energized. Hayden also tried to raise those new recruits a notch in their consciousness and encouraged them to not simply see the Vietnam quagmire as a tragic error but as a logical extension of imperialism and third world revolution.

John Turner, a Black liberationist, also spoke to the young of UC Berkeley and tied the oppression of African-Americans with a foreign policy that trampled on non-white peoples in Asia and other countries. As the meeting ground on into its third hour, someone lit a joint behind the speaker's platform, and simultaneously everyone sniffed and turned their heads.

Strike leaders urged students to attend classes just for the day so they could help lead discussions about the war and the strike. There was supposed to have been an open mike but when the speaking and voting concluded, everyone was desperate to get out of the badly-ventilated gym and off its hard bleachers. People did stop to listen to Mrs. Nikos Kazantzakis, widow of a great Greek novelist. She told the crowd to love freedom as her husband had. "But", she said, "please, please, please, no violence, don't allow somebody to kill you. Don't use violence, they will kill you." A young Black woman far back up in the bleachers yelled out, "Honey, they're killing us now!"

Tuesday, May 12

Tuesday morning, members of a "Spread the Strike" group charged into traffic during rush-hour on a major nearby roadway, blocking vehicles and causing a massive traffic jam. Police moved in, arrested five people and dispersed the group.

Later that day, an overwhelming majority of the athletes at Cal broke a long tradition of athletes being apolitical and approved a resolution that called for "a unilateral withdrawal of all United States forces in Southeast Asia." It also called for "a reconstitution of American universities as centers against the war." Their announcement stated they were "not voicing our protest in opposition to athletics but to the immoral policy of our government. We hereby pledge to use our athletic abilities to voice our opposition to the war and oppression at home." The Cal football team even went further and voted to boycott spring practice in support of the student strike and anti-war movement.

On Thursday, the UC Berkeley Art Museum opened an exhibit entitled "Protest," with all proceeds from art sales going to anti-war activities and legal expenses. And on Friday, UC Berkeley students joined a large anti-draft demonstration at the Oakland Induction Center.

Despite Gov. Reagan's efforts to reopen the campuses, surveys and polls indicated that strikes on the University of California campuses, including Berkeley, were at least 50 percent effective.

Stanford University

On Tuesday the 12th, strikers gave up their long effort to use blockades to shut down Encina Hall, the administration building. And just a warning from a campus official caused a group that tried to close the applied electronics laboratory to disperse. Plus, eight Stanford students tried to attend the University Trustees meeting to present "the problems of the campus," but were denied entrance.

Also on Tuesday, President Kenneth Pitzer announced that departmental requirements and schedules for the rest of the term would be left to the discretion of the faculty. Coincidentally or not, the very same day, university officials declared they were going to "crackdown" on militant students blocking doors of campus buildings. In response to this threat, 400 students marched peacefully and without incident to President Pitzer's mansion to show their opposition but were unable to meet with him. Later in 1970, Pitzer resigned. He'd been worn out by student protests, he conceded. Provost Richard Lyman took over, becoming the second new president in as many years.

With every "revolution," there's a "counter-revolution," and on Tuesday the counter-revolution showed its face at Stanford. Three conservative student groups announced they had filed a $1,500,000 lawsuit against Stanford University, alleging the university had failed to protect them from radicals in 1969. The six plaintiffs included officers and members of the conservative Free Campus Movement, the Campus Young Republicans and the Palo Alto Republican Party. Plaintiffs claimed they had been severely injured when trying to protect campus buildings from demonstrators.

The counter-revolution also appeared at Stanford University Medical Center where a committee in support of Nixon had circulated a letter of approval for the US move into Cambodia, signed by 300 students and faculty at the center and by another 300 residents in the immediate neighborhood outside campus.

Looking back, the rebellion at Stanford during May substantially altered how the university was run. The Board of Trustees was increased by one-third, with eight trustees directly elected by the alumni, and student and faculty representatives added to most board committees. And for the first time ever, Stanford faculty were granted an elected legislature—the Senate of the Academic Council. Students also became involved in both the forming and enforcement of rules of student conduct.

ROTC was eliminated along with classified research. The controversial Stanford Research Institute that conducted national defense work left Stanford in 1970. Changes in dormitory rules and other aspects of student life brought the school up to modern times. The student population moved away from the overwhelming WASP dominance and evolved towards more of a multi-ethnic student body, and Stanford Memorial Church was opened to all faiths. Quotas limiting women enrollment were dismantled and in 1997, women undergraduates outnumbered men for the first time since World War II.

De Anza College—Cupertino

Monday, May 11

On Monday, a group of over one hundred students and faculty set out from the library and marched with arms locked to a nearby campus entrance. At least two dozen sat down at the Stevens Creek and Mary Avenue intersection and blocked three lanes of traffic including the entrance. Fifteen minutes later Sheriff deputies arrived, and a commander ordered them to clear at least one lane. No one moved. As a deputy directed traffic around the sit-in, others began to arrest the demonstrators, yet everyone appeared to be relatively calm. More patrol cars were called in to assist.

A middle-aged man approached the Sheriff's commander and argued with him. "Leave the kids here," he said. "I was talking to them ..., trying to talk them out of this. They want to get arrested. They aren't going to cause any trouble." The commander threw it right back. "There's trouble right now! We can't let them take over like this."

Moments later, a car driven by a De Anza student conveniently broke down in the one open lane, and the driver couldn't get it started. Deputies pushed it out of the way using a patrol car, damaging its transmission in the process. The paddy wagon arrived and one by one those arrested were walked over and placed on board. Supporters and onlookers cheered and applauded each time a demonstrator was walked to the wagon. Once the paddy wagon was full, a bus had to be called in for backup. Those remaining in the intersection continued the sit-in until they too were arrested. In all, 21 students and 2 De Anza faculty members were arrested for obstruction of traffic. Taken to County Jail, they were booked on misdemeanors with a bail set at $315 each.

Tuesday, May 12

A seminar Tuesday on Southeast Asia attended by dozens of De Anza students morphed into a discussion about the killings of six Black men in Augusta, Georgia, the night before. Black students at the seminar expressed deep concerns about white apathy, at which point, it was decided to move the debate to the steps of the library, a common campus rally point.

After an open-mike was set up, a member of the Black Student Union, Cyndy Broussard, urged those in the gathering crowd to "Move up and listen to what I've got to say. You guys keep talking about getting united.

So, let's get united!" Brossard read a newspaper clipping about the killings in Augusta—six Black men fatally shot in the back by white police officers. She noted with approval that the campus flag was already at half-staff in their honor. "But" she cried, "you've got to think about all the other people who have died in the United States in the past 150 years."

Activist Danie Clark was next to speak. He called out, "All you whites who are helping Blacks in the ghetto – get out! Go into your own ghettos and tell them what we've been trying to get into your heads." Another speaker Lennie Wilson said he had rallied behind white students after the Kent State deaths "just like a fool," because he didn't see any white students behind him now. Wilson urged everyone to come back to the library for a rally at 1 pm and "march with these four caskets to the Sunnyvale courthouse."

When once again, students assembled to protest in front of the library, large numbers of African-Americans and Chicanos were in the crowd along with white students. The march took off, led by mock caskets draped in black with members of the BSU and the Mexican-American Student Confederation acting as monitors. As the marchers proceeded north to Sunnyvale, about four miles, several cars plastered with posters followed, with one having a loudspeaker calling out chants.

It was about 3:30 when the column reached city hall, and a dozen police officers and a handful of city hall workers met it on the lawn. Forming two lines, marchers stood aside as the caskets were carried to the front of the municipal building. Chris Cross, assistant multicultural coordinator for De Anza, addressed the crowd of 400 students and faculty members. He said the march and participation by so many students was reassuring to him as it showed De Anza students cared about the country's race problems. Cross invited police officers, community people and everyone at city hall to come to the De Anza campus to check out the teach-ins, to take part in the dialogues, to leave their emotions at home, and to conquer, he said, "the greatest racist enemy of all — ignorance." The event broke up without incident and demonstrators were ferried back to campus by a squad of cars that had followed the march.

San Jose State College

Things heated as soon as the campus reopened on Monday. Antiwar activists wanted to keep the school closed and at noon, several hundred rallied and then occupied the college administration building, blocking entrances and hallways. Tension viscerally mounted when police arrived, while meanwhile 2,000 students marched in long lines around the campus chanting, "On strike! Shut it down!" repeatedly. When dozens sat down in front of the building, one student was grabbed by police and arrested.

That very day, Dr. Hobart Burns, acting president of college, abruptly announced his resignation. He was torn, he explained to the campus press, between his legal responsibilities on one hand, and his sympathy and anti-war sentiment with the students on the other. As an example, he cited the demand by the Academic Council to give striking students passing grades, even though they hadn't attended classes. State law, he claimed, forbid such an arrangement and he had been placed in an untenable position.

Over at the Engineering Department later that day, 300 students voted to recommend a Pass / No Credit grading system. They also voted to support the president, Dr. Burns.

Stanislaus State College – Turlock

The student body president, Tom Pivetti, opened a Monday antiwar convocation at the "Rock" – a common rally site on campus—by urging the 450 students to "unite in our efforts to the end the war." Peaceful dissent must continue, he said, until "the troops are brought home and the nation turns to its problems on the domestic front. It's about time this nation started to clean up its own backyard."

Pivetti continued. "The system creates a bureaucratic mentality. The institution robs us of the opportunity to answer our questions. Our day is so bogged down with thinking other people's thoughts that we don't have time to think our own." The most effective tactic, he said, was to use the strike to oppose the mindset that sent Americans to fight in Southeast Asia. "In doing so, we withdraw our minds and bodies from the same people who have started an illegal war in Southeast Asia." He finished with a flourish. "Strike until every one of your brothers, husbands or friends are united with their families!"

Tuesday, at **Sonoma State College** an estimated 1,800 people attended the second session of an officially-sanctioned Convocation called by the Academic Senate to consider whether the campus should continue the strike. The first session had been held on May 6, and 2,000 members of a student body of 3,500 voted for a class boycott until May 12. The second session voted to continue the strike against business as usual, even though the session was without official authority. Many at the event felt this was a moral decision that re-asserted the compatibility of academia with concern for the state of American society.

When **UC Davis** reopened on Monday, 50 students announced they were conducting a fast until enough signatures had been collected on an anti-ROTC petition being circulated that the administration would consider closing the program. During the week, students at **UC Santa Cruz** collected 200 draft cards to be sent to a national center in Princeton.

UC Santa Barbara – Isla Vista
Monday, May 11

The target for striking students on Monday when the campus reopened was the Computer Center, long-thought to be tied to a CIA-sponsored war research program. A hundred students assembled at the Center and blocked its doors, trying to prevent its use by staff and faculty. Yet, the move to shut it down did not have a strong base among strikers, so when university officials gave assurances about the computer's mundane operations, the blockaders departed.

Later in the day, a faculty group's proposal for a course on the "National Crisis" to cover war, peace and domestic problems was approved by the administration. 2,500 students ended up enrolling.

Tuesday, May 12

On Tuesday night, there was another move to confront administrators over the Computer Center when a hundred students showed up outside its doors. But by midnight after hours of discussions, an impasse was reached, and frustrated students returned to their apartments and dorms.

Wednesday, May 13

On Wednesday, Chancellor Vernon Cheadle was to speak at a campus convocation he had convened to discuss the Cambodia crisis. Cheadle got up to address the crowd of roughly 6,000 when several dozen students attired in outlandish and bizarre costumes began heckling him. Cheadle insisted they let him speak – and an ovation from the audience made clear that most did want him to speak. Just as he was about to talk, however, cherry bombs exploded beneath his chair – and thinking they were gunshots – aides rushed Cheadle off the stage and out of the stadium.

Strikers received some good news when the contractors' association in Santa Barbara announced they would honor future picket lines and would end all construction on campus for the duration of the student strike. Nobody could have known then that the picket lines would not be returning, as the end of the strike was at hand. In addition, the Academic Senate voted to authorize students whose studies had been postponed by campus anti-war activities to enroll for up to twelve units in a special University Extension course.

Thursday, May 14

After splattering themselves with red paint, 13 students on Thursday laid down in front of the administration building to symbolize the deaths of the Kent State Four and all the Cambodian war casualties. Refusing to disperse, campus police moved in and detained all of them.

Friday, May 15

A floor vote by the Academic Senate on Friday recommended the elimination of all credit for ROTC courses, with a final decision to be made by a mail ballot of all members. The balloting form the June mailing, however, defeated the proposal.

San Fernando Valley State

Monday, May 11

Once the campus reopened on Monday, Sociology was one of the first departments to pledge explicit and moral support to students working against the war by not penalizing them and by giving them fair options for grades. Other departments followed suit.

Tuesday, May 12

On Tuesday the associated student government held an intense debate on whether the student body supported the strike. As a compromise, the council voted unanimously to sponsor a special 2-day referendum for Wednesday and Thursday to decide. The council also turned down a proposal from a college official to suspend any student for a week for participating in militant strike activities, such as blockading doors, disrupting classes or throwing rocks.

Also Tuesday, a petition circulated that called for faculty members to work out optional grading policies with students, so they were not penalized for being out of class. In just a matter of hours, it had nearly 5,600 signatures.

Two hundred history students met mid-morning on the lawn east of the library and formed their own strike committee and demanded that History support the optional grade policy. On another lawn, a majority of 150 students from the English Department voted to support the optional grade policy. When the group walked over to Sierra Towers and presented their demands to the department's acting chair, he told them he would cancel morning classes to allow the English faculty to meet. He said he had a "responsibility to hold classes open," but he "recognizes the conscience of students."

Similar ad hoc committees formed in other departments, such as the Art, Anthropology, and Drama, and students passed similar resolutions in support of the optional grading policy. In contrast, Psychology students ran into "some resistance" from faculty. The strike also reached into the campus student body presidential election. At an Open Forum on Tuesday, Ed Nunez, one of the run-off candidates for president, said he supported the strike, condemned the Kent State killings and denounced the presence of police spies on campuses.

Thursday, May 14

Once the balloting for the 2-day referendum was completed on Thursday, the results were made public—a decisive majority voted to support the student strike. (In 1972, the college was renamed California State University, Northridge.)

UCLA

On Tuesday the 12th of May, the campus anti-war movement came surging back when 8,500 students attended a strike rally. Notably, pledges were taken from the crowd to join picket lines of local striking truck drivers. A much smaller crowd of 200 held a peaceful march on the West Los Angeles Federal Building, less than 2 miles to the south.

A UCLA spokesperson told the press that the campus was in a state of "semi-strike." Faculty members had relaxed academic requirements, the grading system itself was in a state of "limbo," and individual students were meeting with faculty to figure out grades. Some departments were on strike, but others – like Engineering – had kept working.

In an unprecedent move, the Academic Senate voted to disarm all campus police. They also approved a resolution to deny academic credit to ROTC programs until the end of the wars. And thirdly, they voted to redirect academic programs to be more in tune with the needs of ethnic groups. The senate did not approve, however, a motion that would have allowed students to finish out the term exclusively with anti-war activities without penalty.

California State University, Long Beach
Monday, May 11

Student strikers kept the pressure on to keep the Long Beach campus closed. On Monday, they distributed flyers calling for a boycott of classes and at a mid-day rally 2,000 people showed up in support. After marching to the administration building, strikers presented acting president Donald Simonson with a list of demands, which included grading options sympathetic to students and a repeat of the demands of the campus Third World movement for increased minority or "third world" studies and faculty. Word came that Simonson would answer students at the Academic Senate meeting the next day and at a campus convocation scheduled for Wednesday.

Tuesday, May 12

In front of a packed house on Tuesday, the Academic Senate approved a motion that called for a three-hour cancellation of classes for Wednesday to hold a campus-wide convocation "to focus on the problem of bringing the issue of the Southeast Asian War to the community."

However, there was controversy even before the meeting started. Conservative faculty members believed hot-headed campus radicals had called the session, and one faculty senator had tried – without success—to organize a boycott of the meeting. To dispel all this, Senate Chairman Edwin Becker at the beginning of the meeting explained its origins had emerged from a Sunday meeting of the student senate, a body usually apolitical.

When the session started, spectators lined the perimeter of the room, dozens of students peered in from the windows, and marchers with strike signs circulated outside. At the end, the Senate voted to allow strikers to have the options of final grades on a pass/fail basis or accept a withdrawal or incomplete in their classes. Yet, students felt this was a defeat as it left out the option of having the final grade based on course work to date. The Senate did pass a motion that called on the administration to keep the campus open in the future and to pledge to never relinquish control of the campus to any police authority.

A noon rally was the jumping-off point for an impressive effort by anti-war students who had formed the Community Information Committee to conduct a door-to-door canvassing campaign with 300 volunteers. The city of Long Beach had been divided up into 20 sectors for the canvassing, and at the specific request of the campus Third World Movement, "minority communities" were not included. Armed with pens and petitions, the canvassers were to present the students' views with the hope of forming some kind of campus-community coming together as part of an all-out effort to "stop the war."

Canvassers, each with a name tag, were instructed to "be polite, don't push, speak plain English and try to relate to each member of the community." Residents would be asked to sign a simple petition that stated, "The United States must immediately withdraw all troops from all of Southeast Asia." One of the organizers, Don Brady, said, "Our aim is not to alienate the community with rudeness or radical talk," but to find common ground where both sides could work together. The committee planned to continue the door-to-door work the rest of the week.

Wednesday, May 13

Wednesday was the day when classes were officially cancelled for three hours to enable the entire college community to attend a convocation on the war with an address by acting-president Simonsen. Before a crowd of 5,000 students, faculty and staff, Simonson announced his approval of the Senate's ideas on grade policies, thus concretizing strikers' defeat on the issue. He also said, "violence has no place in the educational process" either by the government or by protesters but didn't apparently address students' other demands. Once Simonson concluded, the convocation continued with other speakers on the Indochina war and college turmoil.

Upon **California State Fullerton's** official reopening on Monday, students were out picketing in front of all the major campus buildings in efforts to keep the school closed for the remainder of the academic year. But it was bad timing. They faced the beginning of the all-consuming finals week. While some "unrest" still simmered on campus, the intensity of the strike at Fullerton had passed. Yet, the May protests had defined a generation and a new legacy of student activism had been established at the campus, widening the rights of protest and strengthening the First Amendment for future generations.

Many students who had been on strike at **California State College - San Bernardino** returned to class on Monday wearing black armbands. When **UC Irvine** opened back up, anti-war students renewed their strike activities, and on Thursday, faculty and the administration voted to allow students to take part in anti-war actions without being penalized academically. Later during the next week, several UCI students were arrested after they had joined a striking Teamsters' picket line off-campus.

UC San Diego
Monday, May 11

It was an overcast Monday at the La Jolla campus the day the school "officially" reopened, and the dark clouds from grad student George Winne's self-immolation protest just the day before cast its own gloom. At noon, campus minister Lesley Atkinson and New Left philosopher Professor Herbert Marcuse led a solemn memorial for him. In what some described as the largest crowd ever to be seen in Revelle Plaza, students and faculty filed through paying their respects while trying to process the death of a fellow student.

Yet, the gloom was cast aside and the anti-war movement came roaring back to life that same day. Over a hundred students burst into the upper floor of the Applied Physics and Information Science Department and took it over. They taped newspapers and blankets over office and lab windows so they couldn't be identified. At the center of their protest were the contracts that some of the department's professors had with the Department of Defense.

Protesters hung out in the offices and hallways and during the afternoon, their ranks swelled to 250. A student postal worker feigned a mail delivery, got past campus security lines, and delivered a sack full of donated sandwiches and drinks. It was the third non-violent sit-in within two weeks at the campus.

Around 2 pm, dozens from the sit-in barged into the offices of the Institute for Pure and Applied Physical Sciences that was in the same building and forcibly removed two grad students who hesitated leaving. They then had the entire third floor. San Diego Police were nowhere in sight, although school officials had been in contact with them throughout the day.

Dean George Murphy told the campus newspaper that due to Winne's death the administration would not be insensitive to the students conducting their third sit-in. Just the week before, the administration had vowed not to allow another one. He did say the "administration will reduce the time allowed for the sit-in on a gradual basis to end this chicken game." He added, "I think there is a move on this campus to reject the sit-in. We hope to isolate (the protesters)."

A few minutes before 5 pm and just before the sit-in broke up, occupiers donned paper bag masks with large cut-outs of the faces of Chancellor McGill and Governor Reagan. With their numbers around 150-or-so, they left the building via the northwest side door, while a diversionary crowd stood by at the northeast door. The occupation had ended without incident and students believed they had once again shut down business as usual at departments with deep connections to the Pentagon.

Later, Henry Rooker, the department chair for the latest sit-in, downplayed the role of Defense monies. To a campus newspaper, he claimed DoD funds only paid for five graduate students, and that for the last two years, his department had actually been trying to get rid of Defense funding.

Tuesday, May 12

The student-led campaign against war research on campus finally began to resonate with some faculty and resolutions were introduced in the Academic Senate to sever ties to the Department of Defense and for amnesty for students involved in the building take-overs. Both resolutions were ultimately defeated. Instead, the faculty legislative body flexed its muscles and voted to send a note to the trial judge of students arrested during the sit-ins asking him to consider the students' strong moral convictions.

On Tuesday, the second student-faculty delegation sent to Washington by the university had returned. Their primary task was to lobby for the Cooper-Church Amendment and the McGovern–Hatfield Amendment with the region's Congressmen and Senators. Ann Roman and Jim Galloway were two students among the last delegation and both had lobbied San Diego Congressman Lionel Van Deerlin, the area's lone Democrat.

Roman's delegation hit Van Deerlin in two shifts and found out he already supported Cooper-Church. Her group, she wrote in the *Triton Times*, "moved right away" to McGovern-Hatfield, "telling him that supporting the one and not the other was not enough and threatening to work actively against him if he didn't support both amendments." Van Deerlin shot back, "Don't threaten me, I'm from a navy town." Tempers did eventually cool and Van Deerlin ended up allowing the San Diego delegation to work out of his offices. When they left, Roman told the congressman "how disaffected students were, how, if they didn't see some actions to change things rather than words, then all hell would break loose." Van Deerlin responded that if McGovern-Hatfield passed the Senate, he and others would come out of the woodwork and support it. Roman came away from her experience thinking Congressmen needed constant pushing. "We were there to try to turn people around, and not to be fooled by just being listened to; to confront them and to exert as much pressure as possible," she wrote.

Jim Galloway, the other student lobbyist, was totally dissatisfied with the interaction with Van Deerlin. He felt his delegation went in, said nice things and danced around the need to pressure him for the tougher of the two resolutions. "We thank him so much for his time, say good-bye, and then leave with handshakes all around and a couple of friendly pats on the shoulder." But as a lobbying effort, "it was bullshit," Galloway said. "The name of the game is pressure and power, with political blackmail and fear as rules." He wrote in the *Triton Times*, "If you want to try to work within the system, then you have to do it in the manner that the system works. However, if through acts of conscience, you cannot bring yourself to play those nasty games, then you either sit home and let others do your dirty work for you—you are still an accomplice to the crimes by your non-action—or you start reading *The Making of a Counter Culture* by Teodore Roszak, and that's an entirely different scene with entirely different rules."

Friday, May 15

On Friday, there was a rally at Revelle Plaza in protest of shooting deaths of the six Black men in Augusta, Georgia, organized by the Black Student Council and supported by MEChA. Earlier in the week, when BSC member Sidney Glass announced the event, he pointed out that when a white student is killed in antiwar activities, an immediate response is made to protest the murder. Yet, when Blacks are shot outright by "fascist" National Guard or police when protesting the denial of their civil rights, their deaths go unnoticed - "Except by their Black brothers, that is. Today's radicals seek the cooperation of Blacks in their antiwar activities, but they have not lived up to their 'radicalism' by protesting the deaths of Blacks; so therefore, what kind of gratitude do they expect?" Glass also called for an all-day moratorium and a lowering of the Revelle Plaza flag.

San Diego State College
Monday, May 11

The strike reawakened on Monday with an "official" start at a 10 am rally at Aztec Bowl. No class boycott was involved but the widespread and enthusiastic support for campus anti-war actions translated in a strike headquarters being established in Aztec Center, the student union building and a take-over of ROTC facilities. The Associated Student Council met and voted to call upon Nixon to withdraw all troops from Southeast Asia and called upon College President Malcolm Love to end ROTC—along with all war-related research on campus.

In the mid-afternoon, about 150 demonstrators surrounded the campus flagpole and a couple of students lowered the flag to half-staff to honor the Kent State Four. Once they left, however, a 250-pound San Diego football star walked over and raised the flag back to full staff. He then stood by the flagpole for three hours, warding off challenges and threats against him.

Later in the day, several hundred students rushed the doors of the building housing the Air Force ROTC offices and gained entry. Once inside, they locked the doors and announced they were sitting-in until their demands around ROTC and war-related researched were answered. One woman upset with the protest, peered through the locked doors and asked, "Aren't you going to allow education?" A striker inside replied, "This is education, ma'am." The occupiers stayed all night.

Tuesday, May 12

Throughout Tuesday, occupiers were given a series of escalating warnings from administration officials to disperse or face dire consequences. After the last warning, it was near midnight and students were given time to debate the options. Outside hundreds of supporters gathered and chanted anti-war slogans. Finally, a consensus was reached to be peacefully arrested rather than disperse. San Diego police were informed, and officers moved in and took custody of 17 men and 14 women. Those arrested were led out to a cheering crowd of 1,000 supporters, even though it was past midnight. They were arraigned the next day and each released on $250 bail.

Wednesday, May 13

According to the student newspaper, the *Daily Aztec*, class attendance on Wednesday was roughly 90 percent of "normal." Still, the student government supported the strike and one member explained that many students sympathized with strike activities but were still going to class. The faculty – like the students – were likewise divided but did vote to allow students to substitute options for class attendance and grading. Factions among the faculty mirrored the split in the student body, where students opposed to the strike were labeled as "jocks" and "frats" and pro-strikers were "peaceniks" or "hippies."

The well-functioning strike central in Aztec Center organized a letter-writing campaign that collected thousands of antiwar letters sent to government leaders; it organized door-to-door canvassing in the community by teams of students with petitions and information about the war; it organized Free University classes designed to replace 'business as usual'; and was planning a 6-hour teach-in on "political oppression" with films, workshops and speakers for the 18th. It was held, it was a success but it was the last hurrah for the strike at State.

May 16—US Marine Base Camp Pendleton

Just outside **Camp Pendleton**, a large US Marine base north of San Diego, service men and women and their supporters held an antiwar rally and march on Saturday as part of the national campaign on Armed Forces Day. Organizers claimed 5,000 people were in attendance including about 200 Marines and sailors, students from San Diego colleges and many people who drove down from the Los Angeles area. Speakers included national strike proponent Tom Hayden, Black Panther members and local Marine organizers.

Chapter 7
MONDAY MAY 18 – SUNDAY MAY 24

The Third Week of the National Student Strike

Now in its third week, the National Student Strike on many campuses appeared to be waning, a development reflected and expressed in the newsletters and newspapers of striking students. At the same time at other campuses, however, the strike and protests were only in their second week or just getting organized.

On Wednesday, May 20, the Associated Press reported "Eighteen days after President Nixon sent American combat troops into Cambodia, student protest strikes were under way at a reported 265 college." It added, "However, the disorders and scattered violence which characterized the first two weeks of protests have subsided."

Students on many of the campuses that had not experienced militant protests, it reported, "were quietly organizing for political action aimed at forcing a rapid end to American military operations in Indochina," with campaigns for peace candidates or for Congressional amendments that reduced military funding.

The National Strike Information Center at **Brandeis University** confirmed strikes continued at 265 campuses, and that of those, nearly 150 were among the nation's 1,500 four-year colleges and universities. Other campuses included junior colleges and specialized institutions of higher education. And a dozen schools remained closed for the rest of the school year. The Union for National Draft Opposition announced that over the past week, more than 6,000 draft cards had been turned in to their organization.

Colby College – Waterville, Maine

Published Friday, the very last issue of *Strike Notes* reported $154 had been raised from a student strike rummage sale and auction, which brought the total of the Strike Fund to about $1600.

In the face of College President Robert Strider's intransigence on who was allowed to speak at commencement, seniors at Colby circulated a petition which stated, "We the class of 1970, feel that is our right to have a student speaker of our choice at Commencement exercises on Sunday, June 7th."

Dartmouth College – Hanover, New Hampshire

Monday witnessed the last issue of the *Strike Newsletter* and in explaining their reasons for ending publication, the staff conceded, "It is fairly obvious at this point, that there is no strike at Dartmouth. There has been a change in academic requirements, and a number of students have taken advantage of it - either for political or personal ends." Yet, "the aura of social consciousness so prevalent a few days ago has now virtually disappeared, leaving the campus partially deserted, fragmented in activities, and generally very quiet. The need for a daily newsletter has disappeared."

The staff argued that the strike had raised the four issues of war, racism, political and economic repression, and "the value of the present educational system." Everyone had agreed on the first issue because it "was the easiest" and "was far away" but "almost everyone neglected the last three issues because they hit so close to home and pressed the responsibility of everyone here." They did express the hope that the few, small groups working on the issues would continue the "opening up process which began on May 4." Ending on a positive note, the staff announced that they were actually expanding their paper, moving to a weekly and renaming it simply "Newsletter," to facilitate "the open discussion of relevant issues in the community."

University of New Hampshire – Durham

Monday's *Strike Daily* carried a long, desperate plea from a student who had been active in the campus strike. Chuck Theodore gave "one last futile gasp" to convince his fellow students not to give up the fight. "To those of you who are sitting on your fat asses in your little cubicles of this massive prison, ... you who have found yourselves enjoying a vacation free from the task of thinking—thinking of what is happening to this country and this world."

"For the first time in the history of the University of New Hampshire," Theodore wrote, "apathy was thrown to the wind and students united. Students were together. Everywhere eyes were cast, people were seen wearing looks of aliveness, their bodies moved with a destination in mind instead of abstract wandering without direction. People en mass asking what they could do, where they could get information about the strike, passing the Strike Daily around, getting INVOLVED. Students and faculty alike were thinking; they had become sensitive to what had been and what was happening around then. So many wanted to do something, and they were."

The students at Kent State, Theodore claimed, were "murdered not by National Guardsmen or by a commander who gave the order to fire or by Nixon but by a society that is sick, a society that thrives on war and death, a society that cements shut its mind to cries for peace instead of war, to cries of compassion instead of competition, to love, instead of hate." The killings, "made the students of this nation vomit and instantly everyone everywhere was saying 'hey! Wait a minute. Let's do something!'" Then "two students at Jackson State were murdered. And no one gave it a second thought."

"The same thing has happened to the Strike. Two weeks ago ... this campus was awakened and was alive for the first time. In the air was a wind that told of feelings of what was happening to us, to the country, to the world. People wanted to do something that would institute change, that would make this world a place worth living in, that would make life better. But now there is no one, hardly a soul."

Masses of people energized by the strike had departed, leaving all the strike tasks to just a few. "These people have dropped from an Olympus of optimism to a Hades of depression. They have seen thousands on this campus working for common goals simply get up and quit. They now see a desperate chance to save this world die in the blood of apathy." He vowed to stay on and quoted from a Jefferson Airplane song, "We are all outlaws in the eyes of America!"

Other indicators showed the strike in its death throes. At a Monday meeting the strike coordinating committee was "restructured" to be more effective and include more women members. But there was less and less to coordinate. The strike central hall was abandoned and ideas for a long-range strike fell to the wayside. Nominations for at-large members of the strike committee were announced, but in a telling sign, the vote for them was at a "place and time to be announced."

The *Strike Daily* on Wednesday, May 20, reported only, "Thursday 8pm – Workshop or rally. To be announced." The very last issue was published Thursday but it contained nothing by or about local strikers but instead carried a reprint from Bobby Seale's then-forthcoming book *Seize the Time*. There were no reports of mass meetings on campus or actions or of national events.

Still, the activism ignited in Durham and on college campuses across the land burned into the pages of history, wrote John Scagliotti, then a senior at Colby, in a 40 year retrospective of the May protests published in a local New Hampshire newspaper. Scagliotti was the Durham student who had driven to Boston to pick up the three movement celebrities, Hoffman, Dellinger and Rubin for a May 5 speaking engagement on campus. A year after the May rebellion in April and May 1971, the U.S. Senate Foreign Relations Committee held nearly two dozen hearings on the war in which anti-war groups were allowed to give testimony—Scagliotti was one of the witnesses who testified. "They allowed us in the body of Congress," he said, "and that really came from that week a year before."

Bennington College, Vermont

Tuesday's issue of the strike newsletter struck a derisive tone. One article—typed in all caps for emphasis—said it all. "It is becoming increasingly evident, that the fires of energy during the initial stages of the strike have dwindled. One wonders how with such a burst of outrage at this country's government, the student body and faculty can resume 'business as usual.' One wonders why, perhaps, only two people are writing this newsletter. Where is the literature faculty? Where are the community meetings? ... after all this yelling, where is everybody?"

"Where are you, you 400 students who voted for this strike?" it asked. "Are we like spoiled children who make a lot of noise to get what we want then do nothing with what we've gotten? Was all this concern simply an appeasement of middle class guilt? Or was there a real concern that merits real attention and commitment? Commitment involves action. We cannot continue our efforts without your support and commitment." It also described "three bright lights" still shining "in the foggy apathy:" an economy class was conducting an economic survey for the Bennington area, a play on the Vietnam war was staged for the community and a professor was holding an open class on Marx. It was one of the last issues of the newsletter.

University of Massachusetts – Boston

As an indicator of the status of the strike at UMass, the *Mass Media* edition for Monday, May 18, came out with this admonition, "Don't let the workshops peter out," followed by a list of the very same workshops announced the week earlier.

The campus Afro-American Society made an appeal for funds for the National Black Solidarity Day they were organizing, scheduled for the next day, Tuesday, May 19 – Malcolm X's birthday. Black students working with the local African-American community had requested $1,000 to fund presentations by national speakers on issues as, "The war in Indo-China and impact on Black people," "Racism and oppression in the US," and "White nationalism and imperialism."

Generally, workshops and meetings continued on campus through Tuesday, May 26. There was one discussion meeting of note by the police relations group, "an organization of students and faculty who have been meeting with police officials and patrolmen in an effort to bridge the communication gap."

Other Boston Colleges

On Monday, **Brandeis University** students joined a sit-in at West Newton, a western suburb of Boston to non-violently obstruct buses carrying draftees to their physicals. Eighty-seven people were arrested—many from Brandeis.

In a parallel action on Friday morning, May 22, 200 members of the Non-violent Direct Action Group conducted another sit-in at Boston Army Base in front of a bus carrying inductees. 104 were arrested and then arraigned on charges of loitering and "unlawful sauntering."

At **MIT** on Sunday, May 24, the Student Mobilization Committee (SMC) sponsored a rally to protest the legal cases of two students charged with disrupting classes by leafletting and making announcements. At the time, SMC was dominated by members of the Socialist Workers Party (SWP) who had a mutual distain for members of the Progressive Labor Party (PLP) who dominated SDS. During the rally a fist-fight broke out between members of SMC and SDS. The *Boston Globe's* report blamed SDS and PLP, but sources at MIT reported to the Strike Center that an SDS member had been "harassed" by an SMC member. Seven people of various persuasions ended up in the infirmary.

Wheaton College - Norton, Massachusetts

There wasn't much strike visibility on the all-women Wheaton campus on Monday. The phone at Strike Headquarters wasn't answered; the strike newsletter was no longer being published; and only a nucleus of strikers remained on campus – mainly to keep community speaking engagements. Yet, according to the campus Public Relations Director an estimated 800 students had taken part in the strike. Relatively speaking, the strike at Wheaton had been low-key, one without any violence and only one room had been taken over by strikers – the campus newsroom – which had been turned into strike headquarters. By the end of the second week, some strikers had already gone home.

The real visibility of the strike, however, were those who still attended workshops and meetings, and those who canvassed small factories, supermarkets and local neighborhoods. A local Norton newspaper, *The Sun*, observed that this left about 300 students who had not participated in the strike, and the paper asked, 'Why not?' in several interviews with Wheaton students.

Senior Diane Goepel's priority was getting an education, she explained, and because school cost a lot, she wanted to get her money's worth. She sympathized with strikers but couldn't afford the time it took to be involved—she needed that valuable time to study. Plus, things were already tense enough and more polarization would ruin the cordial relationship between strikers and non-strikers. Once her academic work was completed, she said, she did want to get involved.

Carleen Reynolds, a junior, said that she and others were simply just opposed to a strike as a way to show disillusionment with the country. Anne Armitage, a junior, stated she supported Nixon's policies but hadn't wanted to link up with other students who felt the same way because it would only polarize the campus more.

Sophomore Nancy Sinnott supported the strike and said some of those who had gone on strike didn't like the idea of a class boycott but believed it was necessary – and worth it—to demonstrate their disenchantment with the direction the country was taking. Sinnott and another sophomore, Martha Thurber, summarized the process taken by Wheaton strikers. First, they educated themselves in workshops, and second, they went out into the community to get involved by canvasing door to door, "rapping" with people at supermarkets, speaking at club meetings, inviting lecturers to the campus, and speaking at schools and factories.

The newspaper asked, "What will the effects of all this be?" Some of the women replied there had already been positive developments. For one, the relationships between the students, faculty and administration had all changed for the better. The students had also noticed changes in their relationships with parents. Martha Thurber remarked that she had been amazed at the way she talked to her parents about the strike. In addition, the role of the university was changing within the larger community. Nancy Sinnott said she was really pleased by the reception she and other strikers had received from townspeople in nearby Norton. (Wheaton remained one of the oldest institutions of higher education for women in the nation until 1988 when in order to accommodate women high schoolers who wished to attend coeducational schools, it admitted men.)

Students and faculty from **Williams College** joined residents of Williamstown in forming a group called United Advertising Campaign for Peace. They opened an account with a Madison Avenue advertising agency and began a $2-to-3 million anti-war advertising campaign.

On Monday, final exams began at the **University of Connecticut**, and it was reported that many students took exams at home, while impressive numbers didn't take exams at all and elected instead to take an "S" for a strike grade. Later in the week, the Liberal Arts and Sciences faculty met to decide on whether to give academic credit to faculty-supervised community involvement work, including "activities relating to the three national student strike demands." It was voted down by 256 to 118.

New York State
Union College – Schenectady, New York
Monday, May 18

On Monday, the campus newspaper, *Union Press*, published the names of the eight Black Americans killed by police forces within the previous few days: James Earl Green and Phillip L. Gibbs at Jackson State College; William Wright Jr., Sammie L. McCullough, John "Johnnie" Stokes, John Bennings, Mack Wilson, Jr. and Charlie Mack Murphy in Augusta, Georgia. The newspaper found it "curious indeed" that the barrage of police gunfire at Jackson State had lasted 30 seconds, consisted of at least 140 shots, and was aimed in the vicinity of a Black women's dormitory. Besides the two young men killed, nine people had been wounded, it noted, and that "Green was 17 years-of-age, a high school senior, reportedly on his way home from a part-time job."

Union Press also announced that the National Steering Committee of the National Committee for Economic Actions had called for the "immediate cessation" of all consumer boycotts against the Philip Morris Corporation. After meeting with the president of Philip Morris, boycott committee members believed the company had become "enlightened," especially in terms of "internal management," and that Philip Morris had "both directly and indirectly made significant contributions to the community at large. We are further convinced," the statement read, "that Philip Morris will maintain this progressive corporation attitude in the future. There is no doubt that last week's boycott was the motivating factor in the creation of this progressive policy." Absent any tongue in cheek, the statement concluded the national committee "encourages the American public to resume their purchasing of Marlboro and other Philip Morris products." Around this time vending machines on the Schenectady campus that sold Coca-Colas suffered considerable vandalism. To avoid more damage, the local distributor emptied the machines of all their products.

Tuesday, May 19

On Tuesday, anti-war activists found themselves with an organized opposition with the appearance of a new political group, the Student

Committee for an Alternative Viewpoint, formed to "insure the expression of Conservative viewpoints on this campus."

That evening the top administrator of Rotterdam, a town several miles south of campus, had organized a panel of diverse viewpoints on the issue of "student unrest." The panel consisted of a professor, a college news director, students from Union and **SUNY Albany**, including a member of the Third World Liberation Front, local politicians, police officials and school administrators. Union students and administrators took the initiative and explained the issues of the student strike and the basis of students' grievances. Later, one panel member noted the chief value of the meeting was to show Rotterdam town officials what the colleges were doing and that not all students were "bomb-throwers and communists and revolutionaries." Rotterdam representatives – although receptive—still appeared to be uncertain about dialogue between them and the campus.

Wednesday, May 20

At a Wednesday night meeting of the Strike Steering Committee, a statement was released calling for a halt to the Air Force ROTC program on campus. Addressed to the faculty, it stated, "We young Americans are displeased with what we see happening to our country. We see our Presidents pressured by the Pentagon into entering, and then repeatedly escalating on Asian land war that is not in our best interests. Domestically, most agree that the Military-Industrial Complex, by absorbing astronomical sums of money is precluding meaningful action on our problems at home."

It was "imperative to whittle away at the power of the Pentagon, and its associated civilian corporations before they destroy our nation." To give the nation "a new chance for growth, we have set about to 'seek and destroy' within ourselves and our immediate surroundings, all the tentacles of military power. The most obvious of the pillars upon which the Pentagon stands in our community is the Air Force Reserve Officer Training Corps (AFROTC). It is our belief, then, that ROTC should be told to leave Union at the earliest possible date, June 1970."

New York City
Monday, May 18

In the Big Apple, the art community responded to Nixon and his adventure in Cambodia by forming a group called the Art Strike—an "Expression of shame and outrage at our government's policies of racism, war and repression."

On top of that, a broad coalition of artists demanded that museums and galleries display a disapproval of Nixon's policies and the war's effect on intellectual life. In response on Monday, May 18, museums began closing galleries with what was termed, "a preview of the cultural blackout." Two galleries of the Jewish Museum closed after pressure from artists, as did the New York Cultural Center. The sculptor Robert Morris pulled his show from the Whitney Museum, and at the request of staff, the Whitney displayed protest materials and satirical paintings about the Vietnam War.

Some museums, however, resisted the demand to close. The Metropolitan Museum of Art extended its hours as a "positive gesture." In response, 500 artists picketed the Met to have it change its policy. Instead, it issued a statement claiming its "responsibility to the people of New York is best served by remaining open and allowing art to work its salutary effect on the minds and spirits of all of us."

Wednesday, May 20

Nixon-supporter and New York City labor leader, Peter Brennan, orchestrated a series of rallies by construction workers, longshoremen and white-collar workers against liberal mayor John Lindsay. The rallies culminated on Wednesday in a huge pro-Nixon and pro-war march of tens of thousands through the streets of Manhattan. After consulting with police, who openly sided with the organizers, the press reported that "150,000" had been in the march. It was closer to 60,000.

Thursday, May 21

The next day, a group called the Coalition for Peace made up of labor groups and students staged their own demonstration at city hall with an estimated 20,000 people in attendance. After the rally, several thousand protesters tried to march north to Bryant Park but were blocked by police, and several violent scuffles broke out. Within days, 16 complaints of police brutality were filed.

Thursday was another bad day for Wall Street – "one of the worst in months," the press reported. The Dow Jones sank nearly 15 points, hitting its lowest level since March of 1963. Along with inflation and the general state of the economy, analysts blamed the Indochina War and the threat of war in the Mideast for the bleak report. Dow averages during May 1970 dropped to the lowest average in almost 7 years, and since December of 1969, stock prices had dropped by over 30%.

At the usual joyful May commencement at **Union Theological Seminary,** the ceremony was turned into a memorial service for the six slain young people from Kent State and Jackson State.

SUNY Cortland

University students announced they were staging a three-day hunger strike in the campus dining halls for Monday through Wednesday. Any money saved would go to subsidize the strike movement, its canvassing, letter writing and telegram campaigns, and to help repay the student government House of Delegates, which had lent funds to the strike projects.

A rare disclosure was made by Cortland's Registrar that showed the numbers and percentages of students who chose the different grading options of the well-known Cortland Plan. 606 students, or 13.4 percent of the student body, selected Plan I with the expectation of completing their normal academic program. Another 964 students, or 21.2 percent, were assigned to Plan I automatically because they did not submit any preference. And close to two-thirds, 2,972 students or 65.4 percent, selected Plan II with the strike options. Some students selected Plan II as a form of personal protest against the war but actually concluded the semester by auditing their courses.

Tuesday at **Rochester Institute of Technology** was the first official day of the Alternate University which offered a range of courses from "Development of a College Curriculum," "RIT as a Polluter," to "Post Modern Literature" and "Modern Asian Cultures." The essential theme, as one coordinating committee member put it, was that relevant courses should be available to people "who just can't comprehend sitting in an art class while things like politics and race relations are going down around them." The Alternate Institute appeared to have captured the imagination of a large cross-section of both the faculty and the administration, with strong student support. Most courses were composed of subjects students and faculty had suggested and were run along the seminar model, where students were not lectured, but instead engaged in free discussions.

Princeton University, New Jersey

From May 19 to the 21st, a national conference on draft opposition was held at Princeton sponsored by the newly-formed UNDO, the Union for National Draft Opposition, and attended by members of over 130 schools and organizations. Campus representatives came from across the country and delegates included a 'who's who' of established peace groups: the ACLU, American Friends Servicemen's group, the Fellowship of Reconciliation, the New Mobe, National Committee to Repeal the Draft, Peacemakers' Conference and East Coast Resistance.

UNDO had called for a national day of draft resistance for June 10th and its plan was to paralyze the Selective Service System by inundating draft boards with mass applications for conscientious objector status and with registration applications from women. UNDO's operating assumption was that if thousands sent in their draft cards and applications, the federal bureaucracy would break down—and the government could not indict all of them. UNDO had selected Princeton as the mail depository for anyone who wanted to mail in their draft card.

During the strike at Princeton, roughly 80 percent of the student body had chosen to boycott classes. Nearly a dozen campus social clubs had cancelled house parties until Commencement 1970. Yet even Commencement wasn't spared protest. Members of the graduating class of 1970 marched with signs that read "End the War" or walked without cap and gown and wore street clothes with white arm bands. Princeton University president, Robert Goheen, had been one of the 37 university presidents who had formally petitioned the White House and Congress for the ending of American military involvement in Indochina.

During the May turmoil, tough segregationist and white supremacist Sen. Strom Thurmond from South Carolina had raised the issue of work by Princeton students for antiwar congressional candidates. Thurmond publicly questioned whether Princeton students' use of university facilities, including computers, on the campaigns compromised the school's tax-exempt status. President Goheen retorted that, "As a corporate entity," the university would maintain its neutrality on political issues, and none of its funds were involved. The IRS said it was investigating. Despite Thurmond's concerns, the campus' academic calendar for fall of 1970-1971 was revised to allow students to canvass for political change during a two-week recess before the November elections.

Temple University – Philadelphia, Pennsylvania

Temple students joined others from the **University of Pennsylvania** and **Swarthmore** in developing a radical education project and organizing campaign. They planned to form the Philadelphia Regional People's University and open up their respective colleges to the surrounding communities. One of their goals was to study the connections between racism and the war and strategize on effective actions for change. Their list of changes included freeing up college facilities for community use, such as the library, the student activities building and the physical education complex. They wanted a day care center in the student activities building for student and community mothers, a job-placement program for unemployed community youth, and workshops to include film/ lecture programs by Black community groups. However, there is no record that any of these worthy and idealistic ideas were ever put into immediate form.

The Temple Strike Committee leafletted a speech by pro-war Senator Hugh Scott at Temple Sinai in West Oak Lane on Sunday, May 24, and afterwards engaged him in a testy argument. Scott had made statements such as, "I will not be influenced by numbers," and "The war will be forgotten soon!" After Scott refused to answer questions, the students walked out.

Later in the week, the *Strike Bulletin* pondered the status of the strike. "The Strike is still on. The 3 basic demands of the Strike have not been met. ... The war is still on, and Temple still has ROTC, no thanks to the Board of Trustees. Temple is now considering doubling the size of its police force at a cost of almost one million dollars." Then it pleaded, "The Strike Committee needs help. ...Help is needed for leafletting, poster making, ..."

University of Pittsburgh, Pennsylvania

The Pitt News reported, "For the second time in as many weeks, Pitt students gathered to mourn the killing of college students." A Monday, May 18, afternoon rally commemorating the deaths of the two Black men slain at Jackson State was called by the Black Action Society. The 300 people in attendance were scattered across the sun-drenched Cathedral lawn and listened to speakers compare the size of the day's event with the crowds after the killings of white students at Kent State. Paul Carver, history instructor at Carnegie-Mellon, enumerated the incidents of Blacks being murdered at Southern schools, incidents that the public never heard about because of "the racist mass media." He told the crowd, "When they murder Viet Cong, Cambodians, Blacks, they are also shooting us."

Richard Utley from the Black Action Society was critical of white students who had ignored the event. "We called this rally," he said, "to see if whites would help." He urged students to participate in the upcoming one-day strike on Wednesday that his group had called, and to contribute money to the Jackson State Defense Fund. Utley's theme was picked up by David Montgomery, history professor, who said, "The lawn was jammed for the Kent State rally. There isn't quite that feeling here today." The differences in the two responses, he said, was "a division we cannot afford." He continued, "The time is here to do much, much more than protest," and that there was a need for solidarity between Blacks and whites. Closing out the rally, Nate Smith, a local Black leader, volunteered to lead everyone to another a commemoration of the Jackson State killings in a nearby Black community. About 60 people followed Smith and marched to the rally at Centre Avenue and Grove Street.

That same Monday, two dozen women from the Committee for Women's Rights abruptly burst into Chancellor Wesley Posvar's offices and announced they were staging a teach-in right then and there unless their demands were met. Posvar smartly consented to meet and discuss what was on their demands list. At the top - besides no recrimination against any of them—they wanted at least half of the eight high-level administrative positions filled with women; the establishment of a campus interdisciplinary school for women's studies; a day care center for female married students and faculty members—and they wanted the school to commit to act before May 26.

Posvar's first response was that he didn't think the group represented the sentiment of other women on campus. Dr. Ina Braden, president of the committee, explained how over the last few months their written requests for reform had been shunted from committee to committee but acted upon by none. "It is the frustration of going around in circles," she said, "that brought us here today." They wanted Posvar to order department chairs, deans and the department of personnel to hire more women. "We can only replace people at the rate they depart," Posvar replied.

He also failed to see the logic of setting up a separate School for Women's Studies. One woman answered that there was a definite need to investigate woman's role within the various fields of discipline. She emphatically stated that other universities had recognized this, that women's studies had been established at Stanford and at the University of California. The Chancellor grumbled, "The university cannot respond to a set of demands within a given time period."

Dr. Braden said she estimated the reforms would cost the university between two and four million dollars, to which the Chancellor said all funds for the next fiscal year had already been earmarked. As the talk wound down, the chancellor did make some promises. He would appoint three women to administrative posts—a mere tokenism the protesting women thought—and he would initiate a study of establishing a women's study program.

University of Maryland – College Park
Monday, May 18

Two members of the strike steering committee banned from campus, Frank Greer and Elizabeth Miller, went to court Monday and assisted by the ACLU, tried to obtain an injunction against their evictions. Refusing to issue an injunction, the judge did order that appeal hearings for students fighting their evictions required more due process. Faced with the ruling, the university rescinded the orders against Greer and Miller.

Under the martial law imposed by National Guard Commander General Warfield, a "neutral" appeals board for students had been set up by the general, made up of the school vice-president, the campus security director and a National Guard officer. Hardly an impartial panel, the vice-president and the security director were the ones who had provided Warfield with the list of students to ban.

To defy the ban on demonstrations, students had organized a rally for Monday, but a mere half hour before it was to begin, General Warfield rescinded the ban, allowing it to proceed. He said, "student responsibility was beginning to reassert itself." One thousand gathered on the mall, including many who turned out to protest the ban and the military presence on campus. Speakers with the strike committee hailed the victory but warned they had received word that students were being harassed by the FBI. Then, in a significant recognition of the state of the campus, members of the Anthropology, Sociology and Economics departments announced their faculties were on strike and were flatly refusing to teach while the campus was under control of the military.

Wednesday, May 20

At midnight Wednesday, 1,500 students decided to challenge the curfew and staged a peaceful march to President Bull Elkins' house, in memoriam to those killed at Kent State, Augusta, Georgia and Jackson State. There were no incidents nor arrests.

Thursday, May 21

On Thursday, the last member of the "Maryland Ten" to be served with warrants—Larry Babits—turned himself in to police. On May 4, graduate assistant Babits had been wounded by police buckshot during the actions around Route One. Other members of the Maryland Ten included current SDS activists Karen Pomerantz, Mark Woodward, and David Willett, plus Richard Fox of the Revolutionary Youth Movement 2 – a faction of SDS—and Robert Wade, a longtime member of SDS since 1967; also, Steven Cullen, Lawrence Dean and Terry McKeon, leaders of the Vietnam Moratorium Committee. The tenth person was a young woman student who was not an activist but resembled one of the anti-war leaders. Babits was the lone faculty arrested.

Friday, May 22

On Friday, 3,000 students turned out for the last major rally on campus to hear Jane Fonda and author Mark Lane speak about the GI movement. Fonda talked about a series of actions at military posts around the country, including one at Fort Meade that day. Once the rally concluded, about 15 students joined Fonda and Lane and traveled to Fort Meade to try to leaflet soldiers. They were detained and expelled by military authorities.

Ft Meade

The protest at **Fort Meade** was part of the nationwide campaign to support anti-war GIs. About 500 to 600 civilians joined a hundred GIs for a march and rally near the Army post between Baltimore and Washington. There were speeches by Abbie Hoffman, Susan Schnall, an Army nurse jailed for her antiwar efforts, a member of the Black Panther Party, GIs and veteran Spanish revolutionaries. The military had put out an alert that demonstrators would be violent, but the action was entirely peaceful except for authorities kicking Jane Fonda and a few students off the base.

Washington DC

On Monday, a few days after the murders of Black men at Jackson State, President Nixon met with 15 Black university and college presidents, including the president of Jackson State. Veteran civil rights leader and head of the National Urban League, Whitney Young, Jr., had said at the time that, "Southern law officials are almost given license" to kill protesting African Americans due to speeches by Nixon and Agnew. (Less than a year later, Young would drown while swimming in the Gulf of Guinea while attending a conference in Lagos, Nigeria.)

On Wednesday, the New Mobe announced from their DC office that antiwar protests were being planned for Memorial Day, May 30, in atleast eight U.S. cities.

At the **District of Columbia Teachers College**, students and faculty agreed to use the remaining class time in May "for consideration of social, economic, and political issues."

Southeast

Washington and Lee University – Lexington, Virginia

Twenty W&L students joined others from Virginia campuses on Monday, May 18, in lobbying legislators in Washington. Senators Birch Bayh of Indiana and Joseph Tydings of Maryland – both Democrats – were contacted and told students they planned to vote for the McGovern-Hatfield Amendment to end the Vietnam War by the end of the year. The Virginia student lobbying group – made up mainly of W&L and **University of Virginia** students—worked out of the offices of the National Student Association and was considered one of the most important student lobbying groups in DC.

Back on campus, Tuesday's issue of the strike newsletter ran a short article about how the 12 African-American students wounded by police at Jackson State on May 15 were still in the hospital.

North Carolina State University at Raleigh

Beginning Monday, between 250 and 300 students from the Raleigh campus began canvassing local neighborhoods with petitions and postcards. After obtaining "permission" from Raleigh Mayor Seby Jones, canvassers went door to door urging townspeople to express their opposition to the war by signing postcards addressed to North Carolina's senators, and by signing petitions in support of the McGovern-Hatfield Amendment. Over the course of May, students claimed half of Raleigh had been canvassed, that 16,000 signed postcards and over 1,000 signatures in support of the amendment had been collected.

Also on Monday, the much-ballyhooed and administration sanctioned "Peace Retreat" began, and it involved a wide array of campus organizations including some that supported the war. It's guiding principle was based on the premise that higher education did not adequately focus on real world issues, and "that the traditional classroom experience is not relevant, and the methods of teaching are far from adequate." One Christian group proposed "peace through Christ" and another group, American Students for Action, opposed the war but supported Nixon and his policies – and claimed it had collected more than 3,000 signatures on a petition in support of Nixon. The Mobilization for Peace was clearly visible and expressed its purpose was to mobilize anti-war actions focused on the imperialist nature of the war in Indochina, not just on actions deploring U.S. involvement.

The Retreat's Steering Committee also brought in outside activists and speakers to assist with the programs. One group, Guerilla Theater, performed skits throughout the Raleigh area to illustrate the horrors of war. Jerry Lewis, a Kent State faculty member who had witnessed the shootings, spoke on Wednesday, the 20th, and remarked that the Peace Retreat was one of the better student organizations he had witnessed during all his campus visits. Over the next couple of days, the antiwar sentiment at the Retreat was expressed by 100 students who traveled to Washington DC to lobby their Congressional representatives.

"March Against Repression" – Perry, Georgia

With shouts of "Soul power!" and "I am somebody!" more than 300 demonstrators on Tuesday, May 19, joined Rev. Ralph Abernathy, president of the Southern Christian Leadership Conference (SCLC) on a 5-day, 100-mile march across Georgia to the capital in Atlanta. Marchers followed a mule-drawn coffin from the Black Belt Georgia town of Perry in a "March Against Repression." The procession—a protest of the Augusta and Jackson State deaths—was made up mostly of youthful Black marchers except for five white students from the **University of Georgia**. The mules had names — the white one was nicknamed Nixon and the brown one Maddox. Paced by three Georgia Highway Patrol cars, the march was without incident except when youngsters killed a four-foot-long rat snake during a rest period. Few white people were seen along the road, and those that did appear did not seem hostile.

At a Perry town hall meeting before the march began, SCLC organizer Hosea Williams blamed Nixon and Georgia Gov. Lester Maddox for the recent repression that had caused 12 deaths at the hands of law enforcement (six Black men in Augusta, four white students at Kent State, and two young Black men in Jackson). At a press conference, Williams read a telegram he had received from Governor Maddox, in which Maddox tried to persuade organizers to cancel the march. "I urge you to cancel the protest march from Perry to Atlanta," the telegram began. "Previous nonviolent marches and demonstrations by your group and similar groups, all supported by the Communist enemies of freedom in America, have spawned the hate and prejudice among our young and some of your fellows which later led to the violent deaths of six people in Augusta."

Residents of Perry, who made up most of the marchers, were not to be persuaded by Maddox. During previous weeks, they had been protesting the dismissal of two Black teachers and against segregated classrooms in local public schools. During the protests in early May, police had made a mass arrest of 275 African-Americans and had jailed them for three days in a prison camp closed because it was deemed unfit for human habitation. Tuesday's march began on the very street where the mass arrests had occurred.

The night before the march in Athens, Georgia, 400 local residents, Black and white, pledged mass rallies every night of the week in solidarity with the residents of Augusta, a little over 80 miles away. They also expressed support for the planned arrival of the March Against Repression and planned to join mass demonstrations in Atlanta that Saturday. One Black high school student told a reporter from the *Great Speckled Bird*, an Atlanta underground newspaper, "We're prepared, we'll sit in the streets, pack the jails, but we're gonna win."

Florida Memorial College – Miami
Monday, May 18

Students at the historic Black college at Florida Memorial College had been demanding that the administration increase Black enrollment, faculty and Black studies. But when the administration refused to accede to their reforms, several hundred seized a campus administration building. On Monday night police arrived and tried to forcefully evict the occupiers. This resulted in skirmishing between rock-throwing students and club-swinging police for more than an hour. Police resorted to using teargas to disperse the remaining 200 or so demonstrators from the area. All toll, 26 were arrested.

University of Tennessee – Knoxville

Like many colleges across the country, the strike at the Knoxville campus subsided with the onslaught on finals, graduations, fatigue, and summer. Yet the energy and the activism it generated didn't die. It resurfaced at the end of May when it was announced the world-renowned evangelist Billy Graham would be bringing his 10-day crusade to the university's stadium.

Knoxville officials had been planning the event for a year and were all geared up for Graham's visit. During the previous spring, thousands of Knoxville residents had signed a petition to bring him and his crusade to Neyland Stadium and Graham had accepted. One wrinkle—many in the college community didn't think it was appropriate for the university to host a Christian mass meeting like the crusade.

Nevertheless, the crusade opened on Friday, May 22, with plans to run through May 31. On May 24, Johnny Cash played before 62,000 people, and a few days later, it was announced that Nixon himself would be attending. Many assumed that Nixon wanted to show that he could appear on a college campus three-weeks after the Kent State killings. Plus, he knew he had many supporters in that part of the country. Antiwar activists at UT, of course, saw Nixon's visit as a perfect chance to directly confront the president and show opposition to his war policies.

Monday, May 18, at **Fisk University**, a predominantly Black school in Nashville, a fire blamed on arson destroyed Livingston Hall, a four-story campus building.

University of Alabama, Tuscaloosa

On Tuesday, 150 students made one last effort to challenge the curfew and ban on campus demonstrations imposed by Alabama Governor Lester Brewer by holding a rally. Once it began, police and National Guard troops quickly moved in and arrested 37 brave souls for curfew violations. Beginning May 6, the campus had experienced an unprecedented burst of student activism—only to be locked down since and under virtual martial law for most of the period.

Forty years later, former UA antiwar activists recalled those heady days in a local newspaper. Vietnam veteran Tom Ashby had left UA to fight in Vietnam and had returned to the university in time to play a role in anti-war protests. He had blocked out his views on the war, he recounted, until he saw the way students who voiced their opposition were being treated on campus. "Our society was so ignorant about what was going on in Vietnam and the civil rights movement," Ashby said decades later. "I had a responsibility to do what I could to make what I knew we were doing in Vietnam known."

Former Alabama governor Don Siegelman was also a student on the Tuscaloosa campus at the time, and said he was greatly affected by the way students were being mistreated. "We were equally concerned with the attitude that the administration at the University of Alabama held toward students along with the societal issues that could impact the whole community," he said four decades later. Siegelman had been worried about being drafted. "I was lucky enough (to have connections) with the National Guard and I joined up. And that is the only reason I was able to run for public office because I'm sure if I were forced with the decision of fighting in Vietnam or moving to Canada as a conscientious objector, I would have become a conscientious objector."

Former activist Eugenia Croscheck said, "I felt in my heart it was the right thing to do." That was echoed by Carol Self, who said, "It was just an awakening where you start to see what your heart believes."

Auburn University in Auburn, Alabama

Student reaction to Cambodia and Kent State came relatively late to Auburn University. On Thursday, May 21, a day long strike was enacted with marches, speeches, debates, draft counseling, films and petitioning—attended by up to 400 Auburn students.

By 8 am, tables with a multitude of petitions had been set up including one in favor of the McGovern amendment. Others included support for women's liberation, for environmental controls, against bacteriological warfare, against overpopulation, malnutrition, poverty, and for the conservation of wildlife and natural resources. The Young Republican Club set up their table near the McGovern one and claimed by the end of the day they had collected 1,700 signatures endorsing President Nixon's Cambodian policy.

Originally called for by the group, the Human Rights Forum, the strike included picketing at the newly-constructed Haley Center which housed administrative offices. Auburn president Harry Philpott had even attended some strike activities, and members of his administration had provided beverages to participating students. Earlier, Philpott had issued a statement in support of students' freedom of expression, and in fact, had been commended by the American Association of University Professors for his defense of a "Strike for Peace" event as protected free speech.

Strikers staged a militant march through campus while chanting "Peace Now! Peace now!" and wound through Samford Park and ended up at Graves Amphitheatre for speeches and a free concert by Beggar's Opera, a local rock group. One speaker was outgoing Theatre Department head, Dr. Kenneth Campbell, who told the crowd, "You have a Congressman - bug the hell out of him. Don't let your Senator sleep until he has answered your 'whys' satisfactorily." He then read a telegram addressed to President Nixon he wanted people to sign. It read in part, "Our strike was a substitute for violence, a chance for expression of dissent without resorting to the streets.

The strike is a long accepted form of peaceful protest. It binds people together in a common endeavor bringing to bear pressures without violence upon a source of dissatisfaction. ...We urge you to take the required action to end the war and to bring the nation together." Some 550 students and faculty members ended up signing it.

Rev. Kuykendall from the First Presbyterian Church in Auburn spoke of how the nation had reached "the end of the line" in three areas, "leadership, rhetoric and violence." Thursday's strike, he said, was "an occasion to say in a nonviolent fashion that we've reached the end of our rope in these areas." The peace America was seeking, he explained, is represented by the Old Testament term "Shalom – a peace not only as the absence of war, but as a time of well-being for all mankind, a time which is marked by reconciliation, concern for other human beings, freedom, and hope for the future." Kuykendall received a standing ovation.

A representative of a group of Republicans opposed to the war, Michael Brewer, listed several reasons why he supported the McGovern-Hatfield amendment. The Constitution granted Congress the power to raise and control armies, he said, and maintain the balance of powers. If Congress disagreed with Nixon, Nixon should not be able to have complete control of the armed forces. He said McGovern-Hatfield was completely in agreement with the President's objectives, as it merely guaranteed that Nixon follow his original plan of action. Brewer ended with, "the only assured way to bring peace is to work for change in the composition of the House and Senate."

Dr. Joseph Harrison, a professor of history, had similar advice. "Don't re-elect the Congressmen who support the war in Vietnam. Put pressure on Congress. Run peace candidates for office even though they might not win." He urged students to "go out and do the hard, disillusioning and often unrewarding work of supporting a local candidate." Harrison also advised them not to insult the people they're trying to persuade. "Don't antagonize them with words, pamphlets, and salutes. That is not practical politics." Next to speak was a candidate for Georgia governor from the Socialist Party, Linda Jeness. She lectured that universities should be "organizers and participants in the social struggle that we are involved in and not as training grounds for ROTC, CIA or captains of industry, and not havens for counter insurgency programs and germ warfare."

This wasn't the first antiwar protest at Auburn. Until the fall of 1969, students' concerns had focused on racial equity, women's rights, university disciplinary policies, ROTC and student funds. Then during the Moratorium in October '69, Auburn students took on the war in Vietnam, and held a peace vigil and other antiwar activities. These actions rattled the then pro-war administration, and in December it enacted restrictive guidelines that all student protests were expected to follow.

Jackson State College, Mississippi
Monday, May 18

Three days after police shot into a Black girls' dormitory killing two men and wounding another 12 people, across the city, African-American students were on the move. 500 Black school children walked out of their classes and marched to the Governor's mansion where they surrounded it with picket lines. Dozens of Jackson State students also formed picket lines – but in front of stores to enforce a boycott of white businesses.

Fearing another massacre, Jackson community leaders sought to focus the anger and organized a boycott of white businesses, holding church rallies at night. Charles Evers, mayor of Fayette, called for a boycott of all white-owned businesses across the state until May 24, and asked that all colleges close in solidarity with the slain youth.

Other young Black people, however, were in no mood for picket lines and boycotts—including many Jackson State students. Some seethed with rage and threatened to burn downtown Jackson. "Moderate" Black leaders spoke of forming a paramilitary defense group to arm and protect their community and align with the Mississippi United Front, a civil-rights organization.

Many students stayed on the scene at Alexander Hall—both to protest the massacre and ensure that the facade of the women's dorm, pocketed with bullet holes and broken windows, was kept intact to be used as evidence in investigating the tragedy.

Tuesday, May 19

By Tuesday white repair workers and state investigators had twice within 24 hours tried to enter the Alexander Hall dorm—only twice to be turned away by a hundred students. Students posted a sign that read, "No Evidence Is to Be Removed." There was a very real fear that anything turned over to state investigators would end up as part of the cover-up, after all, state police were refusing to cooperate with the FBI.

A couple of defiant campus rallies were held on Tuesday involving from 300 to 700 students—one was held right outside the shattered dorm. Later students gathered at the college football stadium for a meeting with President Peoples, and afterwards a large crowd marched back to Alexander Hall to continue their occupation of the dorm grounds. They chanted and held signs, like, "Shoot Me, My Back Is Turned," "Pigs Watch out!", "Deliver Me From [governor] John Bell Williams."

Jackson Mayor Russell Davis had formed a biracial committee to investigate the incident, and after over a week of hearings and witness testimonies, it issued a majority report. It had three conclusions: 1) students at Alexander Hall had posed no threat to police, despite some objects being thrown; 2) there was no credible evidence of any sniper and police had made no real effort to protect themselves from snipers; and 3) city police had not participated in the fusillade.

This was quite a relief for the mayor. Yet, unbeknownst to the mayor's committee, the FBI had found a type of buckshot at the shooting site that only Jackson city police used. City police had indeed been involved in the massacre.

During the remainder of May, the city of Jackson remained tense. Immediately following the shooting, three white-owned storefronts in Black neighborhoods had been engulfed in fires. Gun shops did a brisk business, National Guardsmen patrolled the streets and bivouacked in local parks, the local white press continued to blame students and snipers for the deaths, and more white storefronts were burned.

Hundreds of Jackson State students stayed camped out in front of the dorm. A court order was engineered to force them to give ground, but in response even more rallied in front of TV cameras and tore the order up. Finally, President Peoples and student leaders and activists came to an agreement with investigators after being convinced that anything collected as evidence would be given to the FBI—and not to the state police. US Attorney General John Mitchell even flew to Jackson to view the damage at Alexander Hall and appeared to be genuinely shocked at the sight of 250 bullet holes in the steel and concrete.

US Senators Walter Mondale and Birch Bayh came to Jackson to attend James Green's funeral and to view the battered dormitory. A reporter asked Senator Bayh if he thought the police had over-reacted even if there had been a sniper. Bayh responded, "I've heard no evidence of a sniper," and noted, "...if you do have a sniper, you don't just shoot everything in sight." Senator Mondale added, "It's a new national syndrome – the unfound sniper. Every time there's an overreaction, that unfound sniper always gets blamed."

The national reaction to the Jackson State killings was not as widespread or intense as the reaction to the Kent State shootings. Rallies and memorial services were held on campuses from New York, Chicago, Utah, and California – and not all of them were peaceful. Some predominately Black colleges closed down and some predominately white colleges cancelled classes. Students at the **University of Southern Mississippi** held a general strike for two days.

In late July, a Hinds County grand jury released its report and criticized Jackson Mayor Davis for contributing to the shootings by not allowing the use of tear gas, instead of bullets. Davis claimed he only delayed the use of tear gas until the arrival of the National Guard and said no other request for its use had been given to him. He also continued to dispute the report that Jackson city police had taken part in the shootings.

In December of 1970, seven months later, a federal grand jury failed to produce any indictments or written findings after it had summoned 49 state patrolmen and 26 Jackson city police officers to testify. The President's Commission on Campus Unrest investigated the Jackson State shootings and concluded, "the 28-second fusillade from police officers was an unreasonable, unjustified overreaction...A broad barrage of gunfire in response to reported and unconfirmed sniper fire is never warranted." Still, there were no arrests in connection with the deaths at Jackson State.

Subsequently, the Jackson City Council voted to close Lynch Street, where the shootings had occurred—Mayor Davis voted in favor. At that same meeting, the council added the initials "J. R." to the existing street signs, denoting J. R. Lynch Street, named after one of Mississippi's leading

Black statesmen during Reconstruction, Congressman John R. Lynch. Today, his full name is on the street signs.

The university memorialized the shootings by naming the area Gibbs-Green Plaza and turning it into a large, multi-level brick patio and mall for the campus. A large stone monument sits in front of Alexander Hall near the plaza honoring the two victims. And damage to the façade of Alexander Hall is still visible. Fifty years after the Jackson State massacre, five of the seven Jackson city council members were African American, and the young mayor was Black with a last name of Lumumba.

The **Loyola University** administration in Louisiana continued to refuse to take a stand on the Southeast Asia war. In response, students set up picket lines, staged demonstrations against ROTC, held fasts – all of which continued up to the end of the academic term, May 19. But not to be forgotten, antiwar protesters appeared at commencement exercises on May 22.

Midwest
Ohio State University – Columbus

The Columbus campus of OSU reopened on Tuesday, May 19, under tight control. President Novice Fawcett had abruptly closed the campus on May 6th after daily protests for a week had resulted in the National Guard coming onto campus and flooding it with tear gas. Classes reopened to enable the university to finish the quarter, and the mood of students was subdued—many appeared to be in a state of shock. They wanted to finish the term and get the hell out of there.

Still, the strike coalition held a noon rally on the Oval Tuesday and returning students were greeted by a "special issue" of the strike newsletter with an editorial entitled "Welcome Back to the Ohio Police State University - Local Prison Reopens." It stated, "They need us back to study their history and learn their skills and get one of their degrees so that we can take our places in their society and serve them better. In other words, they want 'business as usual.'"

The editorial criticized the campus administration for "pushing the same old lies and half-truths about protecting the campus community from a small number of outside agitators and hard-core radicals...." It concluded,

"The pig administration has thus shown us that they will deprive us of our rights, throw us in jail, order armed troops onto campus, or do whatever they think is necessary to ensure that the product that they turn out for the ruling class of rich businessmen continues to crawl off the production lines at the Ohio State University."

Another provocative article headlined, "OSU and the Devil" lambasted the university for its connections to the war machine, the ROTC program and its cooperation with the draft board. The university was engaged in military contracts, it stated, "aimed at developing new and better methods of killing people in Southeast Asia and around the world wherever a national liberation struggle may endanger US corporate super profit-making foreign holdings." It described Ohio State's ROTC program as "the largest in the country, turning out hundreds of officers every quarter to command a war which has already killed over one million Vietnamese people." Ohio State war research was a business. "In the fiscal year of 1967," it reported, "the OSU research foundation had $4,137,000 in contracts with the Department of Defense." It ticked off a number of key military contracts, their values and the names of the professors who worked on them.

For example, three professors were involved in a $220,000 research project funded by the US Army to evaluate combat weapons systems. Another $182,198 contract with the US Army Missile command involved "developing a model capable of evaluating the concept for a target illuminator and other close support weapons." The article continued, "The intricate link of the University with the war machine can no longer be ignored. We must educate ourselves to the extent in which the university has dipped its hands into the blood of the Vietnamese people. We must demand that all war related research be stopped immediately." In giant letters, it screamed, "War is a disaster – not a science." It continued, "The fact that military matters receive higher priorities than the problems of poverty, racism, war, imperialism, and pollution can only by understood when we realize that the university serves the interests of the rich, not the people."

It concluded, "The student strike is an act of resistance against these forces of violence and destruction. We have acted, not because we do not value education, but because we refuse an education which trains officers and strategists; that equips us only to serve business interests as technicians and managers, that produces scholars cut off from social realities. We have acted not because we wanted the university closed down, but because we wanted it opened up. Opened up to blacks and other minorities, opened up to poor whites and working people, opened up to women." Lastly, "The response to our movement was to threaten us, to beat, arrest, gas, and shoot us, and finally to lock us out. But this repression won't work."

On Thursday, May 21, a huge crowd of 8,000 people filled the Oval to listen to speeches from strikers and faculty members. However, it appeared that many in the university community were too exhausted to continue the fight. When a speaker yelled through the microphone to "Shut it down!", there was a massive cry from the crowd, "No!"

At **Kent State University Stark,** the campus newspaper the *Montage* editorialized about the calamity at Kent State. "And who is to blame?" It asked. "The National Guard, the KSU students, President Nixon and his administration, are they to blame? No, the American public is to blame and it is they who must carry the burden of a distressed nation, an unchanging world of false ideals in a changing society." It continued, "It is our obligation to posterity to heal the wounds which have left us a house divided and which necessitates a meaningful adjustment to these recent events. For the whole world is watching."

At a special campus meeting Tuesday, May 19, at **Wittenberg University** in Springfield, Black students pointed to the stark differences in outrage expressed after Kent State and then after Jackson State. President of Concerned Black Students, Peter Davis, described what happened after Kent—a cancellation of classes, teach-ins, protests—and then compared it with the nearly non-existent campus reaction to Jackson State. He said, "Today, a more prevalent and persistent problem exists – Black vs white." He ended with a question for "White Wittenberg." "Where now do your priorities lie?"

By Monday, at the **University of Toledo** there had been no response from President William Carlson to the four demands submitted by the Black Student Union after the deaths at Jackson State—one demand had been for a three-day moratorium. To protest the administration's "indifference," 40 members of the BSU set up blockades and picket lines around campus. Finally, after four hours of protests, Carlson met with them and announced afterwards he had conceded to the moratorium. He claimed he had made the decision Friday but had not gotten around to announcing it. The BSU and Carlson agreed on other demands—$200,000 would be set aside for a Black studies program, and the university would seek more Black professors and graduate students.

Michigan State University – East Lansing
Monday, May 18

On the night of Monday, May 18, some 300 mostly white students met at the Student Union to discuss an appropriate response by the university community to the shootings at Jackson State. Also, on the agenda was a teach-in on racism. Because the university's new president, Clifton Wharton, was the first Black administrator to be named president of a major university, students invited him to join the teach-in.

When the clock hit 11 pm, staff and officials notified students that it was time for the Student Union to close. But they insisted on finishing their discussions in the building that was supposed to be theirs. When the teach-in and talks ended around 1:30 am, students discovered that not only had President Wharton not attended, but he had sent in officers from five police departments who had surrounded the building. Plus, police had blocked off all the doors and windows.

Ken Wachsberger, a junior, had had his suburban consciousness awoken by the Kent State murders, and had attended the discussion on racism. Over fifty years later, he clearly recalled what happened next when the arrests began. "I was the first person busted out of 132 students and outside agitators because I was closest to the door." As students were grabbed and arrested, some went limp, only to be carried and dragged out of the building.

As a university official walked through police lines, he was overheard to say, "It's out of our hands now." Inside a police paddy wagon, Ken and the others were advised by organizers not to sign the arrest forms. Ken remembered, "I was the first called to be arraigned but I got thrown into solitary confinement because I refused to sign my arrest form. I assumed no one would sign, but it turned out, I was the only one. By the time I was released from solitary and sent back to the men's cell, just about everyone had been arraigned. I was the last one." When Ken left the court house, he was met with by supporters and a round of applause as word had spread that he had been in solitary.

The 132 people arrested were charged with loitering and trespassing and sent off to Ingham County Jail. After classmates and supporters raised $4,000 in bail money, they were released shortly afterwards. When the news went out that day across the strike information network, it was reported, "134 white students arrested while attending a discussion on racism."

The next day, the *State News* published a blistering attack on President Wharton's decision to permit state police to make the mass arrests. "The arrested students were in the process of organizing educational workshops and seminars. They were not demonstrating or attempting to occupy the building. They were merely sitting in their Union Building discussing future, non-violent plans." The raid was "ridiculous and uncalled for." The National Student Information Committee asserted the action "showed the lack of power that college officials can exercise over police once they have been permitted on campus."

For Ken Wachsberger, his arrest and the whole affair brought major changes to his life. "My arrest led directly to my dropping out of college and becoming part of the underground press." It was the beginning of his career as a journalist, author, editor, book coach, and community organizer.

Wednesday, May 20, at **Eastern Michigan University**, a memorial service sponsored by the Black Student Association was held for the killings at Jackson State.

Ball State University – Muncie, Indiana

On a hot Thursday afternoon, May 21, a large crowd of faculty members and students stood in the withering heat for a memorial service for the two young men slain at Jackson State, Phillip Gibbs and James Earl Green. After two minutes of silence, speakers—including President Pruis, clergymen and students—paid tribute to them. Father James Bates called Augusta "the Lusitania of Black inequality," and told the gathering, "We are met here today not only to mourn those who die, but those of us who live." He cited the names of all who had passed and said, they "died because they were fighting for what they believed. It is time for us to rededicate ourselves to our own beliefs."

President of the Student Association, Jerry Williams, described how he was becoming more and more disillusioned with memorial services. "They seem to accomplish very little," he said, and felt students were getting wary of their "emotional appeal." The recent service for the Kent State students had "turned into a theological discussion," he said. Williams also complained about the lack of press coverage over the Jackson State tragedy. "I wonder how the event would have been covered if the students killed had been white. I seriously think that it would have made a difference in the type of coverage it received."

On Wednesday, **Purdue University** formally suspended 35 students identified by the administration as "having participated" in a May 1st spontaneous sit-in that had disrupted the president's annual review of ROTC units. Despite the lack of any damage or vandalism, campus police forcibly remove them using batons—one student had been injured—but no arrests were made. Hearings would be held for each student later in the month and any suspensions were to last until January 1971.

Northwestern University – Evanston, Illinois
Monday May 18

The Daily Northwestern on Monday announced that the administration had filed charges against 35 students involved in the Lunt Hall incident for violating campus regulations. On May 13 hundreds of protesters had invaded Lunt Hall which housed the campus Naval ROTC, and some minor trashing had occurred. Eventually Evanston police forcibly evicted them and about 40 people were detained, including a handful of non-students. Students were charged with violating five sections of the student handbook including "obstruction or disruption of teaching, research, administration, hearing procedures, or other university activities, or of other authorized activities on university premises."

Also, on Monday, the associated student government Strike Central Committee announced it was $2,200 in debt and still had to pay a "horrendous" phone bill of at least $2,000 and another bill for paper of $200.

Tuesday, May 19

Early in the week, the College of Arts and Sciences announced that it would be voting on whether to abolish credit for ROTC. University officials responded by ordering Naval ROTC to temporarily suspend all operations until after the balloting. One dean said it was an effort "to restore confidence and to cool the situation off." He also claimed that the suspension of NROTC activities had been under consideration even before the Lunt Hall disturbance, but added "more than anything else," the move was prompted by the disruption. Tuesday was the balloting deadline, and when the votes were counted, the College of Arts and Sciences had voted to abolish the credit for ROTC.

Tuesday evening in Cahn Auditorium, the schools of Music, Speech and other performing arts units gave a combined multimedia production featuring music, theater and film as a "unified expression of all the arts for peace."

Wednesday, May 20

A rally was held Wednesday to inaugurate the New University program for the campus. Established the previous week, many classes were restructured and new ones introduced for the fall term. For two weeks in November, for example, classes would pause to enable students to work for peace candidates. And notably, the new curriculum did not include the NROTC program.

Northern Illinois University – DeKalb
Monday May 18

On Monday night, a well-known civil rights worker, Father James Groppi, gave an impassioned speech at a rally at University Center (renamed the Holmes Student Center in 1974). After his address around 9:45, Father Groppi accompanied a crowd of 1,500 students who marched peacefully through campus, with chants of "Peace now!" and "Remember Kent, Augusta and Jackson!" interspersed with antiwar songs. Student marshals flanked the crowd as it marched from the Center to the campus Free Speech Area.

Around 11 pm, a split among the protest leadership emerged in front of the crowd. Some wanted to march into downtown DeKalb while others wanted to remain at the Free Speech zone. One professor of physics told everyone there was no permit to march into DeKalb. Then a Catholic Peace

Fellowship member got up and declared, "There comes a time when you have to let the community know what is going on." That sealed it—they were going to march into town.

It was 11:30 pm or so when hundreds of students formed a column and began to move towards downtown DeKalb. In order to get there, they had to cross the narrow Kishwaukee River on one of several bridges. This night, they chose the bridge along Lincoln Highway but when they reached it, they ran straight into two lines of police that blocked their way. Undeterred, students simply sat down on the highway and for an hour, there was a stand-off. By then, the crowd had grown to some 600 people. They set up three bonfire barricades in the "liberated zone" to slow police down.

Without warning, President Rhoten Smith suddenly appeared and joined the students. Immediately cheers and applause broke out. For the next several hours, Smith hung out with the demonstrators, moving from group to group to discuss the action.

At 2:30 am, the crowd was addressed by DeKalb City Manager Don Crawford, the same city manager who had marched with students the previous week and ordered to disperse. Nobody moved. Another announcement was made that more state police were on their way and within moments, most of the crowd got up and dispersed. That left roughly 200 to face reinforced police lines. Fifteen minutes clocked by and police advanced on the protesters – most then fled but some remained, and after a brief rock-throwing clash, 35 were taken into custody and loaded onto a bus for a trip to Sycamore County Jail. By 3:45 am, the sit-in had been broken up and any lingering students had been chased from the area. A total of eight injuries were reported; three students were treated for minor injuries at the University Health Center, and the DeKalb Public Hospital reported five policemen had also been treated for minor injuries and released.

Tuesday, May 19

On Tuesday and for the second night in a row, students massed on the south end of the Lagoon, a garden-like series of ponds fed by the Kishwaukee River on the edge of campus. Around 10 pm, hundreds raced over and onto the nearby Lincoln Highway. They shouted, "The streets belong to the people!" and sat down just west of the Kishwaukee River bridge. It appeared to be a repeat of the previous night. Within a handful of minutes, 30 riot-police lined up in front of them. During a half hour stand-off, students chanted and sang songs—"Peace Now!" and "All we are saying, is give peace a chance."

The police line was stationary until they were suddenly barraged with rocks thrown by students hiding in a small, wooded area that bordered the Lagoon. In reaction, officers moved on the sit-in which forced demonstrators to get up and scramble west away from the bridge. When police returned to their original position, students likewise regrouped on the highway. The third time this back-and-forth happened, police charged across the bridge. The crowd of 500 was then pushed back towards campus. As they were forced west, members of the crowd took out windows at University Center, the Fieldhouse and the Village Commons Shopping Center. At one campus intersection, protestors erected a barricade of trash receptacles and set it ablaze. Police lines advanced on the rock-throwers and everyone fell back to an area near Douglas Hall. In the process, four university vehicles were set afire in the middle of the street and the Physical Plant building was ransacked.

Finally, a dozen squad cars roared up. They discharged officers who immediately shot tear gas into the retreating crowds. By 2 am, the roughly 300 students in the "liberated territory" had been routed. Many simply melted away and filtered back to their dorms and nearby homes. Yet, 54 protesters were arrested—all charged with disorderly conduct, except for one woman charged with aggravated assault. Six were nonstudents. Eight people were injured, although none seriously. At the University Health Center two policemen and three students were treated for minor injuries and released. Although no National Guard had been ordered to the campus, the Guard unit at the Sycamore Armory was placed on alert.

Wednesday, May 20

Wednesday, the mayor of DeKalb, Jesse Chamberlain, had a beef with the university and he took his case to the press. Chamberlain announced he was submitting a bill to the university for the damages done to local businesses during disturbances over the last two weeks. Chamberlain said, "NIU has a great impact on the city of DeKalb. It's a state institution with students coming from all parts of this state and others. I don't see that DeKalb should have to bear the expense to maintain order at the university. If the students were all from DeKalb," he said, "it would be a different story. But since they are from all over, we should have some help paying for the damage." Local merchants estimated $7,000 in damages during the May 5 student march through town. On top of that, the city had to pay its police officers time and a half and wanted reimbursement for those costs as well.

During the day, a campus referendum on whether to keep the ROTC program resulted in 7,186 votes for ROTC and 5,197 opposed. When the results were announced at 11 pm to a crowd of 500 students at the University Center, there was plenty of anger. Cries of "Off Rotcee!" reverberated across campus as small groups of students began walking to the Kishwaukee River bridge, site of the two previous nights of sit-ins and clashes.

Yet when students reached the highway this time, there was a busload of state troopers already in position on the bridge. Demonstrators turned around, regrouped three or four blocks away, and then proceeded south and took over a major intersection. With a plan to avoid a direct confrontation with police, the throng surged west along a four-lane highway taking out every window in the businesses that fronted it, including a drug store, laundromat, record store, restaurant and clothing store at University City.

The crowd turned northeast, crossed the campus and returned to Williston Hall, the admissions and records building. A patrol car leading a line of police was hit with rocks, and more windows at Williston were broken. Protesters were pushed pass the library and then scattered and by 2 am, police had cleared the streets of West Campus. Most of the damage was confined to the University City shopping center. Three students were charged with a felony, inciting a riot. Unlike the previous two nights, there had been no direct confrontation between protestors and authorities. The night's busts brought the total number of students arrested over the past three weeks to roughly 140—92 in just the last three nights.

Thursday, May 21

At 4:30 pm Thursday, Kenneth Trantowski, the editor of the campus student newspaper *The Northern Star* was arrested. He was served with a subpoena for failing to turn over negatives of two photos the paper had published the day before and was taken into custody by a county policeman and a university security officer. Released two hours later on his own recognizance, Trantowski had been ordered to turn the negatives over to a district court the next week. If he failed to turn them over, he would be arrested for contempt of court. One photo showed students turning over a university vehicle and in the other, students were marching down a campus street. Police wanted the negatives to identify students involved in the disturbances.

Shortly after he was released, Trantowski stated to *The Star*, "They told me I should produce the pictures because they knew I wanted to see the violence stopped on campus and those responsible for it arrested. I told them I could not produce the pictures." Roy Campbell, the paper's faculty advisor was also adamant. "The negatives are not available, and they will not be available. *The Northern Star* will not be used as part of an investigation by any police agency," he vowed. "It does not mean that the newspaper is against law enforcement, but it does mean that the newspaper is independent in its reporting of the news." The owner of the parent company, *DeKalb County Press*, had its attorney file a motion in district court seeking to quash the subpoena. In addition, the Northern Illinois professional chapter of the Sigma Delta Chi journalism society held a special meeting in DeKalb to investigate the subpoena and arrest.

For the fourth night in a row, state troopers patrolled the campus. Exhausted, city police officers were replaced by additional state police. Despite a curfew, gatherings of students were seen at about 10:00 pm, yet the campus remained peaceful. There was an arrest of one young man at 12:30 am who was charged with possession of marijuana.

Illinois State University – Normal
Monday, May 18

Fifty African-American students met with university officials on Monday and demanded that the flag be lowered for two days in memory of the two young Black men killed by police at Jackson State. President Samuel Braden had already agreed to lower it on May 19 – the next day—to honor Malcolm X's birthday, but this time, he flatly refused. He had Hovey

Hall, the central administration building, locked up for several hours to prevent any sit-ins.

Tuesday, May 19

On Tuesday, the campus experienced a unique confrontation that became known as the famous "flagpole incident." Over the first two weeks of the strike, lowering the American flag to half-staff in honor of the Kent State Four had been a huge issue on campus. During the first week and under student pressure, President Braden had campus flags lowered for several days. They were raised back up on Monday, the 11th. Then Black students demanded two days of lowered flags for the murders at Jackson State. And on Tuesday the 19th as he had pledged, Braden had all campus flags lowered for Malcolm X. But this move did not please hardhat workers at nearby construction sites.

Early in the morning, a group of construction workers barged onto campus and moved to the Quad flagpole. They shoved aside three campus police officers and the president's assistant and raised the flag to its full height. They did the same at two other university buildings and then left campus. The flags were quickly lowered again on President Braden's order. At 9:30, however, upwards of 40 workers reappeared at the main flagpole and defied the president's order to leave the area. While a hundred students looked on, the hardhats raised the flag back up. Campus police then moved in and arrested the apparent leader. Heated exchanges instantly broke out, but no fists were thrown. Before they left for the second time, the workers threatened to return in larger numbers at noon if the flag was lowered again. And again, once the hardhats left, the flag was returned to half-staff.

Students and administrators immediately began preparing for the coming confrontation. Incensed that outsiders were dictating what could be done on campus and deeply concerned that an outright brawl was about to take place, administrators requested police reinforcements from local departments. However, Bloomington police informed them that they had their own troubles with local high school students. And Normal Mayor Baugh refused to give aid unless the flags were raised to full staff after a stormy meeting with President Braden, Only the Sheriff promised assistance. Braden's office also called the governor's office for more help.

In one of the most ironic twists on a college campus during the May rebellion, one hundred state police officers marched onto campus in strict formation wearing full riot gear – to protect students and their flags at half-staff. University officials also got creative and circled the main flagpole with a barrier of 25 cars and trucks, wagon train style.

As the noon hour approached, hundreds of students gathered on the Quad, many of them armed with baseball bats, bicycle chains, and other weapons. Yet, when noon arrived – nothing happened. Nobody showed. Minutes passed and it became obvious the construction workers were not going to appear. Suddenly, the great "flagpole incident" was over. Students drifted away, the state police marched off, and the flag at half-staff, guarded by a ring of steel, fluttered alone in the warm midday breeze.

On May 25, President Braden once again traveled to the state capitol and testified on campus disruptions along with presidents from other universities. Several weeks later, Samuel E. Braden shocked the university community when he announced he was resigning as the university's tenth president. He said he wanted to return to teaching.

The Carbondale campus of **Southern Illinois University** was completely shut down for the balance of the semester and all students were ordered out of their dorms by Monday, the 18th. A Catholic group, the Newman Center, established a bail fund for the hundreds of students who had been arrested over the last couple of weeks, and students from the peace network formed a jail watch to ensure that student prisoners were well treated.

On May 22, the National Strike Information Center reported, "The fight to divest ROTC of academic credit has been won at the **University of Illinois at Chicago Circle**."

University of Wisconsin – Milwaukee

Monday, May 18, striking students maintained their occupation of the student Union building – then in its seventh day. Inside, students played bridge, poker and other card games, a rhythm spoon band played in the snack bar, a guerrilla theater group performed in the lobby, and folk dancing spilled over into the pool hall. In the evening, a general strike meeting was held with the focus of transforming the strike into a campus community movement.

Tuesday morning, students keep up their picketing of campus buildings. They also cleaned up the building they had occupied, and donated food they had collected to the East Side Food Coop. In the day's issue of *Strike!* the question of gay liberation was addressed. There had been an active chapter of the Gay Liberation Front on campus and its members wrote a full-page editorial for the newspaper reminding the university community that as a group and individually, gays had been very prominent in the strike, the occupation, and were generally aligned with the more radical groups.

University of Minnesota – Twin Cities
Monday, May 18

President Malcolm Moos declared Monday a day of mourning in honor of the two slain at Jackson State College. Also Monday's issue of *Strike Action* reported on anti-war efforts at the Medical School where students and faculty members were spreading the word about the strike within the medical community. They had held a teach-in on the medical aspects of the war hosting healthcare professionals who had experienced it. They helped organize a group of health science professionals to fly to Washington DC to consult with the state's congressional representatives. And med students attended the state's Medical Association meeting and spoke about the emergencies occurring on campus and in Southeast Asia.

A brief article reported on employees at Pillsbury in Minneapolis who had formed the Committee to End the War in Indochina at their downtown office and had posted petitions to end the war on all company bulletin boards and in its elevators.

Finally, *Strike Action* included a local sports wrap-up. "Latest softball results from Sunday: Hundred Flowers 15, SDS 9. It must be noted, however, that five of SDS's best hitters are serving time in the Hennepin County Workhouse" for their involvement in actions against the Criminal Justice Studies Department.

Tuesday, May 19

At a noon rally on Tuesday, organizers announced that President Moos continued to refuse to respond to a strike demand for the removal of the ROTC program. In response and carefully orchestrated, up to 100 strikers and non-students moved over to the ROTC Armory and laid "siege."

While picket lines and guerrilla theatre temporarily barred access to the building, scores attacked the outside walls and doors with colorful antiwar slogans, banners and drawings.

Totally unexpected, President Moos arrived and tried to placate everyone with his announcement that the Faculty Senate committee would be making recommendations about ROTC at a meeting in late May – which would then go to the Board of Regents. Once demonstrators had withdrawn, a couple of the banners were ripped down by a campus security officer, and the remaining artwork and drawings were removed by ROTC cadets and Armory workers.

Wednesday, May 20

Wednesday morning, a crowd of 300 returned to the front of the Armory to continue their non-violent protests against ROTC. Chants, dances and the beating of drums were used by students, faculty and clergy members to carry out their public display of opposition. However, a large contingent of police showed up, including 25 campus police officers and declared the assembly to be a violation of the university's policy against the disruption of campus activities. Unfazed, demonstrators refused to leave. Police then moved in, forcibly pushing them back, and arrested two people. One senior, accused of assaulting an officer, was arrested for resisting arrest even though his hands were behind his back, and a former university employee was arrested for "unlawful assembly" while sitting under a nearby tree.

Later that day, President Moos felt compelled to make a statement expressing his regret at the use of police to disperse peaceful demonstrators. He explained that the noise and distraction outside the Armory forced the cancellation or moving of eight Communication classes, disrupted ROTC classes and other activities in the building. It was his intention, he said, to keep the campus open and peaceful.

A student striker editorialized about the incident in the next *Strike Action*. "When people can no longer peacefully assemble, when men no longer receive just rights, when police need trumped-up charges to arrest peaceful demonstrators, then our democratic process does not serve the people. All the more reason, it would seem, to more seriously examine the sensibility of allowing militaristic departments such as ROTC and

[Criminal Justice Studies] — to train their 'humanistic' hirelings to perpetuate this travesty of democratic justice."

Strike Action included a news short reporting on student-led discussions about the Cambodian invasion in the local towns of Burnsville, a few miles to the southwest, and in Golden Valley, directly west. Also, a short blurb implored graduating seniors to donate their cap and gown fees to the strike fund or to a peace candidate's campaign, since they were not required for the graduation ceremony.

The day's schedule of Special Seminars was published which included "Moral and Political Responsibilities of Scientists," the nearby Monticello nuclear generating plant, and a symposium on, "Is the teaching of the English Language and English literature racist?" The most popular seminar of the day, not unexpectedly, was by John Kenneth Galbraith on "Foreign Policy: Causes of the Disaster" before 3,000 people.

Finally, the newsletter carried a poignant piece, "Reflections on the Revolution," by student Robert W. Warrant. "The strike was a wonderfully spontaneous event at the outset. It was a groove to watch it grow inside the union from a few tables manned on the main floor into a huge occupation of that huge building. To see the beautiful red armbands flowering on more and more arms as the days went by. To see earnest spontaneous raps going on between students and professors.

"To hear about people laying their bodies down in front of huge trucks manned by huge truck drivers. To see nurses and older straight people coming to meetings and shouting and laughing. It seemed like that must have been the feeling you got around here back in the thirties when the unions were new and trying to survive the attack on their existence by all the powers that be.

"Back when they weren't supposed to organize because the sons of bitches that controlled their lives (by giving them just enough to stay alive) wouldn't let them, when the coal dust covered everything and hung in the air in the winter, when they were young and trying to have some effect on their own lives.

"I think sometimes those truck drivers have forgotten what happened to them. I think they've forgotten about those times. All they seem to worry about anymore is their color TV and when Spiro is gonna do somethin about those goddam, loudmouth, dope smoking, longhaired, commie, pointy headed, hippie bastards.

"All you union men out there, don't forget that everybody ain't got it good as you do yet, that some people still make a buck an hour and just barely stay alive and that some people aren't free like you are and that some people are still worried about what the hell this country is coming to.

"Don't forget your kids are still trying to grow up in this world and aren't quite sure everything is as groovy as you told them it was. There are some of us with families just like you have who can't even work because our hair is too long to suit the bosses that run things. When all the things that are gonna happen happen, always try to keep this one thing in mind: if you don't understand something don't be afraid of it and don't start hating it, don't fear it until you understand it, and once you give it enough thought to understand it chances are you won't hate it. …

"The strike has its demands, and they are good demands, and they are reasonable demands. But this is only true if you understand one thing: that the thousands of college and university communities in this nation are trying to establish their rightful power as a political and economic force in this country.

"These people are tired of being a closed-off debating club that serves society at large by processing young people through knowledge factories. They are tired of doing research and studies and a hell of a lot of work and then having the military make all the decisions. The intellectual community in this country wants some power and they know that the only way to get any power in this country is to go on strike and that's what is happening. And the people who go on strike gotta remember this too. This isn't some funny little game we've all made up to play with.

"Some of the people involved in this strike have laid their futures on the line. Their futures. That means that if we don't win this thing a lot of good people are gonna get really fucked over. They're gonna lose their jobs, they're gonna be harassed and persecuted. So if your only interest in this strike is playing a few fun games and going to a few demonstrations and standing around for a while making jokes, and then if you go home or go on a vacation or go and have some good times and let those that laid it down get fucked over, then I think we are all in real trouble because we don't have the guts, we can't make a real serious commitment to accomplishing something with our efforts.

"And if that's all that the young people of this country can do, then there is little doubt that we really deserve leaders like tricky Dick Nixon and Spiro T. Agnew. Maybe everybody should go down and get a heinee haircut and move back home and cheer them on as they put the longhairs in concentration camps, as they begin the extermination of the black people and the black movement, as they continue a genocidal war on the oriental and Asian human beings with our awesome war machine.

"If you want to stop the bullshit from coming down, if you want to have a voice in your destiny, then let's get into it. Let's steel ourselves and begin our struggle and continue our struggle. And let it be written that these days in May marked the time when the American people decided that they were going to be free, when they decided that business as usual would stop until the government and the society became once again of the people, by the people, and for the people."

Thursday, May 21

On Thursday—and for the third time that week—protesters returned to the Armory for a demonstration but since it was brief, it was deemed not to constitute a disruption. Later in the day, an exceptionally large crowd of some 5,000 attended a speech on campus by Senator Eugene McCarthy, who had galvanized the youth-based anti-war movement in 1968 with his mercurial run for the presidency.

Friday, May 22

On Friday, another well-known speaker, Dave Dellinger of the Chicago 8, spoke before a crowd of some 2,000 people at a "Festival of Life" which had been partially sponsored by the campus strike committee.

An official university report released publicly estimated that class attendance had been its lowest during the first week of the strike but had returned to "normal" by Friday, the 22nd. The greatest impact of the strike, it stated, was on the College of Liberal Arts where "the strike generated substantial educational innovation, including registration by 700 students in a course on the national crisis." Interestingly, it reported that 6,000 Twin Cities students had taken advantage of the grading options, with 95% receiving a pass/ no credit grade in lieu of a letter grade.

A report from the vice-president's office confirmed that activities in the student Union building were returning to normal but complained that "an undetermined number of persons are remaining in the building during the night, most of them to carry on publishing and planning related to the activities of the Ad Hoc Strike Committee."

Carleton College – Northfield, Minnesota

As the student strike appeared to wane in its third week, sources of funding for strike activities also dried up. All that was left, strike fund treasurer Bonnie Alexander told the campus press, *The Carletonian*, was about $400 and a huge pile of unsold silk-screened "Strike" T-shirts. In a moment of enthusiastic optimism, 600 shirts had been purchased and silkscreened to be sold during the march on St Paul weeks earlier. But the T-shirt market had been "soft" and instead of making a profit, strikers ended up with 400 customized shirts.

Originally, $2800 had been raised for the strike fund and most of it had been dispersed, footing bills for strike actions and events, including "whopping telephone bills, expenses for mimeographing, the glut of paper that has deluged the campus, and, of course, the charge for the buses to the cities," Alexander reported.

$1,600 had been netted for the strike fund from meals sacrificed over strike weekends, $750 had been collected from students riding the buses, several hundred dollars had been made in donations from the campus community including a substantial donation from college President Nason himself, according to Alexander. The last $400 of the fund was earmarked to pay mimeograph expenses for the study groups. "When we're done paying off all the major bills, we'll come out ahead, but barely," pledged Alexander.

Beginning Monday, May 18, **St. Olaf College** students in Northfield began making presentations at high schools, spreading the word about their strike and the war. As part of the outreach, they were in contact with 43 south and southwestern Minnesota high schools and were working with principals and sympathetic teachers, including student teachers. The college presenters wanted in particular to confront opposition to the anti-war movement at the smaller towns in the state.

In Minnesota's northwest quadrant, the administration of the **University of Minnesota at Crookston** reported the campus had remained in operation without incident, with no strike nor grading options sought by students – or given. Class attendance appeared to continue as normal. There wasn't even a Day of Reflection as there had been at other UM campuses. There was an Open Forum on Friday, May 22, when students and faculty numbering up to 80 took part in a discussion on the Cambodian situation.

The president of **Lincoln University** in Jefferson City, Missouri announced, "Upon the request of student leaders ... the University Family will conduct a Memorium which will provide for an opportunity to express its deep concern for recent social occurrences ..." to be held on May 20. The public, historically Black, land-grant university was founded in 1866 by African-American veterans of the American Civil War, the first Black university in Missouri.

University of Nebraska, Lincoln

On Thursday, May 21, the Faculty Senate met to consider several suggestions and proposals put forth by students including the main one of calling for a recess for students to work for peace candidates for the fall November election. The faculty members debated different options: no recess, the two-week original recommendation, a one-week compromise, or no recess but with excused absences for students involved in campaigns. In the end, the faculty majority rejected all of them.

Students responded bitterly. In a letter to the *Daily Nebraskan*, a student organizer of the local campus "New Congress" wrote, "I am sick and tired of people telling me to work within the system and then acting in such a manner as to make it impossible for me to do so." The next day, after a long debate by the Arts and Sciences faculty on credit for the ROTC program, they voted to make changes in the credit but refused to abolish the program.

Rocky Mountains

University of Utah – Salt Lake City

On Tuesday, May 19, about 100 students at the Salt Lake City campus gathered at noon on the Union lawn to protest and discuss the killings of the two African-American men at Jackson State. Hosted by the Black

Students Union, speakers from various persuasions took the microphone. One questioned, "How can we be sure when another group of students gets frustrated with working within the system that they won't be killed, too?" Another speaker emphasized how to get to the many uninvolved students on campus. "We're not talking about philosophical ideas, but six graves, six dead students. If you can't relate with students, who can you relate with?" One speaker turned to the issue of the draft and said, "Lower the voting age to 18 and raise the maximum draft age to 65. See what happens when the middle-class businessmen have to leave their swimming pools to be in the army."

Then a member of the BSU got up and criticized the previous speakers for not dealing with the Jackson State shootings. What was relevant, he said, was a discussion on the Mississippi shootings and not "Kent State, the draft, Cambodia, Vietnam or President Nixon." He continued, "Black people have been killed on campuses in this country ever since they were allowed on campuses. But you don't worry about it until white students start getting killed. Two more Black students have been shot in cold blood, but no one strikes. They all had their strike last week and Black people are killed too often to strike every time a Black student is shot."

In closing a spokesperson for the BSU said that he thought the rally "would have been successful if the students would listen to us. But I don't know what we have to do to get people to listen."

Just after midnight, a memorial service for Green and Gibbs killed at Jackson State was held and attended by some 300 people. On the hour the men died (approximately 12:05 am), people carrying candles met on the Park Building steps. Poetry was read describing the plight of Black people in America, a choir led the group in singing, "Lift Every Voice and Sing," and speeches linked issues of violence, police, and Jackson State with the problems Blacks faced in America.

Pacific

Washington State Univesity – Pullman

Monday, an alliance of Black and Chicano student groups, describing themselves as "Third World," presented the university administration with a list of eleven demands as "a minimum commitment against racism." The demands included the recruitment of more Third World students, faculty and staff, and for program studies for African-American and Chicano students.

That Friday, May 22, President Glenn Terrell made official his rejection of their demands. In response, 250 students staged a sit-in and blocked Stadium Way. The only incident during the hour and half sit-in occurred when a car tried to drive around it and a demonstrator threw a two-by-four through one of its windows. In solidarity, 25 white students withdrew from WSU to protest Terrell's rejection of the Third World student demands.

Also Friday, the right-wing at the Pullman campus reared its head. The *Daily Evergreen* published the results of a student survey it had taken a week earlier. Out of nearly 1120 responses, 57% said they agreed with Nixon's decision to send troops into Cambodia; only 39% agreed US troops should be withdrawn immediately from Southeast Asia; 56% agreed National Guard troops with loaded weapons should be allowed onto college campuses to quell "student violence"; and 62% disagreed with President Terrel's decision to close the university to hold a teach-in. One theory about the campus conservatism was that it was due to the relatively high numbers of military personnel from local communities then serving in Vietnam.

Western Washington State College – Bellingham

On Tuesday, the 19th, the school newspaper, *Western Front*, reported, "The strike movement has apparently lost its appeal to many of its 'fair-weather' followers this past week as freeway blocking and rallies are replaced by work." Yet, in the same paper, student president Greg Baker countered that "150-200 were participating in actual community relations, in the form of information tables downtown and speaking to the high schools." Independent study classes on US foreign policy were also being held during the week.

Western Front also announced that a new state law restricting student demonstrations had just gone into effect – just as the student strike was winding down. Ostensibly aimed at curbing violence on college campuses, it made it a misdemeanor to interfere or intimidate by threat, force or violence any administrator, faculty member or student carrying out their duties or studies. The law, passed by a 1970 Special Session of the legislature, was viewed as a boldface effort by legislators to express their disapproval of the turmoil on campuses.

The results of a poll on the strike conducted by graduate students displayed a split in attitudes. 46 percent agreed that the strike was a necessary and proper action for the college, whereas 43 percent disagreed. Yet, 63 percent generally agreed with the strike cause, while 31 percent disagreed.

On Monday, the situation at **Eastern Washington State College** in Cheney dramatically escalated. Police cracked down on students leafletting cars about the strike during rush hour and arrested 26 students. One account reported that police repeatedly used tear gas to force a crowd that had gathered to disperse.

A protest rally against the shipment of nerve gas through Oregon was held Saturday, May 23, at Holiday Park in Portland and many students from **Portland State University** were in attendance. The keynote address was by former Oregon Senator Wayne Morse, one of the only two United States senators to vote against the Gulf of Tonkin Resolution which allowed President Johnson in 1965 to take military action in Vietnam without a declaration of war.

California
UC Berkeley
Friday, May 22

It was the end of the third week of the strike when the administration made the momentous announcement that there would be no more academic credit for ROTC. In addition, the administration agreed to the demands of campus food service workers, thus averting a boycott of university food services. They had been organized by the Campus Workers Union.

On Friday, *the Berkeley Barb* once again published a report about the strike at UC Berkeley by reporter Phil Pukas. After he had had several encounters with students and a few faculty members, Pukas found there were generally two views of the strike. It wasn't going anywhere or it was the best thing since sliced bread. At Strike Central in Eshleman Hall, a secretary for the student government conceded things had slowed down. There weren't as many phone calls and the national strike report was only sent out twice a week, not daily as it had. Optimistic, she commented, "But we think the slowdown only means that more people know where to go and what to do now. So, they don't need as much direction from us."

Outside one young woman was passing out fliers in Sproul Plaza when Pukas asked her about the so-called "reconstitution" of education being pushed mainly by the administration. "Bullshit," she said. "The talk about reconstituting classes is a farce; they're still going on as usual." But a male student hurrying off to speak at a high school, told him, "You're goddam right the strike is working!"

A philosophy student, Fred Scheuler, told Pukas, "It's going all right, I guess. Anything that works against the war is good. But it's a waste in another way. The strike kind of convinces the already convinced. There are some who won't be persuaded no matter what you say." What about the "reconstitution of U.C.?" There was too much division, Scheuler responded. "Philosophy Department, for example, has a crisis of consciousness right now. There are strong sentiments to radically change the department, and there are others who don't want to move." He worried the reconstitution movement would run out of gas. "It's not going to be done in one big blast. It's going to be one long, hard, sweaty struggle, and I'm not so sure that enough people are aware of the need for work over a long period."

Student Pat Paoli told the reporter the strike was "more together than it's ever been before. Even the fraternities and sororities are getting into action, and that's the first time anybody ever heard of them getting it on." She felt somewhat confused, however. "I feel kind of like a ping-pong ball; I'd like to see it brought together into a big, unified thing. I was at San Francisco State, and this strike isn't like that one. It ought to be all or nothing."

Another student, Deborah Pearson said the strike was "not effective for under-grads. It's like there's a hierarchy, and the thing is being run by the grad students. Some people are involved, but it's hard to find out what to do; it doesn't feel like the mass of the students are involved." A Chicano student agreed. "It doesn't look like much of a strike to me. A lot of the students are using the strike as an excuse to just stay home from school." One undergrad summed up a widespread sentiment. "I think about half the people here are involved with the strike; half are going to classes. But a lot of people are staying home because they're too embarrassed to go on with business as usual and can't get behind the war work. What we need is leadership that can make a more unified effort out of the strike."

David Hensher, a psychology student, said the strike had "been over for two weeks. They've blown their only effective tool, which is boycott." The administration was working overtime to co-opt the strike, he said. "Their loosening up with the pass-fail system for students and allowing late withdrawals takes power away from the strike." Another psych student told Pukas, "A lot of shit has come down that the university hasn't addressed yet. The murders in Augusta and Jackson haven't made any noise here yet, and they should have had us up in arms. More militant action is needed."

A law student was pessimistic. About half the law students were involved, he said, but it would take dynamite to change the constitution of the law school itself. "There's been thought that the law school is a bastion of counterrevolutionary sentiment, and in many ways it's true. Some of the faculty jealously, even insanely, guard the power they have."

The chairman of the Spanish Department was cornered by Pukas. "Some of the faculty feel bewildered," he said. "Their training simply did not prepare them for something as big as the current move to reconstitute the university. They don't know how to react." He had seen this in many other departments. "A number of them would like to be more active, but simply don't know how. They are confused because this is not the way they think of a university. And for many, it has gone much farther than they expected."

Pukas asked a couple of people, 'What about the radicals?' Bill Hastie of the Internal Strike Coordinating Committee opined, "We're just glad that they haven't made any violent moves. It allows us to get that much more together." A psych student, Bruce Mangan, went deeper. "It seems as though the radicals are afraid of losing their legitimacy, or whatever you want to call it. They see that a lot of previously silent people are getting involved now — in some cases more than the 'confirmed radicals' have been — and the radicals don't want to blow their new broader base." He added that the radicals were waiting for the inevitable other shoe to drop—the betrayal by the establishment. "They are going to let the people do their leafletting, petitioning, and all the other sanctioned things, and then, when the people see the failure of the traditional modes of dissent, they'll be radicalized and ready for more militant tactics."

What's to become of the strike? Pukas asked student David Mensher. "People are realizing that they do have the capacity to change institutions around them. If only the momentum can be retained, change may come." Pukas had found this a common theme, 'if only we can keep it going.' There was a fear that everything would slow down by its own weight. Yet others, Pukas discovered, were optimistically making plans. Some were into the "Princeton Plan" to shut down the campuses for two weeks during the fall election season so students could work for peace candidates. Others had plans to keep the strike going through the summer, by continuing the work outside the university in the community.

Bruce Mangan had the best summation of the strike, Pukas thought. "It's a heavy political education for a lot of people. All of those people engaged in strike activity are learning a lot about themselves and their place in the community. Faculty members are forced to look into themselves and the function of the university." There was genuine hope, Pukas found, that "surely some of those people out there will read some of those pamphlets, will listen to some of the anguished pleas to make this more than merely another student movement that died."

Looking back decades later, former strike leader Dan Siegal, then law student and president of the student body – recalled the scene on campus. "The Berkeley campus exploded. We were on strike. There were no classes for the last six weeks of the academic year. The student strike against Cambodia was by far the most inspiring set of activities that I believe every took place at Berkeley. They dwarfed anything that occurred before or since." Siegal—years later – became a well-known Bay Area civil rights lawyer and a one-time candidate for Oakland mayor in 2014.

Back in late May of 1970, with commencement just weeks away, students and teachers began to talk of demonstrating at the ceremony. As a result, Chancellor Roger Heyns canceled the mass commencement usually held at Berkeley's Memorial Stadium, and instead, authorized individual departments to hold small ceremonies - a tradition that continues today. Yet, it wasn't until October 1990 that the Berkeley class of 1970 finally held its graduation ceremony. About 260 members of the class of 3,300 turned out for the belated commencement - so many that there weren't enough caps and gowns to go around and many had to share.

During the commencement, speaker and Berkeley history professor Leon Litwack told the graduates they should be proud that the campus was a key site of anti-war protests and free speech movements during the 1960s and 1970s. "Berkeley has become synonymous around the world with the rights of free expression," Litwack said. "But those rights did not come easily. They had to be fought for. And much of the credit goes to a generation frequently denigrated for its excesses."

Fresno State College
Tuesday, May 19

On Tuesday, acting dean Phillip Walker, laid a bombshell – unrelated to the campus anti-war protests earlier in the month. Representing the administration of Dr. Karl Falk, Walker announced that eight of the 12 lecturers and faculty members of the ethnic studies program would not be rehired, including Richard Keyes, the program's chairman. This decision by Falk, appointed just the previous fall and with a reputation as an authoritarian, reopened wounds that had been festering for months.

In the fall of 1969, the college refused to hire a Black Panther as a lecturer. Then in March 1970 an African-American chemistry professor and five students were criminally charged with detaining Dean Walker – which they had denied. In support of the people being charged, Black residents from West Fresno demonstrated on campus—and the criminal charges were dropped.

Also in March, Chicano students organized a weeklong hunger strike in protest of "the daily oppression of all Chicano people" and the "suppression tactics" of the Falk administration. During the hunger strike, violence broke out between Chicano students and a group believed to be agricultural students, and faculty members physically held the two sides apart by linking arms. Subsequently, Chicano students joined Black students in charging the school administration with attempts to wreck minority-oriented programs.

Late Tuesday night, two firebombs were hurled into a building that housed the school's new $1 million computer center. The fire department dosed the fire in less than 30 minutes and officials said fire damage to the building was minimal—but the firebombs had struck the computer center, causing extensive damage, estimated as much as $750,000. Police had seen several people run from the building, and later an 18-year old suspect was apprehended and charged with arson and conspiracy.

Wednesday, May 20

By Wednesday, there were more repercussions from the decision not to rehire eight staff of the ethnic studies program. A large group of up to 100 students – many African-American – marched through campus, shouting "Strike! Strike!" Windows were smashed, lunch tables overturned, library shelves upended, and furniture damaged. Students were expressing an anger and frustration at an educational system they perceived was failing them. One student was later charged for the window smashing.

All of this - the firebombing and window-smashing—pushed Dr. Falk to the edge and he declared the campus was under a state of emergency – and no assemblies could be held on campus without his approval.

Thursday, May 21

During a press conference, three faculty members from the ethnic studies program said the college had "effectively destroyed" the Black studies program.

Friday May 22

Protests against the Falk administration culminated on Friday. Chicano and Black students had attempted to disrupt classes with protests all week and by Friday, it appeared they had partially succeeded. Many classrooms were empty and hundreds of students milled about campus. Up to 300 white, Chicano and Black students rallied and moved to Shaw Avenue, a major east-west highway that bordered the southern edge of school. There, they sat down three-deep and blocked all six lanes. They piled garbage, a steel bed frame and other debris onto the roadway making a barricade and occupied it for three hours.

Finally, a hundred riot-equipped police showed up. They began a sweep into the crowd to force people off the highway but had to dodge rocks and bottles to make their first arrests. When police retreated, students charged back onto the road. It took police three sweeps and 46 arrests before the highway was reopened. Once those arrested were taken away, a group of 20 construction workers moved onto the traffic divider and taunted demonstrators remaining on the sidelines. In the end, there were no injuries and damage was negligible.

Back on campus, a spokesperson for student protesters announced that a busload of students would be going to the capitol in Sacramento on Monday to meet with Assemblyman Leon Ralph, D-Los Angeles, to discuss the situation at the Fresno college. Ralph had earlier spoken out in favor of firing Fresno State President Dr. Karl Falk.

Los Angeles

At a "Music for Peace" concert at **UCLA** on Wednesday, May 20, 5,000 students listened to the 350-voice, 120-piece university orchestra and choir perform excerpts from Handel's "Messiah." In intervals students chanted, "Peace! Peace!" and many at the UCLA main quad held up the universal two-finger sign of peace.

"Ohio" By Crosby-Stills-Nash and Young

Elsewhere in Los Angeles at the Record Plant Studio 3 in Hollywood on May 21, another musical endeavor produced a song that became the anthem of a generation. A mere 17 days after Kent State, one of the best and most famous rock and roll bands in America recorded "Ohio," and Crosby-Stills-Nash and Young took only three takes to do the recording. The four-piece band was made up of David Crosby, Stephen Stills, Graham Nash and Neil Young. (Crosby passed away in January 2023.)

When Neil Young saw photos of the massacre of the college students at Kent State in *Life* magazine, according to Graham Nash, he went "off into the woods for an hour and wrote the single." Then it was nearly instantly recorded. In the liner notes for the song, Young wrote, "It's still hard to believe I had to write this song. It's ironic that I capitalized on the death of these American students. Probably the biggest lesson ever learned at an American place of learning. My best CSNY cut. Recorded totally live in Los Angeles. David Crosby cried after this take."

The folk-rock group rush-released the single even though they had one out already, "Teach Your Children." They didn't care – they wanted their message to get out there – and fast. Just some 10 days after it was written, the song was released with the B-Side of Stephen Stills' "Find the Cost of Freedom," and it peaked at No. 14 on the Billboard charts.

Due to its "anti-war" and "anti-establishment" sentiments, the song was banned from some AM radio stations and playlists in the United States – including in the state of Ohio. The song received a great deal of airplay, however, on underground FM stations in bigger cities and in college towns. Nixon, to no one's surprise, criticized the song. David Crosby said that Young keeping Nixon's name in the opening line was "the bravest thing I ever heard."

A 2010 article in *The Guardian* said the track was the "greatest protest record" and "the pinnacle of a very 1960s genre." Today, the track is often played on classical rock stations and fifty years after its inception, bands and singers still do covers. In 2009, "Ohio" was inducted into the Grammy Hall of Fame. The lyrics "Four dead in Ohio," which repeats throughout the song, has crystalized its inspiration, and ensures that the Kent State massacre is never forgotten. "Ohio" has proven to have transcended eras and has come to reflect much greater truths about violence, power dynamics and oppression. In July 2023, Neil Young sang it to an enthusiastic crowd at a concert in San Diego, California.

Lyrics

Tin soldiers and Nixon coming
We're finally on our own
This summer, I hear the drumming
Four dead in Ohio.

Chapter 8
MONDAY MAY 25 – SUNDAY MAY 31

Last Week of the National Student Strike Presented in a Day by Day Chronology

Monday, May 25

Union College – Schenectady New York

On Monday, in a sign of the strike's status, the number of editors named in the masthead of *Union Press*, the strike newsletter, was down to three – compared to six when it started. Accused by the conservative campus press of being nothing more than a "clique," the remaining editors responded: "We were not previously aware that once a movement has shrunk down to a small number of enthusiastic people, it automatically becomes a clique. If a dedication of more than three week's duration to what we believe is the most important cause in our society leaves us as members of a tiny clique, then we are proud to be members of it."

What appeared to be going strong, was the campus' lobbying efforts in DC. A group of 35 Union students and four faculty members spent two days, May 25 and 26, "wandering through the cold, long hallways of Congress conversing with numerous legislators and government officials," the *Union Press* reported, "and learning some 'hard' facts about the American political process."

When they first departed Union on Sunday, the student lobbyists were optimistic and exuberant. And when they climbed the stairs of the bus for the eight-hour ride to the Capitol, they felt like they were leaving the "revolutionary" bastion of Union College to go work within the system, as their elders had advised. That night, they were housed by some gracious citizens of Bethesda, the DC suburb, and the next morning, they rose at 6 to begin their anti-war crusade.

Divided up into small groups, they planned to lobby legislators on two bills then before Congress: the McGovern-Hatfield Amendment, which called for an end of economic aid to the war effort by December 31,

1970, and complete withdrawal by June 30, 1971; and the Cooper-Church Amendment designed to hold the President to his plan of withdrawing troops from Cambodia by June 30.

Even though they had several appointments arranged in advance, actual meetings were more hit and miss and even accidental. They did have visits to the office of Senator Strom Thurmond, the arch-reactionary from South Carolina, and the office of Democrat Mendel Rivers, also from South Carolina and chairman of the House Armed Services Committee, plus a visit with a top aide of Vice-President Agnew.

The student lobbyists found that the sentiment among legislators was that neither bill seemed very certain of passing both chambers of Congress. Despite mail strongly opposed to Nixon's policies in Indochina, congressmen weren't convinced that it represented the overall American public opinion – due in large part to the polls showing support for Nixon.

By the time they left Washington, they had mixed reactions. Whereas many felt personally satisfied and enlightened, others were totally dissatisfied and politically depressed. They no longer saw Washington as a source of optimism and could see that the killings and destruction in Southeast Asia would drag on day after day, and that both America and Indochina were in store for a good deal more of the same.

Post-May

The final issue of *Union Press* was distributed on Friday, June 5, and it thanked "all those who have helped in the typing, running off and distribution," especially Bob Krauss "who handled the collation and team of distributors too numerous to mention here," and Terry McManus who was up every night running the mimeograph machine, "a dirty and thankless job."

A damning editorial was also published by one of the last members of the strike committee still on campus. "The Union College year is almost over. A lot of people are moving out already. The strike, less than five weeks old, has been showing increasing signs of senility for the last three weeks. Very few of us show any spark of the anger that ignited the whole thing at the time of the Kent State Massacre. Very few of us are left."

During the strike's last days, the volunteer student radio and ham radio network "were the first to go." And "the Union Press appears today for the first time in a week, and for the last time this year." Strike central "is almost empty — covered with the litter of unsigned petitions, cigarette butts, empty Coke cans and ignored fact sheets. The committee signup sheets are still on the table, giving evidence of a lot of broken promises, a lot of very ephemeral enthusiasm, a lot of words and pitifully little action to back them up."

It commented on the lack of communication between strikers and the administration. "We'd like to give some statistics, but we don't have them." Strikers would have liked to know – "and we'd like everyone to know" – how many students took advantage of the grading options, how many "collected their passes or grades or incompletes and took off for a couple of extra weeks' vacation. But the administration never released them."

"We'd like to know," it continued, "why people are in such a hurry to get out of Union College, why people don't 'give a damn' about what's happened to their country or to their world." It asked where were the "900–odd people" who voted to go on strike? There were "only four people here at Strike Central ... We realize that we might have handled the whole thing all wrong; we realize that we've been disorganized and uncoordinated and stupid and rash quite a lot of the time. But the fact remains that this country is up to its neck in shit and unless someone can do something to pull it out of the mire, we must all go under with it. Which fact makes everything we have done, every ounce of energy expended, in whatever direction, rightly or wrongly, valid."

"Many of us have gotten tired keeping our fist clenched and have let them to go limp and clammy. There is little movement left. ... Strike Center is no longer the center of anything. There are a few of us left" to "virtually wind up the Strike." Yet, "some argued to give it one more try, have one more meeting, see where things were going to go. Needless to say, those 'some' were not at that meeting." Students had planned for the strike to go out with a bang, with a staged guerilla theater skit on Library Plaza against ROTC, but not enough people showed up at the meeting to even form a cast.

"As for us, we're still angry about Cambodia, Kent State, Jackson State, the Black Panthers, and ROTC, but we are disillusioned because no one else seems to be. We want to issue a warning, our last words to a public that is no longer interested: 'You're up against the wall, you mother fuckers!! Tear it down and be free or face the consequences.'"

University of Minnesota – Twin Cities

On Monday, a faculty strike committee released its report on the future of the campus ROTC program and made a number of recommendations. "In brief, we wish the relationship between the US military and the University to parallel that between the Catholic Church, [and] the YMCA." It recommended "the University remove from the campus all military training programs and that all direct ties with such programs be eliminated," but did allow for any department to offer courses of interest to "off-campus military training programs." It called on the university to no "longer cooperate formally with any military training program, e. g., by providing physical facilities or services. That no military personnel, while on active duty, be permitted to serve on the faculty or staff of the University."

The committee also proposed that the approximately $45,000 spent on ROTC programs be used instead on program development for the Afro-American Studies Department and recommended the "Armory building or equivalent space be devoted to activities of special interest to commuter students and for activities such as the Peace College." Lastly, it called for "protections and continuing financial support for students currently enrolled in a ROTC program."

Monday's *Strike Action* newsletter reported on the success of the Strike's Speaker Bureau. Since the beginning of the strike, more than 268 speaking engagements had been filled and people had been sent to "mothers' clubs," businessmen's groups and neighborhood get-togethers.

Washington State Univesity – Pullman WA

At the end of the previous week, university president Glenn Terrell had publicly rejected demands made by a coalition of African-American and Chicano students: an increase in program studies and recruitment of Third World students, faculty and staff. In response on Monday, the coalition started a brand new student strike. Their members engaged in all-day picketing of campus buildings, made plans to withdraw their money from downtown banks and set up a boycott of local businesses who refused to post signs supporting the new strike.

University of Oregon – Eugene

Monday, Tom Hayden and radical writer Robert Scheer appeared at the Eugene campus and gave fist-pumping speeches. At the beginning of May, Hayden had been one of the first national leaders of the anti-war movement to call for a student strike. Yet now in its last week, even Hayden couldn't re-energize the waning movement, and this would be his last public appearance in May 1970.

During the June 13 ROTC commencement ceremony University President Clark reaffirmed his support for the ROTC program.

Tuesday, May 26
University of Maryland – College Park

Reflecting transitions at colleges across the nation, on Tuesday, 20 members of the Strike Steering Committee officially disbanded the group. Yet, unlike many campuses, they immediately reorganized themselves – and they formed the Democratic Radical Union of Maryland (DRUM) with the same platform and demands of the student strike. The group had plans to resume protests in the fall, including being in support of the "Maryland Ten."

The "Maryland Ten" were students targeted by National Guard commander General Edwin Warfield for their involvement in campus actions including occupations of Route One. At first, they had been issued felony warrants alleging breaking and entering and destruction of state property, but in June, the felonies were dropped by the grand jury for insufficient evidence and changed to misdemeanors.

Finally, the long-delayed trials of the "Maryland Ten" began on December 10, 1970, and lasted into early February 1971. Charges against the woman who resembled an activist were dropped; Lawrence Dean, a leader of the antiwar movement, was found guilty of trespassing and forcible entry; Karen Pomerantz, David Willett and Mark Woodward of SDS along with faculty member Larry Babits were acquitted of all charges and set free; strike leaders Robert Wade, Steven Cullen, and Richard Fox pleaded "no contest" and ended up exonerated, as was Terry McKeon. In late February Dean was sentenced to a total of three months in jail. In explaining the difference between his sentence and the others, the judge cited Dean's "insincerity, bad attitude and lack of remorse, and to set an example for other demonstrators." Dean completed his undergraduate program and began serving his three months in June 1971.

Case Western Reserve University - Cleveland

Tuesday's "Strike News" listed the end of the month activities, including an all-day art show by Artists Against the War, the leafletting of anti-war flyers at shopping centers and at college graduation ceremonies around the city, a Tuesday antiwar rally at "People's Park" and another afternoon rally in Union Ballroom "to keep the Union open over the weekend for strike activities." Also listed in "editor's notes" were these: "Whoever stole 2 typewriters and a purse from this office is a Motherfucker. Up against the wall!!!!" And "Bring food – please!!! Anytime of the day or night to strike Central."

Negotiations during the last week of May at **Ohio State University Columbus** between the administration and strike coalition members were supposed to be still going on over ROTC, military research and other strike issues. But it didn't look promising, as neither side on Tuesday could agree on a meeting site.

University of Minnesota – Twin Cities

On Tuesday, 50 protesters lined up in front of Morrill Hall—the administration building – and partially blocked its entrances in an anti-ROTC action. After students were issued a complaint and a verbal warning, campus police moved in and arrested from 14 to 17 people for unlawful assembly. The complaint alleged, "Members of the group were boisterous and making much noise by shouting, blowing whistles and kazoos, banging on a 55-gallon oil drum and throwing water-filled balloons against the building and at persons entering and exiting the building...." As if in retribution, President Malcolm Moos abruptly and unilaterally cancelled an all-university senate meeting scheduled later in the week.

Wednesday, May 27

On Wednesday at **Brandeis University** in Massachusetts, a small core of activists at the National Strike Information Center issued a spirited call for the continuation of strike work through the summer. Entitled "Off the Campus" their statement acknowledged the need for a "new label" to "sum up the current rebellious state of the nation." It was "crystal clear" the strike, now in the fourth week, "is no longer a 'student strike,'" and that "Students are not protesting alone." It ticked off a list of groups and constituencies that had joined students: faculty and administrators, consumers, GIs, labor.

It stated, "over 150 colleges and high schools remain on strike," and that "people are also engaging in selective buying campaigns, mass marches and demonstrations, lobbying for anti-war candidates, non-violent civil disobedience, runs on banks, community political education, etc. In other words, a multiplicity of strategies exists as do a multiplicity of categories of people using them." Then, in a gush of optimistic idealism, it concluded, "For both reasons we no longer should speak of a 'student strike' but of 'A Summer of Resistance and Liberation.'"

Yet, no nationally recognized center existed to use this call to move radicalized students into an inclusive network of activists to build off the historic changes the May Rebellion had wrought. Efforts to form one at the beginning of May had been rejected; plus, SDS was broken, the New Mobe—already on its last legs—collapsed soon after May, and the information networks established over the last four weeks were faltering and falling by the wayside. This call fell on deaf ears.

University of Connecticut - Storrs

In late May, the hammer came down on striking students who had engaged in a spontaneous take-over of the administration building on May 13. Nearly two dozen students had taken part in a rampage of vandalism resulting in $1,500 worth of damages to telephone lines, windows and plastic signs. The University Committee on Student Conduct, composed of three faculty members and two students, held a hearing and 18 students were found guilty and given punishments. Six received disciplinary probation, eleven were suspended, and one was dismissed outright. Hearings for eight others were pending—to be handled over the summer. Nine students ended up being arrested by local authorities, and three had outstanding warrants.

On Wednesday, the National Strike Information Center announced that **Washington and Lee University** in Virginia was the official headquarters for the South and would be open all summer. Students on campus would be pushing the goals of the Movement for a New Congress, plus, the school was setting up a center to train draft counselors through the month of June.

Late in May, the **University of Virginia - Charlottesville** held a two-day seminar attended by over 100 students from 15 Virginia colleges to mobilize support for local and congressional candidates who had taken stands against the war. On Wednesday, the National Strike Information Center reported that, despite finals, support for the strike on the Charlottesville campus was still high.

At **University of South Carolina – Columbia**, the administration of Dr. Thomas Jones

was still dealing with student disruptors—and more was to come before the fall semester. Eventually, 51 students were suspended for two actions that occurred during the first week in May. Of those arrested, most were charged with misdemeanors, paid fines from $25 to $300 and never went to jail.

Ohio State University – Columbus

A flyer was distributed Wednesday that announced a very different type of "memorial service" for the Oval at 2 pm. It was to be held "In honor of OSU graduates *who will be killed* in the war in Indochina - a priest and a rabbi will officiate." Meanwhile, National Guard troops remained on campus and a limited curfew was still in effect.

Also Wednesday was the first day of the Free University and 35 alternative classes were held on the Oval. Organizers described the Free University as an alternative to the mainstream academic menu, and as a "peaceful protest against the administration's indifferent attitude to meeting student demands." The very first workshop was entitled, "Making it under military occupation," and students and instructors planned to eat and sleep on the Oval. A flyer for the Free U stated, "We will not be intimidated by gas, bayonets or bullets; we want simply to live."

However, the administration had other plans for the Free U. It all started early in the evening when the campus Safety Committee recommended to the National Guard commander that the curfew be lifted from the Oval to allow students to continue their exchange of ideas throughout the night. The guard commander took the message to the administration, but the request was denied. In response, nearly a hundred students left the Oval and reconvened their alternative classes in the nearby but off-campus St. Stephens Episcopal Church.

Next and just after midnight, Guardsmen ordered the news media to vacate the Oval, and then swept the area and carted off a few lingering students. The curfew was extended to a wider swath of campus and cordoned off by Guardsmen. Students in the dorms reacted angrily to the forced lock-down with catcalls and jeers yelled from windows. Kicked off the Oval, another 100 students congregated at a major intersection but dispersed after an hour. Organizers pledged the "24 hour Free university" would continue.

Northwestern University – Evanston Ohio

On Wednesday, students at Northwestern coordinated what was called the Illinois Pause for Peace campaign—a one-day shutdown of businesses—by working with other campuses across the mid-west and northeast. The campaign called for businesses to close and place signs in their windows indicating opposition to the war, for workers to call in "sick of war" and for consumers to refrain from buying anything for a day. The record is silent on whether the Illinois Pause for Peace was successful, but the national campaign had closed down earlier for lack of financial and political support.

As students and faculty prepared to leave campus for the summer, *The Daily Northwestern* published "A list of things to do to continue the strike," and it reflected the optimism and hope of a small group of students mesmerized by the prospects of the strike continuing and expanding.

The 'wish list' included a litany of proposed tasks and actions for different groups, such as contacting alumni to explain the strike and getting students and faculty on the Board of Trustees. It contained setting up relevant lecture series and high school programs, conducting Chicago community organizing, working on antiwar referendums and campaigns of peace candidates, reaching out to community "minority groups," a fair for the New University, using art, drama and music for strike and anti-war statements, keeping a continued lobbying presence in Washington DC, a permanent child care center on campus, buying ads in newspapers, magazines and on television with anti-war messages, media projects such as documentary films of the strike to be distributed to groups in Chicago, working with labor and union groups, organizing medics and draft counseling. However, the article ended with a telling concession—"most of the groups ... are badly in need of volunteers."

University of Notre Dame – South Bend, Indiana

After May 1970, Notre Dame changed and dissent was less divisive and even acceptable. Questioning the war as well as its domestic fallout made the campus, by and large, a center of protest against the war—partially because of Father Hesburgh's leadership. The new mood went beyond opposition to the war, and there was more concern for issues related to social justice, poverty law and peace studies. The May rebellion proved there had been a type of maturation across the campus—followed by a period of heightened social concern. The old 'God, Country and Notre Dame' patriotism in place since the mid-1960s—was gone.

University of Minnesota – Twin Cities

On Wednesday, Veterans for Peace distributed a flyer on campus that called on the university to immediately sever all connections with ROTC. It stated: "As former members of the armed forces who have lived under the command of both ROTC and non-ROTC officers, we know the 'liberal officer theory' is a myth. Officers trained at universities are neither more or less humane than officers trained elsewhere." The flyer suggested, "Reserve Officers training can be conducted at military installations as reserve enlisted men's training is." Finally, "the presence of ROTC only causes further polarization of an already divided campus."

Wednesday also witnessed another effort by the administration to undercut the strike movement. Administrators pressured the governing board of the Union student center – where strike headquarters was quartered—to close the building for the upcoming Memorial Day weekend. However, that push was countered by the student-organized Peace College that planned to have a three day event for strikers at the Union over the same weekend. Students worried that closing the building would result in a possible confrontation. Nothing was resolved but tensions continued to mount over strikers' use of the Union.

UC San Diego—California

During Wednesday, three to four dozen students held a militant picket line in front of Chancellor William McGill's office to protest the firing of Angela Davis from UCLA. Called by SDS, the Black Students Council and MEChA in solidarity with the controversial lecturer and former UCSD grad student, the picket line blocked the chancellor from entering his office – but only for a few minutes. Yet, the administration identified 21 individuals (including the author) and later served them with eviction notices and took them to trial for trespass.

That very evening, two groups of radical antiwar students held their own separate meetings on campus. SDS members and supporters were meeting upstairs in a classroom in York Hall, while the more-anarchist, hippie Radical Caucus of about 50 people was meeting in Strike Central on the ground floor of Blake Hall, a dorm. Suddenly a well-known activist burst into the Blake Hall meeting and screamed that police were arresting people at the other meeting. To a person, the entire group jumped up and rushed across campus. When they reached York Hall, they saw campus security officers herding several handcuffed students towards police cars at the loading dock. A German grad student, in a thick accent, yelled, "This is what they did in Weimar Germany!" Campus officers were wrestling with a tall senior who resisted being pushed into a police car but by time people reached the dock, he had been violently thrown into the back seat. The vehicle roared off, followed by the other campus police cars—all on their way to the campus police station across campus.

SDS'ers recounted what had happened. Campus police officers had simply barged into their meeting and arrested two students for an action they had been involved in six months earlier. This account made everyone more outraged, and the entire crowd starting running across campus towards the police station. As people passed through administrative complexes, a few windows and outside furniture were broken or tipped over.

As people moved from Revelle to Third College, someone yelled out that Dean George Murphy, one of the top administrators, was to make a speech on the incident. Outraged radicals regrouped outside the single-story, wooden administration building and Murphy emerged and stood on a poorly-lit deck. In the dark with a few interior lights on behind him, Dean Murphy tried to console the furious students. Everything would be taken care of, people's rights would be respected, proper procedures would be followed. His words fell flat. Then suddenly, Murphy staggered and nearly fell off the deck. Instantly, students realized he was smashed—totally drunk. A small bottle of brown liquor protruded from a back pocket. This made the students – already furious – just livid.

Off in the near distance, a small beige, wooden security building was lit-up with glaring overhead lights – making it an obvious target. There was no discussion or talk about what to do. Students simply began picking up and lobbing rocks at the police station. Volley after volley rained down on the building until finally after a long barrage, the small number of campus cops made a run for it, dashed to their cars and sped off into the night. With this retreat, the mini-riot fizzled, and most drifted back to their dorms or domiciles off campus. A few roamed the school grounds and smashed more windows.

Thursday, May 28
University of Tennessee – Knoxville
In the middle of May, it had been announced that the world-renowned evangelist Billy Graham would be bringing his 10-day crusade to the university's stadium, which would run from Friday, May 22, through Sunday, May 31. However, many in the college community didn't think it was appropriate for the university to host a Christian mass meeting. Then on May 27, the bombshell: Nixon himself would be attending the very next day on the 28th. He wanted to show that three-weeks after the Kent State killings he could appear on a college campus, plus he knew he had many supporters in this part of the country. Yet, for antiwar activists at the Knoxville campus, this was a perfect chance to directly confront the president and show him that opposition to his war policies existed even in Tennessee.

Thursday morning, the 28th, a flyer appeared on campus, bearing large, hand-drawn letters, "Thou Shalt Not Kill – Thursday, May 28 – 4pm in front of the Student Center." It urged students to join the mass rally in the stadium to protest Nixon's appearance, as well as the killings at Kent and Jackson States and Augusta, Georgia. Protesters were asked to wear black and to sit together, "to show Nixon, who will be present, our unified and peaceful opposition." It was signed Students for Peace.

The time approached for Nixon's appearance and several hundred protesters, faculty, and students filed into the stadium—many carried signs that said, "Thou Shall Not Kill." When Nixon finally appeared at the microphone before the packed stadium and began to speak, yells, antiwar slogans, and profanities erupted—signs were held up and shaken. The tumultuous scene continued for minutes and only wound down when police moved in and began making arrests. In the end, 24 students and 2 professors were arrested for disturbing a religious meeting and warrants were issued for another six. Another report of the event claimed between 40 and 50 were arrested.

That night, John Smith, the student government president, was so outraged by the police response, he fired off a critical public statement: "As of today, the right of dissent was jeopardized by an ancient legal code. I am appalled at the arrests today of more than 40 UT students and faculty, due to the delay and the process involved." He accused the administration of "political exploitation," of "betraying their responsibility of academic freedom" and of engaging in "another blatant attempt to purge certain students and faculty." Lastly, he stated, the demonstration had been political "and those involved were not trying to stifle religious freedom."

Quickly, a student-faculty Legal Defense Fund was set up to raise monies for those arrested. In a statement, the Fund group accused law enforcement and jail officials of using improper procedures against those arrested, such as setting high bails, making it difficult to identify those in jail so bail could be arranged, and the use of film and photographs to identify persons to be arrested on 'John Doe' warrants. It mocked Chancellor Charles Weaver's statement that "the University is not a sanctuary for lawbreakers," by reminding him "that persons suspected of breaking the law must be given fair trials and, in every way, afforded due process. However, due process can be expensive even for an innocent person." It ended with a plea, "Will you help us show our young people that this community is committed not only to upholding the law but also to defending orderly legal processes? Please send a contribution."

Ohio State University – Columbus

Fifteen minutes before noon on the last Thursday in May, a group of 150 students paraded around the Oval—it was the newly-formed

Marshmallow Brigade. Precisely at 12, they charged the front of the castle-like library, and with screams and yells, bombarded it with painted marshmallows. The red, white, and blue missives rained down on the building as "ammo bearers" scurried back and forth behind the line of attack and medics stood by to assist with casualties. Administration "insecurity forces" quickly locked the building and called the National Guard – still deployed on campus—to protect them from the marshmallows. A spokesperson for the Brigade stressed that their group was not affiliated with any other campus organization but was a group of seriously concerned students who had respect for the Strike Coalition demands. "We are faced with the absurdity of the administration's refusal to negotiate, and we felt that we should respond with our absurdity," he said.

Over the course of the May rebellion, 600 OSU students had been arrested at Columbus – mostly for curfew violations. In contrast to the memorials built for the dead at Kent State and Jackson State, the Ohio State turmoil—its mass arrests and injuries from buckshot—have largely been forgotten. There are no memorials at Columbus, even though its disturbances were perhaps larger and more violent than at Kent State. It had been an absolute miracle that no one had died.

President Fawcett kept the 5,000 National Guardsmen on campus to maintain security and they weren't withdrawn until Saturday, May 30.

The student population of OSU, like at other college universities, had exploded over the previous decade, and by the spring of 1970, had literally doubled since 1960. However, the school's enormous expansion had not been met with a parallel preparation for that unprecedented growth, and campus facilities had become increasingly strained. Plus, the increase in African American enrollment had not been accompanied by accommodations for a new population. And in 1970, the administrative structure of the university still excluded students from participation, with "business as usual" the implicit motto of the Fawcett regime.

OSU historian Bill Shkurti later observed that the student clashes were especially complex because they weren't about a single issue. "Fundamentally, this was a revolt against the university. There was discontent from the students during a period when the university had to manage enormous growth. They didn't manage the human side very well. The university worked very hard to keep the lid on in terms of student protests. The problem was, they kept the lid on through the use of force. So, when the lid blew, it really blew."

Generally, the student disturbances at Ohio State had all been minimized and downplayed by the university, the City of Columbus, and Governor Jim Rhodes. Nobody wanted news about the violence, the injuries, and arrests – all negative publicity - to go nationwide. The media played a role and helped quash the bad PR, especially the local conservative press. As harsh as it sounds, City and college officials probably breathed some relief when Kent State exploded as it pushed OSU off the front page and off the public's radar. No one in law enforcement involved in the troubles and shootings at OSU was ever prosecuted for the excessive use of force.

Over the years, the memorial gates at the campus entrance, High Street and 15th Avenue, were taken down so students could never close them again. The walkways around the Oval were paved with asphalt so no one in the future could use its bricks for ammunition. OSU administrators did continue to negotiate with students and several changes were made, including the establishment of a Black Studies program and a Women's Studies program, plus the hiring of additional Black campus policemen. The school had the injunctions against students lifted but did not lower student fees and refused to sever ties with the military or to discontinue military research.

At the **University of Minnesota Twin Cities** campus, a Viet Cong flag appeared during an all-University Senate meeting on Thursday and instantly, heated and noisy arguments erupted over its presence. President Moos then used the flag as an excuse to recess the meeting because it "had created an atmosphere in which the business of the Senate could not be conducted." This appeared to be more of Moos' stonewalling of the students and their pesky demands.

Washington State Univesity – Pullman

On the very day that over 1,000 students protested President Glenn Terrell's rejection of students' demands outside the campus administration building, the university announced a new Chicano Studies Program—one of the demands. Others had included the recruitment of more Third World students, faculty and staff and an African-American studies program.

Over the next couple of days, a series of minor vandalism incidents occurred on campus. Bricks with the word "strike" on them were thrown through campus bookstore windows and there was an arson attempt at the football stadium.

On June 1, an agreement between President Terrell and the Third World coalition was announced – and because the university granted enough demands, the strike was called off. On June 7, Commencement went off without a hitch, and in fact, President Terrell was cheered when he commended demonstrators for their dedication to non-violence.

Friday, May 29
Case Western Reserve University - Cleveland

The very last issue of "Strike News" was published on Thursday, and on the front cover was a large cartoon of Nixon holding a smoking rifle while standing on blocks labeled "RIP KSU," "RIP Jackson," and "RIP Augusta." One small article in the issue headlined, "Another Brother Dead" was about Terry Robbins, a local man identified as the third person killed in the accidental explosion of a Weather Underground townhouse in New York City in March. Robbins, a former member of SDS and "active in the Cleveland area in movements against repression," had subsequently joined the Weather organization. (The other two killed were Ted Gold and Diana Oughton; two others, Kathy Boudin and Cathy Wilkerson, fled the scene with minor injuries.)

One long article in "Strike News" bubbled with optimism and ticked off a list of committees and activities that would "be functioning this summer." More of an idealistic "to do" list, it claimed all the strike committees would continue including the communications committee and the speaker's committee. The women's liberation committee made plans "to provide a free babysitting service to free women for other activities, including STRIKE activities," and to continue the education of women on women's oppression. The architecture committee would create "the implementation of environmental ideas concerning the building of an alternative living style" on campus that would include a food and housing cooperative. Other committees, such as the Ohio Peace Committee, the Corporate Action committee, and the free school liaison would all continue. Yet, "Strike News" couldn't bring itself to admit the one dreadful truth – the strike was over.

UC Santa Barbara – Isla Vista

With finals in full swing, Chancellor Cheadle finally allowed Jerry Rubin of the Chicago 8 to speak on campus at the stadium on Friday, May 29. It had been over a month since Cheadle had originally refused to allow Rubin to speak, but now, the atmosphere was "cooler." Yet, the day of the speech, a group of construction workers began to march on the campus in opposition to Rubin's appearance, but a union official, a contractor and the sheriff convinced them to disband.

In early June, students learned that 17 people were being indicted by a county grand jury for the burning of the Bank of America building in February. One of those indicted, a highly-prominent African American activist, had been in jail the night the bank was burned – this was common knowledge among students. Sensing something fishy, 2,000 students rallied in protest on June 5th and demanded all the charges on everyone dropped. Hundreds signed statements saying they were all responsible for the bank burning. Once again, protesters moved over to the bank site and once again rocks flew. In a swift response, the County Board of Supervisors took the drastic step of ordering an immediate curfew for Isla Vista, beginning at 7 pm, and State Highway Patrol officers along with Sheriff's deputies moved in to enforce it.

Saturday, May 30

Washington and Lee University – Lexington, Virginia

The very last issue of "Campus Newsletter" published May 30th included several retrospectives. Editor Griffin wrote, "W&L has long been an isolated, stable community of 'learning' separated from the events and realities of the world by a thick shell. This year, that shell has been cracked, and questions raised as to the validity of a W&L education, or any education of sixteen years duration that prepares you for the day shift."

Griffin went on. "The light from the real world has been brought to this campus, but the cost was high. Misunderstanding, misinterpretation, and polarization was the price. Benefits can be many, and even now appearing, students speak with a new frankness to professors, and the reverse is also true." It ended on a positive note. "The W&L students have arisen from their bed of apathy and have responded to a crisis. This new direction of the campus is both visible and invisible. The dress of ten years ago is gone, and the 'typical' W&L gentleman is no longer a rich, southern, conservative, fraternity playboy, in fact there is no longer a 'typical' W&L student."

Another retrospective by Fran Lawrence, student body president-elect, opined, "There were many mistakes made in these past few weeks by all parties evolved. The student body at times lost sight of its goals and a course of action consistent with those goals. Student leaders failed to grasp the situation entirely and unknowingly helped lead the student body into a cul de sac." Lawrence continued, "The faculty, though ... failed later to fully appreciate student sentiment and the contemporary crisis. Clearly this university must involve itself in the surrounding community and nation and fully involve both students and faculty in the university."

Memphis State in Memphis, Tennessee

On Saturday, a couple thousand students attended a large rally and demonstration in Overton Park. Speakers included two of the Chicago 8, John Froines and Rennie Davis, as well as Coretta Scott King, widow of the famed civil rights leader – and they all spoke of war and repression. (In later years, Froines would focus on occupational and environmental health issues, working in government and academia. He passed away in July 2022.)

A voter registration campaign being organized on campus to unseat Mississippi Senator John Stennis, an arch-conservative and white supremacist, sent out word to recruit volunteers for the summer registration drive planned throughout Mississippi. (Mississippi was less than a dozen miles away from the campus.)

University of Minnesota – Twin Cities

On Saturday, a half dozen faculty members handed out copies of a statement that charged the arrests of 15 students at the anti-ROTC Morrill Hall demonstration on Tuesday had been unjustified. Their statement also strongly criticized the unilateral recessing of a Faculty Senate meeting by President Moos, which had stifled expressions of support for the strike by faculty members.

Post-May

On Monday, June 1, a cooler and vending machine broke down inside Coffman Union, the student center which led the center's director to cancel all food-related privileges for strikers. This sparked a meeting of the Union's Board of Governors where food service workers expressed a litany of complaints about strikers. Chief among them was their inability to access kitchen areas and locker rooms due to strikers' overnight occupancies, and the lack of cleanups after normal closing hours. Their complaints resulted in a resolution by the Board that declared all over-night occupancies of the Union were no longer justified and must cease—students and faculty members could still access the center during normal building hours.

At a June 4 University Senate meeting, the Senate recommended to the Regents that the university join with other colleges and negotiate with the Department of Defense to regularize the approval of courses and instructors for ROTC programs and "move military training aspects of the program off university campuses." However, the Senate defeated a motion to abolish the ROTC program altogether. When Senate members left the meeting, they had to step around a group of anti-ROTC protesters posing as dead and wounded war victims.

On Friday, June 5, just before 11 pm, the last of the occupiers in Coffman Union – 20 to 30 people – were escorted out of the center by two dozen campus police officers. No arrests were made because the group had vowed to leave peacefully but under protest.

In time, the university estimated, "About one-third of the students who participated in the student strike missed 50 percent or more of their classes." However, because of the strike many public forums, teach-ins, independent studies, and community action efforts were begun. A new for-credit course, "A Crisis in America," enrolled 700 students with 50 faculty members teaching seminar sessions. One alternative, the Peace College, stemmed directly out of the strike and highlighted activism and cultural issues. It also allowed staff and non-university locals to participate.

The 15 people arrested on May 26 in front of Morrill Hall, which housed the ROTC, went to trial in late September on unlawful assembly charges. One of those was Bill Tilton, the vice president of the Student Association and a member of the strike leadership. After the campus strike,

Tilton continued to work against the Vietnam War, and he was among seven fellow activists who attempted on July 10 to destroy draft records in three Minnesota towns. After being arrested for attempted sabotage, the men became known as the Minnesota 8, and charges were later reduced to attempted burglary. One pleaded guilty and received probation whereas the other seven, including Tilton, were convicted and sentenced to five years in federal prison, in which they served up to twenty months. After serving his time, Tilton graduated from law school and practiced law in Minnesota for over 40 years, including defense work for the Wounded Knee defendants, and became a well-known civil litigator. In 2001, he was named the Minnesota Lawyer Attorney of the Year.

University of California San Diego
The Memorial Day Yippie Invasion of La Jolla

On Saturday, May 30, Memorial Day, a 1,000 students and young people "invaded" La Jolla, the wealthy seaside community adjacent to UC San Diego, and many came dressed up in outlandish costumes. Flyers circulated at UCSD and other San Diego campuses invited students to converge for the "Yippie Invasion of La Jolla" targeted because "La Jolla owns half the world" and constituted a "major staging area for the enemy." The invasion was to last for "no more than 30 days" and promised to "go no more than 21 miles inland"—mocking references to Nixon's limits in his invasion of Cambodia.

Most in the crowd were not, of course, card-carrying members of the Youth International Party, but identified with its anarchistic, comical confrontational style and counter-cultural trappings. Plus, for strikers, the invasion was a way to let off steam after a month of protests. The parade left the UC campus and trekked down the hill through well-kept tony neighborhoods all the way to downtown La Jolla. People chanted, sang songs, waved peace flags, played kazoos, and some carried toy guns.

As the Yippies passed one front yard with an American flag flying on a pole, a few ran up and lowered it to half-staff. The middle-aged male owner, standing on the front porch, instantly rushed up and raised it back up. A roar of approval erupted from the crowd and he was loudly applauded. A handful of invaders grabbed him and lifted him up on their shoulders – to more hurrahs. He was as surprised as anyone else as he was carried off in the parade and down the street, with both a frown and smile on his face.

When the parade reached a cliff and its beach adjacent to downtown, a couple of marchers stripped nude and jumped into the ocean – to hearty cheers from those on shore. Two lifeguards, however, were not impressed, and immediately jumped in and paddled out to them on boards. The first guard reached one of the swimmers, cold-cocked him and hauled him onto his board. This set off an instant angry cry of protest from the shore. Unable to land in the face of the screaming crowd, the lifeguards paddled their captives north to the next beach at La Jolla Shores. Many "invaders" rushed over to confront the lifeguards but by then, San Diego Police officers had arrived, formed a line on the sand and escorted them and the two swimmers off the beach. After a short stand-off, all the Yippies dispersed.

Post-May

Twenty-one undergrads and grad students (including the author) were selected by the administration to be criminally charged for trespass for participating in a May 27 picket line that had briefly blocked Chancellor McGill from entering his office. The "UCSD 21" became a short-lived *cause celebre* and tried to mount a defense based on their actions being justifiable. But in the end, after a week bench trial, the vast majority were found guilty and sentenced to 5 or 10 days in the old, decrepit downtown San Diego jail (the author was sentenced to 5 days).

On Sunday, June 14, the Class of 1970 had their commencement and Buckminster Fuller gave the commencement address. For many striking seniors, the strike had never formally ended, and some wore strike armbands on their gowns or street clothes with red fists silkscreen on their jackets or shirts. Just before Fuller began speaking, Angela Davis stood up from the audience and loudly announced that there would be an alternative commencement behind Revelle Library. Immediately, 200 rose out of their seats and walked out – and over to the grassy area on the south side of the library. Clusters of graduates and supporters congratulated each other, joints were lit, wine was poured, and Herbert Marcuse walked up and joined the alternative commencement party. It was truly a bittersweet moment.

Over that past year, the investigation into the role of war research at UCSD and the campaign to force the school to cut ties with the Pentagon and war profiteers was a turning point for many students. Up to then, most had held a great deal of respect for the institution, but when student radicals proved UCSD held contracts worth millions of dollars to conduct military and war-related research, the lie was exposed. This betrayal of trust built a supportive base for the May 1970 strike, and the sit-ins organized by a coalition of radicals turned large numbers of students against the war and into the belief that fundamental social and economic change had to come to America.

Some radicalized students turned to trade-union organizing coordinated by small leftwing cadres. A few others turned to community organizing—under the twin beliefs that white radicals needed to organize in their communities, as the Black Panthers had advised, and that if the war was ever truly going to end, a base of opposition had to be built at the community level.

Sunday, May 31
Smith College - Northampton, Massachusetts
Strike activities at the Northampton campus in western Massachusetts continued throughout May, eventually fading as students began to study and take examinations. Even though, commencement exercises brought the strike to a formal close, a number of strike events occurred the week of commencement to show alumnae and parents what the women students had been doing for the past month. Additionally, many organizations and students pledged to remain active through the summer. President Nixon's daughter Julie graduated from Smith that year but neither she nor the president could attend commencement exercises on Sunday, May 31, due to the threat of protests

Purdue University – Lafayette, Indiana
On June 1, the suspensions of 35 students were finalized by the university's Board of Inquiry, having been identified as participants in a May 1st sit-in at the Purdue Armory. They had been violently removed by campus police using riot batons and a number had been injured, including one sent to the university health center.

The University Senate eventually came to question the Board of Inquiry's report that the suspensions were based on, but it wasn't until mid-November in the fall term. During a senate meeting, Professor C. E. Eisinger, chair of a key faculty committee, criticized the panel's inquiry results, particularly on the use of batons by police. Legally, Eisinger asserted, batons were to be used only to prod or move demonstrators, but on at least four occasions, police had "raised batons over their heads and struck at demonstrators in contact with the police." Professor J. J. Stocktown, the panel's chair, responded by claiming the university police officers in question had in fact faced "disciplinary action," and that campus police would in the future use films of the Armory incident in training of new officers.

The president of **University of Akron** in Ohio, Norman Auburn, sent a letter to parents and alumni, dated June 17, proudly informing them that on graduation day in early June the "University commissioned 61 new officers in the Army and Air Force." Boastfully, he contrasted his campus with others, where "graduation ceremonies have been cancelled; others have been sparsely attended, many were disrupted by noisy and unruly students and non-students."

University of Nebraska, Lincoln

Numerous seniors, on Saturday, June 6, wore white armbands of protest on their black gowns at commencement exercises on the Lincoln campus. Four days later, during the early hours of June 10, arsonists lit five fires inside the campus Military and Naval Sciences Building. Originally, the administration reported that flames caused an estimated $15,000 worth of damage. However, a panel instigated by the Board of Regents to investigate the arson determined the damage was less than $1,000.

The same panel also determined that student actions related to the draft board, the ROTC building takeover and student strike had been "improper." The panel did single out one faculty member, Dr. Stephen L. Rozman, assistant professor of political science, whose participation in strike actions, the panel believed, had crossed the line when he sat-in with students during the first week of May. Following a hearing, the Board of Regents ultimately discharged Rozman in June of 1971. Rozman brought a lawsuit in federal district court for reinstatement contending he had been discharged for the exercise of First Amendment rights and without due process. His suit was denied as was his appeal.

None of the students' demands at the University of Nebraska were immediately accepted although in the years since, some were—including that Regents' meetings be made public and that campus police be disarmed.

Decades later, one senior who graduated in 1970, Dan Ladely, spoke of those days on the Lincoln campus. "It was a very interesting time. I think we really felt like we had to do something. My sophomore year here, my roommate flunked out, went to Vietnam and died, was killed. So, it was really affecting us a lot. And we were really wanting to stop it."

EPILOGUE

As we have seen, the May 1970 National Student Strike that exploded in response to President Nixon's invasion of Cambodia and the subsequent government repression brought the nation's higher education system to a halt and created an unprecedented crisis for the Establishment.

The raw numbers from the May 1970 rebellion are consequential – and all speak to the extraordinary nature of the national crisis. The eight deaths, the nearly 1,300 students injured or wounded, the average of 200,000 students who protested daily during the first week, the 1,400 and more colleges and universities affected, the 650 campuses shut down, the nearly 100 violent clashes between students and law enforcement, the arrests of 4,500 students, the two dozen deployments and activations of National Guards in 16 states—make up the staggering statistics.

Estimates of the numbers of students who participated in protests and strikes range from over 1 million to 4 and 5 million. The seminal book *SDS* found there were "protest demonstrations, involving nearly 60 percent of the student population—some 4,350,000 people out of a total of 7.4 million —in every kind of institution and in every state of the Union." *Wikipedia*: "Over a million students participated."

Yet, these are all guesses and speculations. There's simply no record that represents a precise account of the multitudes who participated during May 1970. And the difficulty in accurately setting the record is demonstrated by the daily numbers of people who protested. Our record showed that nation-wide between Monday, May 4 – the day of Kent State—and Sunday May 9 the numbers of protesters were incredible:

- Monday 61,825 to 67,525 participated in some kind of campus protest;
- Tuesday from 198,510—221,410;
- Wednesday from 199,155—231,805;
- Thursday from 111,570—119,310;
- Friday May 8th, from 177,517—202,942;
- Saturday May 9th, 100,000 to 120,000 or more– in Washington

DC alone.

These statistics demonstrate just how massive the involvement of young Americans was during the cataclysmic crisis and are prima facie evidence of the magnitude of the Rebellion, more than reported at the time or since, more than acknowledged by academia, by historians, or by the mainstream media and press.

Scranton Report

Barely two weeks after the dust had settled from May, Nixon established the President's Commission on Campus Unrest, better known as the Scranton Commission after its chairman—former Republican Governor William Scranton of Pennsylvania. Scranton was tasked to lead a study into the myriad of disorders and expressions of dissent that had broken out on college campuses during May, especially the national student strike, and the killings at Kent State and Jackson State.

As soon as the Commission was established, participants and supporters of the rebellion viewed it as an attempt to whitewash the causes and reasons of the explosion of student dissent and disruption. And apparently, they had cause for their cynicism. The White House viewed the Commission as solely a device to tamp all the turmoil down. Nixon warned Scranton, "Just don't let higher education off with a pat on the ass."

The Commission published its report in September 1970, after a jaw-dropping 90 days of preparation, and asserted: "The crisis on American campuses has no parallel in the history of the nation. This crisis has roots in divisions of American society as deep as any since the Civil War. The divisions are reflected in violent acts and harsh rhetoric, and in the enmity of those Americans who see themselves as occupying opposing camps. Campus unrest reflects and increases a more profound crisis in the nation as a whole." (pg. 1) "... If this trend continues, if this crisis of understanding endures, the very survival of the nation will be threatened. A nation driven to use weapons of war upon its youth is a nation on the edge of chaos. A nation that has lost the allegiance of part of its youth is a nation that has lost part of its future." (pg. 5)

Some findings are noteworthy. "In May 1970, students did not strike against their universities; they succeeded in making their universities strike against national policy," and for them, "nothing is more important than an end to the war in Indochina. Disaffected students see the war as a symbol of moral crisis in the nation which ... deprives even law of its legitimacy."

In one of the most important areas the Commission examined, the killings at Kent State, the Stanton Report concluded that the shootings on the Ohio campus were unjustified. While some students were dangerous, violent and criminal, it stated, the random firing into crowds was "unnecessary, unwarranted, and inexcusable." There was no justification for students to face M-1 rifles, the commission iterated, as "...the general issuance of loaded weapons to law enforcement officers engaged in controlling disorders is never justified except in the case of armed resistance that trained sniper teams are unable to handle."

The Commission placed the blame of what happened at Kent State on the Ohio National Guard for not following Army guidelines on civil disorders. "Even if the guardsmen faced danger, it was not a danger that called for lethal force. The 61 shots by 28 guardsmen certainly cannot be justified. Apparently, no order to fire was given, and there was inadequate fire control discipline on Blanket Hill. The Kent State tragedy must mark the last time that, as a matter of course, loaded rifles are issued to guardsmen confronting student demonstrators."

The Commission's members declared that their most important recommendation was to bring the country together and that responsibility "rests with the President. As the leader of all Americans, only the President can offer the compassionate, reconciling moral leadership that can bring the country together again."

Still, the Commission failed to place the blame for the "turmoil" squarely on Nixon's Cambodia invasion, his war policies in Vietnam, and the subsequent domestic repression. Nor did it seriously address the white racism Black and Latino students experienced on campuses. Nor did it critique in a more sweeping overview a system that allowed student and Black "dissent" to be violently suppressed by armed law enforcement. In the end, the report tried to be everything to everybody, but ended up, as one critic said, a "schizoid whitewash."

It didn't matter. Agnew denounced the report and Nixon ignored it. For them, the report failed to excoriate the students and absolve the government. Agnew called the report "imprecise, contradictory, and equivocal." He added, "To lay responsibility for ending student disruptions at the doorstep of the President in office 20 months is scapegoating of the most irresponsible sort." The primary responsibility for the disorders, the vice-president said, laid with faculties and administrators. "The President cannot replace the campus cop," he said.

Nixon responded in a letter to Scranton eleven weeks after the Commission issued its report in which he rejected its principal finding that as president, he must "exercise his reconciling moral leadership." Instead, he placed the responsibility for campus disorders "squarely" on the academic community, and stanchly defended Agnew—who had been targeted in the report as the source of "divisive and insulting rhetoric."

Over the coming months, Nixon's campaign strategy for the GOP clearly showed that not only wasn't he heeding the report, he hadn't even read it. The recommendations of one of the most substantial documents on domestic affairs prepared under his administration fell by the wayside, rejected with a thinly disguised scorn from the White House.

Early Withdrawal from Cambodia

The spontaneous and universal revulsion by students to the Cambodian invasion, however, did hasten the withdrawal of American and South Vietnamese troops from that country, although this was never admitted to by the White House or by Establishment press. Yet, on May 7, three days after Kent State, Nixon issued a directive that limited the distance and duration of US military operations in Cambodia to 30 kilometers (19 miles) and set a deadline of two months – to June 30—for the withdrawal of all US troops back to Vietnam.

At a news conference the next day—May 8—the same day that thousands of demonstrators began to converge on Washington, Nixon stated, "The action actually is going faster than we had anticipated. The middle of next week the first units, American units, will come out. The end of next week the second group of American units will come out. The great majority of all American units will be out by the second week of June, and all Americans of all kinds, including advisers, will be out of Cambodia by the end of June."

Then on the evening of June 3, Nixon again addressed the nation and declared his "Cambodia sanctuary operation" had been successful. He stated, "As of today I can report that all of our major military objectives have been achieved. Forty-three thousand South Vietnamese took part in these operations, along with 31,000 Americans."

The last American advisers and support troops "officially" withdrew from Cambodia on June 30. American casualties in Cambodia, according to the *New York Times* on July 1, 1970, stood at 344 killed and 1,592 wounded. South Vietnamese forces suffered more than 800 killed and 3,500 wounded. American and South Vietnamese generals claimed they had killed 11,349 enemy soldiers and captured another 2,509. The Pentagon was silent on Cambodian civilian deaths.

History is not kind to Nixon's "incursion." Militarily, it realized few strategic results. Nixon proudly boasted of the numbers of enemy weapons captured and tons of rice destroyed, but the operation proved more of a temporary slow-down for Hanoi than a knock-out punch.

For Nixon, the invasion had been the first real test of his new policy of "Vietnamization," under which South Vietnamese forces were supposed to take the brunt of the fighting, and he later claimed it was "the most successful military operation of the Vietnam War." Still, the South Vietnamese army in Cambodia had been substantially assisted by American troops with air and other support.

The domestic costs had been staggering. America's higher education system had been brought to a halt. Students had been shot down by National Guard troops. And, emboldened by the domestic antiwar response, Congress had been spurred into action and legislators reinserted themselves into the decision-making process of U.S. foreign policy.

Tone from the White House: Increased Law Enforcement

When the last lingering protests from May settled down, the President of the nation stood at a crossroads. Should he follow the recommendation of his own Scranton Commission to "bring the country together," or should he follow his conscience and continue on the path he had already set? Should he listen to his Vice-President, Spiro Agnew, who had warned on October 30, 1969, "We cannot afford to be divided or deceived by the decadent thinking of a few young people. We can, however, afford to separate them from our society—with no more regret than we should feel over discarding rotten apples from a barrel." Many had seen this Agnew threat as going beyond the pale, because it raised the idea of concentration camps for dissidents.

Just a month after Kent State, Nixon made his decision and set the tone for the White House. He assembled his intelligence, military and law enforcement team, and instead of brainstorming on ways to bring the country together, he ordered them to address the many threats he perceived as dangerous. The threats came from an array of opponents: anti-war and student activists, members of Congress, businesspeople, media personalities, authors, and even Hollywood celebrities. It was then that Nixon began his infamous "enemies list," a compilation of political opponents, and it was in direct response to the student rebellion and congressional efforts to limit his power.

Its purpose was, as Nixon aide John Dean explained in an internal memo, "to use the available federal machinery to screw our political enemies." That machinery included IRS tax audits, manipulating "grant availability, federal contracts, litigation, prosecution, etc." The initial enemies list included actor Paul Newman, Congressmen John Conyers (D-MI), Allard Lowenstein (D-NY), and Ron Dellums (D-CA), journalists Daniel Schorr and Mary McGrory, Leonard Woodcock—president of the United Auto Workers, philanthropist Stewart Mott, and foreign policy expert Morton Halperin. Eventually, Nixon and his aides assembled a much longer "master list" that contained hundreds of names. The lists became public during the Senate Watergate hearings in 1973.

According to Nixon's aide H.R. Haldeman years later, "Kent State marked the beginning of Nixon's downhill slide toward Watergate." Nixon himself described the days after Kent State as "...*among the darkest*" days of his presidency.

That fall, Nixon wrote an outrageous letter to 900 college presidents and threatened them with a loss of federal funds if they didn't restore "order and discipline" on their campuses. He then proceeded to base the entire Republican Party midterm campaign of 1970 on hyping up public sentiment against students and young people – all part of his scheme to gain the support of white voters, the so-called "silent majority" and key component of his Southern Strategy.

"Law and order" became the White House mantra and the administration geared up the federal machinery of repression. Funds for local law enforcement were increased by 300%—including a national computerized information network. Surveillance operations were expanded to the point where there were federal files "on hundreds and thousands of law-abiding yet suspect Americans," the *New York Times* reported. $20 million was added to the federal budget for riot equipment and training for the National Guard. And the Selective Service Administration was ordered to step up the prosecution of more than 4,000 draft-resistance cases.

Nixon went further. His top priority was turning the Department of Justice into one of the most extensive operations against political dissidence ever seen in America. Its Internal Security Division was built into a full scale national "Red Squad" for the investigation and prosecution of political dissidents anywhere in the country. Special teams of DOJ lawyers were dispatched across the nation to assist and help lead federal grand juries against SDS, Weatherman, and other leftists and peaceniks.

As the Department of Justice's most active branch, the FBI oversaw the Nixon administration's cranked up covert police surveillance, spying and harassment of the student antiwar movement. In 1970, the FBI added 1200 new agents mostly for campus work. And documents liberated from an FBI office in Media, Pennsylvania, showed every single college in America was assigned an agent, each ordered to build elaborate informer networks. They were directed to step up campus operations, to "enhance the paranoia" and get students to think "there is an FBI Agent behind every mailbox."

On top of all this, there was an array of other government programs, some illegal, that were employed by Nixon and his expanded executive branch. And for the first time, the FBI, the Army, the Secret Service, the Narcotics Bureau, and other federal and local agencies began to work together and share files in their spying and intelligence gathering on dissidents.

There was the Huston Plan to coordinate the security agencies in their illegal spying on leaders of the anti-war movement, other "left-wing radicals" and members of the countercultural movement. Most of the plan's components, however, were squelched by Hoover and Attorney General John Mitchell.

Nixon re-energized COINTELPRO, the Counter Intelligence Program, when he politicized the Justice Department. It was comprised of a series of covert and illegal projects by the FBI to surveille, spy, infiltrate, discredit, and disrupt domestic political organizations and movements. There was also the CIA's Operation Chaos, a top secret domestic espionage project run by the CIA from 1967 to 1974 which targeted Americans for possible foreign connections.

Congress Asserts Itself

Emboldened by the mass upsurge against the president for his Cambodia invasion, Congress moved to curtain Nixon's power with the Cooper-Church Amendment, the McGovern-Hatfield Amendment, and the repeal of the Gulf of Tonkin Resolution. Also, Congress lowered the voting age to 18 from 21 for the first time in American history.

Initially, Cooper-Church was defeated in the House, but a revised version made it through both houses of Congress and became law on December 22, 1970. As a result, all U.S. ground troops and advisors were barred from participating in military actions in Laos or Cambodia—while the air war being conducted in both countries by the US Air Force was ignored.

McGovern-Hatfield was a more substantial Congressional defiance of executive power and would have required US military operations in Vietnam to end by December 30, 1970. Known as the "amendment to end the war" it would have also required a complete withdrawal of American forces halfway through 1971. On September 1, 1970, the amendment failed in the Senate by a vote of 55 to 39. Minutes before the voting, its primary sponsor, George McGovern, made a brief but emotional appeal to his Senate colleagues, using the strongest language he had ever used in talking about the war:

Every senator in this chamber is partly responsible for sending 50,000 young Americans to an early grave. This chamber reeks of blood. Every Senator here is partly responsible for that human wreckage at Walter Reed and

Bethesda Naval and all across our land—young men without legs, or arms, or genitals, or faces or hopes.

There are not very many of these blasted and broken boys who think this war is a glorious adventure. Do not talk to them about bugging out, or national honor or courage. It does not take any courage at all for a congressman, or a senator, or a president to wrap himself in the flag and say we are staying in Vietnam, because it is not our blood that is being shed. But we are responsible for those young men and their lives and their hopes. And if we do not end this damnable war those young men will someday curse us for our pitiful willingness to let the Executive carry the burden that the Constitution places on us. So, before we vote, let us ponder the admonition of Edmund Burke, the great parliamentarian of an earlier day: "A conscientious man would be cautious how he dealt in blood."

During the summer of 1970, a bipartisan chorus called for repealing the 1964 Gulf of Tonkin resolution, which had given Presidents Johnson and Nixon broad leeway in conducting military operations in Vietnam and Southeast Asia without a formal declaration of war. On June 24, 1970, the Senate voted 81 to 10 to repeal it, and in mid-January 1971, Nixon signed the repeal.

More protests against the Vietnam war followed in the immediate years to come, 1971 and 1972, but nothing matched the intensity, ferocity, severity and rebelliousness of May '70. Over time, polls showed that the American people turned against the war and agreed with the students. The last draft call was on December 7, 1972, and on January 27 in 1973 the Selective Service announced there would be no further draft calls.

That announcement was dwarfed by the signing of the Paris Peace Accords the same day. Peace talks between Americans and Vietnamese had been going off and on since 1968, and Nixon in early May 1972—under intense domestic pressure to end the war—made a major concession—the US would agree to a cease-fire as a precondition to its military withdrawing from South Vietnam without North Vietnam doing the same. The concession broke a deadlock and on January 27, 1973, National Security Advisor Henry Kissinger and North Vietnamese Politburo Member Le Duc Tho signed the Accords. The peace treaty established a temporary peace, an end to US direct military involvement and led to the removal of all remaining US Forces, including air and naval forces. That year the two men were awarded the Nobel Peace Prize, although Le Duc Tho refused to accept it.

Fighting between the North Vietnamese and National Liberation forces with the government of South Vietnam broke out in March of 1973, and two years later a massive North Vietnamese offensive conquered the south on April 30, 1975. As Saigon "fell" the last few Americans still in South Vietnam were frantically airlifted out of the country. Separated since 1954, the two countries united in 1976 as the Socialist Republic of Vietnam. Saigon was renamed Ho Chi Minh City.

A half century later, on Sunday, Sept 10, 2023, American President Joe Biden came to the Vietnamese capitol of Hanoi to acknowledge Vietnam's elevation of the United States to its highest diplomatic status, a comprehensive strategic partner. The expanded partnership reflected a broad effort by the US to counter China's influence and Vietnam's desire to flex a degree of independence.

In November of 1973, Congress – over Nixon's veto—passed the War Powers Act designed to limit the U.S. president's ability to initiate or escalate military actions abroad without the express approval of Congress. Its goal was to avoid another lengthy conflict like Vietnam. It requires the president, as Commander-in-Chief, to notify Congress whenever armed forces are deployed and imposes a limit of 60 days on any engagements initiated without congressional approval. While it does not outright forbid presidents from taking military action, it does create some sense of accountability. Since its enactment, its effectiveness has been repeatedly challenged by presidents who have mostly ignored the spirt of the Act.

Beginning in May 1973, a special Senate committee began hearings into the Watergate affair and its televised proceedings revealed details of the "White House Horrors." They included the Huston Plan and other elements of the White House arsenal of extra-legal actions: the "enemies list," the covert Plumbers Unit, the proposed fire-bombing of the liberal Brookings Institute, and the burglary of Daniel Ellsberg's psychiatrist's office (Ellsberg leaked the Pentagon Papers). Members of the Plumbers Unit – Nixon's "fixers" – had been ordered to break into the Democratic Party headquarters at the Watergate. And the break-in, of course, led to the exposure of the unprecedented scale of the Watergate scandal and to the eventual resignation of President Nixon in August of 1974.

Consequences of the May Rebellion

The May Rebellion changed America and changed American politics forever – both in the immediate sense and over the ensuing decades. It ushered in a whole new generation of "peace candidates" and was a major step in the creation of the "Vietnam Syndrome" – a public aversion to US military operations overseas that hampered future presidents in deploying ground troops. For two decades, it became a "third rail" in American politics, where any substantive military engagement would be met with immediate grassroots and legislative opposition.

May 1970 was the high-water mark of the greatest anti-war movement in American history. Its demands for peace and an end to the wars molded an anti-imperialist nature into the country's body politic. In terms of its intensity, breadth and universal nature, nothing like it has been seen since. The national strike was the most forceful display of student power in our history, a power that had been developing for a decade, and forecast a new youth bloc in American politics and economy. And significantly, the widespread support for the Black Panthers by white antiwar students demonstrated a dramatic turn among America's young in addressing the system of institutionalized white racism.

As Nixon's aide H.R. Haldeman later speculated, the Kent State shootings were "a turning point" for the president and the "beginning of his downfall slide into Watergate." Because Nixon's trust in the FBI soured in part due to its failure to find the "outside agitators" responsible for provoking the National Guard at Kent State, he turned to the secret "Plumbers group"—which then led to the June 1972 break-in at the Watergate. In short, the repressive abuses of the Nixon administration geared up in the aftermath of the May Rebellion led to Watergate in 1972 – and his resignation in 1974. (But not, of course, before Nixon won a landslide re-election against the Democratic Party peace candidate, George McGovern in November 1972.)

Students embodied the conscience of America.

In the last analysis, students in the rebellion embodied the conscience of America. In disavowing by act and word the imperial ambitions of the

Establishment, students became the first major sector of the public to collectively reject the corporatist narrative of the war and its immorality. And as were seen in polls and legislative reactions, the American people soon followed.

During that fateful May, students were hellbent to force the country to deal with an untenable situation, the crisis of legitimacy and a war that was tearing the country apart. With their resistance to the war policies of the White House, students drew a line in the sand and responded militantly and even violently to the repression that followed. Where one stood on the Vietnam War defined you; there was no more middle ground; you were either against the war or for it.

Flexing their muscles like never before, students and young people in general forced a nation that was in denial about the war and its consequences and 'brought the war home' to the campuses, to the malls and neighborhoods, to the downtowns and state capitols. Students carried out their militant tactics not only to resist imperial ambition but also to awaken the sleeping giant, the American people.

Why has there been a half century of cover-up of what happened?

One of the essential questions of this work is—why has there been over a half century of cover-up and unceremonious entombment of what happened in May 1970? What can be said about the erasure from public memory and this suppression of history—our history, a chapter of our people's history? Why haven't government officials, historians, academicians, media projects, foundations—dug up this history? For over half a century, there has been no significant public, government, academic or media acknowledgement of the severity, breadth and depth of the rebellion, despite a scattering of remembrances at a few colleges for the 50th anniversary of Kent State in May 2020.

Can we simply blame the mainstream media for this? During the protests in May 1970, the media at first acted with bewilderment – they had been led to believe the student anti-war movement was dead—and had to be shaken from their lethargy. And then, once shaken, the media acted with blindness, overlooking and under-reporting the incredible wave of protests, strikes and shut-downs, the massive numbers of students in motion, the violence, the significance of student power and the intransigence of government. At any other moment, just one of these would have rated front-page news. In the end, the mainstream media left the May insurrection as one of the greatest unreported stories of the century.

There have been other periods in American history that have also gone unreported or "blocked out"—such as Shay's Rebellion, the violent insurrections of the great 1877 railroad workers' strike, the official government policies of Native American ethnic cleansings, and the numerous massacres of African Americans like in Tulsa, Oklahoma. And for half a century, the May Rebellion nestled in the ranks of these forgotten episodes.

Perhaps it was to be expected. Seven months after the Jackson State and Kent State killings, investigative journalist, I.F. Stone, uncovered that in both cases, the FBI and other government agencies turned up "evidence that the Guardsmen and law officers who did the shootings also agreed among themselves to tell FBI investigators a false story." How could we expect the truth of what happened in May 1970 to be uncovered when falsehoods and the fabrication of evidence of its most significant and violent incidents were woven into the initial government narrative?

Perhaps it was to be expected when the entire Vietnam conflict itself was built with government lies, as unearthed by the Pentagon Papers. Why, even the Nixon administration itself was woven through with lies, as the Watergate proceedings uncovered. But yet—what of the intervening years between the cleansing of the Watergate era and today? Inexplicably, the voices and actions of May 70 remained interned.

There is no answer to the inquiry. And we are left with speculation.

As Howard Zinn explained in *A People's History of the United States*, "the Establishment has been unable to keep itself secure from revolt." And "To recall this is to remind people of what the Establishment would like them to forget – the enormous capacity of apparently helpless people to resist, of apparently contented people to demand change. To uncover such history is to find a powerful human impulse to assert one's humanity. It is to hold out, even in times of deep pessimism, the possibility of surprise." (Page 573.)

The May Rebellion was indeed such a surprise to the Establishment, with all its violence and mass civil unrest. In the end, May 1970 was simply too violent and tumultuous for the powers that be to glorify by resurrecting any of its true details. The governing elites have consistently downplayed mass, radical movements in the past, and this was no different.

Yet, May '70 exposed the violent underpinnings of our society. For the Establishment, then, this exposure was best forgotten. How modern American society was shaken to its core by a bunch of motley students is not a story to be retold. How the highest levels of academia were brought to a halt and how the institutions were forced to grapple with the realities of a war, an industry and a system they were part of—are accounts worthy only for the archives and PhD theses, and not for public consumption.

But it is our people's history. It's part of the democratic struggles of the nation. Part of a long chain of history that has been submerged by officialdom. And now the record of what happened in May 1970 is revealed to all and for all. It is a beginning.

AFTERWORD for VOLUME 2

Student Anti-War Movement Continued

More protests against the Vietnam war followed in the two years after May, with 1971 witnessing over a thousand Vietnam Veterans Against the War (VVAW) stage "Operation Dewey Canyon III", camp out on the National Mall, throw their medals at the White House, and testify before various congressional panels – including the much-decorated and former Navy Lieutenant John Kerry.

Then on April 24, 1971, from half to three-quarters of a million people marched on the National Mall in Washington DC in a peaceful "Vietnam War—Out Now" demonstration, organized by the People's Coalition for Peace and Justice. That same day, from 150,000 to 250,000 demonstrators swamped San Francisco in the largest West Coast anti-war protest ever held during the entire Vietnam War (the most massive protest the author ever attended). The next month, May Day Protests brought out tens of thousands of protesters who attempted to shut down government operations in the nation's capital by blockading bridges and thoroughfares. Over the three-day protests, 12,614 were arrested, a record in American history.

In the spring of 1972, Nixon resumed the air war against North Vietnam and there was an upsurge in protests and a new wave of massive demonstrations across the country: an estimated 100,000 people marched in New York City, 12,000 in Los Angeles, 25,000 in San Francisco, as well as other cities around the US and the world. More protests broke out in May when Nixon decided to mine Haiphong Harbor off the coast of North Vietnam. 10,000 to 15,000 protested in Washington, DC.

Polls showed American people turned against the war

Over time, the American people began to agree with the students. In just a few months' time, polls of Americans indicated a dramatic turn against the wars. In early November 1969, after a major speech by Nixon on his policy of "Vietnamization," a Gallup Poll indicated that 77% of the American public was in support of his policy in Vietnam. Another poll in January 1970 showed public approval at 65%, although one in April had the approval rating dropping to 48% with 41% disapproving. A few days after Nixon announced the Cambodia invasion – but before shots were fired at Kent State – another Gallup Poll reported that a slender majority of Americans continued to support him.

Then came the full onslaught of the May Rebellion. And by June 1970, opinion polls showed Americans opposed sending GIs "to help Cambodia" by 58% to 28%; favored a December 1971 deadline for total withdrawal by 44 to 33 %; and wanted more than ever, 58 to 24 %, to pull US forces out even if the South Vietnamese government collapsed. Nearly two-thirds polled thought the president should get congressional approval before again sending troops into Cambodia. And by April 1971, a Gallup Poll showed that 73% of the American public was in favor of a withdrawal of all US troops from Indochina by the end of the year.

Students' visible resistance to the wars and the door-to-door campaigns by campuses had laid the groundwork for a turnabout in American public opinion about Cambodia, Vietnam and war in general.

The Pentagon Papers

Some of the turnabout in public opinion was hastened by the release of the "Pentagon Papers" by Daniel Ellsberg and Anthony Russo in June of 1971. Officially titled *Report of the Office of the Secretary of Defense Vietnam Task Force*, and first published in the *New York Times*, the documents represented an official history of the US political and military involvement in Vietnam from 1945 to 1967. They revealed the US had secretly expanded the scope of military operations, none of which had been reported in the mainstream media, and that generals and presidents had repeatedly lied to the American public. The revelations destroyed the so-called "Domino Theory" – one of the main rationales for the war and American involvement—which had been parroted by diplomats, generals, and Cold Warriors for over a decade.

Academic Reform

Importantly, the May Rebellion opened up political space for those pushing for racial and gender equality in academic institutions. Most notably, support and sympathy for the Black Panthers, the most visible African-American organization being persecuted by the government, became a major issue and demand by the mainly white antiwar movement.

This in turn lent encouragement to Black students to intensify their own demands and rights on campus – despite the myopia of latent racism with some white antiwar students – and helped to galvanize the push for the creation of Black studies and increases in Black enrollment, faculty, and employees. Space was also opened up for Black activists to help educate white students to the reality of institutionalized racism and the oppression their communities suffered.

In some western colleges, similar demands were made for Chicano/Mexican-American students' rights, studies, and departments. And on at least one campus, Native American students expressed parallel demands. Clearly, however, the main impetus for these ethnic studies, enrollment and staffing reforms came from the Black, Latino and Native communities themselves.

Likewise, demands and pressure from women students and faculty were made for courses in women studies or departments, and for more women faculty and administrators. In addition, the atmosphere created by the Strike helped lead to a general loosening up of restrictions on women college students, such as dress codes and the curtailing of "co-ed" only curfews. Overall, this period witnessed a widening growth in the consciousness of women's liberation and the formation of campus feminist groups in response to the abject societal male chauvinism, but also partly as a reaction to the male dominance of the New Left and the anti-war movement. Students at all-women schools proved their capabilities in responding to the crisis and organized protests just as substantial as those on mixed campuses.

Also importantly, basic students' rights—or the lack thereof—were pushed to the forefront, especially at those schools where the Berkeley-inspired Free Speech Movement had never reached. Issues of freedom of speech and of assembly were raised dramatically, particularly at schools where regressive administrations ruled. Crack-downs on peacefully protesting students forced an understanding that their own schools lacked an adherence to basic citizen rights as guaranteed in the US Constitution and Bill of Rights, and in response, students demanded those rights. They also pressed for more self-governance and control over their own activities and education, and over student centers and funds.

And at many colleges, faculties were jolted out of their complacency and forced to confront their own complicit roles in the military-industrial-academia complex where university budgets were partially funded by the Pentagon. Plus, on some colleges – even prominent universities—faculties made substantial strides in increasing their own self-governance and enlarging the roles they played in the administration of the campuses.

The crisis was punctuated with an across-the-board demand for more relevant courses and classes, as seen in the creation of "Free Universities," alternative class structures and contents, and the countless teach-ins and seminars organized during May. This was a major cornerstone of the wave of academic reform that swept the country during this period. At the bottom of it all was an effort to change the relationship between student and university, to exert the student's role as more of a co-equal partner in her or his own education.

Lessons in Co-optation, Accommodation and Repression

On the flip side of academic reform, administrators and law enforcement gained important insights during the rebellion over how to control or squelch campus dissent. California governor Ronald Reagan provided a model for many administrations with his abrupt unilateral closure of the entire state-funded higher education system—with hopes the rebellion would go away. It didn't of course.

Other lessons learned by administrators were ones about accommodation and co-optation. Give in to the students, avoid militant protests, sponsor "forums" and campus plebiscites, send telegrams to Nixon asking him to bring the troops home, sign petitions—even talk and hang-out with demonstrators. But never seriously question the role of the university in a militarized society. At times, this tactic backfired, and the hypocrisy of administrators stood out like silhouettes in front of a burning barricade. This occurred when top administrators praised the quiet and calm on numerous campus after the mass arrests of students and the jailings of strike leadership.

The dialectic of accommodation was evident in the widespread efforts to channel student dissent into letter-writing, the campaigns of dovish politicians and bell-ringing projects for antiwar petitions. Yet, so many letters, telegrams and petitions swamped congressional offices that those "dovish" representatives were emboldened in their efforts to reassert Congress into the policy of war-making and the curtailing of executive power. All those petitions, likewise, taken door-to-door in neighborhoods around campuses spread the anti-war message, which – with time—helped turn the tide of public opinion against the war.

Another key lesson was the ability of administrators to encourage the wide-scale lobbying effort by thousands of students and faculty members who roamed the halls of congress to inform legislators about the wide spread anguished opposition of students to the war. It was a way to channel the Rebellion into legal and electoral avenues, particularly on the East Coast. Yet, a good number of those student lobbyists returned to their respective campuses frustrated, demoralized and even embittered at the responses they'd received. Some had become quite turned-off to the whole concept of appealing to the mostly conservative, out-of-touch white male legislators. An aspect of accommodation by Congress itself was seen when it passed legislation lowering the voting age in federal elections from twenty-one to eighteen.

Other lessons learned by the Establishment included the absolute need to coordinate actions between administrators and law enforcement. Once administrators gave in to using the repressive measures of outside agencies, by in large, they gave up control of their campuses and of any moral high ground. Repression against militancy usually spiraled into more violent resistance which garnered increased sympathy from the rest of the campus.

After the Rebellion, administrators looked at their campus grounds and tried to figure out ways to discourage mass protests and give themselves more control over their own environs. Traditional mass assembly sites were broken up with landscaping and walls; cobble stones and bricks were removed from campus pathways; and new administration buildings were designed with more glass to allow wider fields of vision and the ability to view interiors.

Outside Agitators, Snipers and Agents Provocateur

From college administrators, mayors, local politicians and governors to the President of the United States, the real instigators of all the violence and turmoil during May were the outside agitators, the Weathermen, professional instigators and rioters. For example, Kentucky Governor

Louie Nunn blamed "outside agitators" and "professionals" for the disturbances at the University of Kentucky. At Ohio University Athens and at the University of Minnesota in Duluth, outside agitators were blamed for the violence. Chancellor Laurence Chalmers at the University of Kansas claimed that "outside agitators" were the real culprits responsible for creating conflict on his campus. He called them "a small band of itinerants" who, after graduation, would "drift away from KU in colorful mini-buses." And when on May 1 in the city of Kent, Ohio, Mayor LeRoy Satrom declared a state of emergency, he called the governor's office and claimed that SDS had taken over part of his city, even though the KSU chapter of SDS had disbanded a year earlier.

There is absolutely no evidence in the record that groups of professional or otherwise agitators roamed the nation and set fire to ROTC buildings or committed other violent acts to stir up the locals, nor of any cells of SDS or Weathermen nor of any other leftwing group that were instigating the rebellion. Yet, when even the Scranton Report raised the issue of outside agitators, it legitimized the idea. And for his part, Nixon saw a vast, left-wing conspiracy brimming with outside agitators as wholly responsible.

It was apparently too difficult for these administrators, town mayors, governors and politicians to admit that the main source of the turmoil on the campuses were their own students, radicalized and energized, genuine and organic.

However, one source of the turmoil were the actions of *agents provocateur*— undercover law enforcement officers or informants. There were at least three instances during May where it was recorded that undercover agents actively contributed to the violence. At Ohio State University in Columbus, two undercover officers led a crowd to a campus gate and then abruptly closed it triggering a massive violent police attack and confrontation. At the University of Wisconsin in Madison, two undercover cops dressed as students and carrying rocks and protest signs beat up an antiwar activist who had "outted" them. At the University of Alabama, Tuscaloosa, an old, abandoned building that once served as the campus ROTC headquarters scheduled for demolition was destroyed by a fire. A year later, it was uncovered that an FBI informant and agent provocateur had torched the hall.

In the immediate aftermath of the shootings at both Kent State and Jackson State, the initial responses by the authorities and law enforcement were that officers and Guardsmen were responding to one or more snipers. These unfounded claims helped to lower the negative impact and intensity of the immediate public and official responses to the murders. And as with the claims of outside agitators, no snipers or snipers' weapons or any other proof of their existence ever materialized. The Scranton Report even accepted this fact.

In fact, when Senator Walter Mondale came to Jackson, Mississippi to attend James Green's funeral, in response to a reporter's question about the possibility of a sniper, he commented, "It's a new national syndrome – the unfound sniper. Every time there's an overreaction, that unfound sniper always gets blamed."

A New Found Power

College students and in general, young people in America, flexed a new power they found during the Rebellion. They directly experienced the exhilaration, ramifications, consequences and the positive attributes of being part of an oppositional movement to a perceived illegitimate authority. It was empowering to confront college administrators, to create road blockades, erect barricades, to occupy campus buildings, to take over freeways. The young of academia discovered that militant tactics could force a recalcitrant college administration – and even law enforcement—to the negotiating table.

They learned the effectiveness of different tactics—and the limitations of those tactics. The massive base of the movement gave encouragement to the militancy, the building occupations and freeway takeovers, in contrast to more traditional tactics, such as letter-writing, lobbying, petitions, and electoral campaigns. In protest, students came to know their own abilities and strengths; some learned they were excellent orators and writers, or resourceful organizers, or versatile in logistics.

Students also recognized their economic power as a massive bloc of consumers and tried to flex that power with national boycotts of corporate consumer goods in efforts to force companies to reject Pentagon priorities and become more socially responsible, and with local boycotts of merchants to build support for their own campus actions.

One chief lesson from May was the firsthand discovery of the role and power of academic institutions and the power of the government, of the state. Suspensions, curfews, the closing of campuses, arrests, jailings and trials, the injuries and even killings were meted out when push turned to shove. And an entire generation learned these lessons simultaneously.

One of those lessons – difficult to learn at the time – were the limits and extent of students' own power and strength, of the transiency of the nomadic life-styles of modern American college students, and how repression and cooptation, exhaustion and burn-out, had thinned their ranks.

Reasons for the month long tide to finally recede were all tied together: utter exhaustion from the onslaught of weeks of protest after protest, the thousands of arrests and jailings – many of the campus leaderships sidelined – the loss of resources in having to raise thousands of dollars for bail and legal fees, the hundreds of injuries, the threats of future repression, the curfews and suspensions, the cooptation and promises of electoral campaigns, and even a depoliticization that developed from all the turmoil. And of course, there's the schools themselves—many closed for strike reasons but most closed because it was the end of the semester or academic term, the time for finals, and the big one – summer itself.

When the Rebellion died down, there was a vacuum at this unique point in history. Without the lead or participation of a strong radical anti-war student group such as SDS, the rebels were left pretty much on their own. And without any local or national organizational structure, there was a seemingly rapid decline of the May student anti-war movement. A nation-wide group could have transmitted a sense of politics; a collective and organized vision of how to affect real change and provide an institutional framework and network to fall back on, to enable joint strategizing and coordination of campaigns, someone to connect the dots.

Yet without these connections, it was very difficult – if not impossible – to maintain the momentum created during May.

Individuals Affected for Lifetimes

The rebellion in May 1970 deeply affected the hundreds of thousands and even millions of young students who rallied in opposition to the wars and repression. For thousands of those individuals, the effects were so strong that they were transformed forever as their campus experiences and lessons from May stayed with them and shaped the values they would hold for the rest of their lives – becoming a defining moment.

Anna Daniels at the University of Pittsburg said, "On May 4, 1970, I lost my innocence. Something coalesced inside of me that day that would become seminal to the woman whom I have become." Steve Wimmers remembered his first ever demonstration at Ohio State University Columbus, "as a pivotal day in my life. It was the first time this kid from a small city in Ohio ever participated in a demonstration, and it changed my life forever."

An entire generation of American college students were forever and deeply affected by the May Rebellion. And, for thousands, they developed a new consciousness, an awareness of the economic, political, social and cultural conditions that engulfed them and their fellow citizens. This new awareness deepened their understanding of America's imperial, class, racial, sexual, and cultural structures and restrictions.

The immediacy of the Vietnam war exploded this new mass consciousness and yes, even a new radicalization and helped them develop a world view that rejected the tenacles of an American empire that snaked into the affairs of state, economies and militaries of other nations, particularly those in the Third World. It was a world view which held empathy for those countries trying to shake off the shackles of colonialism. In the end, the May movement created by these radicalized students went directly to the heart of the *raison d'etre* of the empire itself.

Significantly, radicalized students saw the need for substantial and deep-rooted change in capitalist America and felt on some level a personal commitment to be supportive of or strive for that change. Where these rebels ended up after the rebellion over the last half century manifested this new consciousness, and their lifestyles, work, jobs, projects, professions, careers reflected this new awareness. And that was the radical aspect of their new consciousness. May 1970 caused them to question their relationships – with the university, with academia, with the militarized state, with the economic system of capitalism, with the "law"—and with other humans.

For many white students, they found themselves questioning—perhaps for the first time—the things they took for granted because they were white. Their support for the Black Panthers, their new found awareness from confronting their own racist beliefs, and their support for colleges developing ethnic study departments – all went against the grain of institutionalized racism that formed a key part of their original indoctrination and which continued to hold the nation in its ugly grip.

The month had also thrown elite schools, middle-class and working class schools, and all-women's colleges into the mix of a national movement. From private and public colleges and local public high schools in working class neighborhoods, the strike united students from across the economic spectrum. Militant strikes, such as the one at the University of West Virginia, were unprecedented in America's heartland. On May 8, in Philadelphia, over 10,000 students from many different backgrounds and neighborhoods marched from five different directions to converge at Independence Hall. The strikes at the University of Nevada and at Portland State University united "cowboys" and "long-hairs" across their cultural divide.

In the end, the Rebellion allowed students to break out of their anomie, their individual isolation in a mass society and form bonds with others on issues that had become dear to them – at least temporarily—that multiplied by hundreds of thousands became the human fabric of the strike movement. And it allowed them to depart from the script and the roles prescribed for them and engage in new possibilities and visions.

Of course, the new mass consciousness was not universal, was not perfect and was unevenly shared. But, for a brief moment, massive numbers of American college students had unity among themselves, stood together and stared down the Establishment. At that moment, moderate students sided with the radicals and for a short time, the tide was turned against the war. In truth, most students were not radicals or activists, and many were politically conservative. With time, many of the old divisions would reappear and assert themselves. But one could not deny, however, that things had changed. And the mass radicalization, in fact, had established a new national reality.

Where did all the rebels go?

Once the rebellion was over, there was no finite record of what happened that summer. The question is then where did all the rebels go? Some obviously stayed on campus—not all veterans of the rebellion were seniors who graduated the spring of 1970. And those who stayed on campus helped provide the leadership and base for anti-Vietnam war outbursts in the springs of 1971 and 1972.

Generally, the May generation of activists took their rebellion-infused consciousness and experiences into the workplace, into community work and projects and professions. The more hardened rebels took their politics immediately into trade union and community organizing. Those who went into trade union and factory organizing, did so usually under the auspices of small Marxist sects, and some of them became union leaders.

Some went into the community, taking on urban issues with an anti-war headset and flavor. They tried to bring their radicalism from the anti-Vietnam war movement into community organizing projects, in efforts to build a more solid base for such a movement. Former campus radicals started organic food stores, alternative education schools, free medical clinics, collectively-owned co-ops and businesses; provided support for farmworker boycotts of grapes and lettuce; grappled with issues around police and prisons, around housing conditions, urban planning, local ecological issues, and around quality of life issues.

Some went into cultural work, becoming artists, writers, reporters, musicians or extending their quests to help people in professions of medicine, teaching and law. Some focused on solidarity work with national liberation movements around the globe.

Some went out to the country and started communes or collective-land-owning efforts or tinkered with alternative economies. There were those who chose electoral reform and focused on the campaigns of a new breed and generation of peace activists and legislative actions that sought to rein in the executive branch war-making powers. Others took their electioneering experiences and ran for local public office themselves – and some became city aldermen, mayors and state representatives

There was an explosion nation-wide of "underground" newspapers in the years following the Rebellion. Former campus activists founded and published hundreds of local, anti-establishment newspapers from coast to coast—which helped to publicize progressive community and labor news with views that challenged the mainstream narrative and nourished the budding counter-culture.

Looking back half a century after the turmoil and radicalization of a generation, we can surmise that along with the unceremonious and unannounced funeral of the May revolt, most of those involved didn't retreat into conservativism but maintained their progressive outlook and values – however much they could.

Yet, for a moment in May 1970 young students grasped the future in their hands. All the resolutions, demands, petitions, strikes, rallies, sit-ins, teach-ins, liberation classes, community canvassing—called for a better world, for peace and an end to the war, for racial and gender equality and an end to racism; they called for a more relevant and democratic college and university system of education, for Black studies, Chicano studies, women's studies, for the university to break its ties to the War Machine and the Pentagon, an end to academia's role in the training of new military officers, and called to erase the boundaries between the community and the university. And finally, they called for a more rationale and humane government and society.

Some of what the young demanded was later put in place. Much was forgotten in the years and decades since. But—for at least a few days, a few weeks, during that month of May 1970, the youth of America grasped the future in their hands and for a moment, lived out their dreams of how things should be.

CHAPTER END NOTES, Volume 2

The following citations are from the first use of the reference.
Introduction
On Strike Shut It Down – The Report on the First National Student Strike, Urban Research Corporation, 1970.

Sale, Kirkpatrick. *SDS*. Random House, New York, 1973.

The Report of the President's Commission on Campus Unrest, William W. Scranton (Chr.). Arno Press, New York, 1970.

Chapter 5 Saturday May 9 – Sunday May 10
Northeast
"On Washington: Off Bullshit", National Strike Information Center bulletin, May 12, 1970.

Dellinger, Dave. *More Power Than We Know: The People's Movement Toward Democracy*. Anchor Press/ Doubleday, Garden City, 1975.

Midwest
Campus Strike Papers: Cornell College, *Kent State University Libraries. Special Collections and Archives.*

"1970 Memories of Violence in City Still Strong", Lawrence Journal, Kansas, April 20, 2010.

Rocky Mountains
Campus Strike Papers: Colorado State University, *Kent State University Libraries. Special Collections and Archives.*

Pacific
Campus Strike Papers: Sonoma State College, *Kent State University Libraries. Special Collections and Archives.*

Owen Joynek, "Student Sets Self Afire- Dies to Protest War", Triton Times, May 12, 1970.

Curtis Yee, "The Death of George Winne Jr. and the Fight for a More Peaceful World", The Triton (UC San Diego), May 10, 2017.

Freilicher, Mel. "Franks Book." Received by author. 16 September 2019. Email Interview.

King, Byron. "Re: Hey Byron Spring 1970." Received by author. 4 November 2019. Email Interview.

Maltz, William. "Re: Chapter 1." Received by author, 5 July 2022. Email Interview.

Chapter 6 Monday May 11 – Sunday May 17

Northeast

Campus Strike Papers: Fitchburg State College, University of Connecticut; Eastern Connecticut State College, Rochester Institute of Technology; SUNY Potsdam, Juniata College, Federal City College, *Kent State University Libraries. Special Collections and Archives.*

Southeast

Campus Strike Papers: Randolph-Macon College, University of South Florida, Loyola University New Orleans, *Kent State University Libraries. Special Collections and Archives.*

Jimmy Higgins, "The forgotten dead of Augusta", Fire on Mountain Series, blog, Georgia, May 18, 2011.

Stacey Eidson, "The Augusta Riots – 45 Years ago", Metrospirit, Georgia, May 2, 2015.

Spofford, Tim. *Lynch Street – The May 1970 Slayings at Jackson State College.* The Kent State University Press, Kent, 1988.

Midwest

Campus Strike Papers: Kent State University at Stark, North Park College, Illinois, Hiram Scott College, *Kent State University Libraries. Special Collections and Archives.*

Gregory A. Fournier, "Ypsilanti, Michigan: EMU - The Turbulent Sixties", Fornology.com, March 5, 2013.

Katelyn Morken, "1970 Student Strike–50 Years Later", *From the Archivist: University of Minnesota Libraries,* June 25, 2020.

Rocky Mountains

Campus Strike Papers: Colorado State University; University of Colorado Boulder, *Kent State University Libraries. Special Collections and Archives.*

Pacific

Campus Strike Papers: Stanislaus State College; Mills College; California State College, Long Beach; San Fernando Valley State College; San Diego State College, *Kent State University Libraries. Special Collections and Archives.*

Chapter 7 Monday May 18 – Sunday May 24

Campus Strike Papers: University of Connecticut, District of Columbia Teachers College, Auburn University, Lincoln University, Missouri, *Kent State University Libraries. Special Collections and Archives.*

"The Collegian", University of Richmond, Volume LVII, Number 30, May 22, 1970.

Wachsberger, Ken. "Hey Ken." Received by author, 16 January 2024. Email Interview.

Chapter 8 Monday, May 25 – Sunday, May 31

Bill Tilton papers, University Archives, University of Minnesota, Twin Cities.

Epilogue

Bingham, Clara. *Witness to the Revolution.* Random House, New York, 2016.

Heineman, Kenneth J. *Campus Wars: The Peace Movement at American State Universities in the Vietnam Era.* New York University Press, New York, 1993.

Unger, Irwin. *The Movement – A History of the American New Left, 1959-1972.* Harper & Row, New York, 1974.

Zinn, Howard. *A People's History of the United States.* Harper Perennial, New York, 1980.

---

[1] Yale University, University of Maryland, University of South Carolina, Jackson State College, University of Alabama, University of Kentucky, Kent State University, Ohio State University Columbus, University of Chicago, University of Illinois Urbana, Northern Illinois University DeKalb, Southern Illinois University in Carbondale, University of Wisconsin Madison, University of Colorado in Denver, and University of New Mexico.

[2] Boston University, University of New Hampshire, Case Western Reserve in Cleveland, Ohio University in Athens, Ball State University in Muncie, Indiana, Northwestern University in Evanston and the City of Chicago generally, University of Iowa, and University of Texas in Austin.

About the Author

Frank Gormlie was a student activist during May 1970 at the University of California San Diego. After graduation he founded an "underground newspaper" called the *Ocean Beach People's Rag* – or *OB Rag* -- named after the San Diego community of Ocean Beach. Art Kunkin, the publisher of the *Los Angeles Free Press*, called the *OB Rag* the best progressive community newspaper in the country. Frank continued as a grassroots community activist and was involved in saving the local ecology, in democratic urban planning, working in solidarity with the Chicano and Mexican-American power movements in the 1970s, supporting people's struggles in Central American and South African, and against apartheid, the draft and nuclear power in the 1980s. In addition, he published and edited a small progressive magazine called *The Whole Damn Pie Shop*. Frank worked for a series of non-profits, including managing a community medical clinic, and then went to law school in the mid-1990s. Upon graduation in 1996, Frank had a 20-year practice in criminal and civil law in San Diego. Retiring from the law, Frank and his partner Patty Jones founded an online version of the former community newspaper, the *OB Rag* in 2007, which he still edited as late as 2024. Frank has one daughter, Michelle Seguin, who lives in Oregon with her husband Forrest and their two children, Skylar and Ronan.

www.ingramcontent.com/pod-product-compliance
Lightning Source LLC
Chambersburg PA
CBHW062005180426
43198CB00037B/2412